Papal Teaching in the Age of Infallibility,
1870 to the Present

Papal Teaching in the Age of Infallibility, 1870 to the Present

A Critical Evaluation with Historical Illustrations

Kevin T. Keating

☙PICKWICK *Publications* · Eugene, Oregon

PAPAL TEACHING IN THE AGE OF INFALLIBILITY,
1870 TO THE PRESENT
A Critical Evaluation with Historical Illustrations

Copyright © 2018 Kevin T. Keating. All rights reserved. Except for brief quotations in critical publications or reviews, no part of this book may be reproduced in any manner without prior written permission from the publisher. Write: Permissions, Wipf and Stock Publishers, 199 W. 8th Ave., Suite 3, Eugene, OR 97401.

Pickwick Publications
An Imprint of Wipf and Stock Publishers
199 W. 8th Ave., Suite 3
Eugene, OR 97401

www.wipfandstock.com

PAPERBACK ISBN: 978-1-5326-3553-3
HARDCOVER ISBN: 978-1-5326-3555-7
EBOOK ISBN: 978-1-5326-3554-0

Cataloguing-in-Publication data:

Names: Keating, Kevin T., author.

Title: Papal teaching in the age of infallibility, 1870 to the present : a critical evaluation with historical illustrations / Kevin T. Keating.

Description: Eugene, OR: Pickwick Publications, 2018 | Includes bibliographical references.

Identifiers: ISBN 978-1-5326-3553-3 (paperback) | ISBN 978-1-5326-3555-7 (hardcover) | ISBN 978-1-5326-3554-0 (ebook)

Subjects: LCSH: Popes—Infallibility. | Papacy—History. | Popes—Temporal power. | Catholic Church—Infallibility. | Catholic Church—Teaching office. | Catholic Church—History. | Catholic Church—Doctrines.

Classification: BX2330 K217 2018 (print) | BX2330 (ebook)

Manufactured in the U.S.A. 06/22/18

For Pam, always

Contents

Introduction: The Pope as Teacher | 1

1. Vatican I: The Definition and Exercise of Papal Infallibility | 11
2. Vatican II: The Announcement of the Infallibility of the College of Bishops | 26
3. Opposition: The Church and Modern Thought | 36
4. Sole Authority: The Bible | 69
5. Contradiction: Religious Freedom | 82
6. Ambivalence: Church and State | 94
7. Silence: The Morality of Wars | 122
8. Development and Discontinuity: Catholic Social Doctrine | 140
9. Confusion: The Necessity of the Catholic Church for Salvation | 172
10. Arrogance: Ecumenism and Interreligious Dialogue | 185
11. Constancy: Human Sexuality—Marriage and Divorce, Birth Control, and Homosexuality | 214
12. Certainty: Murder, Abortion, Euthanasia, and the Death Penalty | 234
13. Not an Option: The Priestly Ordination of Women | 245
14. Avoidance: The Problem of Evil and Suffering | 254

Postscript—Uncertainty: The Boundaries of the Infallibility of the College of Bishops | 263

Bibliography | 273

Introduction: The Pope as Teacher

Catholicism is impelled by its whole history . . . to claim unconditional possession of the truth.

—REINHOLD NIEBUHR

Even when the Church's claim to infallibility is not explicit, it is always subliminally present.

—HANS KÜNG

The Age of Infallibility

I REFER TO THE PERIOD which begins in 1870 as the "age of infallibility," because that year was the first time that a doctrine of infallibility was promulgated as a dogma of the Roman Catholic Church. Actually, the last century and a half comprises two ages of infallibility. The first is the age of papal infallibility, which spans the period from the declaration of the dogma of the Immaculate Conception of Mary in 1854 to the declaration of the dogma of the Assumption of Mary in 1950. These are the only two occasions on which papal infallibility has been exercised, although nothing prevents a future pope from exercising it. The second is the age of the infallibility of the college of bishops, which spans the period from the Second Vatican Council in the 1960s to the present. The two types of infallibility differ in one important respect: whereas an exercise of papal infallibility is easy to spot, the infallibility of the college of bishops may be exercised without the faithful (or even many clergy) realizing that it has taken place. When either type of infallibility is exercised on a matter of faith and morals that is to be believed or held by all Catholics, no dissent or contrary opinion will be tolerated.[1] Additionally, once a doctrine has been declared infallibly, it is settled for all time. Infallibility, once exercised, cannot be undone.[2]

Although papal infallibility has been formally exercised on only two occasions, the dogma looms over most major papal teachings. The Catholic Church often has treated a host of major papal pronouncements as infallible, if not de jure then at least de facto. There has been a growing tendency to refuse to concede that popes may err in their noninfallible teachings, or to countenance dissent from those teachings by Catholic theologians. In the words of Swiss theologian Hans Küng, "Even when the Church's claim to infallibility is not explicit, it is always subliminally present."[3] This presents particular problems when the teaching of a later pope contradicts that of a prior pope. The typical papal reaction to such as dilemma is to act as if the earlier papal teaching had never been made. The contradiction remains unacknowledged, because to acknowledge it would be a tacit omission that a prior pope had erred. If a prior pope could err, then a current pope may err as well. Papal teaching could then be subject to the same skepticism and criticism to which the statements of other religious leaders are subject. To avoid such a possibility, all papal teaching should be accepted as true by the faithful without question, with the result that dissent is not viewed as legitimate theological disagreement, but as disloyalty. This phenomenon, which variously has been dubbed "creeping infallibility," "creeping infallibilism," "creeping pseudo-infallibilism," and "virtual infallibility," renders even noninfallible papal teachings beyond the bounds of theological questioning.

The Papal Office and the Role of the Encyclical

This book will explore the teachings of modern popes through an examination of their major writings, especially papal encyclicals. The papal office is unique, both in the manner in which the pope is selected and in the role that he plays in the life of the institution he leads. He is not a hereditary monarch, a self-proclaimed dictator, or a president. He does not inherit his office, seize it through force of arms, or attain it through a general election of his constituents. Instead, he is chosen by the vote of a group of not more than one hundred and twenty men, those cardinals of the church who have not reached their eightieth birthday.[4] Although it is

1. Ford and Grisez, "Contraception," 274.
2. Sullivan, "Secondary Object," 546–47.
3. Küng, *Infallible?* 23.
4. Weigel, *Witness to Hope*, 828–31.

not a requirement of canon law that the college of cardinals elect one of their own members as the new pope, that has been the uniform practice since the late fourteenth century. In a tradition that has been followed since the late tenth century, the newly elected pope chooses the papal name by which he henceforth will be known.[5]

The pope is the undisputed head of the Roman Catholic Church, but his realm differs markedly from those of secular world leaders. He is the head of the smallest nation in the world, the Vatican City State; it comprises approximately 110 acres with a population of less than 1,000 persons. Although the size of his temporal domain is miniscule, he is the spiritual leader of more than 1.2 billion Catholics—more than 17.5 percent of the world's population.[6]

One of the primary tasks of the modern pope is to teach, a duty not imposed upon other world leaders. This function began to increase in importance during the nineteenth century, when the church was confronted by the intellectual challenges of the Enlightenment and the political fallout from the French Revolution. It perceived both developments as unmitigated disasters, not only for itself but for civil society as a whole. As papal historian Eamon Duffy has noted, "In reality, however, the Catholic Church's actual experience of the birth of democracy was not as enlightenment and liberation, but as a murderous attack on religion in general, and the freedom of the Church in particular."[7] Nineteenth-century popes responded to these events and their consequences by issuing encyclicals condemning the evils of the time, especially liberalism, socialism, and atheism. Jesuit historian John O'Malley has explained how the use of the papal encyclical underwent a profound change in the nineteenth century. "By definition an encyclical is a circular letter, and as such it was used by popes and others from ancient times. But in the nineteenth century its significance changed to such an extent that it emerged as virtually a new genre."[8]

Since the mid-nineteenth century, popes have used this "new genre" to address issues of both local and worldwide concern. Church historian John Pollard has noted that "there was an enormous increase in the 'output' of the most important of all papal public documents in this period, encyclicals."[9] The approximately three hundred encyclicals which have

5. Collins, *Keepers of the Keys*, 86.

6. This number includes not only members of the Roman Catholic Church, but also members of those Eastern Rite Churches who are in communion with the Holy See. Our Sunday Visitor, *2016 Catholic Almanac*, 331–32.

7. Duffy, *Ten Popes*, 94.

8. O'Malley, *Vatican II*, 55.

9. Pollard, *Money and the Modern Papacy*, 8.

been published since the beginning of the reign of Pius IX in 1846 have dealt with issues ranging from the parochial to those of global importance. In the last half of the nineteenth century and the first half of the twentieth century, many encyclicals were addressed to the bishops of a single country and concerned matters particular to the situation of the church in that nation. Those encyclicals focused on such diverse subjects and locales as the selection of bishops for China, marriage and divorce legislation in Ecuador, church-state relations in France, Nazism in Germany, the Soviet invasion of Hungary, Freemasonry in Italy, religious persecution in Mexico, and the growth of the church in the United States in spite of the lack of governmental financial support.

Other encyclicals examined issues of concern to the worldwide Catholic Church and were directed to all bishops, and sometimes to the laity as well. Those encyclicals treated many traditional subjects of faith and morals, devotion and prayer, internal church governance, missionary activity, the Virgin Mary and various saints, ecumenism, theological dissent, and threats to the Catholic faith and the church from a variety of philosophies and social movements. Beginning with John XXIII's encyclical *Pacem in terris* in 1963, some encyclicals began to include within their audience "all men and women of good will." Those encyclicals addressed topics of major import beyond the church: war and peace, workers' rights, the development of nations and peoples, technology, and the environment.

The wider audience to which modern encyclicals are addressed—in conjunction with the expansion of print, television, and digital media—has raised the profile of these papal letters to an unprecedented height. In 1928 the Catholic candidate for the United States presidency, New York governor Al Smith, responded to a question about a papal encyclical by asking "Will somebody please tell me what in hell an encyclical is?"[10] Today, an encyclical issued by Francis is a lead story in the secular media. This rise in the prominence of the encyclical comes at a time when the public has shown an increased curiosity about the papacy. In fact, many people today equate Catholicism with the pope.[11]

There are other papal documents besides encyclicals through which the pope exercises his teaching authority. These include apostolic constitutions, apostolic exhortations, and apostolic letters. Several of these types of papal documents will be examined together with the encyclicals. In addition, the pope also teaches in an indirect manner through doctrinal

10. James Hennessey, "Roman Catholics and American Politics, 1900–1960: Altered Circumstances, Continuing Patterns," in Noll and Harlow, *Religion and American Politics*, 247–65, 258.

11. O'Malley, *Catholic History*, 10.

statements issued by the Congregation for the Doctrine of the Faith with his express approval.[12]

The period under consideration also witnessed two extraordinary assemblies of the world's bishops at ecumenical councils held at the Vatican. The most important achievement of First Vatican Council in 1870 was to define the dogma of papal infallibility. The Second Vatican Council (1963–65) issued sixteen conciliar documents dealing with such topics as the church, scripture, liturgy, religious freedom, ecumenism, and non-Christian religions, among others. The constitutions, decrees, and declarations of Vatican II have been influential in the teaching of John Paul II, Benedict XVI, and Francis. Vatican II for the first time explained the manner in which the college of bishops teach infallibly. What I have termed "the infallibility of the college of bishops" was explained by the council as the exercise of infallibility by an ecumenical council, or by the universal consensus of the bishops throughout the world. Such infallibility is never exercised by the bishops alone; it is only exercised when they act in communion with the Roman Pontiff. However, the council left the boundaries of the infallibility of the college of bishops blurry at best. There is a certain "stealth" quality to the infallibility of the college of bishops, as it can be difficult to recognize which doctrines of the church have been infallibly declared through its exercise.

The Varieties of Papal Teaching

The first two chapters will explore papal infallibility and the infallibility of the college of bishops as declared by the First and Second Vatican Councils, respectively. Vatican I promulgated the doctrine of papal infallibility but did not issue any document concerning the nature and scope of the power of the episcopacy. That topic was on the council's agenda, but the outbreak of the Franco-Prussian War in September 1870 caused a hasty adjournment of the council, as bishops hurried back to their home dioceses. The subject of the episcopacy would not be revisited until eighty-five years later at Vatican II.

The next twelve chapters will examine papal teaching of the last century and a half through a study of papal documents on a variety of doctrinal issues. During this period, papal teaching has run the gamut from constancy to contradiction. The former is represented by papal pronouncements on matters of human sexuality—marriage and divorce, birth control, and homosexuality. In this area, papal teaching today is the same as it was in 1870; what was sinful then remains sinful today. But whereas the church's

12. Sullivan, *Creative Fidelity*, 19–20.

teaching on human sexuality in 1870 was in tune with the mores of that era, the reiteration of that teaching today is not only at odds with the attitude toward human sexuality in the broader culture of the West, it has been met with widespread dissent from Catholics themselves. At the other end of the spectrum is papal teaching on religious freedom. In 1870, papal teaching held that non-Catholic religions had no legal right to exist, because error has no rights; only the Catholic Church, the one true religion, was entitled to legal protection and support. In nations where the Catholic Church was the official state religion, other religions had no right to public worship, although they might be allowed to worship publicly as a matter of sufferance, in order to avoid social unrest. In countries where Catholics were in the minority, on the other hand, popes insisted on legal protection for the rights of Catholics to worship and for the church to own and manage its property. Since Vatican II, popes uniformly have asserted that all peoples have the right to religious freedom, including but not limited to freedom of worship, regardless of their religious affiliation. However, the church has studiously avoided any acknowledgement of the contradiction between its former and current teaching. Between constancy and contradiction lies development, which is best exemplified by Catholic social doctrine, as the popes have dealt with new economic, social, and political issues, for which prior teachings could provide only general guidance.

Modern papal teaching also has displayed a variety of attitudes. For example, teaching on the necessity of the Catholic Church for salvation has been characterized by confusion. The Fourth Lateran Council in 1215 announced the doctrine *extra eccclesiam nulla salus* (outside the church no slavation). That doctrine was interpreted literally until the end of the nineteenth century, when Pius IX became the first pope to acknowledge certain qualifications and exceptions. By the mid-twentieth century, the doctrine was no longer interpreted to mean what it appeared to say. In 1953 a Massachusetts priest was excommunicated for advocating a literal reading of the doctrine, which had been the normative interpretation less than a century earlier. Since Pius XII and the Second Vatican Council, the church has maintained that formal membership in the Catholic Church is not necessary to attain salvation, while continuing to insist that it, in some mysterious and unexplained way, remains necessary for salvation.

In the area of church-state relations, popes have demonstrated a certain ambivalence toward government involvement in church affairs. On the one hand, they have decried attempts by governments to regulate church activities and to dictate the manner in which church property is owned and operated. On the other hand, they have been willing to accept financial support from the state, including the use of state funds to pay for certain church-related facilities as well as the salaries of priests. In spite of the current papal insistence on freedom for all religions, the church is willing to accept financial support that is not made available to some other religions. For example, in Germany a tax is collected which provides government support to the Evangelical (Protestant) and the Catholic Church, as well as to support Jewish synagogues. However, no financial support is offered to Islamic groups.[13] Current papal teaching, although insisting on freedom of religion for all, requires neither equal state treatment of all religions, nor a wall of separation between church and state.

Historical Illustrations

In order to demonstrate that papal teaching is not a sterile, academic theological enterprise without real-world implications, historical illustrations are set forth in each chapter. For example, the discussion of the different approaches of the Catholic Church and Protestant denominations toward the Bible is examined through the prism of the battles in the United States over reading of the Bible and prayer in public schools. American Catholic bishops had spearheaded the nineteenth-century opposition to the practice of requiring Catholic students to read from the King James Version of the Bible in public schools. In doing so, the bishops were implementing papal teaching that did not encourage Bible reading by Catholics, because a lay person could not be expected to correctly interpret its books without the guidance of the church, the sole, authentic interpreter of scripture. However, when the United States Supreme Court in the 1960s ruled that such practices violated the Establishment Clause of the First Amendment to the Constitution, the American Catholic hierarchy joined a chorus of Protestant leaders in decrying such rulings.

Another example of the real-world consequences of papal teaching is in the area of artificial contraception. In the 1960s, a decades-old law in Connecticut made it a criminal offense for a doctor to prescribe contraceptive devices to married patients. The law originally had been passed by Republican legislators, but mid-twentieth-century efforts at repeal were thwarted by Catholic legislators, consistent with the church's teaching that the practice of artificial contraception was gravely sinful. Doctors who worked at Catholic hospitals but supported repeal of the ban found their employment terminated or their admitting privileges revoked. The law finally was ruled unconstitutional by the Supreme Court, which for the first time enunciated the existence of a constitutional "right to privacy." Less than

---

13. Gill, *Political Origins*, 20.

a decade later, that rationale would form the basis for the Court's holding that a woman had a constitutional right to terminate a pregnancy through abortion, a right which Catholic and many evangelical Protestant leaders today continue to seek to limit and, ultimately, eliminate.

Other historical illustrations include: the Church's response to modern secular thought and scientific discoveries, from the 1633 trial of Galileo by the Holy Office of the Roman Inquisition to debates over evolution and the Big Bang Theory; the similarities between the efforts by established churches in the American colonies to impede the religious freedom of dissenters and the Catholic Church's historical approach toward non-Catholic religions; the Catholic Church's shifting position on church-state relations in contrast to the American experience of a "wall of separation" between church and state; the reactions of the churches of the North and South toward the American Civil War and the responses of Benedict XV and Pius XII to the First and Second World Wars, respectively; the contrast in the Catholic response to the Reformation before and after the Second Vatican Council; and the opposition of the German bishops to the compulsory sterilization and euthanasia programs of the Nazi regimes. The illustrations hopefully will show how, in the words of Jewish theologian Rachel Adler, "Theologies have real consequences in history."[14]

The final chapter will explore the uncertain boundaries of the infallibility of the college of bishops, with particular emphasis on a document issued by the Congregation for the Doctrine of the Faith under Cardinal Ratzinger. This document gives numerous examples of matters of faith and morals that have been taught infallibly by the college of bishops, including the invalidity of holy orders in the Anglican Church, the papal canonization of saints, and the grave sinfulness of prostitution. One doctrine that is noticeably absent from this enumeration of infallibly taught doctrines is the sinfulness of the use of artificial contraception.

Conventions Used in Papal Documents

There are eleven popes whose writings will be examined in depth: Pius IX (1846–78); Leo XIII (1878–1903); Pius X (1903–14); Benedict XV (1914–22); Pius XI (1922–39); Pius XII (1939–58); John XXIII (1958–63); Paul VI (1963–78); John Paul II (1978–2005); Benedict XVI (2005–13), and Francis (2013 to the present). John Paul I is not included in this list, because he was

---

14. Rachel Adler, "A Response to Phillip A. Cunningham: Catholicism and the Paths of Righteousness," in Heft, *Catholicism and Interreligious Dialogue*, 47–56, 47.

pope for only thirty-one days in August and September 1978 and did not publish any encyclicals or other significant writings.

All of the encyclicals and other papal documents which I examine are available on the internet. English translations of most encyclicals from 1878 to the present may be accessed at www.vatican.va, the official website of the Holy See. Most papal documents which predate 1878, or which are otherwise not available in English translation on the Holy See's website, may be accessed at www.papalencyclicals.net, a website not affiliated with the Holy See. Quotations from papal documents are taken from the English translations found on the Holy See's web site where possible. All papal and other official Vatican documents referenced in the text are listed in the bibliography with a citation to the on-line address where they may be found.

The overwhelming majority of encyclicals and other papal writings are divided into numbered paragraphs. Numerals in footnote citations to these documents are to these numbered paragraphs rather than to the pages on which the cited material appears. Certain papal speeches and messages are not divided into numbered paragraphs. In such cases, the footnote citation is to the page on which the referenced material may be found. Some documents issued by ecumenical councils and by dicasteries of the Roman Curia—such as the Congregation for the Doctrine of the Faith—are divided into articles, chapters, or sections, followed by a paragraph designation. In those cases, the chapter, section, or other appropriate division, together with the paragraph, is given in the footnote.

A few words on certain conventions used in papal encyclicals may be helpful to the reader. Most encyclicals are issued in an official Latin text, together with translations into several languages. The title of the encyclical is taken from the first words of the Latin text. For example, the first words of the Latin text of *Mysterium fidei*, are "*mysterium fidei*," which are translated into English as "the mystery of faith." The topic of the encyclical is the Eucharist. A handful of encyclicals were issued in a language other than Latin (French, German, or Italian), and the same naming convention is followed. The encyclical *Mit brennender Sorge*, begins with the German words "*Mit brennender Sorge*," which are translated into English as "with great anxiety." The topic of the encyclical is the relationship between the Church in Germany and Hitler's government. All of the encyclicals discussed in this book follow the same format. An English language subtitle for each encyclical, which describes the topic of the encyclical, is found in the bibliography. Other papal documents—such as apostolic letters and apostolic exhortations—follow the same convention.

A common feature of papal documents issued by John Paul II, and by the Congregation for the Doctrine of the Faith under Cardinal Ratzinger, is an increased reliance on the use of italics in the body of text. In order to avoid an endless repetition of the phrase "emphasis in original" in parenthetical references, all italicized words and phrases that appear in quotations from official church documents are italicized in the original; I have added no emphasis of my own to any such quotations.

1

Vatican I: The Definition and Exercise of the Doctrine of Papal Infallibility

> *The bishop of the Roman Church ... is the head of the college of bishops, the Vicar of Christ, and the pastor of the universal Church on earth. By virtue of his office he possesses supreme, full, immediate, and universal ordinary power in the Church, which he is always able to exercise freely.*
>
> —Code of Canon Law

> *Power tends to corrupt, and absolute power corrupts absolutely.*
>
> —Lord Acton

The promulgation of the doctrine of papal infallibility by the First Vatican Council on July 18, 1870 could not have come at a less auspicious time. One day later, Prussia declared war on France, thereby inaugurating the Franco-Prussian War. The outbreak of the war led France to withdraw its troops from Rome, where they had been providing the pope with protection against the threat from Italian forces seeking to establish Rome as the capital of a unified Italy. Following the French withdrawal, Italian troops crossed into the Papal States in early September and their attack on Rome began on September 20. On October 20, Pius declared the council adjourned; it was never reconvened.[1] It had accomplished its main

---

1. Chadwick, *History of the Popes*, 215–21; Chiron, *Pius IX*, 271–74; De Mattei, *Pius IX*, 145; Kertzer, *Prisoner of the Vatican*, 35–58.

objective, however, of declaring as a divinely revealed truth a doctrine with little scriptural or historical support. At a time when the pope was being stripped of his temporal powers by the forces of Italian nationalism, his spiritual power was being declared absolute. In fact, it was the definition of the doctrine of papal infallibility which prompted Lord Acton, an English Catholic Member of Parliament who was in Rome at the time of the council, to pen his famous remark: "'Power tends to corrupt, and absolute power corrupts absolutely.'"[2]

The Medieval Antecedents of the Doctrine

The history of the doctrine of papal infallibility prior to 1870 is sparse. Its roots can be traced to a late thirteenth-century internal dispute between two groups of Franciscans over the proper interpretation of the Rule of St. Francis. The most astonishing aspect of this dispute is that the concept of papal infallibility initially was proposed as a means of constraining papal power, not of enhancing it.

As a mendicant order founded by Francis of Assisi in the early thirteenth century, the Order of Friars Minor, commonly known as the Franciscans, did not own goods individually or in common, relying instead on the kindness of strangers for their subsistence. Francis's will provided that his followers could take no action to change his rule for the order to make it less strict.[3] To one group of Franciscans—the Conventuals—this is all that the rule required. Another group of Franciscans—the Spirituals—interpreted the rule as requiring the friars to practice "severe frugality" in their daily lives.[4] One of the leaders of the Spirituals was Peter Olivi, an eccentric theologian who frequently railed against clergy and bishops who lived a life of luxury, in contrast to the life of poverty that Jesus and his apostles practiced.

The cause of Olivi and the other Spirituals was strengthened when Pope Nicholas III issued the constitution *Exiit qui seminat* in 1279, siding with the Spirituals' interpretation of the rule. Nicholas gave the Spirituals even more ammunition in their dispute against the Conventuals by declaring that his interpretation of the rule was to be binding on the Order in perpetuity. "We judge that this Our constitution, declaration, or ordination is to be observed exactly as such and inviolably by the friars themselves for all time."[5]

---

2. Murphy, *God's Jury*, 170.
3. González, *Early Church to the Reformation*, 360.
4. McClory, *Power and the Papacy*, 23.
5. Nicholas III, *Exiit qui seminat*, 25.

Olivi, however, was not content with this victory. Fearing that a future pope might decline to follow Nicholas's interpretation of the rule, he developed a doctrine of infallibility which would bind the hands of any future pope. A papal decree on a matter of faith or morals, once pronounced, could not be subject to revision by a future pontiff.[6] Under Olivi's proposed doctrine of papal infallibility, no future pope could overturn the judgment set forth by Nicholas. Unfortunately for Olivi and the Spirituals, future popes would not feel so bound. Twenty-five years after Olivi's death, John XXII issued the papal bull *Quia quorundam*. John rejected the Spirituals' understanding of the practice of Jesus and his apostles in connection with the ownership of personal property. John was not perturbed by the fact that his bull contradicted the earlier pronouncement of Nicholas, since Nicholas's teaching itself had been contrary to that of his predecessors. John proceeded to declare that those who teach the erroneous views of Olivi "have fallen into condemned heresy, and [are to be treated] as heretics to be avoided."[7] He would not permit Olivi's notion of papal infallibility to be used as a limitation on the exercise of his papal power. More than five centuries later, an ecumenical council would first proclaim as a dogma of faith a doctrine whose roots lay neither in Scripture nor in the earliest Christian traditions, but rather in a seemingly esoteric thirteenth-century squabble among the followers of St. Francis.

Nineteenth-Century Threats to the Temporal Power of the Pope

The doctrine of papal infallibility lay fallow for several centuries, until it burst forth as a major issue in the second half of the nineteenth century. Why then? Scholars agree that contributing factors include Protestantism, the French Revolution, the rise of liberalism, and threats to the temporal power of the pope. The reaction to these developments led many in the church to seek a counterbalance in the reassertion of papal authority. According to Jesuit theologian Francis Sullivan, due to a combination of political and theological factors, "by 1870 the great majority of Catholic bishops were ready to define papal infallibility as a dogma of faith."[8]

The nineteenth century witnessed a tectonic shift in the status of the pope as a European sovereign. At the start of the century, he ruled over the Papal States, a territory which covered more than 41,000 square kilometers within the borders of modern Italy, with a population exceeding three

---

6. McClory, *Power and the Papacy*, 25.
7. John XXII, *Quia quorundam*, 3–7.
8. Sullivan, *Magisterium*, 94.

million. He had at his disposal 13,000 troops to protect his territory and the income derived therefrom. Nevertheless, from the earliest years of the century, the pope's control over the Papal States was tenuous and his personal safety was often in jeopardy. The Papal States were at times occupied by and at other times protected by French and Austrian troops. As the century wore on, the greatest challenge was presented by Italian nationalists, who eyed Rome as the capital of a new, unified Italy. This was the situation confronting Pius IX when he ascended to the papal throne in 1846, a chair he would continue to occupy until 1878.[9]

According to Swiss theologian Hans Küng, Pius viewed the conflict over the Papal States in nearly cosmic terms, seeing it "as an episode in the age-old struggle between God and Satan."[10] The 1848 Revolution in Rome led Pius to flee to Gaeta, a seaport in the Kingdom of Naples. In 1849 the Second Roman Republic was declared. Pius requested both France and Austria to intervene and restore his temporal power. Austrian forces secured the northern Papal States while those of France secured Rome, allowing Pius to return to the Eternal City in 1850. However, a clash between the papacy and the proponents of Italian unification seemed inevitable, given that each side saw the Papal States as crucial to its mission. Pius viewed this territory as essential to the church's exercise of its spiritual authority; Italian nationalists saw the Papal States as an obstacle to Italian unification.[11] In his 1859 encyclical *Qui nuper*, Pius expresses concern about the revolutionary movements in Italy and their threat to his temporal sovereignty over the Papal States. He criticizes the government of Italy for having "acted as an adversary to the Church and its legitimate rights and sacred ministry." He argues that "temporal power is necessary to this Holy See, so that for the good of religion it can exercise spiritual power without any hindrance."[12]

Although Pius had returned to Rome, peace would be short-lived. Most of the revenue producing lands in the Papal States were lost in 1861 when several provinces were incorporated into the newly-declared Kingdom of Italy. The end of the pope's temporal power was at hand. On September 20, 1870, two months after the First Vatican Council defined the doctrine of papal infallibility, Italian troops conquered papal Rome. The Qurinale Palace ceased to be the papal residence, becoming instead the home of the King of Italy. Pius IX declared himself a "prisoner" of the Vatican. No subsequent

---

9. DeMattei, *Pius IX*, 40; Pollard, *Money and the Papacy*, 21–54.
10. Küng, *Infallible?* 75.
11. Chadwick, *History of the Popes*, 71–94.
12. Pius IX, *Qui nuper*, 1.

pope would set foot outside the walls of the Vatican until the ratification of the Lateran Accords between Italy and the Holy See in 1929.[13]

It is difficult to overestimate the devastation felt by Pius IX upon the loss of the Papal States. On a practical level, their loss deprived the Vatican of the significant income it received from its rural estates.[14] In his encyclical *Respicientes*, published a few weeks after the conquest of Rome, he bemoans their loss and sets forth his theological argument for their return. "As We look back on all things which for many years the government of Piedmont has undertaken in order to overthrow the civil rule which God granted Our Apostolic See, We are moved by profound sorrow. God's purpose in providing the successors of St. Peter with temporal jurisdiction was to enable them to perform their spiritual duties in complete freedom and security."[15] Although Pius's plea for the return of his temporal power fell on deaf ears, his spiritual power would reach unprecedented heights at the First Vatican Council.

Pastor Aeternus: The Definition of the Doctrine of Papal Infallibility

The intellectual and political challenges described above called for a papal response. Pius IX gave an early signal of his intentions in this regard in his first encyclical, *Qui pluribus*. Written five months after his papal election in 1846, Pius uses this encyclical to address the issue of the centrality of papal infallibility to the life of the church. The papacy has been established by God as the true and final interpreter of divine revelation. The pope "judges infallibly all disputes which concern matters of faith and morals." In no uncertain terms, Pius identifies the Catholic Church with the pope. "And the Church is where Peter is, and Peter speaks in the Roman Pontiff. The divine words therefore mean what this Roman See of the most blessed Peter holds and has held."[16]

Not all of the bishops who attended the First Vatican Council shared Pius's view as to the centrality of the doctrine for Catholic faith. At the beginning of the council, a large number of bishops, primarily from Germany and Austria, opposed the doctrine. Some thought it was historically or theologically unsound. Another group—the Inopportunists— accepted the doctrine

---

13. Kertzer, *Prisoner of the Vatican*, 50–58.
14. Coppa, *Politics and the Papacy*, 38; O'Malley, *Catholic History*, 20–21.
15. Pius IX, *Respicientes*, 1.
16. Pius IX, *Qui pluribus*, 10.

but thought that the timing of its pronouncement was inopportune.[17] The American bishops were hostile to any pronouncement of papal infallibility. As the bishop of Rochester, New York wrote to a colleague, "In my humble opinion, and almost every American Bishop whose opinion I have heard agrees with me, it will be a great calamity for the Church." The bishop of Pittsburgh was concerned that a declaration of papal infallibility might increase anti-Catholic sentiment among America's Protestant majority.[18]

Those in opposition to the doctrine drew intellectual support from Ignaz von Döllinger of Germany, the leading church historian of the time and a former teacher of Lord Acton.[19] The historical argument against papal infallibility rested primarily on the case of Honorius I, a pope who was condemned as a heretic in 681 by the Third Council of Constantinople.[20] That council had been called by the emperor to combat the heresy known as Monothelitism. Although the Council of Chalcedon in 451 had defined Christ as having two natures, human and divine, not all Christians accepted the Chalcedonian formula. Monophysitism, which held that Christ had a single divine nature, remained a popular belief. The compromise proposed by Monotheletism was that regardless of whether Christ had one nature or two, all could agree that he had a single will.[21] This compromise satisfied neither side of the debate. The Third Council of Constantinople condemned the Monothelete heresy and its proponents, including Honorius I. Those conciliar decrees were confirmed by Leo II, thus presenting the proponents of papal infallibility with a dilemma.[22] If Honorius was a heretic, then he was not infallible. If he was not a heretic, then the council and Leo II were in error in condemning him. In the words of historian Philip Jenkins, "This precedent would cause real problems for nineteenth-century advocates of papal infallibility."[23]

17. Chadwick, *History of the Popes*, 199–200; Chiron, *Pius IX*, 251; Hasler, *How the Pope Became Infallible*, 147.

18. Kertzer, *Prisoner of the Vatican*, 25–26.

19. Ibid., 26.

20. Third Council of Constantinople, "Condemnation of the Monothelites and of Pope Honorius I," in Denzinger and Hünermann, *Enchiridion symbolorum*, 552; Pelikan, *Christian Doctrine and Modern Culture*, 250; Powell, *Papal Infallibility*, 4.

21. Honorius I, "Letter *Scripta fraternitatis* to Patriarch Sergius of Constantinople: The Two Wills and Operations in Christ," in Denzinger and Hünermann, *Enchiridion symbolorum*, 487; Jenkins, *Jesus Wars*, 259.

22. Leo II, "Letter *Regi regum* to Emperor Constantine IV: Confirmation of the Decisions of the Third Council of Constantinople against the Monothelites and Pope Honorius I," in Denzinger and Hünermann, *Enchiridion symbolorum*, 561–63; Kelly, *Ecumenical Councils*, 59.

23. Jenkins, *Jesus Wars*, 261.

Supporters of papal infallibility—the Infallibilists—relied on the traditional view which understood Honorius's embrace of Monothelitism simply as his personal theological opinion and not an official papal pronouncement.[24] They also argued that Honorius was not a heretic but rather a simple man who did not comprehend the theological issues surrounding the Monothelete heresy.[25] However, the action of Leo II in approving the decrees of the council which had condemned Monothelitism and Honorius unquestionably was an official papal act.

Another potent historical argument against papal infallibility was that the doctrine had not been recognized by the early church.[26] Theologically, although many had held that it is not possible for a pope and a council acting in concert to err, a pope acting apart form a council does not possess the charism of infallibility.[27] Some bishops also were concerned that promulgation of the doctrine would prove to be an obstacle to ecumenical efforts with Protestant and Orthodox communities.[28] In a vote on a preliminary draft of the dogmatic constitution defining the doctrine, eighty-eight bishops disapproved of the document.[29] Prior to the final vote, fifty-seven of the opposition bishops left the council to avoid having to cast a negative vote. The final vote was 533 to two in favor of the dogmatic constitution.[30] One of the two negative votes was cast by Bishop Edward Fitzgerald of Little Rock, Arkansas.[31]

The definition of the doctrine is contained in the dogmatic constitution *Pastor Aeternus*. The terms "to define" and "definition" have technical theological meanings. Francis Sullivan explains that to define a doctrine as a dogma of faith "means to give a definitive judgment which puts an end to freedom of opinion on a question and decisively establishes some truth as an element of the normative faith of the community. For an act of the magisterium to constitute a dogmatic definition, it must be evident that it is intended as such a definitive judgment, obliging the faithful to give their assent of faith to the doctrine so defined." He also stresses the important

---

24. Kelly, *Ecumenical Councils*, 59.

25. Hasler, *How the Pope Became Infallible*, 165; Sullivan, *Creative Fidelity*, 64–65.

26. Sullivan, *Magisterium*, 82; see also Küng, *Infallible?* 202–8; Powell, *Papal Infallibility*, 32–35.

27. Pelikan, *Reformation of Church and Dogma*, 106.

28. Powell, *Papal Infallibility*, 83.

29. Kelly, *Ecumenical Councils*, 171.

30. Chadwick, *History of the Popes*, 213–14; Collins, *Keepers of the Keys*, 445; MacCulloch, *Christianity*, 825.

31. Coppa, *Politics and the Papacy*, 47; Kelly, *Ecumenical Councils*, 171.

distinction between a "doctrine" and a "dogma"; all dogmas are doctrines, but not all doctrines are dogmas.[32]

The council put forth four propositions which must be held by all Catholics. At the end of each proposition, the warning is given that if any Catholic publicly dissents from the proposition, "let him be anathema." This phrase is a formula for pronouncing a sentence of excommunication.[33]

Chapter 1 of *Pastor Aeternus* concerns the primacy of Peter, owing to his selection by Christ to be the head of his church.[34] Chapter 2 moves from the primacy of Peter to the primacy of his successors. Primacy was not personal to Peter; it is institutional, shared by all future popes as well.[35] Chapter 3 deals with "the power and character of the primacy of the Roman Pontiff." The council asserts that the pope possesses supreme power over the church.[36] The council's teaching on this point later would be codified in the Code of Canon Law, as set forth in the first epigraph at the beginning of this chapter.[37] Finally, in chapter 4 of the dogmatic constitution, the council defines "the infallible teaching authority of the Roman Pontiff."

> Therefore, faithfully adhering to the tradition received from the beginning of the Christian faith, to the glory of God our savior, for the exaltation of the Catholic religion and for the salvation of the Christian people, with the approval of the Sacred Council, we teach and define as a divinely revealed dogma that when the Roman Pontiff speaks *ex cathedra*, that is, when, in the exercise of his office as shepherd and teacher of all Christians, in virtue of his supreme apostolic authority, he defines a doctrine concerning faith or morals to be held by the whole Church, he possesses, by the divine assistance promised to him in blessed Peter, that infallibility which the divine Redeemer willed his Church to enjoy in defining doctrine concerning faith or morals. Therefore, such definitions of the Roman Pontiff are of themselves, and not by the consent of the Church, irreformable.
>
> So then, should anyone, which God forbid, have the temerity to reject this definition of ours: let him be anathema.[38]

---

32. Sullivan, *Magisterium*, 102, 131.
33. Sullivan, *Creative Fidelity*, 47.
34. First Vatican Council, *Pastor Aeternus*, chap. 1, par. 6.
35. Ibid., chap. 2, par. 5.
36. Ibid., chap. 3, par. 9.
37. *Code of Canon Law*, canon 331.
38. First Vatican Council, *Pastor Aeternus*, chap. 4, par. 9.

The term *ex cathedra*, Latin for "from the chair," is used to denote an exercise of papal infallibility according to the formula set forth in *Pastor Aeternus*. The conditions for the exercise of papal infallibility laid down by the First Vatican Council in that document have the advantage of being straight-forward and relatively easy to apply.[39] When the pope, in the exercise of his teaching office defines a doctrine concerning faith or morals to be held by all Catholics, he speaks infallibly.

There is disagreement about whether Pius IX himself or Archbishop Manning of England was responsible for the addition of the phrase "and not by the consent of the Church" in the final draft of the dogmatic constitution.[40] However, there is no dispute that the import of the phrase is far-reaching and precipitated the walkout form the council of the minority bishops prior to the final vote. The pope may issue infallible statements *ex cathedra* without either the approval of an ecumenical council or consultation with the world's bishops.[41] Since the pope may act alone, then he alone can also decide whether the statement concerns a matter of faith or morals and whether the statement is made *ex cathedra*.[42] Therefore, although Pius IX could have defined the dogma of papal infallibility in an apostolic constitution without summoning an ecumenical council, he chose the more cautious approach.

The Immaculate Conception of Mary: The First Exercise of Papal Infallibility

It is universally acknowledged by Catholic theologians that the definition of the doctrines of the Immaculate Conception of Mary and the Assumption of Mary as dogmas of the Catholic Church were exercises of papal infallibility in accordance with the formula established by the First Vatican Council in *Pastor Aeternus*. There also is near unanimous agreement that these two doctrinal proclamations have been the only exercises of papal infallibility according to the Vatican I formula. This also is the common understanding of rank and file Catholics. As the Catholic journalist Robert McClory has described, "Practically every Catholic school student for most of [the twentieth] century learned that Mary's Immaculate Conception (1854) and

---

39. Küng, *Infallible?* 81.

40. Compare Powell, *Papal Infallibility*, 67 (attributing the phrase to Archbishop Manning) with McClory, *Power and the Papacy*, 117 (attributing the phrase to Pius IX).

41. Hughes "Hans Küng," 384–85.

42. Powell, *Papal Infallibility*, 80.

her Assumption (1950) represented the only dogmas pronounced by popes *ex cathedra* in the past 150 years."[43]

Before reviewing Pius IX's definition of the doctrine of the Immaculate Conception of the Virgin Mary as a dogma of the church, it is necessary to address a preliminary question. Can papal infallibility be exercised only prospectively after Vatican I, or could a pope prior to that council have made an infallible pronouncement? In other words, may a papal pronouncement made before 1870 be considered an exercise of papal infallibility on a matter of faith or morals that must be definitively held by all Catholics? The council's dogmatic constitution *Pastor Aeternus* provides a clearly affirmative answer to these questions. The council did not believe that it was creating a new doctrine; rather, it was "faithfully adhering to the tradition received from the beginning of the Christian faith" when it defined the doctrine of papal infallibility to be "a divinely revealed dogma" to be definitively held by all Catholics.[44] Since the charism of infallibility has been possessed by all popes back to Peter, even if they were unaware of it, Pius IX could have made an infallible pronouncement when he defined the doctrine of the Immaculate Conception, so long as he satisfied the conditions laid down by the council fifteen years later.

The procedure followed by Pius IX that led up to the definition of the doctrine is instructive; it reveals that Pius chose a much more collegial course of action than the council determined was required of him. Although the council later would say that a pope could act without the consent of the church, Pius took pains to obtain such consent from the bishops around the world. In his 1849 encyclical *Ubi primum*, he addressed the possibility of defining the doctrine of the Immaculate Conception. He indicates that he had received letters from many bishops requesting that he do so. He responds to these requests by appointing a group of theologians and cardinals to make an examination of the issue and prepare a report. He also requests that the bishops advise him as to their views on whether he should define the doctrine.[45] Their responses were overwhelmingly positive, although there was some opposition.

Certain bishops believed that the doctrine could not be defined theologically, since it had been in dispute for centuries.[46] There was no New Testament support for it, and it contradicted the doctrine of the universality of human sin. The view that Mary was free from original sin had

43. McClory, *Power and the Papacy*, 145.
44. First Vatican Council, *Pastor Aeternus*, chap. 4, par. 9.
45. Pius IX, *Ubi primum*, 3–6.
46. González, *Reformation to the Present*, 401–2.

been controversial in the Middle Ages. In fact, Augustine, Bernard, Albert the Great, and Aquinas had expressed opposition to it.[47] In 1486 Sixtus IV addressed the controversy in his constitution *Grave nimis*. He condemns those who asserted that anyone who denied that Mary was conceived without original sin was guilty of heresy, "since the matter has not yet been decided by the Roman Church and the Apostolic See."[48] The Dominican Order, of which Aquinas was a member, continued to oppose the doctrine into the nineteenth century.[49] Some bishops, including Cardinal Pecci—the future Leo XIII—supported the doctrine but thought that its definition at this time was inopportune.[50] In the end, Pius followed the recommendation of the majority of bishops. The result was the definition of the doctrine as a dogma of the Catholic Church in the apostolic constitution *Ineffabilis Deus* on December 8, 1854.

Pius does not simply announce the doctrine, but first sets forth its theological basis. He begins by stating that the Catholic Church has always held the doctrine "as divinely revealed," which is confirmed by the fact that it "did not hesitate to present for public devotion and veneration of the faithful the Feast of the Conception of the Blessed Virgin." He then points to the creation and approval by popes of "confraternities, congregations and religious communities founded in honor of the Immaculate Conception." He relies on the confirmation of the doctrine by numerous popes as well as by the Council of Trent. That council had reaffirmed the doctrine of original sin but expressly excluded Mary from the intent of the decree. Pius then goes on to define the doctrine in the following terms. "We declare, pronounce, and define that the doctrine which holds that the most Blessed Virgin Mary, in the first instance of her conception, by a singular grace and privilege granted by Almighty God, in view of the merits of Jesus Christ, the Savior of the human race, was preserved free from all stain of original sin, is a doctrine revealed by God and therefore to be believed firmly and constantly by all the faithful." The definition of the doctrine is followed by a warning about the consequences of dissent; anyone who disputes the doctrine publicly is subject to excommunication.[51] This exercise of papal infallibility by Pius was a radical move; no previous

---

47. Kerr, *Aquinas*, 92; MacCulloch, *Reformation*, 21–22; Pelikan, *Growth of Medieval Theology*, 71, 164–65.

48. Sixtus IV, "Constitution *Grave nimis*: The Immaculate Conception of Mary," in Denzinger and Hünermann, *Enchiridion symbolorum*, 1425–26.

49. Chadwick, *History of the Popes*, 119.

50. Chiron, *Pius IX*, 153–55.

51. Pius IX, *Ineffabilis Deus*, 1–5.

pope ever had defined a dogma on his own authority and without the concurrence of an ecumenical council.[52]

Pius IX's definition of the doctrine of the Immaculate Conception as a dogma of Catholic faith satisfies the conditions established the First Vatican Council for the exercise of papal infallibility. According to *Pastor Aeternus*, a papal pronouncement must satisfy three conditions in order to constitute an exercise of papal infallibility. First, the pope must be acting "in the exercise of his office as shepherd and teacher of all Christians." Second, "he speaks *ex cathedra* . . . when . . . he defines a doctrine concerning faith or morals." Third, the doctrine so defined is "to be held by the whole Church."[53] An examination of these conditions as applied to *Ineffabilis Deus* reveals that they were satisfied in that apostolic constitution. First, Pius was exercising the papal teaching office when he defines the doctrine of the Immaculate Conception and not simply expressing a personal theological opinion.[54] Second, the doctrine concerns a matter of faith. Theologians universally have held that the papal definition of a doctrine as a dogma of faith is an *ex cathedra* infallible pronouncement. Third, Pius declares that the doctrine is "to be believed firmly and constantly by all the faithful." Therefore, the definition of the doctrine of the Immaculate Conception as a dogma of the Church in *Inefabillis Deus* constitutes the exercise of papal infallibility according to the conditions established by Vatican I.

Subsequent to *Pastor Aeternus*, Pius IX did not issue any *ex cathedra* pronouncements. At the council, however, he took the position that he already had taught infallibly when he had defined the doctrine of the Immaculate Conception. In the run-up to the council, Pius is reported to have made the following comment to a Belgian envoy. "People want to credit me with infallibility. I don't need it at all. Am I not infallible already? Didn't I establish the dogma of the Virgin's Immaculate Conception all by myself several years ago?"[55] According to historian Garry Wills, "Fifteen years on, when some at the Vatican Council argued that the Pope was not infallible, he responded with the assurance that he had already proved he was, in the formula by which he defined the Immaculate Conception. Mary was his Trojan horse for sneaking the dogma of his own power into the citadel by her special side door. When his own Secretary of State told him that he was alienating the world with this drive for a formal declaration of infallibility, he answered,

---

52. González, *Reformation to the Present*, 402.
53. First Vatican Council, *Pastor Aeternus*, chap. 4, par. 9.
54. Sullivan, *Magisterium*, 101.
55. Hasler, *How the Pope Became Infallible*, 82.

'I have the Blessed Virgin on my side.'"[56] A similar judgment has been expressed by John O'Malley. "At Vatican I the definition of papal infallibility was thus to some extent a ratification of a *fait accompli*."[57] From the time of his first encyclical in 1846, Pius had signaled his belief in the centrality of the doctrine of papal infallibility for the church. Therefore, it should not be surprising that he was aware that he was exercising papal infallibility when he defined the doctrine of the Immaculate Conception. When the council defined the doctrine of papal infallibility, it was confirming what Pius IX had known fifteen years earlier. All popes since Peter had the power to make infallible pronouncements, even though for almost two millennia they did not know that they possessed such authority.

The Assumption of Mary: The Last Exercise of Papal Infallibility

Pius XII's first encyclical on the Virgin Mary, *Deiparae Virginis Mariae*, issued in 1946, is a short letter to the bishops concerning whether he should proclaim as a dogma of faith the bodily Assumption of Mary into heaven. He asks the bishops whether they judge that the Assumption should be declared a dogma of faith and whether the clergy and people desire that the dogma should be defined and declared.[58] For some reason, Pius did not authorize this encyclical to be published in *Acta Apostolicae Sedis*, the official repository of papal documents, until four years later.[59]

In light of the positive responses he had received from the bishops, Pius issued the apostolic constitution *Munificentissimus Deus* in 1950. Pius ties together the doctrines of the Immaculate Conception and the Assumption, the two privileges of Mary. Humans are not exempt from original sin or from the corruption of their bodies after death. However, God granted Mary exemption from original sin. It follows, therefore, that her body also should be exempt from corruption after death.

Pius asserts that the doctrine of the Assumption is not a new one, but is "contained in the deposit of Christian faith entrusted to the Church." He cites several examples of how the doctrine has been part of the Catholic Church's tradition for centuries. The Assumption is one of the mysteries of the Rosary and has been commemorated in liturgies. The Fathers of the church "spoke of this doctrine as something already known and accepted by Christ's faithful." He concedes that Aquinas (a Dominican) never dealt

56. Wills, *Papal Sin*, 215.
57. O'Malley, *Vatican II*, 31.
58. Pius XII, *Deiparae Virginis Mariae*, 2–4.
59. Coppa, *Pius XII*, 224.

directly with the doctrine, but he is quick to point out that Bonaventure (a Franciscan) treated it as a certain one. Pius then defines the doctrine in the following terms. "We pronounce, declare, and define it to be a divinely revealed dogma: that the Immaculate Mother of God, the ever Virgin Mary, having completed the course of her earthly life, was assumed body and soul into heavenly glory. Hence if anyone, which God forbid, should dare willfully to deny or to call into doubt that which we have defined, let him know that he has fallen away completely from the divine and Catholic Faith."[60] This definition satisfied the conditions for the exercise of papal infallibility established by Vatican I: in the exercise of his papal office as universal teacher of the Church, Pius XII defined a matter of faith to be definitively held by all Catholics.

The promulgation of the dogma was not universally well-received, especially among other Christian groups. In the words of Protestant evangelical historian Mark Noll and journalist Carolyn Nystrom, "When evangelicals and Catholics think of their differences, the subject of Mary quickly comes to the top of the list."[61] Protestant, Orthodox, and Anglican critics reject the Marian dogmas as novelties with no biblical support and no basis in the tradition of the early church.[62]

The only two universally acknowledged exercises of papal infallibility have involved Marian doctrines which are rejected by most non-Catholic Christians, do not have explicit scriptural support, and have been disputed by many exemplary theologians throughout the Catholic Church's history. The Marian dogmas have continued to be a stumbling block to reconciliation between the Catholic Church and various Protestant denominations, as evidenced during numerous officially sanctioned ecumenical dialogues that have taken place since Vatican II. Noll and Nystrom observe that the issue of Mary is a problematic one for Protestants in ecumenical discussions. "Devotion to Mary, prayers to Mary, the idea that Mary was sinless and was 'assumed' into heaven all made Protestants nervous about the possibility that the Catholic attitude toward Mary crossed the line into idolatry. Most dialogues contained some discussion about Mary, even if only to admit that agreement was impossible."[63] Some non-Catholics believed that Pius's extreme devotion to Mary bordered on Mariolatry.[64]

60. Pius XII, *Munificentissimus Deus*, 4–5, 8, 15–16, 20, 31–32, 44–45.

61. Noll and Nystrom, *Is the Reformation Over?* 133.

62. MacCulloch, *Christianity*, 952; Pelikan, *Christian Doctrine and Modern Culture*, 278–79; Sullivan, *Magisterium*, 114.

63. Noll and Nystrom, *Is The Reformation Over?* 95.

64. Pollard, *Papacy in the Age of Totalitarianism*, 417.

The definition of the doctrine of the Assumption also left unanswered certain details about the doctrine, such as "whether Mary died, was buried, and experienced bodily corruption."[65] Apparently, Pius determined that resolution of these questions was not central to the doctrine.

Conclusion

History has proven that Lord Acton's fears of an unfettered exercise of papal infallibility were unfounded. Two instances of the exercise of papal infallibility over the course of more than one and one-half centuries indicates that popes believe that infallible papal pronouncements should be a rarity. But Acton's wariness about the potential misuse of papal infallibility was not entirely off the mark. Papal infallibility has cast a long shadow over all papal teaching since 1870, as the American jurist and religious scholar John Noonan has noted.

> Nonetheless, ever since the doctrine of papal infallibility had been proclaimed at the First Vatican Council, a kind of creeping pseudo-infallibilism had taken place in which many papal utterances were treated as if they were absolutely dispositive of the issue addressed. A type of fundamentalism thrived in which particular papal utterances were invoked the way a scriptural verse might be cited by a biblical fundamentalist. Hedged about by this quasi-infallibility, the pope had a place and enjoyed greater prerogatives than any secular president in relation to a legislature.[66]

Power does not always corrupt, but once exercised, it may prove difficult to restrain.

---

65. Powell, *Papal Infallibility*, 47.
66. Noonan, *The Lustre of Our Country*, 339.

2

Vatican II: The Announcement of the Infallibility of the College of Bishops

> *Although commentators assess the council's ultimate importance differently, many would agree that it was the most important religious event of the twentieth century.*
>
> —John W. O'Malley

Ever since the close of the Second Vatican Council on December 8, 1965, there has been a lively debate as to what the council had accomplished. John O'Malley argues that one's perspective on the council's achievements frequently is colored by whether one is a theologically liberal or conservative.

> During the council the media often pilloried "the conservatives" for obscurantism, intransigence, for being out of touch, and even for dirty tricks. One thing can surely be said in their favor. They saw, or at least more straightforwardly named, the novel character and heavy consequences of some of the council's decisions. The leaders of the majority, on the contrary, generally tried to minimize the novelty of some of their positions by insisting on their continuity with tradition. It is ironic that after Vatican II, conservative voices began insisting on the council's continuity, whereas so-called liberals stressed its novelty.[1]

There can be little doubt that the church that emerged after the council looked different in important respects from the church over which Pius XII had ruled. The most visible change was the shelving of the Latin Mass

1. O'Malley, *Vatican II*, 114.

in favor of Mass celebrated in the vernacular with the priest facing the congregation. The council also had a profound effect upon parish life beyond the liturgy. Its emphasis upon the church as the entire people of God, rather than just the hierarchy, has been accompanied by increased roles for lay men and women in parish ministries. In the realm of civic life, the church's embrace of religious liberty as a fundamental human right marked a dramatic break from the tradition of seeking state support for the Catholic Church to the detriment of other religions.

But one area in which the council broke new ground often is ignored—infallibility. The council would broaden the doctrine of infallibility in a manner that would render superfluous the conditions for the exercise of papal infallibility established by the First Vatican Council. The Second Vatican Council would expand the manner in which infallibility is exercised to include not only *ex cathedra* papal pronouncements, but also infallible declarations of doctrine by an ecumenical council or by the universal consensus of the worldwide episcopate without a formal declaration.

The exercise of infallibility by an ecumenical council, or by the universal consensus of the bishops throughout the world, is never exercised by the bishops alone; it is only exercised when they act in communion with the Roman Pontiff. It is this exercise of infallibility by the world's bishops in communion with the pope that I have termed the "infallibility of the college of bishops." This term is not found in the documents of Vatican II or in any official papal or curial document. I have chosen it as a shorthand reference for any exercise of infallibility other than by the pope speaking *ex cathedra*. The main difference between papal infallibility and the infallibility of the college of bishops is the manner in which they are exercised. Vatican I set forth in precise terms the manner by which papal infallibility may be exercised. Vatican II, on the other hand, announced the concept of the infallibility of the college of bishops (without using that term), but left uncertain the manner of its exercise. Subsequent developments would show that it can be exercised in such a manner that not only the faithful, but even Catholic theologians, may not be aware of it until the pope or the Congregation for the Doctrine of the Faith announces that it has in fact been exercised. Francis Sullivan has observed that it is no easy task to determine when a doctrine has been taught infallibly by the college of bishops. "The text [of *Lumen gentium*] does not, of course, take up the difficult question, which can be of practical consequence at times, of how this specially qualified unanimity is to be ascertained by the faithful who are bound to believe."[2] Since the announcement of the infallibility of the college of bishops by Vati-

---

2. Sullivan, *Magisterium*, 126.

can II, no pope has exercised papal infallibility according to the conditions established by Vatican I. The doctrine that was so controversial when it was promulgated in 1870 has, as a practical matter, been rendered moot.

Lumen gentium: Article 25 and the Infallibility of the College of Bishops

When the First Vatican Council adjourned on the eve of the Franco-Prussian War, it had not taken up the question of the role of the episcopate. That question would not be addressed until the Second Vatican Council issued its dogmatic constitution *Lumen gentium* almost a century later. Chapter 3 of *Lumen gentium*, entitled "On the Hierarchical Structure of the Church and in Particular on the Episcopate," deals with the issue of the relationship between the pope and the bishops, one which Paul VI "described as the most serious issue before the council."[3] The council in *Lumen gentium* begins by reaffirming the teaching of the First Vatican Council on the primacy and infallibility of the pope. "And all this teaching about the institution, the perpetuity, the meaning and reason for the sacred primacy of the Roman Pontiff and of his infallible magisterium, this Sacred Council again proposes to be firmly believed by all the faithful."[4] It then turns to the somewhat contentious issue of the source of episcopal authority. Two decades earlier, Pius XII had set forth his view that bishops were little more than papal assistants or delegates, exercising only that power which the pope deigns to give them. In the encyclical *Mystici corporis Christi*, he stated that when bishops exercise their office they "are subordinate to the lawful authority of the Roman Pontiff, although enjoying the ordinary power of jurisdiction which they receive directly from the same Supreme Pontiff."[5] In a repudiation of Pius's monarchical ecclesiology, article 21 of *Lumen gentium* states that bishops, as successors to the apostles, receive the full power of their office through episcopal consecration, which empowers them with the threefold office of sanctifying, teaching, and governing.[6]

The distinction between the views of the council and Pius XII may appear subtle, but it is an important one. For Pius, the bishops receive their power from the pope; for the council, the bishops receive full power from the fact of their episcopal consecration. Because bishops possess full power to teach by reason of their episcopal consecration, and not simply by

3. O'Malley, *Vatican II*, 206.
4. Second Vatican Council, *Lumen gentium*, art. 18.
5. Pius XII, *Mystici corporis Christi*, 42.
6. Second Vatican Council, *Lumen gentium*, art. 21.

delegation from the pope, they have a role in teaching doctrines infallibly, as *Lumen gentium* sets forth in article 25. But first, the council examines the larger question of the infallibility possessed by the church as a whole. "The entire body of the faithful, anointed as they are by the Holy One, cannot err in matters of belief. They manifest this special property by means of the whole peoples' supernatural discernment in matters of faith when 'from the Bishops down to the last of the lay faithful' they show universal agreement in matters of faith and morals."[7]

Before turning to the infallibility of the college of bishops, the council examines the issue of the relationship between the pope and the worldwide episcopacy. Although the bishops are not simply assistants or delegates of the pope, the college of bishops can exercise its teaching function "only with the consent of the Roman Pontiff." Likewise, an action of an ecumenical council is not valid "unless it is confirmed or at least accepted as such by the successor of Peter." Outside of a council, the college of bishops can act through their separate but unified teaching on matters of faith and morals, so long as the pope "approves or freely accepts the united action of the scattered bishops."[8]

The necessity for conciliar action to be approved by the pope recalls a medieval dispute between the popes and bishops over the power of an ecumenical council vis-a-vis the papacy, a dispute which goes by the name of "conciliarism." The issue reached a head during the Great Schism following the Avignon papacy in the fourteenth century, a period that saw multiple claimants to the papacy, an intolerable situation which the Council of Constance (1414–18) was called upon to resolve. The council deposed two of the rival claimants (the first John XXIII and Benedict XIII) and the third (Gregory XI) resigned, the last pope to do so until Benedict XVI in 2013. A new pope was elected, Martin V (1417–31), who was universally regarded as legitimate.[9] Prior to Martin's election, the Council of Constance addressed the question of the power of an ecumenical council to issue decrees binding on the pope. In its decree *Haec sancta*, the council declared that its decrees must be obeyed by everyone, even a pope.[10] Not surprisingly, this decree of the Council of Constance was not ratified by Martin V. Later, in the papal bull *Execrabilis*, Pius II rejected conciliarism

---

7. Ibid., art. 12.
8. Ibid., art. 22.
9. Collins, *Keepers of the Keys*, 297–322.
10. Council of Constance, session 5, *Haec sancta*.

in no uncertain terms. He announced that there can be no appeal from a papal decree to an ecumenical council.[11]

Article 25 of *Lumen gentium* expressly deals with the infallibility that can be exercised by the college of bishops. This infallibility may be exercised in one of two ways. It is exercised in an extraordinary manner when a doctrine is proclaimed by an ecumenical council, such as was done at the First Vatican Council when the doctrine of papal infallibility was defined. It also can be exercised in an ordinary manner outside of a council.

The first paragraph of article 25 deals with the noninfallible teaching of the bishops and the pope on matters of faith and morals. Is there a normative way in which Catholics must receive and respond to such teaching? The council does not say that dissent from such noninfallible teaching is impermissible. But it signals that such teaching of the bishops cannot be approached with a closed mind or an attitude of skepticism. Rather, it is to be accepted "with a religious assent." With respect to noninfallible teachings of the pope, the "religious submission of the mind and will must be shown in a special way."[12] However, the council fails to explain how such "religious assent" or "religious submission" is to be demonstrated, or whether principled dissent from such teaching is permissible and, if so, under what conditions.

The second paragraph deals with the exercise of infallible teaching authority by the bishops as a body. The council makes clear that individual bishops do not teach infallibly. Even the pope, when he is acting in his capacity as the bishop of Rome, rather than as the head of the universal church, cannot teach infallibly.[13] The bishops of the world, on the other hand, teach infallibly when they agree on a matter of faith or morals that is to be held definitively by all Catholics. This infallible teaching authority of the episcopate may be exercised when they are gathered together in an ecumenical council (extraordinary universal magisterium) or when they are dispersed throughout the world outside of a council (ordinary and universal magisterium).[14]

The third paragraph appears to limit the subject matter of infallibly defined doctrines. Infallibility extends only "as far as the deposit of Revelation extends." Therefore, the only truths of faith or morals which may be infallibly defined, either by the pope alone or in conjunction with the body of bishops, are those which have been divinely revealed. But if the exercise of infallibility is limited to divinely revealed truths, then how could the doctrines of the Immaculate Conception and the Assumption have been

---

11. Pius II, *Execrabilis*, 1–3.
12. Second Vatican Council, *Lumen gentium*, art. 25.
13. Sullivan, *Magisterium*, 101.
14. Second Vatican Council, *Lumen gentium*, art. 25.

promulgated *ex cathedra*, since they are not mentioned in Scripture? This question is answered by the fourth paragraph of article 25. Revealed truths are not just those found in scripture, since revelation includes both "that which is written" (truths revealed in Scripture) and that which is "orally handed down" (truths revealed in tradition).[15] What the council does not discuss is why it has taken centuries for the church to realize that some matters of tradition, such as the doctrines of the Immaculate Conception and the Assumption, are revealed truths.[16]

Mysterium ecclesiae: Can the Magisterium Err?

Less than a decade after *Lumen gentium*, the Congregation for the Doctrine of the Faith deemed it necessary to issue a declaration clarifying the council's teaching on the church in general and on infallibility in particular. The stated purpose of the 1973 declaration *Mysterium ecclesiae* is to correct the teaching of theologians who "through the use of ambiguous or even erroneous language, have obscured Catholic doctrine, and at times have gone so far as to be opposed to Catholic faith even in fundamental matters."[17] The document does not single out any theologian by name, but it has been assumed that its target was Swiss theologian Hans Küng, whose books *The Church* and *Infallible? An Unresolved Enquiry* were the subject of an investigation by the congregation.[18]

Article 12 of *Lumen gentium* dealt with the theme of the infallibility possessed by the church. However, the congregation is quick to point out that this "shared infallibility" of the people of God does not in any way diminish either the teaching role of the magisterium or its role as the sole arbiter of disputes concerning doctrine. It reiterates the three ways in which the infallibility of the magisterium may be exercised: (i) by the bishops of the world in union with the pope in declaring a doctrine to be held by all Catholics; (ii) by the definition of a doctrine by an ecumenical council; and (iii) by the pope defining a doctrine in an *ex cathedra* pronouncement. The congregation then describes the reach of infallibility on matters of faith and morals. "According to Catholic doctrine, the infallibility of the Church's Magisterium extends not only to the deposit of faith but also to those matters without which that deposit cannot be rightly preserved and expounded. The extension however of this infallibility to the deposit of faith itself is a

---

15. Ibid.
16. Sullivan, *Magisterium*, 130.
17. Congregation for the Doctrine of the Faith, *Mysterium ecclesiae*, 1.
18. Powell, *Papal Infallibility*, 171.

truth that the Church has from the beginning held as having been certainly revealed in Christ's promises."[19] This extension of the subject of infallibility beyond revealed truths to include also "those matters without which that deposit [of faith] cannot be rightly preserved and expounded," is referred to by theologians as the "secondary object of infallibility."[20]

The congregation identifies what it perceives as two erroneous interpretations of the church's infallibility. The first error asserts that even though the church possesses infallibility, history discloses occasions when the magisterium has erred in matters of faith and morals.[21] This discussion appears to be aimed squarely at Küng, who argued that any explication of the doctrine of infallibility must account for errors made by the church's magisterium throughout the centuries. For Küng, infallibility did not mean that the church cannot err, but that its message will endure in spite of the errors which it has committed over the centuries. "To err is human. It is also ecclesiastical. It has recently been pointed out that it is also papal—simply because Church and Pope are human, and human they remain. This has often been forgotten in the Church, and we have been sharply reminded of it."[22] The congregation, however, was unwilling to admit that the church could ever err on a matter of faith or morals.

The second error addressed by the congregation concerns the hierarchy of truths, a concept which was introduced by the Second Vatican Council in its decree *Unitatis redintegratio*.

> Moreover, in ecumenical dialogue, Catholic theologians standing fast by the teaching of the Church and investigating the divine mysteries with the separated brethren must proceed with love for the truth, with charity, and with humility. When comparing doctrines with one another, they should remember that in Catholic doctrine there exists a "hierarchy" of truths, since they vary in their relation to the fundamental Christian faith. Thus the way will be opened by which through fraternal rivalry all will be stirred to a deeper understanding and a clearer presentation of the unfathomable riches of Christ.[23]

---

19. Congregation for the Doctrine of the Faith, *Mysterium ecclesiae*, 2–3.

20. Germain Grisez, "Infallibility and Specific Moral Norms: A Review Discussion," in Curran and McCormick, *Dissent in the Church*, 58–96, 59; Sullivan, *Magisterium*, 131–36.

21. Congregation for the Doctrine of the Faith, *Mysterium ecclesiae*, 4.

22. Küng, *Infallible?* 27–28, 153.

23. Second Vatican Council, *Unitatis redintegratio*, 11.

Some theologians apparently had the temerity to take the council at its word that some doctrines of faith were more central than others. One of the mainstream theologians who advanced such a view was the Jesuit Avery Dulles—the son of United States Secretary of State John Foster Dulles—who was later made a cardinal by John Paul II. For Dulles, the primary truths of the Catholic faith concern the salvific work of God in Jesus Christ, as expressed in the New Testament and the creeds. Other truths which presented the greatest stumbling blocks to reunification of the Christian churches, such as the Marian dogmas and the doctrine of papal infallibility, could be seen as secondary truths.[24] Such an interpretation is one which the congregation wished to quash. "It is true that there exists an order as it were a hierarchy of the Church's dogmas, as a result of their varying relationship to the foundation of faith. This hierarchy means that some dogmas are founded on other dogmas which are the principal ones, and are illuminated by these latter. But all dogmas, since they are revealed, must be believed with the same divine faith."[25] It is difficult to see what remains of the concept of a hierarchy of truths if all dogmas are on a par with one another. The congregation appears to have taken upon itself, with the pope's approval, to interpret a conciliar document in such a way as to rewrite it.

Finally, the congregation addresses the question of the development of dogma. Its fear is that belief in the development of dogma could easily lead to dogmatic relativism. Instead, the congregation asserts that dogmas once formulated are true from the beginning and remain true forever, although their truth may be expressed more clearly as time goes on.[26] There is no development of dogma in any real sense, but only development in the expression of dogma. The congregation's criticism of the notion of the development of doctrine can be viewed as a rejection of the seminal work of theology on that issue, John Henry Newman's *An Essay on the Development of Christian Doctrine*, published in 1845. Newman, an Anglican convert who was made a cardinal by Leo XIII, had argued that all doctrines develop over time.

> Moreover, while it is certain that developments of Revelation proceeded all through the Old Dispensation down to the very end of our Lord's ministry, on the other hand, if we turn our attention to the beginnings of Apostolical teaching after His ascension, we shall find ourselves unable to fix an historical point at which the growth of doctrine ceased, and the rule of faith was

---

24. Powell, *Papal Infallibility*, 147.
25. Congregation for the Doctrine of the Faith, *Mysterium ecclesiae*, 4.
26. Ibid., 5.

once for all settled. Not on the day of Pentecost, for St. Peter had still to learn at Joppa that he was to baptize Cornelius; not at Joppa and Caesarea, for St. Paul had to write his Epistles; not on the death of the last Apostle, for St. Ignatius had to establish the doctrine of Episcopacy; not then, nor for centuries after, for the Canon of the New Testament was still undetermined.... No one doctrine can be named which starts complete at first, and gains nothing afterwards from the investigations of faith and the attacks of heresy.[27]

Mysterium ecclesiae can be viewed as an example of the Congregation, with papal approval, pulling back from the spirit of Vatican II. Many theologians have considered Newman's ideas, even though he had been dead for many decades, to have been among the most influential ones at the council.[28]

Conclusion

It is difficult for infallibility and development to peacefully co-exist. An infallible definition of a doctrine as a dogma of Catholic faith ends all discussion of the issue. John Paul II, in his apostolic letter *Ordinatio sacerdotalis*, declared that the church had no authority to ordain women to the priesthood, and that "this judgment is to be definitively held by all the Catholic faithful."[29] The issue of the power of the church to ordain women to the priesthood is the subject of chapter 13. At this point, John Paul's apostolic letter is raised only to emphasize the lasting implication of any doctrine which is taught infallibly. Since the matter has been settled for all time, there can be no development on the issue. "No genuine development in the church's teaching, once it has been infallibly proposed, can *contradict* what was previously proposed, properly understood in the sense in which it was proposed. If the Church infallibly proposed a teaching at one time and later proposed a contradictory teaching as an authentic development of its basic doctrine, then the Church's teaching would lose its meaning."[30] When John Paul issued *Ordinatio sacerdotalis*, he was not exercising papal infallibility pursuant to the conditions set forth by Vatican I. Rather, he was declaring this to be a doctrine that had been universally taught by the bishops of the world in communion with the pope. It was an exercise of the ordinary and universal magisterium, an instance of John Paul confirming the infallibility

27. Newman, *Development of Christian Doctrine*, 67–68.
28. Hebblethwaite, *Paul VI*, 109.
29. John Paul II, *Ordinatio sacerdotalis*, 4.
30. Ford and Grisez, "Contraception," 293, emphasis in original.

of the college of bishops in declaring that priestly ordination is reserved to men alone. It would not be the last time that the infallibility of the college of bishops would expand the number of doctrines which are to be definitively held by all Catholics.

3

Opposition: The Church and Modern Thought

> *Experience shows, even from the earliest times, that cities renowned for wealth, dominion, and glory perished as a result of this single evil, namely immoderate freedom of opinion, license of free speech, and desire for novelty.*
>
> —Gregory XVI (1832)

> *The Church . . . had from the nineteenth century onwards visibly entered into a negative relationship with the modern era, which had only then properly begun. Did it have to remain so? Could the Church not take a positive step into the new era?*
>
> —Benedict XVI (2012)

The Galileo Affair

THOSE WHO MAINTAIN THAT the Catholic Church, by its very nature, is opposed to advances in science, because such advances threaten revealed truth and Catholic doctrine, often point to the trial of Galileo as prosecution Exhibit No. 1. John Paul II's biographer, George Weigel, has pointed out that the Galileo case has come to symbolize the image of the church as an implacable opponent of science. "As a cultural myth, the Galileo affair had affected far more than the Church's relations with modern science. Scratch the surface of any controversy involving Catholics and modern intellectual, social, or political life, and 'Galileo' was sure to be played as a trump card by the Church's opponents."[1] In 1992, on the 350th anniversary of Galileo's death, John Paul II, in an address to the Pontifical Academy of Sciences, commented on how the Galileo affair continues to reinforce the myth of the Church's antagonism to scientific advances. "From the beginning of the Age of Enlightenment down to our own day, *the Galileo case* has been a sort of 'myth,' in which the image fabricated out of the events was quite far removed from reality. In this perspective, the Galileo case was the symbol of the Church's supposed rejection of scientific progress, or of 'dogmatic' obscurantism opposed to the free search for truth."[2]

The charge that the Catholic Church is anti-science does not withstand scrutiny. The Galileo affair was something of an aberration. Although Copernicus's works had been placed on the Index of Forbidden Books, he was never tried for heresy. In fact, Galileo himself was not found guilty of heresy. His real crime was to challenge papal authority over matters of science. In 1616, Galileo had been enjoined by Cardinal Bellarmine from promoting the Copernican heliocentric theory. In spite of the injunction, Galileo went ahead and published *Dialogue on the Two Chief World Systems, Ptolemaic and Copernican* in 1632. At his trial in 1636, Galileo could not recall whether he had been given the injunction twenty years earlier. It was his violation of the injunction, rather than a charge of heresy, which was at the center of his case.[3] His trial was focused not "on the Copernican system per se" but rather "on the narrow issue of papal authority."[4] The church was not anti-science, but it was determined to exercise its authority to control the publication of scientific discoveries until it could reconcile such discoveries with traditional church teaching.

It is unfortunate that the church's heavy-handed treatment of Galileo has left many with the impression that the church is the enemy of scientific advances. It also is ironic that this impression arose out of a controversy involving astronomy. From the time of Galileo to the present, astronomy is the science with which the Vatican has been most at home. Many of the leading astronomers of Galileo's era were Jesuits.[5] Pius XI, who carried on correspondence with the astronomer Edwin Hubble, established the Pon-

1. Weigel, *Witness to Hope*, 629.

2. John Paul II, *Address to the Plenary Session of the Pontifical Academy of Sciences*, 10.

3. The history of the Galileo affair is detailed in McMullin, *The Church and Galileo* and Rowland, *Galileo's Mistake*.

4. Rowland, *Galileo's Mistake*, 257.

5. Hart, *Atheist Delusions*, 66.

tifical Academy of Sciences in 1936. Its membership has included leading scientists of all religious persuasions, including physicists Max Planck (a Lutheran) and Nils Bohr (an atheist).[6]

While the charge that the church is anti-science is misplaced, the charge that it has been anti-Enlightenment is on the mark. Popes in the nineteenth and early twentieth centuries penned pronouncements rejecting such Enlightenment ideals as freedom of conscience, freedom of speech, freedom of the press, and freedom of religion. Catholic biblical scholars were barred from availing themselves of investigative tools which their Protestant counterparts had been using for decades. Catholic theologians who deviated from the standards of the thirteenth-century Scholastic philosophy of Aquinas were suspect and their writings subject to scrutiny by Rome. By the late twentieth century the church had embraced many of the leading Enlightenment ideals, but then only partially and after decades of resistance.

The Battle to Retain the Papal States

Throughout the nineteenth century the church was confronted by the intellectual challenges of the Enlightenment and the political fallout from the French Revolution. It perceived both developments as unmitigated disasters. In the words of Eamon Duffy, "The Catholic Church's actual experience of the birth of democracy was not as enlightenment and liberation, but as a murderous attack on religion in general, and the freedom of the Church in particular."[7] Nineteenth century popes responded to these events and their consequences by issuing encyclicals condemning the evils of the time, especially liberalism, socialism, and atheism.[8]

A more existential threat to the pope was presented by the proponents of Italian unification, whose armed advocacy of a politically united Italian peninsula included a takeover of the Papal States. A clash between the papacy and the proponents of Italian unification was inevitable, given that each side saw the Papal States as critical to its mission. When the Papal States were lost in 1870, Pius was unable to reconcile himself to this event. According to political scientist David Alvarez, "The demise of the Papal States, lands that had been in the papal domain for a millennium,

---

6. Pollard, *Papacy in the Age of Totalitarianism*, 196–97.

7. Duffy, *Ten Popes*, 94. "In its official pronouncements, the church almost invariably assumed a negative stance toward every aspect of 'the modern world'" (O'Malley, *Catholic History*, 156).

8. O'Malley, *Vatican II*, 55.

was the defining event of the nineteenth-century Papacy."[9] On a practical level, the loss of the Papal States deprived the Vatican of the significant income it had received from its rural estates.[10] The legal status of the loss of the Papal States was codified in the Italian Law of Guarantees, which was enacted on May 13, 1871 and would remain in effect until 1929. The Italian government guaranteed to the pope the use, but not the ownership, of Vatican properties. He was granted the privileges and immunities of a sovereign, but the Vatican was not recognized as a sovereign state. The law contained an annual grant of 3,225,000 lire (approximately $625,000), a stipend which Pius IX refused to accept.[11] The only step that he could take at this point was to lash out at those who had brought about this result. In *Respicientes*, he declares "that any who have invaded or usurped Our provinces or Our beloved City (as well as those commanding these things and their partisans, helpers, advisers, and followers) have incurred excommunication."[12] In *Ubi nos*, issued only two days after the passage of the Law of Guarantees, he remained defiant.

> Reflecting on all these matters, We are compelled to confirm again and profess without change what We have often declared to you and what you have all agreed with. Divine Providence gave the civil rule of the Holy See to the Roman Pontiff. This rule is necessary in order that the Roman Pontiff may never be subject to any ruler or civil power, but may be able to freely exercise his supreme power and authority of feeding and ruling the entire flock of the Lord, and of looking after the greater good of this Church, its well-being, and its needs.[13]

Pius's verbal assaults on the usurpers of the Papal States in these two encyclicals are characteristic of the manner in which he responded to the loss of his temporal power, as noted by papal historian Owen Chadwick. "During the last seven years of Pope Pius IX he did nothing to try to get back a papal State—except protest.... He looked to God, and left it to him, and expected that some time a miracle would occur."[14] But the miracle never came. The political realities in Italy were such that the return of the Papal States never was a realistic possibility.

---

9. Alvarez, *Spies in the Vatican*, 45.
10. Coppa, *Politics and the Papacy*, 38.
11. D'Agostino, *Rome in America*, 48–49; Kertzer, *Prisoner of the Vatican*, 86–87.
12. Pius IX, *Respicientes*, 13.
13. Pius IX, *Ubi nos*, 11.
14. Chadwick, *History of the Popes*, 243.

The status of the Papal States, the so-called "Roman Question," finally was settled by three interrelated treaties (the "Lateran Accords") entered into in 1929 between the Holy See and the Kingdom of Italy. With the signing of the Lateran Accords, the bonds that had joined the papacy and the government of Italy were broken. From that point forward, relations between the Holy See and Italy would be conducted at arm's length. The Holy See would be a "foreign power" in the eyes of the Italian government.

The *Conciliation Treaty* recognizes (i) the Catholic religion as the only state religion of Italy, (ii) the sovereignty of the Holy See , and (iii) the Holy See's ownership of and jurisdiction over the Vatican. It also establishes normal diplomatic relations between the Holy See and the government of Italy. The Holy See "declares the Roman Question to be definitively and irrevocably settled and therefore eliminated, and recognizes the Kingdom of Italy under the Dynasty of the House of Savoy, with Rome as the capital of the Italian State."[15] In the *Financial Convention*, Italy agrees to pay to the Holy See 750,000,000 Italian lire (approximately $90 million at 1929 exchange rates) and one billion lire in Italian state bonds as compensation for the loss of the Papal States, which the Holy See accepted as a final financial settlement.[16] The third treaty was the *Concordat*, which regulates relations between the Catholic Church and the Italian government. Italy assures the church freedom of public worship. The state recognizes the feast days established by the church. Before the appointment of bishops, the Holy See will communicate the name to the government to determine whether there is any political objection to the appointment. All bishops are required to take an oath of allegiance to the state. Bishops and pastors must speak Italian. The state recognizes the civil consequences of sacramental marriage, thereby making divorce unavailable. Religious instruction in public primary and secondary schools shall be under the authority of the bishops. Catholic Action must conduct its activities outside of political parties and under the control of the church, and clergy are prohibited from belonging to or campaigning for any political party.[17] With the *Conciliation Treaty* and the *Concordat* both declaring the Roman Question to be settled, Pius XI became the first pope since 1870 to be free of this issue.

---

15. Lateran Accords, *Conciliation Treaty*, arts. 1–3, 12, 26.

16. Lateran Accords, *Financial Convention*, arts. 1–2. For a discussion of the impact of the Lateran Accords on Vatican finances, see Pollard, *Money and the Modern Papacy*, 138–67.

17. Lateran Accords, *Concordat*, arts. 1, 11, 19, 22, 34, 36, 43.

The Lateran Accords were signed in February, 1929. In July of that year, Pius XI became the first pope to set foot outside the Vatican since 1870.[18] From that point, the pope was no longer a prisoner of the Vatican.

The Opening Attacks on Modern Thought

On the fiftieth anniversary of the opening of the Second Vatican Council in 2012, Benedict XVI noted that the attitude of the church toward the modern world had changed dramatically from the nineteenth century to the time of the council. "The Church, which during the Baroque era was still, in a broad sense, shaping the world, had from the nineteenth century onwards visibly entered into a negative relationship with the modern era, which had only then properly begun. Did it have to remain so? Could the Church not take a positive step into the new era?"[19] If Benedict's question had been asked of the nineteenth-century popes, their answer would have been a resounding no. A biographer of Pius IX has characterized his pontificate as "encapsulating the clash between the Catholic Church and the modern world."[20] This clash did not begin with Pius IX, since his predecessor Gregory XVI already had sounded the alarm in his most famous encyclical, *Mirari vos*, issued in 1832. "Now we consider another abundant source of the evils with which the Church is afflicted at present: *indifferentism*. This perverse opinion is spread on all sides by the fraud of the wicked who claim that *it is possible to obtain the eternal salvation of the soul by the profession of any kind of religion, as long as morality is maintained.*" If religious indifferentism were acceptable, it would imply that liberty of conscience was a fundamental human right. Gregory makes it clear, however, that Catholic doctrine recognizes no such right. "This shameful font of indifferentism gives rise to that absurd and erroneous proposition which claims that *liberty of conscience* must be maintained for everyone. It spreads ruin in sacred and civil affairs, though some repeat over and over again with the greatest impudence that some advantage accrues to religion from it."[21]

Pius IX continued Gregory's assault on Enlightenment thought in *Qui pluribus*. The errors of modern thought are inalterably opposed to the teachings of the church. He accuses the enemies of the church of waging "war against the whole Catholic commonwealth . . . . They teach that the most holy mysteries of our religion are fictions of human invention, and

18. D'Agostino, *Rome in America*, 202; Kertzer, *Prisoner of the Vatican*, 292.
19. Benedict XVI, *Reflections*, 2.
20. De Mattei, *Pius IX*, xiii.
21. Gregory XVI, *Mirari vos*, 13–14.

that the teaching of the Catholic Church is opposed to the good and the prerogatives of human society. They are not even afraid to deny Christ Himself and God." They reject faith, because they see it as "opposed to human reason."[22] Pius subscribed to the medieval understanding of the relation between faith and reason, *fides* and *ratio*. For medieval theologians, there could be no contradiction between faith and reason, because each had a common source.[23] "For although faith is above reason, no real disagreement or opposition can ever be found between them; this is because both of them come from the same greatest source of unchanging and eternal truth, God." Pius also echoes Gregory's total rejection of indifferentism.[24]

It is apparent that Enlightenment ideas about inalienable human rights, which played a central role in the philosophy behind the Declaration of Independence and the Bill of Rights, formed no part of Pius's thinking. To him, the Enlightenment was the father of the terror and anti-clericalism of the French Revolution, rather than a source of civic peace founded on political democracy and religious freedom.[25] Enlightenment thinkers had as little use for Pius as he had for them, as Benedict XVI—writing as Joseph Ratzinger—has noted. "As early as the eighteenth century, the Enlightenment was announcing that the Pope, that the Dali Lama of Europe, was inevitably doomed to disappear one day."[26]

In *Nostis et nobiscum*, Pius returns to the theme of *Qui pluribus* and its attack on modern thought. The church's enemies "say that Protestantism should be brought in, set up and increased to replace Catholicism. Then Italy could once more acquire its former splendor of ancient, that is, pagan, times." Pius, on the other hand, is convinced that Italy's true splendor is due to the fact that "Christ placed the holy See of Peter there," an argument which is unsupported by any historical evidence. He expresses the hope that Italy's political leaders will protect the church's spiritual and temporal rights, a hope which would be dashed twenty-one years later with the loss of the Papal States.[27]

The most important document issued by Pius IX attacking the errors of modern thought is not an encyclical, but the *Syllabus of Errors*, which was issued on December 8, 1864, the tenth anniversary of his infallible pronouncement of the Immaculate Conception of Mary. The idea that Pius

22. Pius IX, *Qui pluribus*, 4–5.
23. Pelikan, *Growth of Medieval Theology*, 98–99.
24. Pius IX, *Qui pluribus*, 6, 15.
25. O'Malley, *Vatican II*, 38–39, 54.
26. Ratzinger, *Light of the World*, 134.
27. Pius IX, *Nostis et nobiscum*, 3–4, 32.

should issue a compilation of the errors of modern times was suggested to him in 1849 by Cardinal Pecci.[28] The precipitating event which prompted Pius to publish the *Syllabus* was a conference in Belgium in 1863 at which a French Catholic aristocrat, Charles Montalembert, opined that the church should reconcile itself with democracy, a suggestion which Pius found abhorrent.[29] The propositions contained in the *Syllabus* were not new, but represented an amalgamation of ideas from earlier writings of Pius.[30] The *Syllabus* set forth eighty erroneous propositions, without commentary, under the following ten headings:

1. Pantheism, Naturalism and Absolute Rationalism (prop. 1–7);
2. Moderate Rationalism (prop. 8–14);
3. Indifferentism, Latitudinarianism (prop. 15–18);
4. Socialism, Communism, Secret Societies, Biblical Societies, Clerico-liberal Societies (unnumbered);
5. Errors Concerning the Church and Her Rights (prop. 19–38);
6. Errors About Civil Society, Considered Both in Itself and in its Relation to the Church (prop. 39–55);
7. Errors Concerning Natural and Christian Ethics (prop. 56–64);
8. Errors Concerning Christian Marriage (prop. 65–74);
9. Errors Regarding the Civil Power of the Sovereign Pontiff (prop. 75–76); and
10. Errors Having Reference to Modern Liberalism (prop. 77–80).

Rationalism is rejected, because it treats scriptural revelation, including the person of Jesus Christ himself, as myths. Even moderate rationalism is in error, because it completely divorces philosophy from revelation. Latitudinarianism and indifferentism mistakenly treat Protestantism as on an equal footing with the Catholic Church. Errors concerning the church and her rights include the notion that the church has no temporal power and may not use force, and that the power of the papacy may be transferred by the decree of a general council from the bishop of Rome to the bishop of another city. Errors about civil society include the view that supervision over public education belongs completely to the state and should be free from ecclesiastical control. Marriage is erroneously viewed as a contract only,

---

28. Chiron, *Pius IX*, 192; De Mattei, *Pius IX*, 115.
29. Duffy, *Saints and Sinners*, 295.
30. Chiron, *Pius IX*, 201.

so that divorce may be sanctioned by civil authority. It is error to propose that the abolition of the temporal power of the pope would be beneficial to the church, and that the pope should "come to terms with progress, liberalism and modern civilization."[31] Owen Chadwick has characterized the last quoted condemned error—Proposition 80—as incredibly damaging to the image of the papacy. "No sentence ever did more to dig a chasm between the pope and modern European society."[32] Pius succumbed to none of these errors, refusing to find any redeeming value in contemporary philosophical, scientific, political, or religious thought. Historian John Ratté has remarked that Pius's worldview was shared by many Catholic thinkers of his time. "Nineteenth-century Catholic social theory . . . saw the middle ages as the model for a re-Christianized Europe and pointed, not to errors *in* the modern world, but to the modern world (that is, the world of the Enlightenment and the French Revolution) as error itself."[33]

On the same day that the *Syllabus* was issued, the encyclical letter *Quanta cura* was published. Unlike the *Syllabus*, the encyclical does not contain a list of specific errors, but sets forth in narrative paragraphs certain modern errors of a general nature. Pius begins by reminding the bishops that he had already "condemned the chief errors of this most unhappy age" in his inaugural encyclical eighteen years earlier. It was now time for him to address certain "other evil opinions, which spring forth from the said errors as from a fountain." These errors include the view that there is no distinction between religions and the notion that liberty of conscience and worship are rights enjoyed by each individual. Communism and socialism are particularly pernicious, because they seek to remove the influence of religion from the family, the education of youth, and society as a whole. Some go so far as to suggest that the church is subordinate to civil authority. Not only does Pius condemn these errors, but he demands that all Catholics do the same.[34] The encyclical stops short, however, of detailing the punishment for Catholics who dissent from its teaching or who embrace the errors denounced in the *Syllabus*.

---

31. Pius IX, *Syllabus of Errors*, props. 7, 14, 18, 24, 35, 45, 47, 67, 76, 80.

32. Chadwick, *History of the Popes*, 176.

33. Ratté, *Three Modernists*, 10, emphasis in original. "Gregory XVI and Pius IX . . . were hardly alone among religious figures in their fear of Liberalism" (O'Malley, *Vatican II*, 60).

34. Pius IX, *Quanta cura*, 2–6.

The Confrontation with Freemasonry

Leo XIII focused his attacks against the errors of modern thought on a particular target. Freemasonry, which historian Gordon Wood has characterized as "a surrogate religion for an Enlightenment suspicious of traditional Christianity," was the most frequent target of Leo's wrath.[35] He penned over two hundred documents in which Freemasonry was condemned.[36] Modern Freemasonry began in London in 1717 and spread to the Continent and the Americas. The first papal condemnation of the association is found in Clement XII's 1738 papal bull *In eminenti*. A "papal bull" is a category of important papal documents that are sealed with a *bulla*, a lead seal. All such sealed documents previously were referred to as papal bulls. Today, such documents are designated as apostolic constitutions, apostolic exhortations, apostolic letters, or encyclicals.[37] Clement forbade Catholics from joining Masonic lodges "under pain of excommunication."[38] Freemasonry was irreconcilable with Catholic doctrine. It constituted a religious sect which proclaimed God as the "Great Architect of the Universe," did not accept the divinity of Christ, and treated all religions as competing belief systems seeking an unattainable absolute truth.[39] An association that regarded the church as merely one way among many in the search for answers to the questions of life could not be countenanced by a church firmly convinced that it had a monopoly on such answers.

Leo XIII's opening salvo against Freemasonry was fired in 1882 through his encyclical *Etsi nos*. He does not mention Freemasonry by name, but attacks the views of a "pernicious sect" and its impact upon the church in Italy. He asserts that the goal of this sect is the overthrow of the church and all religion. He believes that the problems besetting the church will have a negative impact on Italian civil and political life, without demonstrating the causal connection between the two.[40] Leo continued the attack on Freemasonry two years later in *Humanum genus*. In spite of papal pronouncements forbidding Catholics from joining these societies, their growth had not been stanched. He describes the purpose of Freemasonry as "the utter overthrow of that whole religious and political order of the world which the Christian teaching has produced, and the substitution of

---

35. Wood, *American Revolution*, 223.
36. Kertzer, *Prisoner of the Vatican*, 314 n. 5.
37. Sullivan, *Creative Fidelity*, 21.
38. Clement XII, *In eminenti*, 1.
39. For an examination of the religious beliefs of Freemasonry, see Whalen, *American Freemasonry*, 100–114.
40. Leo XIII, *Etsi nos*, 2–4, 8.

a new state of things in accordance with their ideas, of which the foundations and laws shall be drawn from mere naturalism." These naturalists "allow no dogma of religion or truth which cannot be understood by the human intelligence." They seek to destroy the papacy and foster indifferentism. They advocate civil marriage and divorce and attempt to put control of education in the hands of laymen. He urges the bishops to instruct Catholics about the evils of Freemasonry and to announce the prohibition against Catholics joining the society.[41]

Leo's next three attacks were directed specifically at Italian Freemasonry. Freemasons had not been a power in Italian politics during the reign of Pius IX, but they were becoming more influential in the late 1880s.[42] *Dall' alto dell' Apostolico Seggio*, published in 1890, is addressed not only to bishops and clergy, but also to the people of Italy. Leo blames Freemasonry for the loss of the Papal States and the pope's temporal power, the suppression of religious orders, the confiscation of church property, and compulsory military service for ecclesiastics. The features of the Masonic program in Italy were the removal of religious instruction from schools, an atheistic state, the regulation by the state of ecclesiastical property and, most ominously, "*the abolition of the Papacy*."[43] Freemasons had played a role in ending compulsory religious education in public schools and in extending conscription to the clergy.[44] Leo urges the Italian people to be mindful of their historic debt to the Catholic Church.[45]

Two years later, Leo returns to the theme of Freemasonry in Italy with a pair of encyclicals issued on the same day. In *Inimica vis*, which is addressed to the bishops of Italy, he expresses concern that "those who wage war on religion seem to show more energy than those who repel it." He urges the bishops "to inflame souls by persuasion, exhortation, and example; nourish in the clergy and our people a zeal for religion and salvation which is active, resolute, and intrepid."[46] *Custodi di quella fede* is addressed to the Italian people. He deplores the fact that Freemasonry "has finally come to dominate Italy and even Rome." Once again, he outlines the evils of the society: the substitution of naturalism for Christianity; the supremacy of reason over faith and material progress over spiritual progress; and the removal of Christian influence from public life. On a practical note, he warns the faithful to

41. Leo XIII, *Humanum genus*, 6–7, 10, 12, 15–16, 21, 31.
42. Kertzer, *Prisoner of the Vatican*, 110–12, 125.
43. Leo XIII, *Dell' alto dell' Apostolico Seggio*, 6.
44. Kertzer, *Prisoner of the Vatican*, 117–19.
45. Leo XIII, *Dell' alto dell' Apostolico Seggio*, 13.
46. Leo XIII, *Inimica vis*, 9.

be suspect of any groups "that remove themselves from religious influence," because they could become dominated by Freemasons.[47]

In *Spesse volte*, he recounts the ills which have beset the church in Italy following the loss of the Papal States, and then launches into a typical attack on Freemasonry. "Persistent efforts were made to deprive all public institutions of their religious and Christian character; dissident religions were favoured; and whilst the widest liberty was given to the masonic sects, intolerance and odious repression were reserved for the one religion which was ever the glory, the stay and the strength of the Italian people." He refers specifically to the forced dissolution of "many Catholic charitable societies . . . without any proof of their guilt."[48] He does not offer any new prescriptions for dealing with the problem, simply referring back to two of his earlier encyclicals on Freemasonry.

The church continues to be suspicious of Freemasonry. In 1983, the Congregation for the Doctrine of the Faith issued a declaration in which it upheld the continuing validity of the church's ban on Catholic membership in Masonic societies.[49] In spite of the church's unequivocal condemnation of Freemasonry, unsubstantiated allegations continue to surface from time to time to the effect that high-ranking Freemasons occupy positions of power in the Vatican.[50]

The Campaign against Modernism

Historian Marvin O'Connell has noted that "the very word 'Modernism,' in its Catholic context, defies precise definition."[51] It was not a term which Catholic writers used to describe themselves. Instead, as explained by journalist Cullen Murphy, it was a pejorative term applied by Pius X as a catchall category for ideas which were in conflict with traditional Catholic doctrine. "Modernism had no single source or target, and was not really a movement until labeled a deviant phenomenon by the Church—a textbook instance of the power of a name to define a foe into existence."[52]

---

47. Leo XIII, *Custodi di quella fede*, 3–4, 13.

48. Leo XIII, *Spesse volte*, 4, 15.

49. Congregation for the Doctrine of the Faith, *On Masonic Associations*, 1.

50. For example, investigative journalist David Yallop has claimed, without citation to any evidence, that John Paul I "had been given a secret list of 121 alleged Masons, many working close to him in the Vatican" (Yallop, *Power and Glory*, 33).

51. O'Connell, *Critics on Trial*, xi.

52. Murphy, *God's Jury*, 171.

Pius X's lengthiest encyclical, *Pascendi dominici gregis*, issued in 1907, is a blistering broadside against Modernism. When Leo XIII took on Freemasonry, his target was the enemies who were threatening the church from without. When Pius sets his sights on the Modernists, he trains his guns on the enemy within. For him, "every Modernist sustains and comprises within himself many personalities; he is a philosopher, a believer, a theologian, an historian, a critic, an apologist, a reformer."[53]

The philosophical foundation of Modernism is agnosticism. Modernists reject everything in history "suggestive of the divine," the person of Christ is reduced to a historical figure, and all of his words and deeds which do not fit comfortably in the context of the first-century Jewish homeland are excluded. They believe that dogma must evolve and change, being "*under the sway of a blind and unchecked passion for novelty*."[54]

As believers, Modernists separate faith and science, which permits them to take seemingly contradictory positions depending upon from which of the two sides they are viewing an issue, such as miracles. For the Modernist as theologian, the church and the sacraments were not instituted by Christ but are merely symbols. Scripture is a work of human beings, simply a collection of experiences. The state and the church must be separate and "in temporal matters the Church must be subject to the State." Modernists believe that everything in the church is subject to development, including dogma.[55]

As an historian, the Modernist views the sayings of Jesus from the standpoint of Jesus's time, place, and circumstances. As a critic, the Modernist does not read the books of scripture as having been written by those whose names they bear; rather, they are the products of a development from primitive oral narratives to the completed books we know today. As an apologist, the Modernist accepts as a fact that Christ "erred in determining the time when the coming of the Kingdom of God was to take place." Finally, as a reformer, the Modernist treats Scholastic philosophy as an obsolete system, questions clerical celibacy, and believes that the lower ranks of clergy and even the laity should have a share in church governance. Pius attributes the cause of Modernism to "curiosity and pride;" the latter "leads them to hold themselves up as the rule for all." They wage war on Scholasticism, tradition, and the magisterium of the church.[56]

---

53. Pius X, *Pascendi dominici gregis*, 5.
54. Ibid., 9, 13.
55. Ibid., 16–26.
56. Ibid., 30, 34, 36, 38, 40, 42.

Pius advances several proposals to counter the influence of Modernism. He decrees that Scholastic philosophy, in particular Aquinas, should be the foundation of theology. Modernists are ineligible to serve as professors in seminaries and Catholic universities; if they already hold such positions, they are to be removed. Bishops must prevent Modernist writings from being published or read, and Catholic booksellers may not sell books condemned by the bishops. Official censors are to be appointed in each diocese to examine writings prior to publication. Conferences of priests have been used by Modernists as venues "to propagate and defend their opinions"; therefore, bishops should permit them only in rare circumstances. Finally, in each diocese a "Council of Vigilance" is to be established to "watch most carefully for every trace and sign of Modernism both in publications and in teaching, and, to preserve from it the clergy and the young, they shall take all prudent, prompt and efficacious measures."[57]

In light of the draconian nature of Pius's solutions, it is not surprising that his anti-Modernist crusade has been characterized as "a form of theological McCarthyism."[58] Two examples will demonstrate that this comparison is neither gratuitous nor exaggerated. First, Pius established a group within the Secretariat of State, the *Sodalitium Pianum* (Sodality of Pius V), which employed a network of informants to root out suspected Modernists throughout Europe.[59] Second, it is reported that Pius's successor, Benedict XV, discovered a denunciation of himself in Pius's papers.[60]

Although the Modernist crisis generally was limited to Catholic intellectual circles, Pius proscribed a far reaching remedy when he issued the *Oath against Modernism* in 1910.[61] The oath was "to be sworn to by all clergy, pastors, confessors, preachers, religious superiors, and professors in philosophical-theological seminaries." The oath taker must swear to reject the view that dogmas change, reject textual criticism as a norm for scriptural interpretation, reject that the writings of the Fathers should be interpreted like any other human document, and be "completely opposed to the error of the modernists."[62] The campaign against Modernism succeeded, and the movement was dead by 1910.[63] However, the effect of the measures taken by Pius X to combat Modernism would be felt for decades. According to

57. Ibid., 45–55.
58. Wills, *Papal Sin*, 44.
59. O'Malley, *Vatican II*, 71.
60. Pollard, *Unknown Pope*, 44–45.
61. O'Connell, *Critics on Trial*, 347–48.
62. Pius X, *Oath against Modernism*, 1.
63. Ratté, *Three Modernists*, 25.

Rembert Weakland, the former Archbishop of Milwaukee, "The theological suppression of the first decade of the century and the fears it instilled resulted in a total lack of theological creativity in the U.S.A. for half a century."[64] The *Oath against Modernism* was not abolished until 1967.[65]

The Modernist movement never took hold in America, in large part because the American Catholic Church "lacked a native intellectual tradition which would make it receptive to Modernism."[66] However, there was an American Protestant counterpart to the campaign against Modernism, a movement which would give rise to the term "fundamentalism." From 1910 to 1915, leading evangelical Protestant scholars, seeking to stem the influence of liberalism on Protestant theology, published a series of twelve paperback volumes entitled *The Fundamentals*. The project was financed by two Southern California oilmen, the Stewart brothers, who paid for the distribution of three million volumes free of charge.[67] The purpose of the project was to reassert the "'five points of fundamentalism': the verbal inspiration and inerrancy of the Bible, the deity of Christ, the virgin birth of Christ, the substitutionary doctrine of the atonement, and the physical resurrection and bodily return of Christ."[68] Also like Pius X, the authors of *The Fundamentals* displayed little concern for social ethics.[69]

American fundamentalism also had its own version of the Galileo affair. In the immediate aftermath of the First World War, fundamentalists turned their attention to the teaching of evolution in public schools.[70] The result was the introduction in several southern states of antievolution legislation. In 1925, Tennessee passed a law making it a criminal offense to teach about evolution in the public schools.[71] A test case was brought in Dayton, Tennessee against John Scopes, a twenty-four-year-old science instructor, who had used a textbook which discussed evolution.

Although Scopes was the defendant, in reality it was fundamentalism—especially its emphasis on a literal reading of the Genesis accounts of creation—that was on trial. Each side was represented by an iconic American figure. The prosecution was assisted by William Jennings Bryan, a

---

64. Rembert G. Weakland, "The Price of Orthodoxy," in Curran and McCormick, *Dissent in the Church*, 184–88, 187.

65. Talar, "Swearing against Modernism," 566.

66. Ratté, *Three Modernists*, 291.

67. Lambert, *Religion in American Politics*, 107; Marsden, *Fundamentalism*, 118–23.

68. Pelikan, *Christian Doctrine and Modern Culture*, 326.

69. Marsden, *Fundamentalism*, 120.

70. Ibid., 141.

71. Larson, *Summer for the Gods*, 31–59.

former progressive Democratic presidential candidate and secretary of state under Woodrow Wilson. Bryan was an evangelical Christian who believed that the majority had the right to control what was taught in public schools at taxpayers' expense. He had supported a law that would not prohibit all teaching about Darwinism, but only would prevent teachers from claiming that the theory of evolution was true.[72] Bryan's approach was similar to that adopted by the church in its dealings with Galileo in 1616; Galileo was not forbidden from proposing the Copernican hypothesis, but only from making the claim that it was true.[73] The Tennessee statute that was enacted, however, went further than Bryan had advocated, by banning all mention of evolution in classrooms. The lead defense counsel was Clarence Darrow, who had made his reputation defending labor radicals and wealthy murderers. An avowed atheist, Darrow saw it as his duty to "'prevent bigots and ignoramuses from controlling the education of the United States.'" The trial was covered by all of the nation's leading newspapers, one going so far as to compare it to the church's trial of Galileo.[74]

The highlight of the trial was when Darrow called Bryan as an expert witness on the Bible, and subjected him to two hours of withering cross-examination. He ridiculed Bryan's literal interpretation of such biblical stories as Jonah living for three days in a whale and Joshua making the sun stand still. Bryan was forced to concede that the "six days" of creation in Genesis were ages or periods of time rather than twenty-four hour segments. Darrow succeeded in making Bryan, and by extension fundamentalism, look silly, but he lost the case. The jury found Scopes guilty after deliberating for only nine minutes, and the judge imposed a fine of one hundred dollars on him. Darrow had won, however, in the sense that after the trial, fundamentalists would withdraw from political activities for decades. They instead would focus on establishing their own schools or opting for home schooling, places where they could be free from Darwin's influence and his threat to scripturally-based science.[75]

The Catholic Church was noticeably absent from the battle over evolution in America's public schools. Most of the antievolution activities were in the South, a region where the Catholic presence was not significant. Although the church did not embrace evolution, some Catholics saw the dispute not as one between religion and science, but as an examples of

---

72. Ibid., 6.

73. Michel-Pierre Lerner, "The Heliocentric Heresy: From Suspicion to Confirmation," in McMullin, *The Church and Galileo*, 11–37.

74. Larson, *Summer for the Gods*, 6, 89–93.

75. Ibid., 170–93, 229–34.

Protestants using the public school system to promote their religious beliefs. In addition, Catholics already had control of their own parochial schools and colleges.[76] The church had no reason or desire to insert itself into a second Galileo trial; one had been enough.

The Enlightenment Reconsidered

A new attitude toward the modern world was signaled by Paul VI in his inaugural encyclical *Ecclesiam suam*, which was published between the first and second sessions of the Second Vatican Council. It is addressed not only to the bishops but also to "the clergy and faithful of the entire world, and to all men of good will." At the beginning of the encyclical, Paul sets forth its purpose in clear and straightforward terms. "The aim of this encyclical will be to demonstrate with increasing clarity how vital it is for the world, and how greatly desired by the Catholic Church, that the two should meet together, and get to know and love one another." Unlike some of his predecessors, Paul's approach to the modern world was not one of disdain but openness. He is equally clear that the goal of the encyclical is a modest one. "Nor do We propose to make this encyclical a solemn proclamation of Catholic doctrine or of moral or social principles. Our purpose is merely to send you a sincere message, as between brothers and members of a common family."[77]

He identifies three principal policies of his pontificate as it relates to the church. The first is self-knowledge. The second concerns renewal of the church. The third is for the church to establish dialogue with the modern world, the particulars of which he will leave to the determination of the council. He then goes on to analyze each of these policies in turn.

The self-knowledge which the church must deepen is a direct response to the threat of "secular philosophies and secular trends" with which it is confronted. The remedy is a familiar one. "The Church must get a clearer idea of what it really is in the mind of Jesus Christ as recorded and preserved in Sacred Scripture and in Apostolic Tradition, and interpreted and explained by the tradition of the Church under the inspiration and guidance of the Holy Spirit."

The second policy, renewal of the church, has as a prerequisite a proper understanding of the relationship between the church and the world, because "the Church does not exist in isolation from the world." Renewal does not involve any change in the church's "essential nature," but rather

---

76. Ibid., 126, 262.
77. Paul VI, *Ecclesiam suam*, 3, 7.

a restoration of the church to its original ideal. Restoration, however, does not consist in adapting the church to secular modes of thought. In this effort of renewal, the church must be guided by the two fundamental gospel principles, the spirit of poverty and charity.

Finally, Paul addresses the dialogue which the church must enter into with the modern world. Such dialogue is required if the church hopes to influence the world at large. "The Church must enter into dialogue with the world in which it lives. It has something to say, a message to give, a communication to make." Pius XII also believed that the church had a message for the world; but for him this message was delivered as a sermon, not a dialogue. The role of the pope was to teach; the role of the world was to listen and docilely obey. Paul, on the other hand, realizes that such an approach cannot succeed in the second half of the twentieth century. This dialogue must respect the intelligence and dignity of those non-Catholics whom the church wishes to engage. Such dialogue "is demanded by the pluralism of society, and by the maturity man has reached in this day and age. Be he religious or not, his secular education has enabled him to think and speak, and conduct a dialogue with dignity."[78] The importance of "dialogue" for Paul is highlighted by the appearance of the word more than seventy times in the encyclical.[79]

Paul is aware that this dialogue is not without danger, particularly the danger of relativism as the church attempts to come to terms with the challenges of the modern world. He singles out atheism as "the most serious problem of our time." He emphatically rejects Communist ideology, although he does not close the door on dialogue with its proponents. Dialogue is possible because modern atheists often are "fired with enthusiasm and idealism, dreaming of justice and progress and striving for a social order which they conceive of as the ultimate of perfection, and all but divine." Dialogue also is possible with followers of non-Christian religions, due to the shared values of all religions.[80]

The openness which Paul displayed toward the modern world was echoed by the Second Vatican Council the next year in its pastoral constitution *Gaudium et spes*. The council addressed itself "not only to the sons of the Church and to all who invoke the name of Christ, but to the whole of humanity." It unequivocally declares that the concerns of the modern age are shared by the church. "The joys and the hopes, the griefs and the anxieties of the men of this age, especially those who are poor and in any

---

78. Ibid., 9–14, 26, 42, 46–56, 65, 78.
79. O'Malley, *Vatican II*, 204.
80. Paul VI, *Ecclesiam suam*, 87–88, 100–104, 108.

way afflicted, these are the joys and hopes, the griefs and anxieties of the followers of Christ."[81] The council indicates that its focus will not be limited to matters of church doctrine, discipline, and governance. This was a radical change, since prior councils typically limited their scope to matters of internal concern for the church.[82] The council views its task as one of "scrutinizing the signs of the times and of interpreting them in the light of the Gospel." Contemporary people have been confronted with a myriad of changes, some of them negative and others positive. Such changes include the growing number of poor, hungry, and illiterate; the calling into question by the young of established values; the growth in the number of people who have abandoned religious practices; and the achievements of women in their efforts to attain legal equality with men. One of the most troubling developments has been the growth of atheism, which often arises from both a reaction against religion as well as a "violent protest against the evil in this world." One of the hallmarks of Enlightenment thought that the council embraces is freedom of thought and expression. "But it is necessary to distinguish between error, which always merits repudiation, and the person in error, who never loses the dignity of being a person even when he is flawed by false or inadequate religious notions."

The council displays an openness to advances in science and philosophy that had been noticeably absent from prior Church teaching. The council "affirms the legitimate autonomy of human culture and especially of the sciences," while warning against a positivism which believes that only what can be observed and scientifically proven deserves to be called the truth.[83]

The church in the twenty-first century has come to appreciate the contributions of the Enlightenment to the development of human rights and religious freedom. In his 2006 Christmas address to the curia, Benedict XVI stated that "one must welcome the true conquests of the Enlightenment, human rights and especially the freedom of faith and its practice, and recognize these also as being essential elements for the authenticity of religion."[84] The nineteenth-century condemnations of liberty of conscience and freedom of religion have been relegated to historical footnotes, with no effort made to reconcile the traditional teaching with the contradictory current one.

---

81. Second Vatican Council, *Gaudium et spes*, 1–2.
82. O'Malley, *Vatican II*, 233.
83. Second Vatican Council, *Gaudium et spes*, 4–9, 19, 28, 44, 57–59.
84. Benedict XVI, *Christmas Message*, 8.

The Rejection of Modern Philosophy

Popes have struggled not only with modern political thought. They also have resisted embracing contemporary philosophies, viewing them both as a threat to Christian doctrine and as a refutation of the philosophy of Aquinas that had reigned for centuries as the basis of Catholic theology. The late nineteenth century saw the growth of a renewed interest in the Scholastic philosophy of Thomas Aquinas, a development generally referred to by the name "neo-Scholasticism".[85] Leo XIII was an unabashed supporter of neo-Scholasticism, especially its emphasis on the manner in which the philosophy of Aquinas could provide intellectual justification for Catholic doctrine. Owen Chadwick has portrayed Leo as "a pope who loved the Middle Ages and wished to revive their impact in the modern world tried to make the supreme exponent of a medieval philosophy the only reliable exponent of modern philosophy."[86] The appeal of Aquinas to Leo and future popes was the manner in which Aquinas was able to integrate philosophy and theology, always giving pride of place to the latter.[87] For Aquinas, philosophy and theology have the same end—which is God—but they proceed through different methodologies. A philosopher's principles are developed through reason, whereas a theologian's principles are received through revelation and accepted by faith. For example, philosophy can lead a person to knowledge that God exists, as exemplified by philosophical proofs for the existence of God. But philosophy has its limits and must be completed by theology.[88]

Leo's support for Scholastic philosophy is evident from one of his earliest encyclicals, *Aeterni Patris*. It will be cited frequently by future popes in support of their recommendation of Aquinas as the preeminent role model for Catholic philosophers and theologians. The encyclical, however, was not without its critics. Even at the time of its publication, many viewed its principles as "boldly anachronistic and irrelevant."[89]

For Leo, philosophy can serve as a gateway to revealed truth as it "tends to smooth and fortify the road to true faith, and to prepare the souls of its disciples for the fit reception of revelation; for which reason it is well called by ancient writers sometimes a steppingstone to the Christian faith." Philosophy is especially useful in "disproving those things which are repugnant to faith and proving the things which conform to faith." Aquinas

---

85. This discussion of the philosophy and theology of Aquinas is taken from Copelston, *Medieval Philosophy*, 20–42; see also Kerr, *Aquinas*, 31–101.
86. Chadwick, *History of the Popes*, 281.
87. Kelly, *Ecumenical Councils*, 150.
88. Copelston, *Medieval Philosophy*, 35.
89. O'Connell, *Critics on Trial*, 34.

is the best example of this use of philosophy in his theology, so "that he is rightly and deservedly esteemed the special bulwark and glory of the Catholic faith." Scholastic philosophy is useful principally as a tool to refute the arguments of those who attack the truths of religion.[90] According to Dominican Thomistic scholar Fergus Kerr, "For Thomas, as for any medieval theologian, it is by refuting plausible opposing theories that the correct view is reached."[91] The reverence in which Aquinas is held by the church was confirmed for Leo by the fact that, at the Council of Trent, the bishops had available for reference copies of Scripture, papal decrees, and Aquinas's *Summa Theologiae*.[92]

Leo's admiration for the philosophy of Aquinas was also evidenced by his establishment in 1879 of the Pontifical Academy of St. Thomas Aquinas, which grants graduate degrees in Thomistic philosophy. In his apostolic letter *Inter munera academiarum*, John Paul II renews the statutes of the academy which Leo had founded 120 years earlier. John Paul notes that the list of the academy's graduates includes Pius XI and Paul VI, each of whom had earned their doctorate in Thomistic philosophy there. In John Paul's vision, the academy should "serve as a central and international *forum* for studying St. Thomas' teaching better and more carefully." Like Leo, John Paul firmly believed in the continued relevance of the teachings of Aquinas. "In the cultural conditions of our time, it seems truly appropriate to develop further this part of Thomistic doctrine which deals with humanity, given that his assertions on the dignity of the human person and the use of his reason, in perfect harmony with the faith, make St. Thomas a teacher for our time."[93]

Pius XII's 1950 encyclical *Humani generis* is considered by many to be his most influential and far-reaching one. It narrowly circumscribes the role of Catholic theologians, establishing the degree of deference which they must give to pronouncements contained in papal documents.[94] Pius uses this document as a forum in which to attack certain false opinions in modern thought, including evolution, existentialism, and historicism. He is disturbed that some theologians wish to discard the classical philosophical terminology through which dogma has traditionally been expressed (i.e., Scholasticism) and to express dogma instead through the terminology of modern philosophy. He sees a direct link between this approach to theology

---

90. Leo XIII, *Aeterni Patris*, 4, 9, 17, 27.
91. Kerr, *Aquinas*, 91.
92. Leo XIII, *Aeterni Patris*, 22.
93. John Paul II, *Inter munera academiarum*, 4.
94. Talar, "'The Synthesis of all Heresies,'" 503.

and a rejection of the church's teaching authority.⁹⁵ John Paul II will share Pius's devotion to the philosophy of Aquinas and treat it as de facto normative for Catholic theologians.

Pius attempts to curtail the freedom of theologians to debate issues that have been definitively addressed in papal encyclicals. "But if the Supreme Pontiffs in their official documents purposely pass judgment on a matter up to that time under dispute, it is obvious that that matter, according to the mind and will of the Pontiffs, cannot be any longer considered to be a question open to discussion among theologians."⁹⁶ He does not expressly claim that such papal pronouncements are infallible. However, if the matters on which the pope pronounces judgment in an encyclical are no longer subject to dispute or even discussion, then such pronouncements function as infallible, at least de facto if not de jure. Creeping infallibility seeks to immunize all papal pronouncements not only from criticism but even from question. John Pollard cites *Humani generis* as an example of Pius's belief in "virtual infallibility," the view "that *all* papal pronouncements shared in the authority of the infallible *magisterium*."⁹⁷

Pius makes sure that theologians understand their place. "This deposit of faith our Divine Redeemer has given for authentic interpretation not to each of the faithful, not even to theologians, but only to the Teaching Authority of the Church."⁹⁸ This encyclical reinforces the paradigm under which the role of the theologian is solely to "cooperate with the magisterium by explaining and defending what the magisterium has taught.⁹⁹ One result of the encyclical was that certain prominent theologians were targeted by the Holy Office for expressing opinions which were suspected of being heterodox.¹⁰⁰

Pius then sets forth certain false opinions in a manner reminiscent of the *Syllabus*, although not expressed in a series of numbered propositions. He singles out two errors in particular. First, he takes issue with theologians who find the doctrine of transubstantiation to be an outmoded way to describe the Eucharist. Second, he castigates those who fail to treat the "Mystical Body of Christ and the Roman Catholic Church as one and the same."¹⁰¹

---

95. Pius XII, *Humani generis*, 5–7, 15–18.
96. Ibid., 20.
97. Pollard, *Papacy in the Age of Totalitarianism*, 415, emphasis in original.
98. Pius XII, *Humani generis*, 21.
99. Jon Nilson, "The Rights and Responsibilities of Theologians: A Theological Perspective," in Curran and McCormick, *Dissent in the Church*, 5–34, 9.
100. Orsy, "Magisterium," 495.
101. Pius XII, *Humani generis*, 26–27.

Paul VI's encyclical *Mysterium fidei* demonstrates how popes have continued to assert the adequacy of thirteenth-century Scholastic concepts as the most adequate expressions of doctrine. The purpose of the encyclical is to dispel certain new theological ways of describing the Eucharist which run counter to the decrees of the Council of Trent.

The term "transubstantiation" had been employed by the Fourth Lateran Council in 1215 to describe what took place in the Eucharist. Christ's "body and blood are truly contained in the sacrament of the altar under the forms of bread and wine; the bread being changed (*transsubstantiatio*) by divine power into the body, and the wine into the blood."[102] The term transubstantiation relies upon the Aristotelian distinction between "substance" and "accidents", a distinction used by Aquinas in his *Summa Theologiae*.[103] The consecrated host retains the taste and feel of bread and the consecrated wine retains the taste and feel of wine—taste and feel being "accidents"—but their "substance" has been transformed. The Council of Trent relied on this Aristotelian and Thomistic terminology when it defined the doctrine of transubstantiation in the following terms:

> And because that Christ, our Redeemer, declared that which He offered under the species of bread to be truly His own body, therefore has it ever been a firm belief in the Church of God, and this Holy Synod doth now declare it anew, that, by the consecration of the bread and of the wine, a conversion is made of the whole substance of the bread into the substance of the body of Christ our Lord, and of the whole substance of the wine into the substance of His blood; which conversion is, by the holy Catholic Church, suitably and properly called Transubstantiation.[104]

According to Paul, all Catholics are firmly bound to this Tridentine formula, which remains valid always and everywhere.

> ... It cannot be tolerated that any individual should on his own authority take something away from the formulas which were used by the Council of Trent to propose the Eucharistic Mystery for our belief. These formulas—like the others that the Church used to propose the dogmas of faith—express concepts that are not tied to a certain specific form of human culture, or to a certain level of scientific progress, or to one or another theological

---

102. Fourth Lateran Council, *Canons*, canon 1.
103. Kerr, *Aquinas*, 97–100; McGrath, *Historical Theology*, 164.
104. Council of Trent, Thirteenth Session, *Decree concerning the Eucharist*, chap. 4.

school.... For this reason, these formulas are adapted to all men of all times and all places.[105]

It would have been instructive if Paul had expounded on the terminology which the church used prior to the thirteenth and sixteenth centuries to describe the Eucharist and had explained either why that terminology was insufficient, or in what manner the terminology of the Fourth Lateran Council and the Council of Trent was superior. If the Council of Trent represented an advancement over earlier formulations of the doctrine, then why is it impossible to imagine that a future formulation might better explain the Eucharist to a modern world than the formulation of a sixteenth-century council using thirteenth-century terminology? As Francis Sullivan has argued, "To agree that up to the time of Trent this term was 'very fitting' does not exclude the possibility that, in another time and culture, this might not be the most fitting term, and that another term might be preferable to it."[106] Avery Dulles has noted that dogmatic promulgations of ecumenical councils are always expressed through philosophical concepts, which concepts themselves are not dogmatic proclamations. "Since the first ecumenical councils the Catholic Church, in its creedal and dogmatic utterances, has deliberately taken over the language of classical ontology. These doctrinal definitions, in my opinion, do not require under pain of heresy an acceptance of the technical terms and concepts that are employed, but they do require those terms and concepts to be regarded as serviceable in the sense that they can illumine, and do not necessarily distort, the Christian message."[107] Nevertheless, the *Catechism*, issued almost thirty years after *Mysterium fidei*, reaffirms the validity of the Tridentine formula of transubstantiation as the proper expression of what occurs in the Eucharist.[108]

John Paul II took aim both at dissent from official church teaching expressed by certain Catholic moral theologians and at contemporary philosophical systems that had abandoned the methods of Aquinas and the other Scholastics. In his encyclical *Veritatis splendor* he assails what he considers certain errors that have crept into moral theology. He identifies these errors and places strict limits on Catholic moral theologians. Although moral theology is a highly specialized discipline, the questions with which the moral theologian struggles are the same as those asked by all people. "No one can escape from the fundamental questions: *What must I do? How do I distinguish good from evil?*" He is troubled by the manner in which some moral

105. Paul VI, *Mysterium fidei*, 24.
106. Sullivan, *Creative Fidelity*, 123.
107. Dulles, *Craft of Theology*, 127.
108. *Catechism*, No. 1376.

theologians answer these questions, particularly in their seeming rejection of certain unspecified concepts of traditional Catholic moral theology. He emphasizes the continuing validity of the Decalogue. As Jesus said in the Sermon on the Mount, he did not come to abolish the Law but to fulfill it.[109] The *Catechism* also maintains that the Ten Commandments "are fundamentally immutable, and they oblige always and everywhere."[110]

The proper interpretation of the Commandments and the Beatitudes is the task of the church's magisterium, and John Paul is quick to point out that not all manner of expression is acceptable. "The Magisterium has the duty to state that some trends of theological thinking and certain philosophical affirmations are incompatible with revealed truth." Any theological system which posits the primacy of freedom over truth, or which grants to individual conscience the right to determine moral law, is unacceptable. In this regard, he understands God's command to Adam and Eve not to eat of the tree of knowledge of good and evil (Genesis 2:16–17) as a divine limitation on human freedom.[111]

A system of moral theology which refuses to accept that the precepts of natural law are universal and immutable is fundamentally flawed. Just as there are doctrines of faith which are true for all people and all times, so there are universal moral proscriptions. Some moral theologians make a distinction between a person's "fundamental option" and his or her "particular acts." For these theologians, particular acts are not right or wrong in themselves. Rather, their morality depends upon their relationship to one's fundamental option for good or for evil. For John Paul, this distinction is at odds with traditional Catholic teaching that certain acts are always and everywhere morally wrong. He reminds the bishops that theologians who do not accept the distinction between mortal and venial sins espouse teachings which are contrary to the still binding decrees of the Council of Trent. "The Church teaches that 'there exist acts which *per se* and in themselves, independently of circumstances, are always seriously wrong by reason of their object.' . . . Circumstances or intentions can never transform an act intrinsically evil by virtue of its object into an act 'subjectively' good or defensible as a choice." He is troubled by the prevalence of a secularism which seeks to separate not only freedom from truth, but also faith from morality.[112]

The moral theologian cannot be simply an independent thinker or scholar, but rather must be an expositor of the teachings of the church on

---

109. John Paul II, *Veritatis splendor*, 2, 4, 12–16.
110. *Catechism*, No. 2072.
111. John Paul II, *Veritatis splendor*, 25–26, 29, 32–35.
112. Ibid., 51–53, 67, 70, 80–81, 88.

moral issues. As a result, dissent is incompatible with the role of the moral theologian. "While exchanges and conflicts of opinion may constitute normal expressions of public life in a representative democracy, moral teaching certainly cannot depend simply upon respect for a process: indeed, it is in no way established by following the rules and deliberative processes typical of a democracy. *Dissent*, in the form of carefully orchestrated protests and polemics carried on in the media, *is opposed to ecclesial communion and to a correct understanding of the hierarchical constitution of the People of God.*"

In a not so veiled threat to Catholic institutions which might be tempted to stray from the church's teachings, he reminds bishops that it is their prerogative "to grant the title 'Catholic' to Church-related schools, universities, health-care facilities and counseling services, and, in cases of serious failure to live up to that title, to take it away."[113] John Paul does not share John XXIII's openness to theological debate. In his first encyclical, *Ad Petri cathedram*, John signaled that the time had arrived for a free and frank discussion of theological issues. "For discussion can lead to fuller and deeper understanding of religious truths; when one idea strikes against another, there may be a spark."[114] For John Paul, however, the first sign of a theological spark sounds the alarm to grab the Vatican fire extinguisher.

In *Fides et ratio*, John Paul's penultimate encyclical, he undertakes to delineate the proper role of philosophy as an aid to theology. Philosophy asks the most fundamental questions of human existence. "*Who am I? Where have I come from and where am I going? Why is there evil? What is there after this life?*" More precisely, John Paul believes that these are the questions philosophy always should ask, but which are not being addressed by contemporary philosophers. They reject metaphysics and ontology, while concentrating their research on epistemology, a narrowing of the philosophical focus which John Paul fears may lead to relativism and agnosticism.[115]

The encyclical displays an almost complete disregard for contemporary philosophy, coupled with unqualified admiration for the philosophy of Aquinas and for those few contemporary philosophers—all Catholic—who practice philosophy in the Thomistic tradition. Philosophy and theology both seek to discover "the ultimate purpose of personal existence." Philosophy relies on reason alone to answer this question, whereas theology, which also proceeds by way of reason, is aided in its quest by divine revelation and faith. "Of itself, philosophy is able to recognize the human being's ceaselessly self-transcendent orientation towards the truth; and, with the assistance of faith,

---

113. Ibid., 110, 113, 116.
114. John XXIII, *Ad Petri cathedram*, 71.
115. John Paul II, *Fides et ratio*, 1, 5.

it is capable of accepting the 'foolishness' of the Cross as the authentic critique of those who delude themselves that they possess the truth." Faith deals with universal truths, whereas modern philosophy is unwilling to make claims of universality for its conclusions. In this way, modern philosophy comes up short in the quest for truth. "Every truth—if it really is truth—presents itself as universal, even if it is not the whole truth. If something is true, then it must be true for all people and at all times."[116]

John Paul traces the historical development of the use of philosophy by theologians, a practice which, he acknowledges, did not begin with the first generation of Christians. For them, the Gospel answered the fundamental questions of human existence, so that they had no need for philosophy. Eventually, for reasons which John Paul does not explain, theologians began to make use of philosophical concepts and systems in constructing their theology. As examples, he cites to Clement of Alexandria, Origen, and Augustine.[117] Moving into the Middle Ages, he singles out Aquinas for special commendation.

> A quite special place in this long development belongs to Saint Thomas.... In an age when Christian thinkers were rediscovering the treasures of ancient philosophy, and more particularly of Aristotle, Thomas had the great merit of giving pride of place to the harmony which exists between faith and reason. Both the light of reason and the light of faith come from God, he argued; hence there can be no contradiction between them....
>
> This is why the Church has been justified in consistently proposing Saint Thomas as a master of thought and a model of the right way to do theology.[118]

However, John Paul does not want to give the impression that Scholastic philosophy is normative for Catholic theologians. "The Church has no philosophy of her own nor does she canonize any one particular philosophy in preference to others."[119]

In light of the manner in which John Paul extols Scholastic philosophy and dismisses modern philosophy, this statement appears to be a hollow formula. His stated position is that the role of the magisterium with respect to philosophy is strictly a negative one. It should not endorse any particular philosophy, but properly can instruct theologians concerning which philosophical systems are off-limits. Examples of Rome's exercise of

---

116. Ibid., 15, 23, 27.
117. Ibid., 38-40.
118. Ibid., 43.
119. Ibid., 49.

this function include Pius X's condemnation of Modernism, Pius XI's rejection of Marxism and communism, Pius XII's warnings about evolutionism, existentialism, and historicism, and the Congregation for the Doctrine of the Faith's criticism of the use of Marxism by liberation theologians. In practice, however, popes have done more than simply point out errors in certain philosophical schools of thought. He credits Leo XIII's encyclical *Aeterni Patris* with promoting a renewed interest in Thomism, a revival which he claims produced many of the most influential theologians at the Second Vatican Council.

Once again, he is quick to add that he has "no wish to direct theologians to particular methods," a statement that becomes difficult to take at face value with each successive endorsement of Scholastic philosophy and each successive rejection of other philosophical approaches. For John Paul, the achievement of Aquinas was his use of philosophy "to confirm the intelligibility and universal truths of [theology's] claims." He points out the errors of eclecticism, historicism, scientism, pragmatism, and nihilism, and does not recommend any current philosophy as appropriate for use by theologians.[120] John Paul's treatment of modern philosophy has prompted one theologian to ask whether "*Fides et ratio* is simply a restatement of Thomism, an updated endorsement of *Aeterni Patris*?"[121]

The most recent official Church pronouncement on the deference due to the philosophy of Aquinas is found in a 2011 decree by the Congregation for Catholic Education. The congregation states that "The Church's preference for his method and his doctrine is not exclusive, but 'exemplary.'"[122] This recommendation of Aquinas's philosophical method as worthy of imitation would appear to make it a "safe harbor" for Catholic theologians. It is less clear whether the church's preference for the Thomistic method implies that reliance on a different philosophical method by a Catholic theologian would be presumptively suspect. Such an interpretation would be consistent with *Fides et ratio*, but it would be a perversion of the spirit of Aquinas. He did not base his system on a Christian philosophical foundation, but took his inspiration from pagan Greek philosophy. He relied on the philosophical concepts employed by Aristotle in constructing his Catholic theology. The Jesuit historian of philosophy Frederick Copleston has argued that a true Thomist should approach the works of modern secular philosophers with an attitude of openness. "It would seem that a Thomist should expect to find fresh intellectual illumination in the pages of the modern philosophers

---

120. Ibid., 50–58, 64, 77, 86–90.
121. Guarino, "*Fides et ratio*," 680–81.
122. Congregation for Catholic Education, *Reform of Studies*, 12.

and that he should approach them with an initial sympathy and expectancy rather than with an *a priori* suspicion, reserve, and even hostility."[123]

The suspicion and hostility which John Paul displayed toward contemporary philosophy are absent in the writings of Benedict XVI, who demonstrated his familiarity with and regard for many of the leading philosophers of the last four centuries. This new attitude is most evident in the second of Benedict's three encyclicals, *Spe salvi*. The first part of the encyclical is a general discussion of the virtue of hope, whereas the second part explores certain concrete "settings" in which Christians have manifested hope in the face of some of history's most tragic moments.

Hope is a virtue that distinguishes the Christian outlook on life from others. "Here too we see as a distinguishing mark of Christians the fact that they have a future: it is not that they know the details of what awaits them, but they know in general terms that their life will not end in emptiness." Early Christians were particularly open to the message of hope, because many of them "belonged to the lower social strata." But unlike the message of other charismatic figures of the time, the hope offered by Jesus was not one of political liberation. "Jesus was not Spartacus, he was not engaged in a fight for political liberation like Barabbas or Bar-Kochba."[124] The Christian vision is not one of political revolution but a promise of eternal life. Benedict acknowledges in rather stark terms why the promise of eternal life is often not warmly embraced. "Perhaps many people reject the faith today simply because they do not find the prospect of eternal life attractive. What they desire is not eternal life at all, but this present life, for which faith in eternal life seems something of an impediment. To continue living for ever—endlessly—appears more like a curse than a gift. Death, admittedly, one would wish to postpone for as long as possible. But to live always, without end—this, all things considered, can only be monotonous and ultimately unbearable."[125]

For previous popes, the golden age of philosophy was the Middle Ages; any new philosophies thereafter were treated as either unhelpful to theology or detrimental to Catholic faith. They characterized such philosophies in pejorative terms, but seldom discussed the works of particular philosophers. Benedict, on the other hand, is well-versed in modern philosophy and mentions the works of several major philosophers from the sixteenth to

---

123. Copelston, *Medieval Philosophy*, 38.

124. Benedict XVI, *Spe salvi*, 2–5. Simon Bar-Kochba was the leader of the Second Jewish Revolt against Roman rule in Judea and was considered by many to be the Messiah. The revolt, which began in 132 CE, was crushed by Roman troops under Emperor Hadrian in 135 CE. See Brettler, *Jewish Bible*, 278; Rubenstein, *After Auschwitz*, 5.

125. Benedict XVI, *Spe salvi*, 10.

the twentieth centuries, including Francis Bacon, Immanuel Kant, Friedrich Engels, Karl Marx, Max Horkheimer, and Theodor Adorno.[126] Moreover, he finds positive messages in each of these writers, even those who are unabashedly atheistic. Benedict views philosophy as a discipline in its own right and not simply as a handmaiden to theology. The philosopher raises the most profound questions of human existence, to which the theologian provides answers from the Christian tradition.

Benedict distinguishes between the early Christian and modern understandings of salvation. In the early church, both sin and salvation were viewed socially rather than individualistically. "Sin is understood by the Fathers as the destruction of the unity of the human race, as fragmentation and division. . . . Hence, 'redemption' appears as the reestablishment of unity." In modern times, however, salvation is viewed by Christians as something involving the individual's soul, without social or political ramifications. For non-Christians, and some Christians as well, the message of salvation has been replaced by faith in progress. This view of progress, which was associated with the rule of reason and political freedom, became ascendant around the time of the French Revolution. In the nineteenth century, faith in progress gave rise to the writings of Marx and Engels, in particular *The Communist Manifesto* (1848). He praises Marx for having correctly analyzed the plight of industrialized workers and for accurately describing the path which the communist revolution would take. But this praise is mixed with criticism of Marx's view of the person. "His real error is materialism: man, in fact, is not merely the product of economic conditions, and it is not possible to redeem him purely from the outside by creating a favourable economic environment." He also criticizes certain strains of Christian thought for limiting their focus to the individual's personal salvation. The only hope which can sustain people is God.[127]

Evolution and the Big Bang Theory Embraced

The church's opposition to modern philosophical, social, and political thought should be contrasted with its willingness to accept the findings of modern science concerning the origins of the human species and the universe. Evolution is a hot-button issue in American religion and politics, with the religious right accepting the literal Genesis story of human origins and the secular left embracing evolution. "Over three-quarters of the most religious reject evolution altogether, and believe instead that

126. Ibid., 16–42.
127. Ibid., 14–21, 25, 31.

God created human beings less than ten thousand years ago."[128] The battle over evolution played a major role in the development of American fundamentalism in the early twentieth century, as fundamentalists led the fight to keep the teaching of evolution out of public schools.[129] After the Scopes trial, the fundamentalist movement turned away from the public square, concentrating instead on building up their own institutions. They would return to take a leading role in the culture wars of the late twentieth and early twenty-first centuries.[130]

The fundamentalists who oppose evolution often are allies with the Catholics in the fight over other culture wars issues, such as abortion and same-sex marriage, but find scant support from the church in their anti-evolution campaign. American Catholic legal scholar and ethicist Cathleen Kaveny has noted that, "the theory of evolution is largely a problem for evangelical Protestants, not for Catholics."[131] Only one encyclical deals directly with the question of evolution. In *Humani generis*, Pius XII expresses a somewhat ambivalent position on the subject. On the one hand, he criticizes those who "hold that evolution, which has not been fully proved even in the domain of natural sciences, explains the origin of all things." On the other hand, he does not subscribe to a literal interpretation of the creation stories in Genesis. Although the Church does not forbid research and discussion about the theory of evolution, it continues to firmly believe that "original sin . . . proceeds from a sin actually committed by an individual Adam and which, through generation, is passed on to all and is in everyone as his own."[132]

John Paul II, on the other hand, accepted the scientific proof of evolution without reservation. In a 1996 message to the Pontifical Academy of Science, he applauds the Academy's choice of the theme of the origins of life and evolution. He states that Pius XII affirmed in *Humani generis* that there was no opposition between the theory of evolution and Catholic faith, an overstatement of what the encyclical had stated on that subject. John Paul acknowledges that whereas Pius had considered evolution to be only a serious hypothesis, today it is accepted as established science.[133]

---

128. Putnam and Campbell, *American Grace*, 21–22.

129. Marsden, *Fundamentalism*, 164.

130. Jacoby, *Freethinkers*, 245–52; Marsden, *Fundamentalism*, 184–95.

131. Kaveny, *Culture of Engagement*, 199.

132. Pius XII, *Humani generis*, 5, 36–38.

133. John Paul II, *Message du Saint-Père Jean-Paul II aux Membres de L'Assemblée Plénière de L'Académie des Sciences*, 3–4. The *Message* is available on the Vatican's website only in French, Italian, and Spanish.

The openness of the Church to scientific advances—in contrast to its opposition to modern philosophical, social, and political thought—is evident in its embrace of modern scientific theories concerning the origin and age of the universe. Many fundamentalists reject the Big Bang Theory as incompatible with the accounts of creation set forth in Genesis. This fundamentalist reading of the Bible, while being in opposition to modern thinking, is far from traditional. For centuries, theologians such as Augustine and Aquinas have warned against treating the creation accounts in Genesis as setting forth scientific or historical facts.[134]

In a 2005 document, the International Theological Commission identified several scientific conclusions which the church accepts: the universe was born approximately fifteen billion years ago in an explosion known as the "Big Bang"; the earth was formed 4.5 billion years ago; and "physical anthropology and molecular biology combine to make a convincing case for the origin of the human species in Africa 150,000 years ago in a humanoid population of common genetic lineage." The Big Bang Theory and the doctrine of creation out of nothing (*creatio ex nihilo*) are not in opposition to one another, because "God is the cause not only of *existence* but also the cause of *causes*. . . . Through the activity of natural causes, God causes to arise those conditions required for the emergence and support of living organisms, and, furthermore, for their reproduction and differentiation."[135] Thus, the relative papal silence concerning evolution and the origins of the universe may be explained by the fact that the church views these questions as matters for scientific investigation to be proven or disproven, rather than as matters of religious belief.

The "New Atheists" on Science and Religion

The so-called "New Atheists" of the twenty-first century view all theistic religions as opponents of science. The screeds which these writers have published dismiss all religions as purveyors of superstition and delusion to people who are unwilling to accept the findings of modern science. To them, science and Christian religious belief are fundamentally incompatible; since the functioning of the world can be explained by science alone, God is unnecessary. For example, to Sam Harris, a neuroscientist and author of *The End of Faith: Religion, Terror, and the Future of Reason*, religion and science are incompatible because "there is surely an opposition between reason and faith." "In fact, it is difficult to imagine a set of beliefs more

---

134. Hart, *Atheist Delusions*, 63.
135. International Theological Commission, *Communion and Stewardship*, 63, 68.

suggestive of mental illness than those that lie at the heart of many of our religious traditions."[136] Richard Dawkins, an Oxford don and author of *The God Delusion*, notes the scarcity of believers among the faculty of leading research universities. Those few brave faculty members who break with their colleague's atheism "stand out for their rarity and are a subject of amused befuddlement to their peers in the academic community."[137] The late journalist Christopher Hitchens, author of *God is Not Great: How Religion Poisons Everything*, claims that science has proven that religion is false. "Between them, the sciences of textual criticism, archaeology, physics, and molecular biology have shown religious myths to be false and man-made and have also succeeded in evolving better and more enlightened explanations."[138]

These book have certain features in common besides their deliberately provocative titles. The authors share a firm belief that the world would be a better and more enlightened place if religion would wither and die, the sooner the better. In staking out this position, they fail to distinguish among religions, as if there were no difference between the approach to science taken by the Catholic Church or mainline Protestant denominations, on the one hand, and that taken by churches who preach biblical literalism and whose followers eagerly await the Rapture and the End Times. They rig their arguments by contrasting the best in science against the worst in religion. They focus on those who read scripture literally, and then they insist that Christians who deviate from such a literalist interpretation are not being true to their religious tradition. It is somewhat comical for people who disclaim any religious beliefs to set themselves up as arbiters of authentic Christianity. The New Atheists are correct, however, to note that even today, many Christians reject the findings of science, especially those relating to the age of the universe and the origin of the species. The Big Bang Theory and the theory of evolution threaten the worldview of those for whom the first three chapters of the Book of Genesis are a historical account of the creation. But they pose no threat to Catholic doctrine.

---

136. Harris, *End of Faith*, 165, 72.
137. Dawkins, *God Delusion*, 125.
138. Hitchens, *God is not Great*, 151.

4

Sole Authority: The Bible

> *But the task of authentically interpreting the word of God, whether written or handed on, has been entrusted exclusively to the living teaching office of the Church, whose authority is exercised in the name of Jesus Christ.*
>
> —Second Vatican Council

> *Since every Protestant has the right to interpret the Bible, a wide range of interpretations cannot be avoided.*
>
> —Alister McGrath

Someone—the identity of the author is in dispute—once quipped that the United States and England are "two nations divided by a common language." In a similar vein, Catholics and Protestants could be described as two groups of Christians divided by a common book—the Bible. Since the Reformation, Catholics and Protestants have been at odds over the role of the church in the interpretation of Scripture. May an individual read the Bible and correctly interpret it without the aid of the church? Protestants always have answered this question affirmatively, a response which the hierarchy of the Catholic Church has consistently rejected. According to the Anglican historian and theologian Alister McGrath, "The idea that lay at the heart of the sixteenth-century Reformation . . . was that the Bible is capable of being understood by all Christian believers—and that they all have the right to interpret it and to insist upon their perspectives being taken seriously."[1] The Protestant belief that Scripture is the sole authority (*sola scriptura*) was at the core of the Reformation. The Catholic Church, on the other hand, has maintained that it is the sole and final authority on the interpretation of scriptural texts.[2]

The Battle over the Bible in America's Public Schools

In the nineteenth and early twentieth centuries, Protestant and Catholic Americans disagreed over whether Bible reading and prayer in public schools were legitimate educational activities or impermissible Protestant religious instruction masquerading as education. This controversy has been called "arguably the most important church-state issue of the nineteenth century."[3] Although the battle would be resolved as a legal matter in the 1960s, it remains alive as a flashpoint in the culture wars in the United States.

Public schools were unknown at the founding of the republic; what educational facilities for children existed were provided by religious institutions, and such education naturally included religious instruction and readings from the Bible. When public schools came into being in the early nineteenth century, such religious practices were maintained. Religious instruction in public schools did not raise any issue under the First Amendment's religious clauses. The First Amendment, by its terms, only constrained the federal government. "Congress shall make no law respecting an establishment of religion, or prohibiting the free exercise thereof." Education did not implicate the federal government, since it was in the exclusive control of state and local governments. The religious instruction that was provided in the public schools was Protestant; Catholics and Jews were distinct minorities, and freethinkers were virtually nonexistent. The guiding principle was that such instruction must remain "nonsectarian" in order to appeal to all Protestants and to avoid conflicts between denominations. Bible reading and prayer in the public schools were something on which all Protestants agreed.[4]

Since the instruction was Protestant, it was natural that the Bible readings would be from the King James Version. "Fully 90% of the 1,784 separate editions of Scripture published in America from 1776 to 1865 were of the King James Version. Only 6% were Catholic translations, mostly Douay-Rheims; the rest represented unsuccessful efforts by Protestants to improve upon the

1. McGrath, *Christianity's Dangerous Idea*, 2.
2. Küng, *Infallible?* 171–73.
3. Green, *Second Disestablishment*, 251.
4. Green, *Bible, School, and Constitution*, 11–44.

King James."⁵ Use of that translation, however, was more controversial than the proponents of nonsectarianism had expected. They failed to take into account the sensibilities of Catholic parents whose children attended public schools. Catholics did not view Bible readings from the King James Version as nonsectarian, but rather as Protestant sectarianism forced upon Catholic students.⁶ Such Bible readings were unacceptable to Catholic parents and the American hierarchy for two reasons. First, the only English language translation that had received church approval was the Douay-Rheims translation, which was based on the Latin Vulgate.⁷ Second, the notion that schoolchildren could understand the meaning of the Bible without the guidance of church authorities flew in the face of Catholic teaching dating back to the time of the Reformation. American Protestants, on the other hand, shared an implicit trust in the Bible as a plain book which could be understood by everyone.⁸ This dispute soon became politically significant, as the growth in the Catholic population of the country exploded during the immigration boom of the 1830s and 1840s.⁹ At the founding of the United States, there were only 35,000 Catholics in the country; that number increased to 300,000 by 1830 and to more than 3,000,000 by 1860.¹⁰

One solution, of course, would have been for Catholic parents to send their children to the Catholic schools which were being established in the major cities of the country. But that would impose an economic burden upon Catholic parents, who would be required to pay for their children's education in Catholic schools and eschew the tax-supported education provided in the public schools. Archbishop John Hughes of New York led a push for Catholic schools to receive an equitable share of public school funds. This proposed solution was not legally feasible, as many state constitutions forbade the use of public funds to support church-affiliated schools.¹¹ The development of the parochial school system would not be the answer, as a

5. Noll, *America's God*, 372.

6. Feldman, *Divided by God*, 12.

7. The name "Douay-Rheims" derives from the cities in France in which the translations were first published by English Catholics. The New Testament translation was published at Rheims in the late sixteenth century and the Old Testament translation was published at Douay at the beginning of the seventeenth century. Gerald P. Fogarty, "The Quest for a Catholic Vernacular Bible in America," in Hatch and Noll, *Bible in America*, 163-80, 166.

8. Noll, *Civil War*, 20; Timothy P. Weber, "The Two-Edged Sword: The Fundamentalist Use of the Bible," in Hatch and Noll, *Bible in America*, 101-20, 111-12.

9. Feldman, *Divided by God*, 61-71.

10. Noll, *History of Christianity*, 205.

11. Green, *Bible, School, and Constitution*, 45-91; Hamburger, *Separation of Church and State*, 219-29.

majority of Catholic schoolchildren continued to attend public schools.[12] The debate over Bible reading in public schools would continue throughout the nineteenth century, with state courts divided as to whether such practices violated state constitutions.[13]

Papal Denunciations of Protestant Bible Societies

Meanwhile, back in Rome, the papacy was decrying Protestant efforts to disseminate vernacular translations of the Bible to the masses. In 1546 the Council of Trent rejected vernacular translations of the Bible and held as authentic the Latin Vulgate edition. Most significantly, the council decreed that no one should presume to interpret Scripture contrary to the interpretation of the church. "Furthermore, in order to restrain petulant spirits, It decrees, that no one, relying on his own skill, shall,—in matters of faith, and of morals pertaining to the edification of Christian doctrine,—wresting the sacred Scripture to his own senses, presume to interpret the said sacred Scripture contrary to that sense which holy mother Church—whose it is to judge of the true sense and interpretation of the holy Scriptures—hath held and doth hold."[14] The strictures of the Council of Trent against vernacular translations of the Bible were enforced by placing such translations on the Index of Forbidden Books.[15] As a result, in the two hundred years following the Council of Trent, "not a single edition of an Italian-language Bible was printed anywhere in the Italian peninsula."[16] However, the mere act of placing a vernacular translation of the Bible on the Index could not prevent its sale and distribution in Protestant areas.

In the nineteenth century, Protestant Bible societies widely distributed copies of the Bible in vernacular translations. In 1844, Gregory XVI condemned such societies in his encyclical *Inter praecipuas*. He describes such societies "an army on the march, conspiring to publish in great numbers copies of the books of divine Scripture. These are translated into all kinds of vernacular languages for dissemination without discrimination among both Christians and infidels. Then the biblical societies invite everyone to read them unguided."[17] Such societies threatened the Catholic Church's asserted monopoly on scriptural interpretation by distributing

---

12. Feldman, *Divided by God*, 88.
13. Green, *Bible, School, and Constitution*, 240.
14. Council of Trent, Fourth Session, *Decree concerning the Sacred Books*, 2.
15. O'Malley, *Trent*, 160.
16. MacCulloch, *Reformation*, 406.
17. Gregory XVI, *Inter praecipuas*, 1.

Bibles to people in their own language and encouraging them to read it and interpret it for themselves.

Like Gregory, Pius IX saw nothing salutary about the work of Bible societies. In *Qui pluribus* he is especially critical of those Protestant associations that "force on people of all kinds, even the uneducated, gifts of the Bible. They issue these in large numbers and at great cost, in vernacular translations, which infringe the holy rules of the Church." He also echoes the spirit of Trent when he derisively refers to "the great error of those others as well who boldly venture to explain and interpret the words of God by their own judgment."[18] In *Nostis et nobiscum*, he states that the principle tenet of Protestantism is that "the holy scriptures are to be understood by the personal judgment of the individual." He renews his attack on Bible societies and their distribution of vernacular translations of the Bible. "No man, relying on his own wisdom, is able to claim the privilege of rashly twisting the scriptures to his own meaning in opposition to the meaning which holy mother Church holds and has held."[19]

Before the First Vatican Council tackled the issue of papal infallibility, it reaffirmed the role of the Catholic Church as the sole and authentic interpreter of scripture in its dogmatic constitution *Dei Filius*.

> Now since the decree on the interpretation of Holy Scripture, profitably made by the Council of Trent, with the intention of constraining rash speculation, has been wrongly interpreted by some, we renew that decree and declare its meaning to be as follows: that in matters of faith and morals, belonging as they do to the establishing of Christian doctrine, that meaning of Holy Scripture must be held to be the true one, which Holy mother Church held and holds, since it is her right to judge of the true meaning and interpretation of Holy Scripture.
>
> In consequence, it is not permissible for anyone to interpret Holy Scripture in a sense contrary to this, or indeed against the unanimous consent of the fathers.[20]

Therefore, as the nineteenth century was drawing to a close, the Catholic and Protestant positions on the role of the church as the ultimate interpreter of Scripture had not changed since the mid-sixteenth century.

---

18. Pius IX, *Qui pluribus*, 1, 19.
19. Pius IX, *Nostis et nobiscum*, 6, 14.
20. First Vatican Council, *Dei Filius*, chaps. 2, 8–9.

The Church Confronts Modern Scriptural Scholarship

By the end of the nineteenth century, the trend in Protestant theological faculties in universities was to interpret Scripture in the same manner as other ancient texts.[21] Scholars in Germany were championing the use of the historical-critical method, examining biblical texts in light of the place and time of their composition, without regard to religious norms or traditions.[22] But Leo XIII was not prepared to embrace the use of such methods by Catholic scholars. His encyclical *Providentissimus Deus*, issued in 1893, contains a wide-ranging discussion of the proper method for the study and interpretation of Scripture. The encyclical will be the most influential one on Scripture until the publication of Pius XII's encyclical *Divino afflante Spiritu* fifty years later. In his apostolic exhortation *Verbum Domini*, Benedict XVI hails Leo's encyclical as having "the merit of protecting the Catholic interpretation of the Bible from the inroads of rationalism."[23]

Leo begins his encyclical by setting forth those opinions of the rationalists which he will refute.

> ... They deny that there is any such thing as revelation or inspiration, or Holy Scripture at all; they see, instead, only the forgeries and the falsehoods of men; they set down the Scripture narratives as stupid fables and lying stories: the prophecies and the oracles of God are to them either predictions made up after the event or forecasts formed by the light of nature; the miracles and the wonders of God's power are not what they are said to be, but the startling effects of natural law, or else mere tricks and myths; and the Apostolic Gospels and writings are not the work of the Apostles at all.

In order to rebut such beliefs, clergy must be properly trained in Scripture. Certain priests should be selected who will devote themselves exclusively to its study. The seminarian first should be "taught how to prove the integrity and authority of the Bible, how to investigate and ascertain its true sense, and how to meet and refute objections."[24]

The purpose of biblical study then is to provide the Catholic biblical scholar with arguments to support the church's interpretation of the texts and to rebut contrary views. Advances in scriptural scholarship in the nineteenth century had nothing to offer to the Catholic exegete. Leo saw no need

---

21. Ahlstrom, *Religious History*, 772–74.
22. Brettler, *Jewish Bible*, 16.
23. Benedict XVI, *Verbum Domini*, 33.
24. Leo XIII, *Providentissimus Deus*, 10, 13.

for them to even study the works of their Protestant colleagues, much less employ their methods. In fact, he labels it as "unbecoming" to rely on the works of non-Catholic biblical scholars if the work of a Catholic scholar on an issue is available. "The sense of Holy Scripture can nowhere be found incorrupt outside of the Church, and cannot be expected to be found in writers who, being without the true faith, only gnaw the bark of the Sacred Scripture, and never attain its pith." He probably would be shocked to learn that one of his successors, Benedict XVI, would publish three books on Jesus in which he both discusses and relies extensively on the works of Protestant biblical scholars. Leo acknowledges that although certain texts may have been subject over time to scribal errors, this does not mean that the writer of the text had committed error. There can be no error in Scripture, because all of the books were written by the Holy Spirit.[25]

Leo uses the encyclical *Caritatis stadium*, whose primary subject is the church in Scotland, to reiterate the role of the magisterium as the sole interpreter of Scripture. He again displays disdain for the work of contemporary scriptural scholarship. Because Scripture is not self-explanatory, an interpretive aid is necessary, which is the role of the magisterium. "And since the faithful must learn from the 'magisterium' of the Church whatever pertains to the salvation of their souls, it follows that they must learn from it the true meaning of Scripture."[26]

Pius X escalated the attack on modern biblical scholarship in *Lamentabili sane*, which was issued in 1907. Unlike the *Syllabus* of Pius IX, *Lamentabili sane* was not issued under the pope's signature but by the Sacred Congregation of the Holy Roman and Universal Inquisition—commonly referred to as the Holy Office, the predecessor to the Congregation for the Doctrine of the Faith—with the approval of Pius X. For Pius, novelties, innovations, and progress have no place in Catholic doctrine, whose unchanging character he defends and safeguards. Because Modernism advocated scholarly methods which Pius found to be flatly contrary to Catholic teaching, Modernism "became an obsession with him."[27]

Lamentabili sane lists sixty-five propositions which, according to the preamble, "by this general decree . . . are condemned and proscribed." It contains no category headings, although the propositions are not arranged haphazardly. Several of the condemned propositions concern the manner in which Modernists treat Scripture. They allege that the church's interpretation of Scripture is subject to correction as a result of the findings of

---

25. Ibid., 14–15, 20–21.
26. Leo XIII, *Caritatis studium*, 5–6.
27. Pollard, *Unknown Pope*, 23.

contemporary scholarship. God cannot be considered the true author of Scripture. The exegete "must first put aside all preconceived opinions" about Scripture and interpret the texts in the same manner as other ancient documents. The Fourth Gospel was not written by the Apostle John, but by a Christian writer at the end of the first century. Jesus did not claim to be the Messiah. Jesus erred in preaching that the time of his second coming was imminent. The resurrection of Jesus is not a historical fact.[28]

The most problematic of these condemnations concern propositions which can be proven by historical research to be true to a high degree of probability. For example, Proposition 18 condemns those who claim that the author of the Fourth Gospel was not the Apostle John, but an author who wrote several decades after the events described in that book. No leading biblical scholar of the last fifty years—whether Catholic, Protestant, or Jewish—accepts the idea that the writer of the Gospel of John was an eyewitness to the events recorded in that Gospel. It is almost universally agreed that the Gospel of John was written after the other three Gospels, near the end of the first century or early in the second century.[29] Even Benedict XVI—writing not in his capacity as pope, but under his given name—concedes that the Gospel of John was written near the end of the first century and that the final form of the Gospel was not written by the Apostle John.[30]

Pius's condemnation of the methodologies employed by modern biblical scholarship also is problematic. If the exegete does not "put aside all preconceived notions" while performing research, then he or she is not performing exegesis but theology. If all available scientific evidence indicates that the Fourth Gospel could not have been written by one of Jesus's apostles, then, according to Pius, the Catholic exegete must ignore this evidence because it conflicts with a traditional teaching of the church. The Pontifical Biblical Commission, which had been established by Leo shortly before his death, faithfully ignored historical research which threatened the magisterium's interpretation of scriptural texts. For example, in the first decade of the twentieth century, the commission decreed that Moses was the author of the first five books of the Bible and affirmed the historical

---

28. Holy Office, *Lamentabile sane*, preamble, props. 2, 9, 12, 18, 28, 33, 36.

29. See, e.g., Crossan, *Who Killed Jesus?* 20 (dating the Gospel of John to 90 CE); Koester, *Paul and his World* (asserting that none of the New Testament authors were among Jesus's first disciples); Vermes, *Changing Faces*, 8 (opining that the Gospel of John was authored by "a Christian writer who lived three generations after Jesus and completed his Gospel in the opening years of the second century AD"); White, *From Jesus to Christianity*, 307 (dating the Fourth Gospel to 95–120 CE).

30. Ratzinger, *Jesus of Nazareth*, 223–27.

character of the first three chapters of the Book of Genesis.[31] The manner in which the commission had retarded the growth of Catholic exegesis has now been acknowledged by the church. Cardinal Ratzinger, who as prefect of the Congregation for the Doctrine of the Faith was the ex officio president of the Pontifical Biblical Commission, noted in 2003 that decisions of the commission under Pius X had contributed to the impression that "Catholic exegetes were hindered from carrying out unrestricted scientific work."[32] Cardinal William Levada, the prefect of the Congregation for the Doctrine of the Faith under Benedict XVI, said that such statements issued by the commission during Pius's pontificate are "now viewed as transitory judgments."[33] Those not trained in Vatican-speak simply would call these judgments wrong, since they were in direct conflict with the consensus of contemporaneous scriptural scholarship.

The current state of Catholic biblical scholarship is dramatically different from what it was in the first decade of the twentieth century. To take just one example, it is almost impossible to determine by a review of the text alone whether a work of current biblical scholarship is written by a Catholic or a Protestant scholar.[34] That change began with publication of the encyclical *Divino afflante Spiritu* in 1943. Pius XII for the first time permitted Catholic biblical exegetes to use the tools of modern scholarship. The encyclical commemorates the fiftieth anniversary of the publication of Leo XIII's encyclical *Providentissimus Deus*. Pius wishes to follow in the tradition of Leo and other predecessors by laying down "safe rules of Catholic exegesis." The need to update Leo's guidelines was due to the advances in biblical studies and biblical archaeology over the preceding fifty years. Knowledge of Greek, Hebrew, and other Middle Eastern languages had become widespread. Textual criticism had become an accepted technique of scriptural interpretation.[35]

Pius is much more comfortable than his predecessors with the use of translations of Scripture directly from the original Hebrew and Greek texts. Although the Council of Trent had decreed the Latin Vulgate to be the authentic version of the Bible, that decree "applies only to the Latin Church and to the public use of the same Scriptures." In addition, it is not "forbidden by the decree of the Council of Trent to make translations into

---

31. Pontifical Biblical Commission, "The Mosaic Authorship of the Pentateuch," in Denzinger and Hünermann, *Enchiridion symbolorum* 3394-97; Pontifical Biblical Commission, "The Author and Historical Truth of the Fourth Gospel," in ibid., 3512-19.

32. Ratzinger, *On the One Hundredth Anniversary*, 2.

33. Levada, *Dei Verbum*, 2.

34. Pelikan, *Christian Doctrine and Modern Culture*, 305.

35. Pius XII, *Divino afflante Spiritu*, 5, 11-17.

the vulgar tongue, even from the original texts themselves." In other words, the Vulgate is normative only for the Latin liturgy and other public prayers in that rite. For other purposes, such as scriptural scholarship, resort to the original Hebrew and Greek texts is legitimate. It is appropriate for the exegete to interpret the texts in the context of the times in which they were composed, the literary devices employed by their authors, and the oral and written sources on which they relied. He permits the exegete wide latitude in interpreting biblical texts, since there are few texts on which the teaching of the Church is definitive. Finally, he directs bishops to support societies which distribute copies of the Bibles to the laity, and he urges the laity to read scripture daily.[36] This position is far removed from those of Gregory XVI and Pius IX, who feared Protestant Bible societies and their widespread distribution of vernacular translations.

Benedict XVI has hailed *Divino afflante Spiritu* as "an important milestone for Catholic exegesis,"[37] because it opened the door to the use by Catholic exegetes of the historical-critical method and other modern tools of biblical exegesis. It may be more appropriate to characterize the encyclical as the lifting of a millstone, rather than as a milestone. Protestant exegetes had been using the historical-critical method since the nineteenth century. Catholic exegetes had been blocked from using such tools due to the strictures imposed on them by Leo XIII and Pius X. Pius XII was not blazing a new trail in scriptural scholarship but simply allowing Catholic biblical scholars to employ the same methodologies that their Protestant peers had been using for decades.

The Second Vatican Council and Post-conciliar Papal Teaching on Scripture

The Second Vatican Council dealt extensively with scripture in its dogmatic constitution *Dei Verbum*. The word of God is found both in scripture and tradition, and it belongs to the Catholic Church to be the final interpreter of God's revelation. "But the task of authentically interpreting the word of God, whether written or handed on, has been entrusted exclusively to the living teaching office of the Church." The council endorses the use of modern tools of scriptural scholarship, but always subject to the final judgment of the church's magisterium. Contrary to the view of nineteenth-century popes, the council approves of the widespread dissemination of vernacular

---

36. Ibid., 21–33, 47, 51.
37. Ratzinger, *Jesus of Nazareth*, xiv.

translations of the Bible, including translations developed in cooperation with non-Catholic Christians.[38]

John Paul II and Benedict XVI have followed *Dei Verbum* in their support for vernacular translations of the Bible and their dissemination by Bible societies. In his apostolic exhortation *Ecclesia in Africa*, John Paul emphasizes the important role which vernacular translations of the Bible, including those prepared in cooperation with Protestant denominations, play in the church's evangelization efforts on the African continent.[39] In his apostolic exhortation *Ecclesia in Asia*, he reiterates the importance of vernacular translations. "Efforts to translate the Bible into local languages need to be encouraged and supported."[40]

In his apostolic exhortation *Verbum Domini*, Benedict echoes John Paul's call for translations made in cooperation with Protestant denominations. "Promoting common translations of the Bible is part of the ecumenical enterprise." He also endorses the activities of Biblical societies in distributing such translations.[41] Like the council, neither John Paul nor Benedict made any reference to the contrary teachings of Gregory XVI and Pius IX prohibiting vernacular translations of the Bible and castigating the wide dissemination to the public of such translations. The dramatic change in papal teaching from the mid-eighteenth century to the present is not explained, but simply ignored.

The Demise of Bible Readings in the Public Schools

Returning to the controversy over Bible readings in American public school classrooms, the issue would not be finally resolved until the second half of the twentieth century. In 1940 the Supreme Court unequivocally declared for the first time that the Free Exercise and Establishment Clauses of the First Amendment were enforceable against the states and their political subdivisions (such as school districts) through the Due Process Clause of the Fourteenth Amendment.[42] In the 1960s, the practice of Bible reading and prayer in the public schools were definitively foreclosed by the Court. First, the Court struck down the recitation of the following prayer at the start of each school day by children in New York public schools. "Almighty God, we acknowledge our dependence upon Thee, and we beg

---

38. Second Vatican Council, *Dei Verbum*, 10, 12, 22.
39. John Paul II, *Ecclesia in Africa*, 58.
40. John Paul II, *Ecclesia in Asia*, 22.
41. Benedict XVI, *Verbum Domini*, 46, 115.
42. *Cantwell v. Connecticut*, 310 U.S. 296 (1940).

Thy blessings upon us, our parents, our teachers and our Country." Neither the nondenominational quality of the prayer, nor the fact that student recitation of the prayer was voluntary, could save it under the Establishment Clause.[43] Next, the Court outlawed the practice in Pennsylvania and Maryland public schools of opening the school day with the reading of a Bible verse and recitation of the Lord's Prayer.[44]

Whereas the nineteenth-century challenges to Bible reading were led by Catholic parents encouraged by the hierarchy, the twentieth-century challenges were spearheaded by parents who often were professed atheists. The reaction of the American hierarchy to the twentieth-century Court rulings outlawing Bible reading was vastly different from the reaction of their nineteenth-century counterparts. In the nineteenth century, the hierarchy felt threatened by the perceived tyranny of the Protestant majority; today the enemy is the perceived ascendency of radical secularism, a fear shared by leading Protestant evangelicals. As a result, the two groups of American Christian leaders joined in criticizing such Court decisions. Cardinal Cushing of Boston went so far as to bring the rulings to the attention of the pope, informing John XXIII that "it is a great tragedy that the greatest book ever published and a constant best seller cannot be read in the public school system." He and Cardinal McIntyre of Los Angeles joined with evangelical Protestants in calling for a constitutional amendment to permit Bible reading in public schools. This effort had popular support, as 70 percent of Americans expressed their disapproval with the Court's decisions. Versions of a prayer amendment made their way through Congress, but ultimately were defeated. These defeats would not stop the calls for such an amendment. It became a part of the Republican platform at the 1980 convention, and President Reagan repeatedly called upon Congress to take up the issue. None of these efforts, however, would bear fruit.[45]

The debate over Bible reading in America's public schools demonstrates how much the Catholic Church's approach to the Bible has slowly and cautiously shifted over the course of a century. The church has come to reconcile itself with scientific study of the Bible, vernacular translations, and encouraging Catholics to read the Bible. However, the church has continued to assert that the magisterium is the sole authority and has the final word on the interpretation of Scripture. If the church's interpretation of the Bible may not be contradicted or even challenged, then such teaching claims de facto infallible status. Unlike a truly infallible teaching, it may be revised at some

---

43. *Engel v. Vitale*, 370 U.S. 421, 422, 430 (1962).
44. *Abington School District v. Schempp*, 374 U.S. 203 (1963).
45. Kruse, *One Nation under God*, 200, 203–7, 275–79.

later date; but unless and until that occurs, the church's interpretation is final and unassailable. Finality and infallibility bear more than just a passing resemblance. As United Supreme Court Justice Robert Jackson once famously remarked when describing the Court, "We are not final because we are infallible, but we are infallible only because we are final."[46] In its more than two hundred year history, the Supreme Court has reversed more than two hundred of its precedents.[47] As Justice Jackson's dictum suggests, the Court is not infallible because its rulings are always right; it is infallible only because it has the last word. Its rulings remain the law of the land until it alone says otherwise. Over its history, the Church has moved 180 degrees away from certain prior teachings. Popes have been loath to acknowledge that the prior teaching was wrong, or even that it has been changed due to new circumstances. But hiding behind euphemisms such as "transitory judgments" only serves to impair, not enhance, papal credibility.

---

46. *Brown v. Allen*, 344 U.S. 443, 540 (1953) (Jackson, J., concurring).
47. Urofsky, *Dissent and the Supreme Court*, 408.

5

Contradiction: Religious Freedom

> *It is quite unlawful to demand, to defend, or to grant unconditional freedom of thought, of speech, or writing, or of worship, as if these were so many rights given by nature to man.*
>
> —Leo XIII

> *The curtailment and violation of religious freedom are in contrast with man's dignity and his objective rights.*
>
> —John Paul II

New England Puritan Theology and Nineteenth-Century Papal Teaching: More Similar Than You May Think

One of the most enduring American beliefs is that the Puritans who established a colony in Massachusetts Bay had left England, where they had been persecuted because of their religious beliefs, in order to establish a haven for religious freedom in the New World.[1] According to Steven Green, "The narrative that America was founded, in large part, upon an impulse of religious liberty is generally unquestioned."[2] This myth has persisted in spite of the fact that the reality of religious life in that colony, and in other colonies as well, was characterized by intolerance toward those who were not members of the majority religious sect.[3] The principles that became

---

1. Lambert, *Founding Fathers*, 1.
2. Green, *Inventing Christian America*, 20.
3. Gardella, *American Civil Religion*, 4.

enshrined in the federal constitution—no involvement of the federal government in religion and freedom of religious belief and practice—do not have their genesis in Puritan theology or practice; they resulted from the concerted activity of religious dissenters (primarily Baptists) and rationalists such as Thomas Jefferson and James Madison.[4] The Puritans came to the New World seeking religious liberty, but only for themselves. As political scientist Anthony Gill has pointed out, "This portrait of early religious liberty in Britain's American colonies was a romantic notion at best. The harsh truth . . . was 'religious freedom for me, but not for thee.'"[5]

The Puritan agenda was to wipe out all vestiges of Catholic doctrine and practice from the Church of England. When it became clear that this goal could not be accomplished in their native England, certain Puritans set off for the New World, landing in what is now Massachusetts.[6] Once they were established in the colony, the only freedom they gave to adherents of other religions was the freedom to depart to a more hospitable place.[7] In Puritan theology, error could not be permitted to exist in the colony; those who held erroneous views and would not leave were subject to persecution.[8] As historian Frank Lambert has described it, "The Puritans persecuted dissenters in their midst just as they had been persecuted as English Dissenters."[9] Religious persecution, not religious toleration, was at the heart of Puritan theology. Massachusetts Puritans were particularly harsh in their treatment of Quakers. For example, a 1658 law prescribed the death penalty for Quakers who reentered the colony after having been exiled twice.[10] Religious freedom came to Massachusetts involuntarily; it was imposed upon the colony by England with the enactment by Parliament of the Act of Toleration in 1689 and with the new charter granted to the colony in 1691 by William and Mary. The colony's Puritan religious hegemony ceased to exist. Religious freedom for all Protestants was guaranteed, but the same protection was not extended to Catholics.[11]

Although the established Protestant denominations in colonies such as Massachusetts infringed upon the religious rights of others, they did

4. Hamburger, *Separation of Church and State*, 89–107.
5. Gill, *Political Origins*, 61.
6. Gottschalk, *American Heretics*, 10; Noll, *History of Christianity*, 32–35.
7. Hutchinson, *Religious Pluralism in America*, 51.
8. Gottschalk, *American Heretics*, 13; Lambert, *Founding Fathers*, 3.
9. Lambert, *Founding Fathers*, 75.
10. Gottschalk, *American Heretics*, 24.
11. Gill, *Political Origins*, 1–3; Kaveny, *Prophecy without Contempt*, 133–34; Lambert, *Founding Fathers*, 98–99.

not view themselves as enemies of religious liberty; that role they reserved for the Catholic Church.[12] But Catholics in colonial America were on the receiving end of religious intolerance, not its practitioners. In Virginia, for example, any Catholic priest who arrived in the colony was subject to immediate deportation.[13] Prohibitions against Catholics holding public office were common. Partially as a result of various civil disabilities to which Catholics were subject, "the colonial history of the Roman Catholic church is almost non-existent" outside of certain pockets in Maryland, Pennsylvania, and New York. The Catholic Church was forced to lead an almost clandestine existence from 1692 until the American Revolution.[14]

Papal teaching on religious liberty in the nineteenth and most of the twentieth century bears an uncanny resemblance to seventeenth-century Puritan theology. The Catholic Church was the one true church and had a right to religious freedom everywhere. As a result, the only religious liberty which needed to be protected was that of Catholics in countries where they were a minority and the church did not enjoy state patronage. Popes were steadfast in holding that non-Catholics in Catholic countries had no inherent right to freedom of religion or worship. The duty of the Catholic state was straightforward—to protect the Catholic faith and, if necessary, to suppress other religions.[15] In countries which were majority Catholic, the government had the duty to suppress other religions, so long as such suppression could be accomplished without threat to the social order. The guiding principle, like that of the Puritans in Massachusetts, was that error has no right to religious liberty.

> The erroneous conscience has no right to external social freedom. That is, it has no right to public expression or manifestation of its beliefs in worship, witness, or teaching. In particular, it has no right publicly to propagate or disseminate its beliefs. The reason is that error has no public rights; only the truth has public rights . . . to be exercised within society. . . .
>
> . . . Whence it follows immediately that the public powers may never positively authorize the public existence of religious error. The legal attitude towards error can only be one of tolerance.[16]

---

12. Noll, *History of Christianity*, 123–26.
13. Lambert, *Founding Fathers*, 68.
14. Ahlstrom, *Religious History*, 330–42.
15. O'Malley, *Vatican II*, 212.
16. Murray, "Problem of Religious Freedom," 507.

The foregoing summary of the traditional papal stance on religious liberty was published in 1964 by John Courtney Murray, a Jesuit professor of theology in Massachusetts. In that same article, Murray made the following statement about the current state of Catholic teaching on religious liberty. "Today, religious freedom, as a human and civil right, personal and corporate, which requires the protection of a legal institution, has emerged as an exigence of the personal and political reason. As such, it claims the sanction of Catholic doctrine."[17] One year later, the Second Vatican Council would issue the declaration *Dignitatis humanae*, a document which would turn the Church's teaching on religious liberty on its head. The primary impetus for this rejection of traditional teaching had come from the American bishops, who had enlisted Murray to be the principal drafter of the declaration.[18] This was not only a momentous change in church teaching, but also a personal triumph for Murray. Less than ten years earlier, he had been instructed by his order to stop publication of articles on religious liberty, unless the articles were pre-approved by Jesuit censors in Rome. His writings had been under scrutiny for years from traditionalist forces in the Vatican, led by Cardinal Alfredo Ottaviani, head of the Holy Office.[19] When Murray inquired of a Jesuit superior in Rome as to the subjects on which he was permitted to publish, he was told "I suppose you may write poetry."[20] Murray declined the invitation, biding his time until he could return to writing on the subject of religious liberty, free from the constraints of the Holy Office and his own order. His contributions to the council's implicit rejection of nineteenth-century papal teaching on religious freedom were enormous. According to Murray's biographer, Barry Hudock, "*No American Catholic has—by a long shot—had greater impact on the doctrinal beliefs of the global Roman Catholic Church than Fr. John Courtney Murray, SJ.*"[21]

The papacy of John XXIII and the Second Vatican Council brought about official Vatican recognition of the individual's right to religious freedom and a shift in the role of the state. Government is to be a supporter of religious freedom rather than the endorser of one religious tradition at the expense of others. Governmental coercion in matters of religious faith (even when done in the name of the one, true religion), is declared to be a violation of human dignity. Subsequent papal teaching has unequivocally upheld

---

17. Ibid., 570.

18. Hudock, *Struggle, Condemnation, Vindication*, 140.

19. Hebblethwaite, *Paul VI*, 247; McGreevy, *Catholicism and American Freedom*, 207–8.

20. Hudock, *Struggle, Condemnation, Vindication*, 90–100.

21. Ibid., xiv, emphasis in original.

the inalienable right of all people to practice their chosen religion, or none at all. This was not a development of Catholic theology on religious liberty; it was an outright rejection of nineteenth-century papal teaching. But it was a rejection which would be made only implicitly. Neither the Second Vatican Council nor post-conciliar popes would explicitly acknowledge that the old teaching was no longer valid.

The *Syllabus of Errors:* No Right to Religious Freedom for Non-Catholics

One and a half centuries removed from the *Syllabus* of Pius IX, its most controversial propositions are those which deal with church-state relations and freedom of religion. The *Syllabus* rejects each of the following propositions as being contrary to papal teaching: that every person is free to profess the religion of his or her choice; that separation of church and state is the ideal relationship; that the Catholic Church should not be the sole religion of the state; that all people should enjoy freedom of religious worship; and that freedom of religious thought and expression will not corrupt public morals.[22] Pius's belief that the above propositions deserved condemnation was not out of the mainstream of religious thought in the 1860s. As Diarmaid MacCulloch has noted, at that time, and continuing through the end of the First World War, "virtually everywhere in Europe still had an established Church whose establishment owed itself to an equally long-established monarchy."[23]

In his encyclical *Quanta cura*, issued the same day as the *Syllabus*, Pius castigates those who have the temerity to espouse the notion that freedom of religious belief and practice is an inalienable human right. "From which totally false idea of social government they do not fear to foster that erroneous opinion, most fatal in its effects on the Catholic Church and the salvation of souls, called by Our Predecessor, Gregory XVI, an 'insanity,' viz., that 'liberty of conscience and worship is each man's personal right, which ought to be legally proclaimed and asserted in every rightly constituted society.'" Although Pius does not state that his condemnation of freedom of religion has been declared infallibly, he demands that all Catholics condemn the errors he has enumerated.[24]

---

22. Pius IX, *Syllabus of Errors*, props. 15, 55, 77–79.
23. MacCulloch, *Christianity*, 817.
24. Pius IX, *Quanta cura*, 3, 6.

Leo XIII: Freedom of Religion for Non-Catholics may be Tolerated if Politically Necessary

Leo XIII was no more supportive of religious freedom than was his predecessor. In the encyclical *Libertas*, he discusses three modern liberties in relation to Catholic doctrine: liberty of worship, liberty of speech and press, and liberty of teaching. First, he examines the concept of liberty itself in light of natural law. Liberty and law are not antagonistic, because liberty needs something to direct it toward good and away from evil, which is the function of law. The law to which he refers is not positive or man-made law, but natural or eternal law. Natural law governs not only the actions of individuals, but also those of civil societies. It follows that if civil society is subject to natural law, positive laws which are in violation of natural law cannot bind individuals in conscience. In order to ensure that positive law is in accord with natural or eternal law, the state has need of the church.[25]

He begins his discussion of the individual liberties with liberty of worship. This liberty is opposed to the virtue of religion, because it is based on indifferentism, the view that no one form of religion is superior to any other. Leo also gives short shrift to the liberty of speech and press, as well as the liberty of teaching, because people only have the right to promote opinions which are true; the state has the right and duty to suppress "lying opinions." He sums up his discussion of these liberties in the following terms.

> From what has been said it follows that it is quite unlawful to demand, to defend, or to grant unconditional freedom of thought, of speech, or writing, or of worship, as if these were so many rights given by nature to man. For, if nature had really granted them, it would be lawful to refuse obedience to God, and there would be no restraint on human liberty. It likewise follows that freedom in these things may be tolerated wherever there is just cause, but only with such moderation as will prevent it degenerating into license and excess.[26]

Thus, although Leo does not reject these liberties outright, he accepts them not as inalienable human rights, but only as accommodations that may be permitted or denied by governments at their discretion.

---

25. Leo XIII, *Libertas*, 7–8, 10.
26. Ibid., 21, 23, 42.

John XXIII and the Second Vatican Council: Nineteenth-Century Papal Teaching Ignored

The views of Pius IX and Leo XIII on religious liberty would not be challenged by the next four popes. In the 1960s, however, John XXIII and the Second Vatican Council would reverse church teaching on religious liberty in dramatic fashion. Human rights is the subject of John's most famous encyclical, *Pacem in terris*, published less than two months before his death in 1963. It would be difficult to overstate the importance of this encyclical for the future of church teaching on religious liberty. As John Hehir, president of Catholic Charities USA, has explained, "Finally, for the first time in an authoritative Catholic document, there is a clear statement of the right to religious liberty."[27] This also was the first time that an encyclical was addressed to "all Men of Good Will," rather than being limited to a Catholic audience.[28] The central premise of the encyclical is that peace and order are inextricably connected. "Peace on Earth—which man throughout the ages has so longed for and sought after—can never be established, never guaranteed, except by the diligent observance of the divinely established order." He contrasts the perfect order of the natural universe with the disorder that prevails among individuals and nations.[29]

He begins his analysis with an enumeration of the rights of each person, which "are universal and inviolable, and therefore altogether inalienable," language reminiscent of the Declaration of Independence. The most fundamental right is the right to live, which includes the right to "food, clothing, shelter, medical care, rest, and finally, the necessary social services." There is a right to freedom of speech and publication, as well as the right to pursue a chosen profession. The right to share in the benefits of culture includes the right to an education. Unlike his predecessors, who displayed little concern for the religious freedom of non-Catholics living in Catholic countries, John emphasizes that religious freedom is a right possessed by all people. He makes it clear that those who hold views which the church may consider erroneous do not thereby forfeit their human dignity. "It is always perfectly justifiable to distinguish between error as such and the person who falls into error—even in the case of men who err regarding the truth or are led astray as a result of their inadequate knowledge, in matters either of religion or of the highest ethical standards. A man who has fallen into error

---

27. John Hehir, "Catholicism and Democracy: Conflict, Change, and Collaboration," in Curran, *Catholic Moral Teachings*, 20–37, 26–27.

28. Clark, *Catholic Social Thought*, 12.

29. John XXIII, *Pacem in terris*, 1, 4.

does not cease to be a man. He never forfeits his personal dignity; and this is something that must always be taken into account."[30]

John's views on religious liberty would prevail over those of Pius IX and Leo at the Second Vatican Council. In *Dignitatis humanae*, the council set forth a broad statement on religious freedom that would relegate the beliefs of nineteenth-century popes to the status of a historical curiosity.

> This Vatican Council declares that the human person has a right to religious freedom. This freedom means that all men are to be immune from coercion on the part of individuals or of social groups and of any human power, in such wise that no one is to be forced to act in a manner contrary to his own beliefs, whether privately or publicly, whether alone or in association with others, within due limits.
>
> The council further declares that the right to religious freedom has its foundations in the very dignity of the human person as this dignity is known through the revealed word of God and by reason itself. This right of the human person to religious freedom is to be recognized in the constitutional law whereby society is governed and thus it is to become a civil right. . . .
>
> . . . No merely human power can either command or prohibit acts of this kind. The social nature of man, however, itself requires that he should give external expression to his internal acts of religion: that he should share with others in matters religious; that he should profess his religion in community. Injury therefore is done to the human person and to the very order established by God for human life, if the free exercise of religion is denied in society, provided just public order is maintained.[31]

The propositions which Pius IX condemned in the *Syllabus* as "errors" have become official church teaching. In fact, one of the leading theologians at the council, the French Dominican Yves Congar, made the following observation concerning the contrast between *Dignitatis humanae* and the *Syllabus*. "'It must be acknowledged that what this text says is materially different from the 1864 Syllabus and is even practically opposed to what is asserted in Propositions 15, 77 and 79 of that document.'"[32] Archbishop Marcel Lefebvre, Superior General of the Holy Ghost Fathers, recognized the contradiction. "'If what is being taught is true, then what the Church has taught is false.'"[33] Of course, neither John nor the council ever criticized the

30. Ibid., 9, 11–14, 158.
31. Second Vatican Council, *Dignitatis humanae*, 2–3.
32. Chiron, *Pius IX*, 305.
33. Noonan, *Lustre of Our Country*, 346.

Syllabus or *Libertas* or indicated that their teachings were no longer valid; they simply ignored them. The Vatican habit of contradicting prior papal teaching with no explicit acknowledgement of the divergence between the old and new teaching has been commented on by John Noonan.

> The old message of intolerance, massively delivered over fifteen hundred years, might itself have been understood as a development of doctrine that was irreversible. How could it be swept away by one pope and council? Vatican II itself did not attempt to grapple with this question. *Dignitatis humanae personae* did not mention the teaching of the past. . . .
>
> Admitting individual mistakes and identifying individual perpetrators was not the same as explaining how the Church could teach one thing in the past, another thing today. . . . The dilemma seemed inescapable: Admit it, you were wrong then, or you are wrong now. The dilemma made the council uncomfortable. Vatican II made the change and left it to be explained.[34]

The council's declaration also worked a profound change in Catholic teaching on church-state relations, a topic which will be examined in depth in the next chapter. This change was made possible by the positive experience of Catholics in the United States.[35]

Post-Vatican II: Papal Acknowledgement of the Benefit of Religious Freedom for Catholics

Recent popes have embraced the "errors" regarding religious freedom which Pius IX had condemned in the *Syllabus* while steadfastly refusing to criticize the prior teaching. In John Paul II's first encyclical, *Redemptoris hominis*, he deals at some length with the violations of human rights, including the right to religious freedom, which were endemic in the last century. He describes the twentieth century as one "of great calamities for man, of great devastations, not only material ones but also moral ones, indeed perhaps above all moral ones." It is a century that has seen gross violations of human rights through "concentration camps, violence, torture, terror, and discrimination in many forms." Among the rights which must be safeguarded for the good of society are "the right to religious freedom together with the right to freedom of conscience." In line with the teaching of *Dignitatis humanae*, he argues that any infringement on religious freedom, regardless of a person's

---

34. Noonan, *A Church that Can and Cannot Change*, 157–58.
35. Noll, *Turning Points*, 293.

religious affiliation, is "in contrast with man's dignity and his objective rights."[36] This statement exemplifies how dramatically the church's teaching on religious liberty had changed over the past century. In Proposition 78 of the *Syllabus*, Pius IX had condemned as error the belief that "it has been wisely decided by law in some Catholic countries, that persons coming to reside therein shall enjoy the peculiar exercise of their particular worship."[37] In other words, if a non-Catholic immigrates to a country with a Catholic majority, he or she has no inherent right to practice non-Catholic worship. Pius's position cannot be reconciled with that of the council or of John Paul. This is another example of a pope contradicting the teaching of a prior pope, while the contradiction goes unacknowledged.

In *Centisimus annus*, John Paul notes the threat to religious liberty which fundamentalism poses for religious minorities.[38] He also expounds on the theme of religious freedom in some of his apostolic exhortations. A problem related to religious fundamentalism is the proselytizing activities of certain sects, which he criticizes in *Ecclesia in America*.[39] Such criticism is somewhat disingenuous, since no group ever views its own missionary activities as proselytizing which impinges upon the religious freedom of others. In fact, John Paul does not indicate whether any activities of Catholic evangelization can be characterized as impermissible proselytism.

One of the reasons behind the church's current emphasis on religious liberty is the difficulties faced by Catholics in Asia and Africa due to their minority status in many countries on those continents. John Paul addressed these difficulties in *Ecclesia in Asia*. He notes that in some countries only one religion is recognized and Christians are forbidden to practice their faith publicly. In others, all religions are suppressed. "In many parts of Asia, our brothers and sisters continue to live their faith in the midst of restrictions or even the total denial of freedom. . . . I appeal to governments and the leaders of nations to adopt and implement policies that guarantee religious freedom for all their citizens."[40]

The apostolic exhortation *Ecclesia in Europa* was a product of the 1999 synod of European bishops. One of the issues at that meeting had been the increasing presence of Muslims on the European continent due to immigration from Africa and Asia, which many perceived as a challenge to the church's efforts at a new evangelization. John Paul views the relationship

---

36. John Paul II, *Redemptoris hominis*, 17.
37. Pius IX, *Syllabus of Errors*, prop. 78.
38. John Paul II, *Centesimus annus*, 29.
39. John Paul II, *Ecclesia in America*, 73.
40. John Paul II, *Ecclesia in Asia*, 8, 28.

between Christians and Muslims in Europe as also implicating the religious freedom of Christians in Muslim lands. "It is on the other hand understandable that the Church, even as she asks the European institutions to ensure the promotion of religious freedom in Europe, should feel the need to insist that reciprocity in guaranteeing religious freedom also be observed in countries of different religious traditions, where Christians are a minority."[41]

Benedict XVI, in his apostolic exhortation *Africae Munus*, expresses similar concern about the plight of Catholics who reside in countries in which Islam is the official religion. In such countries, restrictions on the right to confess the Christian religion and to participate in public life are severely curtailed, both as a matter of law and of practice.[42]

The main theme of Francis's first apostolic exhortation, *Evangelii gaudium*, is the new evangelization, which was the subject of the Thirteenth Ordinary Synod of Bishops in 2012. Francis devotes several paragraphs near the end of the document to the subject of religious freedom. He reiterates Benedict's plea concerning the plight of Christians in Islamic countries, calling upon those governments "to grant Christians freedom to worship and to practice their faith, in light of the freedom which followers of Islam enjoy in Western countries!" This argument, however, is likely to be unpersuasive in undemocratic countries whose leaders share the Puritan and nineteenth-century papal theology that error has no rights of public expression. For these rulers, Islam is the one true religion; it mandates intolerance of other religions wherever politically feasible. Francis also warns of an additional threat to Christians posed by the tendency of secular society to trivialize religion and to limit it to the private sphere.[43]

Conclusion

Puritan theology and traditional papal teaching demanded religious freedom for their beliefs and practices while denying the same freedom to others. The fundamental principle in each case was that error had no rights, and the faithful must be protected from those who would attempt to lead them astray. Both the seventeenth-century Puritan and the nineteenth-century papal theologies of religious freedom have been abandoned. Since the mid-1960s, the Catholic Church has become a champion of religious freedom for all as a basic human right, which freedom encompasses not just belief, but witness and worship as well. Such freedom also includes the right

---

41. John Paul II, *Ecclesia in Europa*, 57.
42. Benedict XVI, *Africa munus*, 94.
43. Francis, *Evangelii gaudium*, 253, 255.

to reject any and all religious beliefs. The American religious experience has followed a similar trajectory, although its embrace of religious freedom began much sooner, as exemplified by the ratification of the First Amendment in 1791. Today, American law on religious freedom and current papal teaching are fully compatible.

However, the manner in which Americans and the Vatican have dealt with their history diverges. The American imagination has rewritten the nation's history of religious freedom, casting the Puritans as exemplars of religious freedom rather than its opponents. The Vatican, on the other hand, has chosen to ignore its history, treating *Dignitatis humanae* and subsequent papal teaching as timeless church doctrine. A review of these modern texts without knowledge of their precursors could lead a reader to reasonably conclude that the *Syllabus* and the nineteenth century encyclicals had never existed or had been expressly repudiated by the Church. But no attempt to reconcile the traditional and modern teaching on religious freedom has been attempted, probably because none would be credible. Although recent popes have contradicted their predecessors, they have refused to expressly admit that a prior teaching has been superseded or is no longer valid, if it ever was. The new teaching is taught, while the old one simply is ignored as if it never existed.

No pope has never claimed that any of the Catholic Church's teachings on religious freedom have been proclaimed infallibly. Therefore, they are subject to change, correction, and even outright contradiction. Nevertheless, Pius IX demanded that all Catholics condemn the errors that he enumerated in the *Syllabus*. Does that injunction remain in effect? In light of *Dignitatis humanae*, it is difficult to make a case that it is. The consistent refusal of recent popes to acknowledge the contradictions between the old and new teachings on religious freedom deals a serious blow to papal credibility. Archbishop Lefebvre's statement has gone unrebutted. "If what is being taught is true, then what the Church has taught is false." Could a future pope decide that Pius IX and Leo XIII were correct in teaching that only Catholics have the right to religious freedom?

6

Ambivalence: Church and State

> *Hence the Roman Pontiffs have never ceased, as circumstances required, to refute and condemn the doctrine of separation of Church and State.*
>
> —Pius X

> *The State may not impose religion, yet it must guarantee religious freedom and harmony between the followers of different religions.*
>
> —Benedict XVI

Separation of Church and State

THE METAPHOR MOST COMMONLY used to describe the relation between church and state in the United States is a "wall of separation." The phrase was coined in 1640 by Roger Williams, one of the founders of Rhode Island.[1] Williams had been banished from Massachusetts due to his belief that government should not exercise any control over a person's religious beliefs or practices, a view at odds with that colony's Puritan religious conformity. In Rhode Island, Williams established a colony in which freedom of religion was the distinguishing feature.[2]

---

1. Joe L. Coker, "Isaac Backus and John Leland: Baptist Contributions to Religious Liberty in the Founding Era," in Dreisbach and Hall, *Faith and the Founders*, 305–37, 310.

2. Ahlstrom, *Religious History*, 108.

The phrase "wall of separation" does not appear in the First Amendment to the Constitution of the United States, but it was borrowed by Thomas Jefferson in 1802 to explicate his interpretation of that amendment's religion clauses. President Jefferson had received a petition from the Baptists of Danbury, Connecticut, who resented that their tax money was being used to support the established Congregational churches.[3] The First Amendment by its express terms prevented Congress from establishing a national religion; existing state religious establishments, on the other hand, were unaffected. Jefferson, however, viewed the amendment more broadly, believing that even state establishments were injurious to religious freedom.[4] "I contemplate with sovereign reverence that act of the whole American people which declared that *their* legislature should 'make no law respecting an establishment of religion, or prohibiting the free exercise thereof,' thus building a wall of separation between Church and State."[5] Contrary to the hopes of the Danbury Baptists, Connecticut's establishment would continue until 1818, when it was abandoned due to the efforts of a "coalition of Jeffersonian Republicans and religious dissenters."[6] The last state to discontinue its religious establishment was Massachusetts in 1833, as a growing rift between Trinitarian and Unitarian Congregationalists had rendered that state's establishment unsustainable.[7]

The "wall of separation" metaphor did not become a part of First Amendment jurisprudence until the 1940s. In *Cantwell v. Connecticut*,[8] a case involving the conviction of Jehovah's Witnesses for soliciting contributions and distributing pamphlets in an overwhelmingly Catholic neighborhood, the United States Supreme Court for the first time held that the First Amendment is applicable to the states through the Due Process Clause of the Fourteenth Amendment. In *Everson v. Board of Education*,[9] which concerned the reimbursement of parents by a school board for the cost of busing their children to Catholic schools, the Court interpreted

---

3. Feldman, *Divided by God*, 22–23; Hamburger, *Separation of Church and State*, 155–62; T. Jeremy Gunn, "The Separation of Church and State versus Religion in the Public Square," in Gunn and Witte, *No Establishment of Religion*, 15–44, 28.

4. Ralph Ketchum, "James Madison, Thomas Jefferson, and the Meaning of 'Establishment of Religion' in Eighteenth-Century Virginia," in Gunn and Witte, *No Establishment of Religion*, 158–79, 172.

5. Hamburger, *Separation of Church and State*, 161, emphasis in original.

6. Green, *Second Disestablishment*, 121.

7. Ibid., 131–45.

8. 310 U.S. 296 (1940).

9. 330 U.S. 1 (1947).

the First Amendment as creating a Jeffersonian wall between government and religion.

> The "establishment of religion" clause of the First Amendment means at least this: Neither a state nor the Federal Government can set up a church. Neither can pass laws which aid one religion, aid all religions, or prefer one religion over another.... No tax in any amount, large or small, can be levied to support any religious activities or institutions, whatever they may be called, or whatever form they may adopt to teach or practice religion. Neither a state nor the Federal Government can, openly or secretly, participate in the affairs of any religious organizations or groups and vice versa. In the words of Jefferson, the clause against establishment of religion by law was intended to erect "a wall of separation between Church and State."[10]

Papal experience with established religions in the nineteenth and twentieth centuries was more complex than the American experience, due to the number of governments with which the Vatican had diplomatic relations. In addition, the Vatican was forced to defend the church against the efforts of certain European governments to restrict Catholic religious practices, including the expulsion of religious orders and confiscation of church property, challenges which the church in America never had to face. In nineteenth-century Europe, the region which remained the focus of the Vatican's attention, separation of church and state was the exception rather than the rule; most European nations had religious establishments, including Catholic establishments in France, Italy, Portugal, and Spain.[11] Popes during the age of infallibility also have been confronted by a variety of political systems. Nineteenth and early twentieth-century popes were comfortable with monarchy, the most common political system in Europe. But one by one those monarchies began to disappear, replaced by Fascist, Nazi, Communist, or democratic systems. While Pius XI was at home with Italian Fascism, he denounced the ideology of Nazism, although he did not bar Catholics from joining Nazi Party. All popes have rejected the legitimacy of Communism. Pius XII threatened excommunication of any Catholic who was a member of the Communist Party or who read Communist publications. Beginning with him, popes have shown an increasing preference for democracy as the system that provides the best safeguards for human rights, including religious freedom.

10. Id. at 15–16.
11. Witte, "Introduction," in Gunn and Witte, *No Establishment of Religion*, 3–14, 3.

Popes have been ambivalent concerning the appropriate degree of state support for religion. The idea of separation of church and state was condemned in the nineteenth century as a grave error, since it could mean an end to government support, both political and financial, for the church in Catholic countries. Although the Second Vatican Council did not endorse the separation of church and state, neither did it repeat earlier papal condemnations of that arrangement.[12] Moreover, as an increasing number of Catholics now reside in countries where Christians are a religious minority, popes have recognized that separation of church and state may be the best way to protect the religious freedom of Catholics. In countries with Catholic majorities, however, the church has continued to seek privileges for itself through concordats—treaties between the Holy See and sovereign nations—a practice which the council blessed. Before Vatican II, such concordats sometimes contained provisions suppressing other religions, but these provisions are absent from post-conciliar concordats.

This chapter is closely related to the previous one, although the emphasis is different. The subject of the former chapter was the individual's right to religious freedom, including the freedom to practice, witness, and worship according to the dictates of one's conscience. The subject of the current chapter is the church's relation to the institution of the state. There is a logical relationship between the two chapters, because church teaching on religious liberty has influenced its understanding of the proper relationship between church and state; as the former has changed over time, the latter has followed suit.

Pius IX and the Defense of Catholic Religious Establishments

Pius IX issued several encyclicals to the bishops of individual countries addressing governmental action directed against the Catholic Church and its activities. His primary concerns were to protect the established rights of the church in those countries where it enjoyed a special status and, in countries where the rights of the church were not favored by law, to prevent governmental interference in church affairs.

In *Probe noscitis venerabiles*, he praises the recently concluded concordat between the Holy See and Spain. Although the encyclical does not set forth the details of the concordat, an examination of the concordat discloses the manner in which the church enjoyed special status in Spain. The Catholic Church is declared "to be the sole religion of the Spanish nation." Teaching in all schools and universities, whether public or private, must conform

---

12. Noonan, *Lustre of Our Country*, 348–53.

to Catholic doctrine. The Spanish government undertook to pay the salaries of bishops and parish clergy and to provide funds for the maintenance of churches, seminaries, and religious houses. The government also agreed to respect the church's right to own and administer its property.[13]

In *Inter multiplices*, addressed to the bishops of France, Pius attributes the "peace, tranquility, and good will" enjoyed by the Catholic Church in France to Napoleon III, who had become emperor the previous year. He admonishes French bishops to aim for unity. He also condemns a book on the church in France and orders that this publication be placed on the Index of Forbidden Books.[14] It is rare for a pope to use an encyclical to single out a book for condemnation; the result could be counterproductive, as Pius should have learned from the experience of his predecessor. In 1834 the French Catholic writer Felicité de Lamennais published the book *Paroles d'un Croyant* (*Words of a Believer*), in which he railed against monarchy and espoused democracy. Gregory XVI saw the book as an open attack on the teachings of *Mirari vos*. Two months after publication of the book, Gregory issued the encyclical *Singulari nos*, devoted to pointing out the errors of Lamenais. He characterizes the book as "small in size [but] enormous in wickedness" and declares the book condemned.[15] This papal response practically guaranteed that it would become a best-seller.[16]

In *Optime noscitis*, Pius recalls the recently concluded concordat with Austria. The Holy See had entered into the concordat with Austria to "better protect the freedom of the Catholic Church and her rights." In accordance with the concordat, he reminds the Austrian bishops that in making ecclesiastical appointments and choosing seminary professors, they must inquire first whether the emperor has any political objections to the candidate.[17] The situation in Austria had changed dramatically by the time of the publication of *Vix dum a nobis* nineteen years later in 1874. The nation had adopted a liberal constitution in 1866, some of whose provisions on religious liberty contradicted portions of the concordat.[18] The Austrian imperial assembly was proposing to abrogate the concordat.[19] This action was in response to Vatican I's declaration of the dogma of papal infallibility, which was opposed by many

---

13. Pius IX, *Probe noscitis venerabiles*, 1; *Concordat between the Holy See and Spain*, arts. 1, 2, 31–41.

14. Pius IX, *Inter multiplices*, 3–7.

15. Gregory XVI, *Singulari nos*, 2.

16. Chadwick, *History of the Popes*, 15–31.

17. Pius IX, *Optime noscitis*, 2, 6.

18. Chadwick, *History of the Popes*, 247.

19. Pius IX, *Vix dum a nobis*, 9–10.

in Austria.[20] The effect of the proposed laws would be to subjugate the church to civil authorities. Pius viewed such efforts as an infringement on church authority. He compares these proposed laws to those that had been enacted in Germany as part of the *Kulturkampf*,[21] which had resulted in the expulsion of priests and nuns and the jailing of bishops.[22]

In *Incredibili*, Pius laments the passage of laws in New Granada (present-day Colombia) that put the exercise of ecclesiastical functions under government control, resulting in the confiscation of church property, the banishment of religious communities of men and women, and the grant of certain rights to non-Catholics.[23] In *Quod nunquam*, he deplores the imprisonment of two bishops and the occupation of parish churches in Prussia by persons who undertake ministry under authority of the government.[24]

The common thread in all of these encyclicals is Pius's effort to defend the rights of the Catholic Church vis-a-vis the state. In countries where Roman Catholicism is the established religion, he seeks to strengthen that establishment. In countries where Catholics are a minority, he decries any persecution of the church. In neither situation did Pius view the proper position of the state toward the church to be one of neutrality.

Leo XIII: The State as the Supporter of the Catholic Church

Leo XIII wrote prolifically about church-state relations. He emphasizes the duty of Christians to obey their rulers, who have received their authority from God, as well as the duty of rulers to govern their subjects justly. He is particularly concerned that civil strife should be avoided, viewing such strife as a result of the implementation in the political realm of the principles of freedom and equality which were the legacy of the Enlightenment and the French Revolution. The proper relationship between church and state is not one of neutrality; rather, the duty of the state is to support the Catholic Church, the one true religion. He expresses contempt for individual liberties and rejects the notion that they constitute inalienable rights. One of his most important encyclicals was addressed to the bishops of the United States, in which he displays a willingness to accept the separation of church and state

---

20. Hasler, *How the Pope Became Infallible*, 239–40.

21. Pius IX, *Vix dum a nobis*, 2–8.

22. Coppa, *Politics and the Papacy*, 51–52; Duffy, *Saints and Sinners*, 303; O'Connell, *Critics on Trial*, 25.

23. Pius IX, *Incredibili*, 1.

24. Pius IX, *Quod nunquam*, 3–7.

as a matter of local necessity; but he does not recommend such an arrangement as a template for other countries to follow.

In *Diuturnum*, he insists that the power to rule comes from God and not from the will of the people, but he also indicates that democratic forms of government do not necessarily contravene Catholic doctrine. He begins and ends the encyclical by arguing that attacks on the church inevitably lead to civil strife, pointing both to the recent assassination of Tsar Alexander II of Russia and the strife that engulfed Germany following the Reformation.[25] In the main body of the encyclical, he argues that the failure of people to submit to civil authority is a violation of the natural social order.[26] It is difficult to reconcile what appear to be two contradictory positions. On the one hand, political power and the right to rule come from God. On the other hand, people have the right to choose the form of their political institutions and to elect those who will govern them. Leo makes no attempt to explain in what manner both of these seemingly contradictory propositions can be true, nor does he resolve this problem in any of his future encyclicals.

The focus of *Immortale Dei*, written in 1885, departs from that of his earlier encyclicals. Its primary theme is the duty of the state to its subjects, rather than the obedience owed by subjects to the state. Rulers should dispense "evenhanded justice" and govern with the well-being of their subjects as their paramount interest, as opposed to personal gain. But he does not indicate whether there is any legitimate action which a country's subjects may take if their rulers fail to work for the common good, leaving it to God to dispense justice to unjust rulers in the afterlife. Later in the encyclical, he again repudiates the notion that "all government is nothing more nor less than the will of the people, and the people, being under the power of itself alone, is alone its own ruler." It now appears, however, that his reluctance to embrace Enlightenment principles of self-governance may not be primarily theologically motivated, but grounded instead in the fear of the civil strife that could emerge if those principles were universally put into practice. "For the opinion prevails that princes are nothing more than delegates chosen to carry out the will of the people; whence it necessarily follows that all things are as changeable as the will of the people, so that risk of public disturbance is ever hanging over our heads."[27] Leo's concern that the political discord associated with democracy could threaten the fabric of society is a theme that will reappear in future encyclicals.

---

25. Leo XIII, *Diuturnum*, 2, 29.
26. Ibid., 4–7.
27. Leo XIII, *Immortale Dei*, 5, 24, 31.

This encyclical is also the first one in which Leo tackles the issue of the proper relationship between the Catholic Church and the state. The attitude of the state toward the church should be one of support rather than neutrality.

> As a consequence, the State, constituted as it is, is clearly bound to act up to the manifold and weighty duties linking it to God, by the public profession of religion. . . . Since, then, no one is allowed to be remiss in the service due to God, and since the chief duty of all men is to cling to religion in both its teaching and its practice—not such religion as they may have a preference for, but the religion which God enjoins, and which certain and most clear marks show to be the only one true religion—it is a public crime to act as though there were no God. . . . All who rule, therefore, would hold in honour the holy name of God, and one of their chief duties must be to favour religion, to protect it, to shield it under the credit and sanction of the laws, and neither to organize nor enact any measure that may compromise its safety.[28]

By "religion," Leo is referring solely to the Catholic faith, "the only true religion . . . established by Jesus Christ Himself."[29] The implication of this approach for church-state relations is that, where Catholics are a minority, the duty of the state is to preserve their religious freedom and liberty of worship; where Catholics are in the majority, the duty of government is to favor the Catholic Church over other religions. In countries where no single religion predominates, religious freedom is appropriate. But if Catholics predominate in a country, then the state should support the Catholic Church and, if possible, deny freedom to other religions.[30] In other words, the traditional papal approach to church-state relations "prescribes intolerance whenever possible; it permits toleration whenever necessary."[31]

In *Libertas*, in addition to Leo's discussion of liberty (which was examined in the last chapter), he sets forth Catholic teaching on the proper relationship between the church and the state. For Leo, separation of church and state has no place in Catholic social teaching. "Hence follows the fatal theory of the need of separation between Church and State. But the absurdity of such a position is manifest. Nature herself proclaims the necessity of the State

---

28. Ibid., 6.
29. Ibid., 7.
30. Charles Curran, "Churches and Human Rights: From Hostility/Reluctance to Acceptability," in Curran, *Change in Official Catholic Moral Teachings*, 38–61, 48–49.
31. Murray, "Problem of Religious Freedom," 509.

providing means and opportunities whereby the community may be enabled to live properly, that is to say, according to the laws of God."[32]

Liberty of worship is inimical to the proper relationship between the church and the state. The state has duties toward God and is bound to support the one true religion. Moreover, the church has something to offer the state as well. "Religion, of its essence, is wonderfully helpful to the State. . . . It admonishes subjects to be obedient to lawful authority, as to the ministers of God; and it binds them to their rulers, not merely by obedience, but by reverence and affection."[33] Leo's view on the ability of religion to keep social unrest in check was shared by many nineteenth-century rulers. Napoleon Bonaparte, for example, "saw religion, especially in the form of an established Church, as one of the chief means of social control."[34] As historian Mike Rapport has noted, "In trying to mobilise the population, the conservatives had a great moral weapon at their disposal—religion—which in some areas of Europe was *the* decisive factor in keeping the population loyal to the old order."[35] In other words, if the state supports the church, the church will keep the flock in line.

The stated purpose of *Sapientiae Christianae* is "to define more in detail the duties of the Catholics, inasmuch as these would, if strictly observed, wonderfully contribute to the good of the commonwealth." However, when Christian duty and civic duty conflict, Christian duty takes precedence, and resistance to a civil law may be required. Leo returns to a theme that he previously had explored in *Diuturnum*, the forms of civil government compatible with Catholic faith. "On like grounds, the Church, the guardian always of her own right and most observant of that of others, holds that it is not her province to decide which is the best amongst many diverse forms of government and the civil institutions of Christian States, and amid the various kinds of State rule she does not disapprove of any, provided the respect due to religion and the observance of good morals be upheld." Although the church may not have a preference for which particular form of government a country chooses, this does not imply that it must remain silent about political matters.[36] Leo himself did not remain aloof from the political fray, issuing a *non expedit* (it is not expedient), forbidding Italian Catholics

---

32. Leo XIII, *Libertas*, 18.

33. Ibid., 21–22.

34. William Roberts, "Napoleon, the Concordat of 1801, and its Consequences," in Coppa, *Controversial Concordats*, 34–80, 36.

35. Rapport, *1848*, 267, emphasis in original.

36. Leo XIII, *Sapientiae Christianae*, 3, 10, 28, 37.

from engaging in national party politics.[37] Pius X and Pius XI also will inject themselves into matters of Italian politics.

Longinqua, the subject of which is Catholicism in the United States, is one of Leo's most important encyclicals. Issued in 1895, it contains an express acknowledgement of the conditions under which Catholicism can grow even without the kind of government support to which the church in predominantly Catholic countries had become accustomed. He claims that the American colonies had achieved independence with Catholic aid, although he does not specify whether he is referring to the aid of Catholics in America or those from other countries.[38]

In an oft-quoted section of the encyclical, Leo focuses on the unique situation of the Catholic Church in the United States. Although it receives no financial assistance from the government, it is not burdened by governmental interference in its internal affairs. The church in America continued to grow and flourish under these conditions, but Leo expresses the belief that it would benefit from some measure of governmental support.

> . . . But, moreover, (a fact which it gives pleasure to acknowledge), thanks are due to the equity of the laws which obtain in America and to the customs of the well-ordered Republic. For the Church amongst you, unopposed by the Constitution and government of your nation, fettered by no hostile legislation, protected against violence by the common laws and the impartiality of the tribunals, is free to live and act without hindrance. Yet, though all this is true, it would be very erroneous to draw the conclusion that in America is to be sought the type of the most desirable status of the Church, or that it would be universally lawful or expedient for State and Church to be, as in America, dissevered and divorced. The fact that Catholicity with you is in good condition, nay, is even enjoying a prosperous growth, is by all means to be attributed to the fecundity with which God has endowed His Church, in virtue of which unless men or circumstances interfere, she spontaneously expands and propagates herself; but she would bring forth more abundant fruits if, in addition to liberty, she enjoyed the favor of the laws and the patronage of the public authority.[39]

Leo's evaluation of the American experiment in church–state relations appears to be at the same time both enthusiastic and lukewarm. He considers

---

37. O'Connell, *Critics on Trial*, 205.
38. Leo XIII, *Longinqua*, 4.
39. Ibid., 6.

the experiment to be a success peculiar to America, rather than an arrangement to be recommended to other nations.

Testem benevolentiae nostrae, written in 1899, is not an encyclical addressed to all the bishops of the United States, but a letter addressed only to Cardinal Gibbons, the Archbishop of Baltimore and the leading spokesman for the church in America. Leo makes it plain in the first paragraph of the letter that its tone will be different from that of *Longinqua*. "This letter is not intended, as preceding ones, to repeat the words of praise so often spoken, but rather to call attention to some things to be avoided and corrected." The dangers with which Leo takes issue are viewed by him as a grave threat to the church. "These dangers, viz., the confounding of license with liberty, the passion for discussing and pouring contempt upon any possible subject, the assumed right to hold whatever opinions one pleases upon any subject and to set them forth in print to the world, have so wrapped minds in darkness that there is now a greater need of the Church's teaching office than ever before, lest people become unmindful both of conscience and of duty." Leo lumps these dangerous opinions under the term "Americanism."[40]

The "Americanist" controversy reflected a divergence between the traditional and modern views of the manner in which the church should confront the world.[41] For traditionalists in Rome, and some conservatives in America, certain principles of American life, such as democracy, freedom of religion, and church-state separation could not be reconciled with Catholic doctrine. American bishops, on the other hand, "were committed to democratic institutions and the full-scale participation of Catholics in American life."[42] The timing of Leo's letter was occasioned by the publication of a biography of Father Isaac Hecker, a liberal American convert to Catholicism and co-founder of a religious community of priests, the Missionary Society of St. Paul the Apostle, commonly known as the Paulist Fathers. In 1865, the order began publication of the *Catholic World*, an influential monthly magazine.[43] According to Leo, the publication of Hecker's biography "has excited not a little controversy, on account of certain opinions brought forward concerning the way of leading Christian life."[44] Although the letter was addressed only to Cardinal Gibbons, copies were distributed to all of the bishops of the United States. A number of them responded by letter, claiming that they

40. Leo XIII, *Testem benevolentiae nostrae*, 1–2, 4.

41. For a discussion of the Americanist controversy, see Ahlstrom, *Religious History*, 546–54 and Morris, *American Catholic*, 106–12.

42. Ahlstrom, *Religious History*, 828–30.

43. Ibid., 553.

44. Leo XIII, *Testem benevolentiae nostrae*, 1.

did not know anyone in America who held the doctrines which Leo had criticized. The Americanist controversy quickly faded.[45]

In the early 1950s John Courtney Murray published a series of articles in the Jesuit journal *Theological Studies* examining Leo's teaching on church-state relations and religious liberty. According to Murray, Leo's writings should be read as critiques of nineteenth-century rationalism and anticlericalism, which sought to remove the influence of the church from the public sphere, rather than as a criticism of church-state separation as practiced in the United States.[46]

Leo was concerned about the deteriorating state of church-state relations in France. In *Nobilissima Gallorum gens*, he declares that when religion is removed from a nation's public life, its citizens may be "seduced into sedition and revolt."[47] The theme of the effort to eliminate Christianity in France is developed in more detail in *Au milieu des sollicitudes*, which was written in French and addressed "to the Bishops and Faithful of France." He refers to "the depths of the vast conspiracy that certain men have formed for the annihilation of Christianity in France." These enemies of the church repeat the old lie that it wishes to dominate the state politically. He notes that during the last century, France had gone through three forms of government: empire, monarchy, and republic. He is careful not to endorse one of these forms of government as superior to the others. The concept of the separation of church and state, on the other hand, he labels as an "absurdity." At best, it is a condition to be tolerated if the alternatives might prove worse for the church.[48]

Pius X Addresses Deteriorating Church-State Relations in France Italy, and Portugal

Pius X shared his predecessor's concern with the condition of the Catholic Church in France. Relations between France and the Holy See were governed by a concordat between the two sovereigns ratified in 1801. The government of France acknowledged the Catholic religion as "the religion of the great majority of French citizens." The church would enjoy the free exercise of religion in the country. The government was given the right to appoint bishops and archbishops. All bishops were required to take an oath

45. Morris, *American Catholic*, 109.
46. Hudock, *Struggle, Condemnation, Vindication*, 57–67; Noonan, *Lustre of Our Country*, 28.
47. Leo XIII, *Nobilissima Gallorum gens*, 2.
48. Leo XIII, *Au milieu des sollicitudes*, 2, 9, 14, 28.

of loyalty to the government. The church was given control of all property used for worship.[49] Tensions between the French Republic and the Vatican intensified at the beginning of the twentieth century. In 1904, France banned monks and nuns from teaching, confiscated property of disbanded religious communities, and broke off diplomatic relations with the Vatican.[50] In 1905 France passed the Law Concerning the Separation of the Churches and the State. The government gave up its right to appoint bishops, but the law put church property under the control of associations of laymen. Such associations went by the name of *associations cultuelles*.[51] Pius refused to accept this state of affairs, issuing three encyclicals condemning the law.

Vehementer nos was Pius's first encyclical concerning a law which he dubbed "as disastrous to society as it is to religion." The fundamental flaw of the French law is that by dictating a total separation of church and state, it limits the role of the state to the temporal sphere, whereas the state also has a necessary role to play in its citizens' spiritual lives. Leo XIII had found that the separation of church and state which prevailed in America was an acceptable arrangement, even though the church received no support from the government. Pius is not willing to make any such accommodation for France. The difference likely is attributable to the different models of church-state relations present in the two countries. In the United States, the government's attitude toward religion was one of neutrality, whereas in France it was one of hostility. For Pius, the actions of the French government were a direct violation of the concordat. The law gave assemblies of laymen control over public worship in derogation of ecclesiastical authority. Such a result turned upside-down the relation between clergy and laity. "It follows that the Church is essentially an *unequal* society, that is, a society comprising two categories of persons, the Pastors and the flock, those who occupy a rank in the different degrees of the hierarchy and the multitude of the faithful. . . . The one duty of the multitude is to allow themselves to be led, and, like a docile flock, to follow the Pastors."[52]

Gravissimo officii munere deals specifically with the *associations cultuelles*. Pius refuses to recognize the legitimacy of such bodies. "We decree that it is absolutely impossible for them to be formed without a violation of the sacred rights pertaining to the very life of the Church."[53] Owen Chad-

---

49. *Concordat between the Holy See and France*, preamble, arts. 1, 4, 6, 12.

50. Chadwick, *History of the Popes*, 388–91; Pollard, *Money and the Modern Papacy*, 102–3.

51. Roberts, "Napoleon, the Concordat of 1801, and its Consequences," in Coppa, *Controversial Concordats*, 74–75.

52. Pius X, *Vehementer nos*, 1, 3, 5, 8.

53. Pius X, *Gravissimo officii munere*, 3.

wick has labeled the consequences of this encyclical as "disastrous." Since there was no legal entity authorized by Pius to assume ownership of church property in France, the French government stepped in to fill the void. The state ejected bishops, priests, and seminarians from their properties and assumed control of them. It is unlikely that this was a result that Pius had foreseen when he issued the encyclical, if he had given any thought to its political consequences. "His sense of right was such that he cared nothing for the practical."[54] Pius's final encyclical in the French trilogy, *Une fois encore*, again rejects the validity of those associations, which exercise "powers which are the exclusive prerogative of ecclesiastical authority."[55]

The Catholic Church in America had faced a similar dispute over the ownership and management of church property more than half a century earlier. The issue of "trusteeism" in America was able to be resolved favorably to the American church without Vatican intervention. By the 1850s, most states required that all religious property, not just Catholic, be owned and managed by lay trustees in order to prevent churches from becoming a political force due to the extent of their land holdings. Archbishop Hughes of New York simply ignored the New York trustee law and took title to church property in his own name. Other bishops followed Hughes's lead, and the laws fell into desuetude through lack of enforcement.[56]

In *Il fermo proposito*, Pius commends the works of the laity in Italy performed under the umbrella of "Catholic Action," which activities are directed toward "the solution to the social question."[57] However, he is conflicted on the role that Catholic Action should play in the political life of Italy, due to a decree of his predecessor. Leo XIII had issued a *non expedit*, which forbade Italian Catholics from engaging in national party politics.[58] Pius, on the other hand, sees a need for a less restrictive rule. In order to keep control over the activities of Catholic Action, he reiterates that such groups are subject to control by the bishops.[59]

In 1908, the king and the crown prince of Portugal were assassinated, and a republican regime was established in their place.[60] In *Iamdudum*, Pius discusses the ills that have befallen the church in Portugal following the

---

54. Chadwick, *History of the Popes*, 396–97.

55. Pius X, *Une fois encore*, 12.

56. Hamburger, *Separation of Church and State*, 240–43; Morris, *American Catholic*, 74–75.

57. Pius X, *Il fermo proposito*, 20.

58. O'Connell, *Critics on Trial*, 205.

59. Pius X, *Il fermo proposito*, 18–22.

60. Chiron, *Pius IX*, 270.

loss of the monarchy. A new law on the separation of church and state had resulted in "the deletion of the feast days of the Church from the number of public festivals, the abolition of religious oaths, the hasty establishment of the law of divorce and religious instruction banished from the public schools." Two other negative effects of the law were similar to those in France. First, property was confiscated from the church, and property acquired by the church in the future would become public property. Second, associations of laymen were put in charge of public worship. The Portuguese law went further than the French one, in that it gave the state the right to approve seminary textbooks and outlawed publication of papal decrees without government permission. Pius finds the Portuguese law no more acceptable than the French one, so he declares it "null and void."[61]

One may legitimately wonder what power Pius thought he possessed to declare the law of a sovereign nation null and void. Obviously, this declaration had no legal effect in Portugal. But prior popes had taken pains to remind Catholics of their duty to obey the laws imposed on them by civil authority. By declaring the Portuguese law null and void, Pius in effect was freeing Catholics from their moral obligation to obey such a law. An earlier example of such a declaration is found in the papal bull *Regnans in excelsis*, issued by Pius V in 1570. In addition to excommunicating Elizabeth I of England, Pius V freed English Catholics from any duty owed to her.[62]

Pius XI Confronts Nazism, Communism, and Fascism

Pius XI faced several situations which required him to address various aspects of the question of the proper relation between the Catholic Church and the state: repeated violations by the Third Reich of the concordat between the church and Germany; the threat posed to the social order by the Communist form of government; the proper limits of state control over the education of children; a new proposal in France for lay control over church property and worship; attacks by the Mussolini government upon the activities of Catholic Action in Italy; and persecution of the church in Mexico.

In March 1937, Pius issued a pair of encyclicals directed against totalitarianism. The first dealt with the situation in Germany and the second with atheistic Communism. The publication of *Mit brennender Sorge* was precipitated by the Third Reich's repeated violations of the terms of a concordat that had been entered into between the Holy See and the German Reich in July 1933, only months after Adolf Hitler became chancellor. The concordat

---

61. Pius X, *Iamdudum*, 1, 4–9.
62. Pius V, *Regnans in excelsis*, 3–5.

was negotiated on behalf of the Holy See by Pius's Secretary of State, Cardinal Pacelli, who previously had negotiated concordats with Bavaria and Prussia during his tenure as papal nuncio to those German states.[63]

The concordat guaranteed to the church certain freedom from interference by the Reich in matters of worship and internal church administration. In exchange, the church agreed to refrain from participation in German politics. Germany guaranteed freedom of religion to the church and acknowledged the church's right to regulate its own affairs. The Holy See was to enjoy freedom of communications with bishops and clergy. Only German citizens could function as clerics within the Reich, and bishops were required to take an oath of loyalty. The property rights of the church were secured. The right of the church to establish and operate parochial schools, where instruction is given by Catholic teachers in accordance with Catholic principles, were preserved. The church, for its part, agreed that Catholic organizations must "conduct their activities outside all political parties." Finally, "the Holy See will enact regulations to exclude the clergy and members of religious orders from membership in political parties and from working on their behalf."[64]

The Vatican and the Reich entered into the concordat for vastly different reasons, as described by German historian Hubert Wolf.

> ... Two points that were crucial to both partners soon crystallized, which in the end led to a sort of quid pro quo. For the Catholic Church ... what was most important was to ensure the continued existence of Catholic associations and organizations, which were the backbone of German Catholic life. Only if those institutions were exempted from the government's policy of forced coordination with Nazi principles could German Catholicism survive a totalitarian state as an independent and halfway intact institution. What was most important to Hitler and the National Socialists, by contrast, was to rid themselves of all inconvenient political competition.... Catholicism as a political force needed to be eliminated.[65]

Less than two months after the concordat's ratification, Pacelli lodged formal protests against Nazi violations of its provisions.[66] Complaints surfaced that the Reich was oppressing Catholic organizations that had a strictly religious purpose and was discriminating against Jewish converts

63. Coppa, *Pius XII*, 74–112; Duffy, *Saints and Sinners*, 340.
64. *Concordat between the Holy See and Germany*, arts. 1, 4, 14–17, 21–25, 31–32.
65. Wolf, *Pope and Devil*, 172.
66. Lewy, *Catholic Church and Nazi Germany*, 177.

to Catholicism.[67] The concordat contained a protocol which provided that "Should differences of opinion arise regarding the interpretation or execution of any of the articles of this concordat, the Holy See and the German Reich will reach a friendly solution by mutual agreement."[68] In accordance with this protocol, the bishops' complaints went to the Holy See, which then brought them to the attention of representatives of the Reich. In essence, the Reich proceeded as it wished regardless of the express terms of the concordat, knowing that any disputes over its violation would be tied up in diplomatic wrangling between the parties. Pius sent dozens of complaints to the Reich, which the German government failed to address. He considered renouncing the concordat, but Pacelli dissuaded him from doing so.[69]

Relations between the Reich and the Vatican had deteriorated so badly by the time of the encyclical that it had to be smuggled into Germany and printed secretly. It was read from all pulpits in Germany on Palm Sunday, 1937.[70] Pius begins the encyclical, which was written in German rather than Latin, by recounting that he had entered into the concordat reluctantly in order "to spare the Faithful of Germany, as far as it was humanly possible, the trials and difficulties they would have had to face, given the circumstances, had the negotiations fallen through." But the Reich's violations of the concordat had convinced him that it was engaged in "a war of extermination" against the church. He was especially concerned about the Reich's interference with Catholic schools.[71]

He attacks National Socialist ideology head on, although he avoids mentioning National Socialism by name.

> Whoever exalts race, or the people, or the State . . . whoever raises these notions above their standard value and divinizes them to an idolatrous level, distorts and perverts an order of the world planned and created by God; he is far from the true faith in God and from the concept of life which that faith unfolds. . . .
>
> None but superficial minds could stumble into concepts of a national God, of a national religion; or attempt to lock within the frontiers of a single people, within the narrow limits of a single race, God, the Creator of the universe, King and Legislator

---

67. Cornwell, *Hitler's Pope*, 160.
68. *Concordat between the Holy See and Germany*, art. 33.
69. Coppa, *Pius XII*, 114–15.
70. Ibid., 116; Lewy, *Catholic Church and Nazi Germany*, 156; Passelecq and Suchecky, *Hidden Encyclical*, 102.
71. Pius XI, *Mit brennender Sorge*, 3–5, 31.

of all nations before whose immensity they are "as a drop of a bucket" (Isaiah 40:15).[72]

Pius decries efforts to banish the Old Testament from churches and schools as well as "the so-called myth of race and blood," although he makes no specific condemnation of anti-Semitism. Finally, he warns German Catholics not to be seduced by the prospect of a German national church.[73] Hitler responded by ordering the closing of Catholic publishing houses, prohibiting the publication in Germany of future encyclicals, and threatening to reveal instances of sex abuse on the part of Catholic clergy.[74]

This is the last encyclical of Pius XI to address National Socialist ideology. In the months before he died in 1939, he had commissioned a draft of another encyclical that would condemn both racism and anti-Semitism. The drafter of the encyclical was American Jesuit John LaFarge, who recently had published a book about racial prejudice in the United States entitled *Interracial Justice*.[75] The working title of this encyclical was *Humani generis unitas* (*On the Unity of Humankind*). The draft was still on Pius's bedside table at the time of his death.[76]

Divini Redemptoris is devoted to explaining why Communism is not the answer to the problems of the working class. The goal of Communism is "upsetting the social order and . . . undermining the very foundations of Christian civilization." Communists reject any type of hierarchy and preach absolute equality. Three reasons that Communism has spread far and wide are the "religious and moral destitution" of workers resulting from the devastating effects of capitalist economic policy, Communist propaganda, and the silence of the non-Catholic press. Pius contrasts the false equality preached by Communism with Christian equality. Communism has flourished because rulers have scorned the teachings of the church.[77]

Divini illius magistri sets forth Pius's pedagogic approach to education in primary schools, with particular emphasis on the respective roles of the church and the state in education. There is no doubt in his mind that the role of the state is subordinate, since "education belongs preeminently to the

---

72. Ibid., 8–11.

73. Ibid., 15–17, 22.

74. Coppa, *Papacy in the Modern World*, 115; Kertzer, *Pope and Mussolini*, 259–60.

75. Passelecq and Suchecky, *Hidden Encyclical*, 35–36.

76. Coppa, *Pius XII*, 122–23; Fattorini, *Hitler, Mussolini, and the Vatican*, 152–54, 188; Phayer, *Catholic Church and the Holocaust*, 2–4. The complete text of the draft encyclical is reprinted in Passelecq and Suchecky, *Hidden Encylical*, 176–275.

77. Pius XI, *Divini Redemptoris*, 3, 10, 16–18, 36–38.

Church."⁷⁸ Pius argues that the state does not have the right to force children to attend public schools, citing for support not a previous encyclical or other religious text, but a decision of the United States Supreme Court.⁷⁹ In *Pierce v. Society of Sisters*, the Court reviewed the Oregon Compulsory Education Act of 1922.⁸⁰ The act required all children between the ages of eight and sixteen to attend public schools. The primary advocate of the referendum which resulted in passage of the act was the Ku Klux Klan.⁸¹ The law was challenged by the Society of the Sisters of the Holy Name of Jesus, a religious order which operated primary and secondary schools in the state. The Court invalidated the law, in part because it unreasonably interfered with the right of parents to direct the education of their children. Pius does not merely uphold the right of Catholic parents to send their children to parochial schools; he forbids them from doing otherwise.⁸² However, Pius XI's own successor was not a product of the Catholic school system. Pacelli's father Filippo, a canon and civil lawyer, sent his sons to state-run secular schools in which religion was not taught. Pacelli attended such a school in Rome from the ages of nine through eighteen. Filippo believed that the secular school system would provide his sons with a better foundation for the legal careers he hoped that they would pursue.⁸³

Pius laments the fact that Catholic families in some countries (such as the United States) must bear the entire financial burden of educating their children in Catholic schools with no governmental support.⁸⁴ He expresses no similar concern for non-Catholic parents who are forced to support Catholic schools in countries where such schools are state-funded. In the United States, the duty of Catholic parents to send their children to parochial schools had been decreed by the Third Plenary Council of Baltimore in 1884.⁸⁵ In spite of this directive, a majority of American Catholic children always have attended public schools.⁸⁶

In *Maximam gravissimamque*, Pius returns to the theme of *associations cultuelles*, those lay-controlled organizations in France which were to

---

78. Pius XI, *Divini illus magistri*, 15.

79. Ibid., 37 n. 28.

80. 268 U.S. 510 (1925).

81. Hamburger, *Separation of Church and State*, 412–18.

82. Pius XI, *Divini illus magistri*, 79.

83. Coppa, *Pius XII*, 30–32; Pollard, *Papacy in the Age of Totalitarianism*, 292; Wolf, *Pope and Devil*, 34.

84. Pius XI, *Divini illus magistri*, 82.

85. Sehat, *Myth of American Religious Freedom*, 167–68.

86. Steinfels, *People Adrift*, 211.

be given jurisdiction over church property and worship. These associations previously had been condemned by Pius X in a series of encyclicals. The associations never became a reality. Pius XI now examines a new proposal for "diocesan associations" to determine whether they can exist in France consistent with church law. Unfortunately, the encyclical does not detail how these new associations differed from those that Pius X had proscribed. For Pius XI, these new associations are permissible, due to changed circumstances in France and a thawing of relations between the French Republic and the Holy See. Such associations are permitted on an experimental basis, subject to two conditions. First, the statutes of the associations must conform to church law. Second, certain unspecified guarantees must be given to insure that the legal rights of these associations would be protected in the event of a change in the leadership of the French Republic that was hostile to the church.[87] It is difficult to envision how this second condition could ever have been enforced as a practical matter.

Although the Roman Question had been settled, relations between the Vatican and the Italian government were not without strife. *Non abbiamo bisogno*, issued in 1931, was written in Italian and first published in foreign newspapers, due to a concern that Mussolini's censors would not permit its distribution in Italy.[88] Pius pleads the case that Catholic Action in Italy has abided by the terms of the 1929 concordat. That treaty required Catholic Action to conduct its activities outside of political parties and under the control of the church. Nevertheless, certain acts of violence had been perpetrated against members of Catholic Action, violence which Pius believes had been ordered by Mussolini himself. He interprets these attacks on Catholic Action as attacks on himself. He believes that Mussolini's government had resolved to monopolize the lives of the young for the sole benefit of the state. Pius is aware that membership in the Fascist Party is a career necessity for many people. He proposes the following compromise for Catholics who must take an oath to the party. "It seems to Us that such a means for those who have already received the membership card would be to make for themselves before God, in their own consciences, a reservation such as 'Saving the laws of God and of the Church' or 'In accordance with the duties of a good Christian,' with the firm proposal to declare also externally such a reservation if the need of it arose."[89] The Fascist Party was not happy

---

87. Pius XI, *Maximam gravissimamque*, 11.
88. Kertzer, *Pope and Mussolini*, 161.
89. Pius XI, *Non abbiamo bisogno*, 7, 11, 34, 44, 9.

that Pius had authorized Italian Catholics to take the oath while harboring reservations which could render the oath nugatory.[90]

Between 1926 and 1937 Pius issued three encyclicals dealing with the persecution of the Catholic Church in Mexico. *Iniquis afflictisque* provides a summary of the troubles facing the church in Mexico. The Mexican Revolution of 1917 had the effect of ending the legal existence of the Catholic Church in Mexico, a situation which persisted until 1992.[91] The 1917 Mexican Constitution declared the separation of church and state, gave civil authorities the right to limit the number of priests, outlawed the taking of religious vows, and declared church buildings to be state property. Religion could not be taught even in private schools. Bishops were arrested, seminaries and schools closed, and foreign priests and religious have been expelled from the country.[92] Six years later, when *Acerba animi* was published, the situation had not improved. In response, the bishops of Mexico had suspended public worship and went into exile. Religious instruction in schools remained forbidden. The number of priests permitted to exercise their ministry was severely limited. In the State of Veracruz, for example, there was only one priest permitted for every 100,000 inhabitants.[93]

Firmissimam constantiam was issued in the same month as Pius's encyclicals against Nazism and Communism. On the surface, this encyclical appears to have little in common with *Mit brennender Sorge* and *Divini Redemptoris*. The timing of its issuance may be explained by the fact that Pius viewed the events in Russia and Mexico as part of the same international Communist conspiracy.[94] The "reforms" that had taken place in Mexico represented for him "the dechristianization of a people that owes to religion its greatest glories." He is especially concerned about the education of future priests, due to the closing of seminaries by the government. A partial solution was to educate a number of Mexican seminarians in Rome and the United States. Dechristianization was most prevalent among workingmen, peasants, and Native Americans. He warns Mexican parents about the corrupting influence on their children of state-run schools and directs them to take charge of their children's religious education. Finally, he urges citizens to vote in elections "when the good of the Church or of the country requires it."[95]

90. Hebblethwaite, *Paul VI*, 111.
91. Gill, *Political Origins*, 114–16.
92. Pius XI, *Iniquis afflictisque*, 8–14.
93. Pius XI, *Acerba animi*, 4, 9–10.
94. Fattorini, *Hitler, Mussolini, and the Vatican*, 100–101.
95. Pius XI, *Firmissimam constantiam*, 1, 4, 16–17, 22, 31.

In the 1933 encyclical *Dilectisssima nobis*, Pius criticizes certain laws that were enacted by the Spanish Republic following the collapse of the monarchy. Church and state were officially separated, a situation which Pius considers intolerable. This separation led to a host of ills. All church buildings were declared to be public property subject to taxation, clergy were deprived of their income, and divorce was permitted.[96] As of the date of this encyclical, the papal stance on the separation of church and state had not moved beyond that of Pius IX and the *Syllabus*.

Pius XII's "Obsession" with Communism

Toward the end of the Second World War, Pius XII expressed the view that democracy may be the best guarantee of future peace. In his Christmas message for 1944, he praises democracy as an antidote to the type of state absolutism that prevailed in Nazi Germany and Fascist Italy.

> Moreover—and this is perhaps the most important point—beneath the sinister lightning of the war that encompasses them, in the blazing heat of the furnace that imprisons them, the peoples have, as it were, awakened from a long torpor. They have assumed, in relation to the state and those who govern, a new attitude—one that questions, criticizes, distrusts.
>
> Taught by bitter experience, they are more aggressive in opposing the concentration of dictatorial power that cannot be censured or touched, and call for a system of government more in keeping with the dignity and liberty of the citizens.[97]

As far back as Leo XIII's encyclical *Libertas*, papal teaching was not opposed to democratic forms of government. But no previous pope had given such an unqualified endorsement of democracy. "Prior to the Christmas Addresses of Pius XII, Catholic teaching on democracy was ambivalent."[98] Future popes would express no ambivalence toward democracy but only support.

Following the war, Pius wrote several encyclicals directed at Communism. Two of them concern the unique problems faced by the Catholic Church in China following the defeat of Chiang Kai-shek's Nationalist forces by Mao Zedong's Chinese Communist Party. *Ad Sinarum gentem*, written in 1954, is addressed to the bishops, clergy, and faithful of China.

---

96. Pius XI, *Dilectissima nobis*, 6, 9–10, 14, 24.

97. Pius XII, *Democracy and a Lasting Peace*, 11–12.

98. John Hehir, "Catholicism and Democracy," in Curran, *Change in Official Catholic Moral Teachings*, 23.

With the Chinese Communist Party in control of the country, the church in China was beset by adversity, including the expulsion of the papal nuncio. The party falsely accused Chinese Catholics of disloyalty. Some Chinese had proposed the establishment of a national church. Pius refuses to accept this proposal, because it would negate the universality of the church.[99]

Ad Apostolorum Principis is the final encyclical written by Pius before his death in 1958. He addresses the problem of patriotic associations which Chinese Catholics were forced to join. The true purpose of these organizations is to persuade Catholics to "embrace the tenets of atheistic materialism." These associations attempt to subject the church to civil authorities. Some Chinese took the position "that Catholics have the power of directly electing their bishops." Pius finds this position unacceptable, contrasting it to the legitimate right granted in concordats to the rulers of certain countries to nominate bishops or to oppose episcopal candidates chosen by Rome.[100]

From October 28 to November 5, 1956, Pius issued three encyclicals dealing with the massacre of thousands of Hungarians by Red Army troops. Throughout his pontificate, Pius believed that Communism was the greatest threat to the church. Historian Michael Phayer has gone so far as to say that "Pius XII's obsession with communism is the key to understanding his papacy."[101] This obsession led the Holy Office in 1949 to issue a decree which forbade Catholics, on pain of excommunication, from joining the Communist Party, defending Communist doctrine, or even reading Communist publications.[102] No similar decree had been issued during his papacy concerning Catholics who joined the Nazi Party.[103] Pius himself had explained the reason for the different treatment afforded to Catholics who supported Nazism from those who supported Communism, as historian Frank Coppa has observed. "As pope he noted that the Nazis, despite their pagan beliefs and racist ideology, unlike the Bolsheviks, had not outlawed religion, closed churches, or suppressed the faith, and therefore represented less of an immediate threat than Bolshevik Russia for the institutional Church."[104] This distinction also explains in part why he rejected the Allies' calls for the church to excommunicate Hitler, a baptized Catholic.[105] In fact,

---

99. Pius XII, *Ad Sinarum gentem*, 2, 6, 15, 22.

100. Pius XII, *Ad Apsotolorum Principis*, 10–11, 13, 36, 38.

101. Phayer, *Pius XII*, 259.

102. Holy Office, "Decree against Communism," in Denzinger and Hünermann, *Enchiridion symbolorum*, 3865.

103. Coppa, *Politics and the Papacy*, 155; Pollard, *Papacy in the Age of Totalitarianism*, 376.

104. Coppa, *Pius XII*, 201.

105. Ibid., 146; Wolf, *Pope and Devil*, 270–71.

none of Hitler's books had been placed on the Index of Forbidden Books, whereas some publications from other high ranking Nazis had been.[106]

In *Luctuosissimi eventus*, Pius laments the brutality of the attacks. He describes the Soviets as "the champions of atheistic communism [who] attempt with every possible stratagem to despoil the minds of the religion of their forefathers."[107] Three days later, he follows up with the encyclical *Laetamur admodum*. Polish and Hungarian cardinals had been expelled and war menaced the Middle East. Once again, he pleads for prayers.[108] Four days later, he issued *Datis nuperrime*, in which he prays that God will move the hearts of the Soviet oppressors to end the violence, and includes a threat if they do not. "And even though God often punishes private individuals for their sins only after death, nonetheless, as history teaches, He occasionally punishes in this mortal life rulers of people and their nations when they have dealt unjustly with others."[109]

The Second Vatican Council and Concordats: The Church Seeks Governmental Preferences

The emphasis in modern papal teaching on the need for a country to guarantee freedom of religion and worship within its borders necessitates a certain degree of separation between church and state. According to the Second Vatican Council, it is not permissible for a nation to declare one religion to be the sole religion of that state to the exclusion of other religions. This practice had prevailed in countries such as Italy and Spain, where churches other than the Catholic Church had no legal rights. The council's declaration *Dignitatis humanae* put an end to this practice.[110]

Although the church now condemns such arrangements, neither church teaching nor practice contemplates the type of separation which would ban any state preference for one religion over another, or which would bar all government support for religion. The complete separation of church and state dictated by the First Amendment to the United States Constitution is not viewed by the Holy See as the most beneficial to either church or state. The church is more comfortable with arrangements such as the one present in Germany. In that country, a person is assessed a fee of 8 or 9 percent of what he or she owes in federal income taxes. The fee is

106. Lewy, *Catholic Church and Nazi Germany*, 152.
107. Pius XII, *Luctuosissimi eventus*, 5.
108. Pius XII, *Laetamur admodum*, 2–6.
109. Pius XII, *Datis nuperrime*, 5–6.
110. McBrien, *Catholicism*, 676.

paid over to the Evangelical (Protestant), Catholic, or Jewish community to which the person belongs and accounts for 80 percent of the income of these communities. However, only religious communities which have public corporate status participate in the church tax system (*Kirchensteuer*). Since the Muslim community lacks such status, its mosques receive no financial support from the German government, even though Muslims constitute 4 percent of the German population.[111] The size of the tax collected has given the Catholic Church the financial resources to become Germany's second largest private employer.[112]

The right of the church to seek favorable accommodations from the state was sanctioned by the Second Vatican Council in *Dignitatis humanae*.

> Government is also to help create conditions favorable to the fostering of religious life, in order that people may be truly enabled to exercise their religious rights and to fulfill their religious duties, and also in order that society itself may profit by the moral qualities of justice and peace which have their origin in men's faithfulness to God and to His holy will.
>
> If, in view of peculiar circumstances obtaining among peoples, special civil recognition is given to one religious community in the constitutional order of society, it is at the same time imperative that the right of all citizens and religious communities to religious freedom should be recognized and made effective in practice.[113]

"In other words, although DH shows the influences of the free exercise clause of the First Amendment on its drafters, neither DH nor John Paul has accepted the other half of the wisdom of the American experiment, namely, that disestablishment best protects religious freedom."[114]

The concordats entered into by the Holy See during the pontificate of John Paul II evidence the church's practice of seeking advantages for itself from nations in which Catholics constitute a majority of the population. Post-conciliar concordats were entered into with Italy, Hungary, Malta, Poland, Croatia, and Slovakia. Common features of these concordats include: the recognition of Sundays and holy days as national days of rest; financial assistance for Catholic schools and universities; and the teaching of the

---

111. Monsma and Soper, *Challenge of Pluralism*, 183–89.
112. Allen, *Future Church*, 194.
113. Second Vatican Council, *Dignitatis humanae*, 6.
114. Leslie Griffin, "Commentary on *Dignitatis humanae* (*Declaration on Religious Freedom*)," in Himes, *Modern Catholic Social Teaching*, 245–65, 259.

Catholic religion in state schools, subject to the right of parents to decline such instruction for their children.[115]

John Paul II: Totalitarianism as the Enemy of Human Rights

John Paul II was as outspoken as Pius XII in his condemnation of totalitarian governments. Such an attitude is hardly surprising, since John Paul experienced the Communist regime in Poland first-hand as a student, college professor, and bishop, experiences that led him to an appreciation for democratic systems of government. He clearly signals his preference for democracy in *Centesimus annus*, written shortly after the fall of Communism. Although the church's social doctrine does not endorse any particular political or economic system, totalitarianism is inherently opposed to the church's teaching due to the former's denial of the transcendence of God and its rejection of the church. He stops short of endorsing capitalism as an economic system for developing nations, but expresses a preference for the democratic political system as a guarantor of human rights.[116]

Benedict XVI: Government as the Guarantor of Religious Freedom

In *Deus caritas est*, Benedict XVI's first encyclical, he discusses the ideal relationship between church and state. His views are antithetical to those of Leo XIII, who saw the function of the state as support for the Catholic Church. For Benedict, on the other hand, the state is to serve rather as the guarantor of the rights of individuals to religious freedom.[117] Benedict reflects the tectonic shift that occurred in the church's teaching on church-state relations with Vatican II's declaration *Dignitatis humanae*. John Courtney Murray described that shift in the following terms.

> This progress reached its inevitable term in the *Declaration on Religious Freedom*. The sacrality of society and state is now transcended as archaistic. Government is not *defensor fidei*. Its duty and rights do not extend to what had long been called *cura religionis*, a direct care of religion itself and of the unity of the church within Christendom or the nation-state. The function of government is secular: That is, it is confined to a care of the

---

115. The concordats may be accessed at www.concordatwatch.eu.
116. John Paul II, *Centesimus annus*, 42–47.
117. Benedict XVI, *Deus caritas est*, 28.

free exercise of religion within society—a care therefore of the freedom of the church and of the freedom of the human person in religious affairs.[118]

Governmental Support for Religion: Be Careful What You Wish For

Many early American churchmen feared that the churches could not financially survive without tax dollars to pay the salary of ministers and the support of church buildings. History has proven those fears to be unfounded. Religious belief and practice in the United States is flourishing, while in most other developed countries they have been in a sharp decline for decades. Robert Putnam and David Campbell have documented the vibrant state of religious belief in America. "In general, Americans have high rates of religious *belonging, behaving,* and *believing*—what social scientists call the three Bs of religiosity. Eighty-three percent of Americans report belonging to a religion; 40 percent report attending religious services nearly every week or more; 59 percent pray at least weekly; a third report reading scripture with this same frequency. Many Americans also have firm religious beliefs. Eighty percent are absolutely sure there is a God." Americans attend weekly religious services at a higher rate than any other developed western nation, with the exception of Poland.[119]

Historian Martin Marty has pointed out that, far from helping religion and churches to prosper, government financial aid to religion actually may have negative unintended consequences.

> . . . It should occur to any Christian that with any hint of establishment they would be buying into something detrimental to their own Christian faith and churches. Almost all sociologists of religion, theologians, demographers, and other students of comparative destinies among nations agree that the drastic decline of Christian participation and belief in Europe results in no small measure from the fact that the churches were and sometimes even still are favored by the state. . . . That is, having all religions and non-religion on the same legal and cultural basis has led to energetic activity by church people, and contributes to a self-reforming character among religions.[120]

---

118. Murray, "The Declaration of Religious Freedom," in Curran, *Change in Official Catholic Moral Teachings*, 3–19, 5–6.

119. Putnam and Campbell, *American Grace*, 7, emphasis in original, 9.

120. Martin E. Marty, "Getting Beyond 'The Myth of Christian America,'" in Gunn

Rodney Stark and Roger Finke are two sociologists of religion who share the view that state financial support for religion has a negative effect on religious practice. "Throughout Scandinavia, and in Germany as well, the clergy of the state churches are civil servants as well as union members. As such, they cannot be expected to exhaust themselves in an effort to attract large numbers to worship services, for their incomes and tenure are secure regardless of attendance."[121] If the European churches were forced to compete in the religious marketplace like American churches, the religious decline which the European continent has been experiencing since the end of the Second World War might be halted and perhaps reversed. "The heart of our position is that Europeans are poor attenders because of the ineffective efforts of their churches, and that faced with American-style churches, Europeans would respond as Americans do."[122]

Leo XIII did not recommend American-style separation of church and state as a template for other countries. As John Courtney Murray wryly noted, Leo XIII's "Roman advisers . . . had probably never heard of the *Federalist* papers."[123] Even the bishops at the Second Vatican Council were unwilling to forego the privileges that many countries afforded to the church. But history suggests that atheists and agnostics are not the only groups that benefit from separation of church and state. Roger Williams and Thomas Jefferson may have been on to something.

---

and Witt, *No Establishment of Religion*, 364–78, 375.

121. Stark and Finke, *Acts of Faith*, 230.
122. Ibid., 237–38.
123. Murray, "Church and Totalitarian Democracy," 551.

7

Silence: The Morality of Wars

> *It is pointed out that the Holy Father appears to be occupying himself exclusively with spiritual matters, charitable acts, and rhetoric, while adopting an ostrich-like policy toward the notorious atrocities.*
>
> —Harold Tittman, Summer 1942

> *While the world is in flames, in the Vatican they meditate on eternal truths and pray ardently.*
>
> —Antonio Santin, bishop of Trieste, December 1943

The American Civil War: The Churches as Regional Cheerleaders

When Northern and Southern Americans found themselves facing each other across the battlefields of the Civil War, it was the culmination of a decades-long dispute over slavery that had divided the country since the adoption of the Constitution. The Bible figured prominently in the pre-war debates over slavery, but not in a way that would do Christians proud. Northerners and Southerners did not look to the Bible to be informed by its teachings on the morality of slavery; rather, they seized upon those texts that appeared to support their preconceived views, be they pro-slavery or anti-slavery. Southerners cited chapter and verse from Genesis, Leviticus, Deuteronomy, First Corinthians, Romans, Colossians,

First Timothy, and Philemon in support of their position that slavery had been divinely sanctioned. Northerners, on the other hand, had to settle for distinguishing the letter of the Bible from its spirit, an argument that proved to be unconvincing to anyone other than abolitionists.[1] The issue tore apart Protestant denominations, as Methodists and Baptists split into Northern and Southern divisions.[2] Catholic clergy either mirrored regional positions or avoided the issue of slavery altogether.[3]

When the dispute over slavery in America devolved into armed conflict, the churches did not turn to the Bible or the just war tradition to critically examine the morality of the war; instead, the clergy assumed the role of ecclesiastical cheerleaders for their region and its armies.[4] Northerners and Southerners were equally convinced that God was on their side.[5] A logical corollary is that God would not reward their enemies with victory but would ensure their defeat. The Catholic hierarchy also reflected these regional prejudices. Southern bishops supported the Confederate cause, while Archbishop Hughes of New York regularly preached sermons calling for men to volunteer for the Union cause.[6] Abraham Lincoln, in his Second Inaugural Address— delivered only a month before the end of the Civil War and less than six weeks before his assassination—commented on how Northerners and Southerners read the same book but reached opposite conclusions. "Both read the same Bible and pray to the same God, and each invokes His aid against the other."[7] In the assessment of Mark Noll, "The Book that made the nation was destroying the nation; the nation that had taken to the Book was rescued not by the Book but by force of arms."[8] A book which calls upon people to love their neighbors as themselves was invoked as a justification for the annihilation of those neighbors who lived on the wrong side of the Mason-Dixon Line.

Unlike many of his contemporaries, Lincoln did not blindly assume that God was on the side of the Union. According to historian George Rable, Lincoln as president "grew impatient with clerical delegations lecturing him about God's will."[9] In his Second Inaugural, which Noll characterizes

1. Noll, *America's God*, 388–91; Noll, *Civil War*, 33–36.
2. Noll, *America's God*, 185.
3. Noll, *Civil War*, 125–32.
4. Stout, *Altar of the Nation*, xvi–xvii.
5. Ibid., xiv; Rable, *God's Almost Chosen Peoples*, 68.
6. Rable, *God's Almost Chosen Peoples*, 192.
7. Lincoln, *Second Inaugural*, 2.
8. Noll, *Civil War*, 8.
9. Rable, *God's Almost Chosen Peoples*, 187.

as "a theological statement of rare depth,"[10] Lincoln disclaimed any special knowledge as to what God had in mind for either the Union or the Confederacy. In the words of Cathleen Kaveny, "As his faith deepened over the course of his presidency, Lincoln increasingly saw himself as an instrument of the divine will.... At the same time, Lincoln grew increasingly uncertain about the precise shape of God's will."[11] He posited, however, that the Civil War was the price that Americans, Northerners and Southerners alike, were being made to pay for slavery, which he viewed not as a particular sin of the South, but as the nation's original sin.

> ... If we shall suppose that American slavery is one of those offenses which, in the providence of God, must needs come, but which, having continued through His appointed time, He now wills to remove, and that He gives to both North and South this terrible war as the woe due to those by whom the offense came, shall we discern therein any departure from those divine attributes which the believers in a living God always ascribe to Him? Fondly do we hope, fervently do we pray, that this mighty scourge of war may speedily pass away. Yet, if God wills that it continue until all wealth piled by the bondsman's two hundred and fifty years of unrequited toil shall be sunk, and until every drop of blood drawn with the lash shall be paid by another drawn with the sword, as was said three thousand years ago, so still it must be said "the judgments of the Lord are true and righteous altogether."

Lincoln expressed his hope that in the postwar era, one which he would not live to see, the people of the North and South would reconcile, treating each other as reunited brothers rather than as victor and vanquished, and that peace would come not only to the nation but to all nations. "With malice toward none, with charity for all, with firmness in the right as God gives us to see the right, let us strive on to finish the work we are in, to bind up the nation's wounds, to care for him who shall have borne the battle and for his widow and his orphan, to do all which may achieve and cherish a just and lasting peace among ourselves and with all nations."[12]

---

10. Noll, *Civil War*, 89.
11. Kaveny, *Prophecy without Contempt*, 387.
12. Lincoln, *Second Inaugural*, 2.

The Wars of the Twentieth Century: No Moral Judgments from the Vatican

Unfortunately, Lincoln's hope for peace among nations would not come to pass. The Civil War was the world's first total war, claiming the lives of more than 600,000 Union and Confederate troops.[13] Mass armies of citizen-soldiers fought and died in battles of unprecedented scope and ferocity which did not spare civilian populations. Less than fifty years after its conclusion, the First World War would break out in Europe, with the Second World War following close on its heels. How would the Catholic Church respond to total warfare on a scale that would make the Civil War look like a series of minor skirmishes? Catholic bishops in the combatant European nations would react much like their American counterparts had in the Civil War. Believing that God was on the side of their countries, they would pray for divine assistance in vanquishing their enemies. Would Benedict XV and Pius XII, who represented not only the diocese of Rome but, more importantly, the universal church, respond in a less parochial manner? Would they examine the morality of the conflicts and issue pronouncements denouncing the aggression on one side or the other, or would they maintain a policy of strict neutrality? As we will see, they would choose the latter course. While they would bemoan the suffering that the wars inflicted on civilian populations, and occasionally would condemn military excesses and atrocities, they would do so only in general terms without naming names. In one respect though, they would emulate Lincoln. Both Benedict and Pius believed that a lasting peace following the wars could never be achieved if the victorious nations were to treat the vanquished nations as defeated enemies rather than welcome them back as separated brothers to the community of nations.

The number of people killed in the wars of the twentieth century will never be known with any certainty. Military and civilian deaths in the Second World War have been estimated at fifty to sixty million people.[14] Twentieth-century popes frequently decried the brutality of modern warfare, especially the suffering inflicted on civilian populations. They steadfastly urged combatant nations to put down arms and work to build a lasting peace in which resort to war would no longer be the normal method for settling disputes among nations. But they provided little guidance as to how particular wars should be evaluated from a moral standpoint. Benedict XV and Pius XII were unwilling to pass judgment on the morality of the First

---

13. Stout, *Altar of the Nation*, 447.
14. Hastings, *Inferno*, xv; Keegan, *Second World War*, 590.

and Second World Wars, respectively, refusing to take sides in conflicts with large Catholic populations on each side. This refusal to weigh in on the morality of the most lethal conflicts in human history was not because Catholic teaching had nothing to say about the morality of wars. Indeed, the "just war" doctrine has been around since the time of Augustine in the fifth century; but one will look in vain for a discussion of it in modern papal encyclicals. A church which believes it can speak authoritatively on every aspect of the human condition suddenly loses its voice in the face of the destruction wrought by modern warfare.

This omission will be corrected by the Second Vatican Council and the *Catechism* in a manner which, intentionally or not, would exonerate Benedict XV and Pius XII by providing a principled basis for their silence. The price for this exoneration has been to cede to civil authorities the sole duty to make judgments upon the morality of war, exempting not only the church from judging the morality of particular conflicts, but also freeing individual Catholics from the need to inquire into the morality of their participation in wars waged by their countries.

Benedict XV and the First World War: The Policy of Papal Neutrality

The First World War had begun less than one month prior to the election of Benedict XV, whom theologian Richard McBrien has dubbed "perhaps the most underrated of the modern popes."[15] His first encyclical, *Ad beatissimi Apostolorum*, addressed the destruction that the war was wreaking upon Europe. Although the encyclical was written less than three months after the beginning of hostilities, the combatant nations already had suffered several hundred thousand casualties.[16] Benedict portrays the horrible consequences of the war in stark language.

> ... For what could prevent the soul of the common Father of all being most deeply distressed by the spectacle presented by Europe, nay, by the whole world, perhaps the saddest and most mournful spectacle of which there is any record.... The combatants are the greatest and wealthiest nations of the earth; what wonder, then, if, well provided with the most awful weapons modern military science has devised, they strive to destroy one another with refinements of horror.... Yet, while with numberless troops the furious battle is engaged, the sad cohorts of

---

15. McBrien, *Lives of the Popes*, 436.
16. Keegan, *First World War*, 135–36.

war, sorrow and distress swoop down upon every city and every home; day by day the mighty number of widows and orphans increases, and with the interruption of communications, trade is at a standstill; agriculture is abandoned; the arts are reduced to inactivity; the wealthy are in difficulties; the poor are reduced to abject misery; all are in distress.

He considers the root cause of the war to lie in the failure of the combatant nations to observe "the precepts and practices of Christian wisdom." His prognosis is a bleak one: "unless God comes soon to our help, the end of civilization would seem to be at hand."[17] He then identifies four causes of the war.

The first cause is the absence of brotherly love, which manifests itself in race hatred and class envy.[18] Benedict uses the word "race" not in the ethnic sense, but as a synonym for "nationalism."[19] The second cause is "the absence of respect for the authority of those who exercise ruling powers." The third cause is the injustice in relations between the classes. Benedict here is not referring to the injustice of the ruling class, but rather to what he sees as the overreaching of the working class.[20] Benedict shared Leo XIII's view that God created some men rich and other men poor. He believed that the poor "need to resign themselves to their lot."[21] The fourth cause is the striving for earthly goods, which are illusory. The task of the bishops, the clergy, and the faithful is to work for an increase in faith, the outcome of which "will be the decrease of that feverish striving after the empty goods of the world, and little by little, as brotherly love increases, social unrest and strife will cease." Benedict ends his encyclical by combining a plea for a cessation of hostilities with a plea for restoration of the pope's temporal power. The two are united for Benedict, because limiting papal power to the spiritual realm is "very harmful to the very peace of nations."[22]

The causes of First World War have been debated by historians for almost a century without a consensus having been reached. Growing nationalism, an out of control arms race among the European powers, and a lack of diplomacy in the weeks leading up to August 1914 all have been advanced as major factors that contributed to a situation in which war appeared to be inevitable. The causes suggested by Benedict do not find their way onto any

17. Benedict XV, *Ad beatissimi Apostolorum*, 3, 5.
18. Ibid., 7.
19. Pollard, *Unknown Pope*, 86.
20. Benedict XV, *Ad beatissimi Apostolorum*, 9, 12.
21. Pollard, *Unknown Pope*, 177–78
22. Benedict XV, *Ad beatissimi Apostolorum*, 17–18, 31.

historian's list. How then, should one read Benedict's analysis? He is writing not as a historian but rather as the pastor of the world's Catholics writing to its bishops, a fact which has certain implications. First, he is not addressing the causes of the war in a historical sense. Instead, he is describing a spiritual malaise which may have given rise to those historical factors that led to the conflict. Second, many of the bishops to whom he is writing were citizens of nations on opposite sides of the conflict. More than 25 percent of the cardinals who were eligible to vote at the conclave at which Benedict was elected were from the combatant nations.[23] Austria-Hungary, one of the Central Powers, was predominantly Catholic, and southern Germany had a sizable Catholic population. On the Allied side, France had a large Catholic majority. The bishops of these countries, like their American counterparts half a century earlier, did not refrain from leading prayers to God for the victory of their side. As historian Guenter Lewy has observed, "In practice, however, few bishops have ever failed to support the wars waged by their own governments."[24] The clergy followed the lead of their bishops, as "nationalism everywhere swallowed the basic tenets of Christianity."[25] The existence of established churches in the combatant nations partly explains the hierarchy's hesitancy to take a position against a state that "gave financial support and controlled appointments."[26] Benedict faced the dilemma of how to be a moral voice in a global war where there were large Catholic populations on each side. Historical precedent suggested that he remain on the sidelines, as was the papal tradition in wars between nations with large Catholic populations.[27] He was uneasy about injecting himself into the conflict, lest he be accused of favoring one side over the other. Instead, he elected to stay above the fray, urging a restoration of brotherly love as the only sure remedy for a lasting peace.[28]

The chief architect of Benedict's policy of strict Vatican neutrality or impartiality toward the combatant nations was Cardinal Gasparri, the Secretary of State. Gasparri was assisted in this endeavor by his top aide, Monsignor Eugenio Pacelli, who as Pius XII would follow the same policy in the next war. Frank Coppa explains the rationale behind this policy.

> The vast majority of the Vatican's "diplomatic experts" concurred with Gasparri, Benedict, and Pacelli that impartiality was the

23. Pollard, *Unknown Pope*, 60.
24. Lewy, *Catholic Church and Nazi Germany*, 224.
25. Kershaw, *To Hell and Back*, 431.
26. Jenkins, *Great and Holy War*, 66–67.
27. Duffy, *Saints and Sinners*, 258.
28. Benedict XV, *Ad beatissimi Apostolorum*, 6.

only policy the Vicar of Christ could and should pursue, for the faithful were found in both camps and only an impartial pope would he be trusted and able to broker a settlement between the combatants. Furthermore, supporting one side against the other would jeopardize the unity of the Church and require Benedict to firmly establish the political, legal, and moral guilt of one camp and the innocence of the other—clearly not his principal aim. Pacelli steadfastly supported this stance during the course of the First World War, and later as Pope Pius XII, adopted, and adhered to it during the Second World War. Adherence to impartiality provided the rationale for Pius XII's public silence during the latter war and the Holocaust.[29]

Benedict's primary wartime efforts were directed at offering the services of the Vatican to bring about an end to the hostilities. In the words of historian Philip Jenkins, "By far the most significant center of Christian antiwar activism was the Vatican."[30] Benedict authored a Peace Note in August 1917 which contained the following points that should govern any future peace conference: decrease of armaments; international arbitration; freedom of the seas; renunciation of war indemnities; restoration of occupied territories; and an examination of competing territorial claims. None of the parties responded favorably. Britain merely acknowledged receipt of the note, France did not reply, and Germany and the United States rejected his proposal.[31]

Benedict's hope that he could use his papal office to act as a mediator to resolve an international dispute was not without precedent. The most famous example involved the Borgia pope, Alexander VI, who at the end of the fifteenth century had settled competing Spanish and Portuguese colonial claims in Africa and the Americas.[32] In the late nineteenth century, Leo XIII had mediated a dispute between Germany and Spain over the Caroline Islands in Micronesia, and even had offered to mediate the conflicting claims of Spain and the United States over Cuba.[33] In our own time, both the United States and Cuba publicly have acknowledged the pivotal role played by Francis in the reestablishment of diplomatic relations between the countries. Benedict's peace efforts, however, were doomed from the start. Neither the French nor the German governments trusted him. "The French

---

29. Coppa, *Pius XII*, 53–54; see also Wolf, *Pope and Devil*, 38–43.
30. Jenkins, *Great and Holy War*, 65.
31. Alvarez, *Spies in the Vatican*, 111; Pollard, *Unknown Pope*, 125–28.
32. McBrien, *Lives of the Popes*, 268.
33. Alvarez, *Sspies in the Vatican*, 62.

called him the 'Boche pope', the Germans the 'French pope.'"[34] In addition, unresolved issues between the Vatican and the Italian government over the Papal States would serve to keep the Vatican on the sidelines during any future peace conference.

The Vatican had opposed Italy's entry into the war on the side of the Entente (France, Great Britain, and Russia). It feared that Italy's intervention might threaten the Austro-Hungarian Empire, which Benedict considered to be the last great Catholic power in Europe. The 1915 Treaty of London, which governed the conditions under which Italy would enter the war on the side of the Entente, contained a secret provision which precluded any papal involvement in a future peace conference. Italy was concerned that, if the Vatican were to participate in the peace conference, it would seek to include on the conference's agenda the question of the restoration of the Papal States. The combatant nations had no interest in addressing the Roman Question, and an armistice was concluded without any input from the Holy See.[35]

Following the war, Benedict turned his attention to the suffering of the victims of the conflict. *Quod iam diu* was published less than one month after the armistice. In contemplation of the peace conference which would soon be convened, Benedict directs the bishops to order public prayers in each parish of their dioceses for the success of the conference.[36] In *Paterno iam diu*, he confronts the sufferings of the children of postwar Central Europe who still lack adequate food and clothing. He directs the bishops to order public prayers and to gather collections of money, food, medicine, and clothing.[37] He followed up on this directive one year later in *Annus iam plenus*. Although substantial money had been collected following Benedict's previous appeal, he laments the lack of improvement in the lot of the children of the region. He appeals to the children of the wealthier cities in Europe to contribute part of their savings to this effort.[38]

The theme of *Pacem, Dei munus pulcherrimum*, issued in 1920, is that the enmity among people and nations can be overcome only by "a return of mutual charity to appease hate and banish enmity." In a prescient statement, he cautions that the armistice alone cannot bring lasting peace if "latent hostility and enmity were to continue among the nations." He extends the commandment of mutual charity beyond individuals to nations.

---

34. Kershaw, *To Hell and Back*, 432.
35. D'Agostino, *Rome in America*, 103–31; Pollard, *Unknown Pope*, 95–107.
36. Benedict XV, *Quod iam diu*, 2.
37. Benedict XV, *Paterno iam diu*, 1, 3.
38. Benedict XV, *Annus iam plenus*, 1–2.

He desires that nations come together in a league to safeguard order and to reduce military expenditures.[39] But the League of Nations proved to be a failure, and the world was plunged into the chaos of the Second World War less than twenty years later.

Pius XII and the Second World War: Neutrality Becomes Silence

Pius's first encyclical, *Summi pontificatus*, was issued in October 1939, only weeks after the start of the Second World War. Pius's concern with "the dread tempest of war" permeates the document. He attributes the "ultimate cause" of the ills of the present day to "the denial and rejection of a universal norm of morality as well for individual and social life as for international relations." He traces the cause of this denial in Europe to the Reformation. By separating themselves from Rome, some unidentified Protestants went so far as to deny the divinity of Christ and "hastened thereby the progress of spiritual decay." It is difficult to figure out what linkage Pius is trying to make between the Reformation and the Second World War, since he does not develop the argument in either this or any later encyclical. One of the errors which has flowed from this denial "is the forgetfulness of that law of human solidarity and charity." This forgetfulness has led to the deterioration of peace among nations. An additional error has been to divorce civil authority from dependence upon God, which "elevates the State or group into the last end of life." He emphasizes that there are moral limits on the power of the state. It can demand taxes and military service from its citizens, but it has no legitimate claim on their souls.[40]

It was reported in the press soon after the publication of *Summi pontificatus* that Vatican sources had indicated that "'the theme of the encyclical, especially as regards the totalitarian states, was inspired by an unpublished piece that Pius XI, his predecessor, wrote before he died.'"[41] This report was confirmed by an article which appeared in *L'Osservatore Romano* in 1973, which noted that portions of the draft encyclical "can easily be discovered in Pius XII's documents, beginning with the encyclical *Summi Pontificatus*."[42] Although Pius appears to have borrowed certain themes from Pius XI's planned encyclical, "he ignored its explicit condemnation of

---

39. Benedict XV, *Pacem, Dei munus pulcherrimum*, 1, 4, 14, 17.

40. Pius XII, *Summi pontificatus*, 23, 28–29, 35, 51, 53, 66.

41. Fattorini, *Hitler, Mussolini, and the Vatican*, 248 n. 35 (quoting an article from the *New York Times* published a week after *Summi pontificatus*).

42. Passelecq and Suchecky, *Hidden Encyclical*, 4–5.

anti-Semitism."[43] Pius XII may have decided to honor his predecessor by including a discussion of the illegitimate claims of totalitarian states in his first encyclical. However, the German authorities did not react to *Summi pontificatus* with the outrage that they had displayed after the publication of *Mit brennender Sorge*, permitting it to be read from German pulpits.[44]

Pius XII wrote no encyclicals dealing with the war between *Summi pontificatus* and *Communium interpretes dolorum*, which was issued less than one month before the termination of the war in Europe. In the latter encyclical, he merely urges prayers for an end to the conflict.[45] His decision not to address either the war in general, or the Holocaust in particular, has led to speculation about the reasons for his silence. He was informed of Germany's mass extermination of Jews at least as early as May 1942.[46] To his supporters, such as Margherita Marchione, Pius's silence was a product of the Vatican's longstanding and wise policy of neutrality toward belligerents during armed conflicts. She has argued that "the Catholic Church is not a political institution but a spiritual one whose mission is to obtain the eternal salvation of all men, of every race and country. For this reason, the traditional policy of the Church in time of war is neutrality. It cannot ally itself with or against any nation or nations."[47] Pius rejected the characterization of his stance as one of "neutrality," preferring the term "impartiality," because neutrality could be misconstrued as indifference.[48] Critics would see this as a distinction without a difference. In December 1942, Pius informed Harold Tittman, a member of the United States delegation to the Vatican, "that he could not condemn Nazi atrocities without also condemning Soviet atrocities, 'which might not be wholly pleasing to the Allies.'"[49] Pius entertained the unrealistic hope that he might serve as a peacemaker between the Allies and the Axis powers, a position which would have been jeopardized if he appeared to favor one side over the other.[50] As early as April 1939 he had sent out diplomatic feelers to determine whether France, Germany,

---

43. Coppa, *Politics and the Papacy*, 124; see also Passelecq and Suchecky, *Hidden Encyclical*, 166.

44. Lewy, *Catholic Church and Nazi Germany*, 245.

45. Pius XII, *Communium interpretes dolorum*, 5.

46. Coppa, *Pius XII*, 158–61; Lewy, *Catholic Church and Nazi Germany*, xxiii; Phayer, *Catholic Church and the Holocaust*, 47–48.

47. Marchione, *Man of Peace*, 24. Marchione is by no means an unbiased commentator. "One of Pius XII's most ardent defenders has been Margherita Marchione, one of the Filipinni Sisters, who has long pressed for his beatification" (Coppa, *Pius XII*, xvii).

48. Blet, *Pius XII and the Second World War*, 65.

49. Phayer, *Catholic Church and the Holocaust*, 56; see also Coppa, *Pius XII*, 145.

50. Phayer, *Catholic Church and the Holocaust*, 57.

England, and Poland would be amenable to a conference aimed at avoiding war. Although his efforts were rebuffed, he did not let go of this hope.[51] "Pius continued to believe, almost to the end of the war . . . that the Holy See had the capacity to act as an intermediary to bring about peace, even if that might only be a separate peace for Italy. In consequence, the diplomat in Papa Pacelli triumphed over the prophet, the papacy's international diplomatic role over its moral primacy."[52]

The Vatican was in a precarious position based on its location. It was dependent on Fascist Italy for all of its essential services, including food, water, electricity, and communications.[53] There also was the fear that speaking out against the Holocaust might lead to additional reprisals against noncombatants.[54] To his detractors, Pius's silence was symptomatic of his "policy of appeasement" toward Nazis and Fascists. The concordat that he had negotiated with Nazi Germany bound him, as well as the German bishops, to remain silent on issues the Nazis deemed to be political.[55] He was more concerned with the ability of the Church to be able to freely administer the sacraments in Germany, and with the ability of Catholics in Germany to continue to practice their religion without state interference, than he was with the fate of European Jews.[56]

Pius's 1942 Christmas message, *The Internal Order of States and Peoples*, contains the only statement in a wartime pronouncement of Pius which may be construed as referring to the Holocaust. He makes a single mention of "the hundreds of thousands of persons who, without any fault on their part, sometimes only because of their nationality or race, have been consigned to death or to a slow decline."[57] The vagueness of this statement drew protests from a number of ambassadors to the Holy See.[58] Although Pius carefully avoids any express reference to the Nazis, the death camps, or the Jews, he was convinced that the message "was an unequivocal and outspoken condemnation of Nazi genocide against the Jews. Few people then or since have agreed."[59]

51. Blet, *Pius XII and the Second World War*, 10–13.
52. Pollard, *Papacy in the Age of Totalitarianism*, 340–41.
53. Alvarez, *Spies in the Vatican*, 211; Pollard, *Money and the Modern Papacy*, 187.
54. Blet, *Pius XII and the Second World War*, 66; Phillips, *Tragedy of Nazi Germany*, 123; Phayer, *Pius XII*, 44.
55. Cornwell, *Hitler's Pope*, 153, 222–23; Phayer, *Catholic Church and the Holocaust*, 74–75.
56. Lewy, *Catholic Church and Nazi Germany*, 244.
57. Pius XII, *Internal Order of States*, 5.
58. Pollard, *Papacy in the Age of Totalitarianism*, 334–35.
59. Duffy, *Ten Popes*, 111.

Mystici corporis Christi, published in 1943, is a pure piece of theological exposition with little apparent connection to present day realities. It contains only fleeting, oblique references to the war and its effects. There is no small measure of self-aggrandizement in Pius's belief that all would be well if only people would turn to him as the answer to the world's discord and strife.[60] Pius's critics, on the other hand, compared him to Nero, "fiddling in Rome while the world exploded and burned."[61] In the summer of 1942, Tittman complained to United States Secretary of State Edward Stettinius "that the Holy Father appears to be occupying himself exclusively with spiritual matters, charitable acts, and rhetoric, while adopting an ostrich-like policy toward the notorious atrocities."[62] Similar frustration was expressed the following year by Antonio Santin, the Bishop of Trieste. He had sought assistance from the Vatican to lodge a protest with German authorities over the arrest of Trieste's Jews and the expropriation of their property. He travelled to Rome in late November 1942 to discuss his concerns with the pope and the secretary of state. On his return trip, he wrote a letter to the priests of his diocese in which he complained of the seemingly detached attitude of the Vatican toward the Nazis treatment of Jews. "'I found in the house of the pope the solemn silence of the spiritual holy offices. While the world is in flames, in the Vatican they meditate on the eternal truths and pray ardently.'"[63]

There have been scores of books published both defending and criticizing Pius's insistence on remaining neutral or impartial during the war. In reality, Pius found himself in an untenable situation, faced with alternatives whose outcomes he could not predict. Historian José M. Sánchez, who has surveyed the literature surrounding Pius's "silence" in the face of Nazi atrocities, has opined that Pius had two obligations. Under Catholic theology, the sacraments administered by the church are an essential aid to salvation. Any criticism of the Nazi regime might result in reprisals against the church, including arrests of priests and confiscation of church property, which could deny or impair access to the sacraments for German Catholics. On the other hand, as Vicar of Christ, Pius also had a duty to decry crimes against humanity which were gross violations of the commandment to love one's neighbor as oneself.[64] Pius could satisfy one or the other, but not both. Choosing the latter may have been the more courageous course,

---

60. Pius XII, *Mystici corporis Christi*, 6.
61. Hebblethwaite, *Paul VI*, 181.
62. Phayer, *Pius XII*, 48.
63. Zuccotti, *Under His Very Windows*, 276–89.
64. Sánchez, *Pius XII and the Holocaust*, 37.

but choosing the former at least offered at least offered a reasonable chance of success. On the other hand, if he had spoken out emphatically against the Nazi atrocities, the reaction this might provoke in Berlin was not foreseeable. But a definitive assessment of Pius's silence during the war cannot be made until all the papers relating to his pontificate in the Vatican Archives are opened to scholars.[65]

The Second Vatican Council and the Catechism: Theological Support for Papal Silence

The just war doctrine, as it was developed by medieval writers, has two components: *jus ad bellum* (the justice of war) and *jus in bello* (justice in war). The former determines whether the reasons for pursuing war are justified; the latter examines the justice of the means by which a war is fought. The distinction between *jus ad bellum* and *jus in bello* has been summarized by political philosopher Michael Walzer. "*Jus ad bellum* requires us to make judgments about aggression and self-defense; *jus in bello* about the observance or violation of the customary and positive rules of engagement. The two sorts of judgment are logically independent. It is perfectly possible for a just war to be fought unjustly and for an unjust war to be fought in strict accordance with the rules. . . . The dualism of *jus ad bellum* and *jus in bello* is at the heart of all that is most problematic in the moral reality of war."[66]

In *Gaudium et spes*, the Second Vatican Council spoke to both *jus ad bellum* and *jus in bello*. First, it recognizes the right of legitimate self-defense possessed by nations.

> Certainly, war has not been rooted out of human affairs. As long as the danger of war remains and there is no competent and sufficiently powerful authority at the international level, governments cannot be denied the right to legitimate defense once every means of peaceful settlement has been exhausted. State authorities and others who share public responsibility have the duty to conduct such grave matters soberly and to protect the welfare of the people entrusted to their care. But it is one thing to undertake military action for the just defense of the people, and something else again to seek the subjugation of other nations.

Second, it acknowledges that there are limits to the manner in which a just war may be fought. After declaring immoral all forms of genocide, the

---

65. Pollard, *Papacy in the Age of Totalitarianism*, 4.
66. Walzer, *Just and Unjust Wars*, 21.

council is unequivocal that the aerial bombardments of civilian populations, whether by conventional or nuclear weapons, is morally indefensible.[67]

The *Catechism* also discusses both the conditions under which self-defense is legitimate and the means which must be avoided in its conduct.

> The strict conditions for *legitimate defense by military force* require rigorous consideration. The gravity of such a decision makes it subject to rigorous conditions of moral legitimacy. At one and the same time: the damage inflicted by the aggressor on the nation or community of nations must be lasting, grave, and certain; all other means of putting an end to it must have been shown to be impractical or ineffective; there must be serious prospects of success; the use of arms must not produce evils and disorders graver than the evil to be eliminated. The power of modern means of destruction weighs very heavily in evaluating this condition. . . .
>
> Non-combatants, wounded soldiers, and prisoners must be respected and treated humanely.[68]

Gaudium et spes and the *Catechism* provide a principled basis for the position of neutrality or impartiality taken by the Benedict XV and Pius XII during the two world wars. According to the *Catechism*, it is the duty of the leaders of combatant nations to judge the morality of entering into a war, as well as the morality of the tactics by which a war is fought.[69] They, rather than religious officials, possess the information necessary to weigh the factors required to make a just war determination. The council in *Gaudium et spes* affirms that public officials, rather than the magisterium, bear responsibility for the common good.[70] The pope may issue general doctrinal statements concerning *jus ad bellum* and *jus in bello*, but he has no role to play in judging the morality of particular conflicts. The *Catechism* also relieves Catholic members of the armed forces of the responsibility to make personal decisions about the morality of wars in which they are called to fight. If the public authorities require soldiers to fight, they can proceed to battle with a clear conscience.[71]

With respect to *jus ad bellum*, since medieval times it has been assumed that a war cannot be just on both sides.[72] Under any application of the just war

---

67. Second Vatican Council, *Gaudium et spes*, 79–80.
68. *Catechism*, No. 2309.
69. Ibid.
70. Second Vatican Council, *Gaudium et spes*, 74.
71. *Catechism*, No. 2310.
72. Lewy, *Catholic Church and Nazi Germany*, 244; Walzer, *Just and Unjust Wars*,

doctrine, the war of aggression conducted by Germany and Japan in the 1930s and 1940s was immoral, and the war of self-defense fought by the Allies was justified. Walzer, in his influential book *Just and Unjust Wars*, has described the threat of Nazism in terms that leave little doubt as to which side was fighting a just war. "Nazism was an ultimate threat to everything decent in our lives, an ideology and practice of domination so murderous, so degrading even to those who might survive, that the consequences of its final victory were literally beyond calculation, immeasurably awful."[73] Nevertheless, Pius XII did not condemn the war fought by Germany and its ally Japan, limiting his criticism to decrying atrocities without naming names.

In *Gaudium et spes* and the *Catechism*, the church has taken a position which would insulate a pope from criticism if he refrains from taking sides in any future armed conflict. The magisterium has voluntarily relinquished the right to judge the morality of international conflicts, placing it solely in the hands of those public authorities who must make the decision whether to take up arms against another country. Leaving the decision about the morality of war solely to the leaders of the combatant nations opens the church to the legitimate criticism that it cannot exercise its moral authority by remaining silent. Whether intended or not, the teachings of *Gaudium et spes* and the *Catechism* provide retroactive justification for the decision of the German bishops during World War II to remain silent when confronted with the reality of the concentration camps and the Third Reich's planned extermination of European Jewry, as explained by historian Michael Phayer.

> Once the war began, patriotism became another factor that kept the bishops from forthright statements about the atrocities committed against Jews. After the debacle of the Great War, German bishops no longer posed the question of whether there was such a thing as a just war, a traditional tenet of Catholic morality. Saying that it was no longer possible to determine whether a war was or was not just, German church leaders abandoned this moral question and left judgment up to the state, at the same time warning the faithful to obey its decision.[74]

A perhaps unintended consequence of this position is that, if a pope chooses to raise a concern about the morality of a threatened or current conflict, he becomes subject to the legitimate criticism that he is speaking on

---

59.

73. Walzer, *Just and Unjust Wars*, 253. Walzer's book has been characterized as "something of a contemporary classic, as the starting point for understanding just war" (Bell, *Just War*, 75–76).

74. Phayer, *Catholic Church and the Holocaust*, 71–72.

a subject the church has acknowledged is outside of his purview. In the run-up to the 2003 American invasion of Iraq, influential American neoconservative Catholics—such as the former Lutheran Richard John Neuhaus, the former liberal Michael Novak, and papal biographer George Weigel—found themselves in a quandary. These papal supporters regularly applauded John Paul II's denunciations of aggression and oppression by the Soviet Union and Communist leaders in Eastern Europe. This time, as supporters of the Bush administration, they found themselves in the uncomfortable position of taking the pope to task for not following the church's own teaching on the just war doctrine. In spite of the teaching of *Gaudium et spes* and the *Catechism* that it is the role of the leaders of combatant nations, and not the church, to determine the morality of any planned armed conflict, John Paul did not hesitate to inject himself into the controversy. In his annual address to the Vatican diplomatic corps in January, 2003, John Paul expressed dismay about the threatened invasion.

> "*No to war*"! War is not always inevitable. It is always a defeat for humanity. . . . And what are we to say of the threat of a war which could strike the people of Iraq, the land of the Prophets, a people already sorely tried by more than twelve years of embargo? War is never just another means that one can choose to employ for settling differences between nations. As the Charter of the United Nations Organization and international law itself remind us, war cannot be decided upon, even when it is a matter of ensuring the common good, except as the very last option and in accordance with very strict conditions, without ignoring the consequences for the civilian population both during and after the military operation.[75]

John Paul's erstwhile cheerleaders, now turned critics, rightly pointed out that the *Catechism* left the decision about war to public authorities rather than the magisterium.[76] A pope who regularly made pronouncements about the morality or immorality of a wide swath of human conduct was uncomfortable remaining silent in the face of an imminent invasion of a sovereign nation. But the neoconservatives had the better side of the argument; Catholic teaching since Vatican II clearly left to the leaders of the combatant nations decisions relating to the morality of war.

---

75. John Paul II, *Address of His Holiness Pope John Paul II to the Diplomatic Corps*, 4.
76. Cornwell, *Pontiff in Winter*, 260–67.

Conclusion

The teaching of *Gaudium et spes* and the *Catechism* assumes (or hopes) that world leaders will critically examine the just war doctrine before initiating an attack on another country. This assumption (or hope) may prove to be unfounded; few world leaders can be expected to exhibit the sober analysis and theological profundity of Abraham Lincoln. Even Lincoln's somber assessment only came after four years of bloody struggle, not at the start of the hostilities. But the church's teaching on the morality of war does provide the pope with a principled basis for not calling out one side to a conflict for its unjustified aggression. When it comes to the morality of war, the pope either can avoid making criticisms that may have political consequences or he can exercise a prophetic function, but he may not be able to do both. The dilemma faced by Pius XII is inherent in the church's teaching on the morality of war. Papal silence in the face of war may be principled, but it is not without consequences, not only for the victims of aggression but also for the moral authority of the papacy.

8

Development and Discontinuity: Catholic Social Doctrine

> *I wish . . . to reaffirm the continuity of the social doctrine as well as its constant renewal. In effect, continuity and renewal are a proof of the perennial value of the teaching of the Church.*
>
> —John Paul II

> *In reality, significant discontinuities exist in the body of Catholic social teaching. . . The credibility of Catholic social teaching would only increase if popes were to openly recognize their differences with their predecessors.*
>
> —Charles Curran

Catholic Social Doctrine: An Overview

THE GREAT SOCIAL ISSUE facing the churches of Europe and North American in the latter third of the nineteenth century was the plight of urban workers and their struggle for shorter working days, safer working conditions, and a living wage. What would be the response of the church to the host of challenges brought about by the Industrial Revolution?

Beginning with Leo XIII, popes have addressed the challenges posed by rapid changes in the socio-economic and political arenas. He was the first pope to uphold the right of labor to organize and to insist that employers have a moral obligation to pay their employees a living wage. Pius XI expanded on Leo's teaching, emphasizing that the goods of the earth should be distributed so as to benefit all people, and acknowledging that certain limits may be placed on the use of private property. John XXIII, the son of sharecroppers, applied Catholic social doctrine to the struggles of the rural poor. Paul VI and his successors have broadened the scope of the doctrine to encompass the plight of persons in developing nations and the struggle of those countries to take their place as part of the world economy.

As new social and economic conditions give rise to new problems, Catholic social teaching must of necessity develop.[1] The fact that Catholic social doctrine develops, however, is often not acknowledged in papal documents, as ethicist Charles Curran has noted. "The documents themselves downplay change and development; they frequently cite earlier documents, insist on continuity within the tradition, and never explicitly disagree with previous documents."[2]

A disquieting element of Catholic social doctrine is that there is neither continuity nor development in the papal methodology used to examine social questions. Some popes have used a deductive approach, applying traditional principles of Catholic teaching to new situations; others have used an inductive approach, allowing new conditions to inform the answers to the questions they raise. Whereas some popes rely on local churches to discern the situation in their country and apply the Gospels to the historically conditioned situation, others adopt a top-down approach, stressing the overriding role of the magisterium in the development of the church's social doctrine. There is no development in the methodology employed, but only expressions of individual papal preferences.

Leo XIII and the Birth of Catholic Social Doctrine

Leo's most important encyclical, *Rerum novarum*, was concerned primarily with the "social question," which in Leo's time meant the plight of urban workers due to the changes wrought by the Industrial Revolution. But Leo was not a proponent of liberal social thought. A review of his other encyclicals indicate that he possessed a mind firmly rooted in the medieval past and uninfluenced by Enlightenment views. For him, the source of political authority was not the consent of the governed but God, who created a static world of rich and poor, rulers and ruled. It was the duty of those in the lower classes of society to accept their lot and, above all, to obey those in authority

---

1. Clark, *Catholic Social Thought*, 10.
2. Curran, *Catholic Social Teaching*, 15–16.

and to refrain from fomenting social unrest.³ According to historian Peter Phillips, the Church undertook to provide theological justification for the rigid, hierarchical structure of much of European civil society. "Besides giving spiritual consolation to souls in jeopardy, the Church provided intellectual support for authority as one of its prime functions. It explained and justified a hierarchical, aristocratic society in which each person had his defined place; why obedience was owed to superiors, to the law, and to morality; and why the poor are always with us."⁴

The social order was the theme of Leo's first two encyclicals. In *Inscrutabili Dei consilio*, he laments the civil strife which he views as the scourge of the age. The source of this strife is the rejection of the authority of the church—and, in particular, the authority of the papacy—resulting in the unlawful taking of church property and the abolition of the pope's temporal rule. Echoing his immediate predecessor, he vowed to do all in his power to restore the Papal States.⁵ In this endeavor, however, he would be no more successful than Pius IX.

In *Quod apostolici muneri*, Leo focuses on the right to private property, a concept which is central to all of his social encyclicals. Socialists "assail the right of property sanctioned by natural law; and . . . they strive to seize and hold in common whatever has been acquired either by title of lawful inheritance, or by labor of brain and hands, or by thrift in one's mode of life."⁶ In his view on the right to ownership and enjoyment of private property, he found himself in accord with John Locke, a leader of the Enlightenment who "more nearly personifies the reigning spirit of the eighteenth century than any other thinker."⁷ But he did not share Locke's political philosophy. Locke believed that the source of governmental authority is the consent of the governed, which led to his rejection of monarchy as a legitimate form of government.⁸ Leo, on the other hand, rejects the belief that rulers do not derive their "power of governing from God, but rather from the multitude, which, thinking itself absolved from all divine sanction, bows only to such laws as it shall have made at its own will." The natural ordering of society has no place for notions of equality, which Leo equates with Socialism. The encyclical contains no

---

3. Thomas A. Shannon, "Commentary on *Rerum novarum* (*The Condition of Labor*)," in Himes, *Modern Catholic Social Teaching*, 127–50, 135.

4. Phillips, *Tragedy of Nazi Germany*, 34.

5. Leo XIII, *Inscrutabili Dei consilio*, 3, 12.

6. Leo XIII, *Quod apostolici muneris*, 1.

7. Ahlstrom, *Religious History*, 353.

8. Copleston, *Modern Philosophy*, 139–43.

mention of the rights of workers, but only a reminder to the rich that they must provide for the poor or risk eternal damnation.[9]

In *Rerum novarum*, issued in 1891, Leo gives unprecedented Vatican support to workers' rights at a time when labor movements in Europe and America were struggling to gain a foothold. At the same time, however, he is steadfast in his support of the right of private property and in his complete rejection of Socialism and Communism as legitimate solutions to the plight of the working classes. *Rerum novarum* has served as the inspiration for several other encyclicals which are central to the church's social doctrine. When the Pontifical Council for Justice and Peace issued its *Compendium of the Social Doctrine of the Church* in 2004, it gave *Rerum novarum* pride of place.

> The term "social doctrine" goes back to Pius XI and designates the doctrinal "corpus" concerning issues relevant to society which, from the Encyclical Letter *Rerum Novarum* of Pope Leo XIII, developed in the Church through the Magisterium of the Roman Pontiffs and the Bishops in communion with them. The Church's concern for social matters certainly did not begin with that document, for the Church has never failed to show interest in society. Nonetheless, the Encyclical Letter *Rerum Novarum* marks the beginning of a new path. Grafting itself onto a tradition hundreds of years old, it signals a new beginning and a singular development of the Church's teaching in the area of social matters.[10]

Rerum novarum tackles a social issue not treated directly in any prior encyclical, the plight of the working classes, which Leo refers to as "the pressing question of the hour." He begins his analysis by examining a remedy which will not solve the problem, the Socialist proposal to collectivize the ownership of the means of production. Rather than being the problem, private property is the means by which the working class may achieve some measure of security.[11] This argument is curious. Leo is discussing the plight of workers in industrialized societies who, unlike many small family farmers, had no ownership of the means of production and no ability to acquire such ownership. His defense of the right to private property is based on an agrarian model, a form of ownership not available to the urban workers whose rights he is defending.[12] However,

---

9. Leo XIII, *Quod apostolici muneris*, 2, 5–6, 9.
10. Pontifical Council for Justice and Peace, *Compendium of Social Doctrine*, 87.
11. Leo XIII, *Rerum novarum*, 60, 4, 13.
12. Curran, *Catholic Social Teaching*, 174–75.

believing that he has shown conclusively that Socialism is not the answer, he proceeds to propose a remedy.

He discusses the reciprocal duties of workers and employers. Workers must perform their workplace duties and refrain from violence. Employers must not overwork their employees, have them perform activities not suited to their age or gender, or defraud them of their wages. Employers also have the positive duty to grant workers time off to attend to their religious duties. Since there is unequal bargaining power between employers and employees, government has a duty to address this imbalance. He rejects the argument that since wages are freely agreed upon between employer and employee, the employer's sole obligation is to pay the agreed upon wage. Justice requires more than simply honoring contractual obligations. It is in this context that Leo introduces the concept of a "living wage."

> Let the working man and the employer make free arrangements, and in particular let them agree freely as to the wages; nevertheless, there underlies a dictate of natural justice more imperious and ancient than any bargain between man and man, namely, that wages ought not to be insufficient to support a frugal and well-behaved wage-earner. . . .
>
> If a workman's wage be sufficient to enable him comfortably to support himself, his wife, and his children, he will find it easy, if he be a sensible man, to practice thrift, and he will not fail, by cutting down expenses, to put by some little savings and thus secure a modest source of income.

He also advocates increasing the number of labor unions and the creation of some form of workers' compensation and social security.[13]

Ten years after *Rerum novarum*, Leo returns to the theme of the working class, but this time with an emphasis on their participation in the political process while avoiding partisan politics. In *Graves de communi re*, he applauds the actions which have been undertaken to implement the teachings of *Rerum novarum*, such as the establishment of rural banks, mutual aid societies, and labor unions. He then distinguishes between two forms of political action, Social Democracy and Christian Democracy. He criticizes the former, because it seeks to abolish private property as well as class distinctions. Christian Democracy, on the other hand, supports the right to the ownership of private property. He cautions that social action should not become involved in partisan politics. The social question is at its core a religious one and cannot be solved without the involvement of religion.[14]

---

13. Leo XIII, *Rerum novarum*, 20, 37, 45–46, 49, 58.
14. Leo XIII, *Graves de communi re*, 3, 5–7, 11–12.

The next two popes would not issue any encyclicals on social issues. Pius X did not share Leo's concern for the rights of workers; in fact, his view toward trade unionism was one of open hostility.[15] Benedict XV's pontificate would be consumed with the First World War and its aftermath. It was not until after Pius XI had concluded the Lateran Accords in 1929—thus ending the "Roman Question" and settling once and for all the issue of the Papal States—that a pope would return to the theme of the rights of workers.

Pius XI and the Limitations on the Right of Private Property

Quadragesimo anno was issued in 1931, forty years to the day after the publication of *Rerum novarum*. Pius XI refers to Leo's encyclical as "the *Magna Carta* upon which all Christian activity in the social field ought to be based."[16] But Pius's encyclical is more than an homage to Leo's seminal work. He moves beyond Leo's medieval mindset, displaying a greater understanding of the economic realities of modern capitalism and of the great divide between the wealthy few and the struggling masses.

Pius begins the encyclical by examining the economic and social conditions at the time of Leo's encyclical. "For toward the close of the nineteenth century ... society was clearly becoming divided more and more into two classes. One class, very small in number, was enjoying almost all the advantages which modern inventions so abundantly provided; the other, embracing the huge multitude of working people, oppressed by wretched poverty, was vainly seeking escape from the straits wherein it stood." Not surprisingly, this state of affairs was quite acceptable to the upper class, who thought that the problems of the poor should be left to charity. Pius, on the other hand, was unwilling to accept "that so enormous and unjust an inequality in the distribution of this world's goods truly conforms to the designs of the all-wise Creator."[17]

He announces that "new needs and changed conditions of our age have made necessary a more precise application of Leo's teaching or even certain additions thereto." He reiterates the position established by Leo that the pope has "the right and duty to pronounce with supreme authority upon social and economic matters."[18] Although he reaffirms Leo's defense of the right of private property, his view of the purpose of private property and the role it plays in the distribution of goods is far more nuanced than Leo's,

15. Pollard, *Unknown Pope*, 13.
16. Pius XI, *Quadragesimo anno*, 39.
17. Ibid., 3–5.
18. Ibid., 40–41.

as Charles Curran explains. "Pius XI emphasizes the social dimension of property more than Leo XIII, who in the context of providing private property for all workers emphasized the individual aspect of property."[19] Private property has a "twofold character of ownership, called usually individual or social according as it regards either separate persons or the common good." Because "the right of property is distinct from its use," government does not violate the right of private property when it sets limits on its use. Additionally, justice demands that goods be distributed in such a way that all may benefit from them.[20]

Contrary to Leo's vision, neither urban industrial workers nor rural wage workers had any hope of becoming property owners in any real sense. As a solution, Pius proposes that workers be given a share in ownership, management, or profits of the enterprises in which they work, although he does not provide any examples of how such arrangements could be implemented. He reiterates Leo's call for workers to receive a living wage, one which will permit a father to provide for his family without the need for the mother or the children to work outside of the home.[21]

Pius acknowledges that capitalism, Communism, and Socialism have changed since the late nineteenth century. "Economic dictatorship is consolidated in the hands of a few," who by their control of credit control the economic lifeblood of the world. Leo had treated Communism and Socialism as virtually indistinguishable, but Pius sees an important distinction between the two systems. "Communism teaches and seeks two objectives: unrelenting class warfare and absolute extermination of private ownership," as well as displaying open hostility to the church and God. Socialism is more moderate, and even bears a resemblance to Christianity. "Socialism inclines toward and in a certain measure approaches the truths which Christian tradition has always held sacred; for it cannot be denied that its demands at times come very near those that Christian reformers of society justly insist upon." However, at its core, Socialism and Catholicism cannot be reconciled, because Socialism views material advantage as the sole end of humans and society. Therefore, "no one can be at the same time a good Catholic and a true socialist." Pius concludes by emphasizing that although economic justice is required, it is not sufficient, since it alone "can never bring about union of minds and heart."[22]

---

19. Curran, *Catholic Social Teaching*, 179.
20. Pius XI, *Quadragesimo anno*, 45–49, 57.
21. Ibid., 59, 65, 71.
22. Ibid., 105–6, 112–13, 118, 120, 137.

Although Pius points out the theoretical errors and practical shortcomings of both Socialism and Communism, Italian Fascism escapes his criticism in this encyclical. The Italian government had been Fascist since Benito Mussolini became prime minister in 1922. In fact, portions of the encyclical suggest approbation of certain aspects of Fascist labor policy, including syndicates of workers and employers. According to Italian historian Emma Fattorini, the encyclical "praised fascist corporativism, with its emphasis on class collaboration and the repression of socialist organizations, as a model much in keeping with Catholic social doctrines."[23] Some contemporaries disparaged the encyclical due to its perceived approval of certain elements of fascism.[24]

Pius XII: No New Social Teaching

Pius XII did not author an encyclical devoted principally to social concerns. *Sertum laetitiae*, which is addressed solely to the bishops of the United States, is the only one of Pius's encyclicals which includes a discussion of social problems, and that discussion is limited to a few paragraphs. It breaks no new ground, simply reiterating principles that had been enunciated by Leo XIII and Pius XI.

The guiding principle of the church's social doctrine is "that the goods created by God for all men should in the same way reach all, justice guiding and charity helping." He echoes Leo's view that the division of the human race into rich and poor is part of God's plan. Workers' salaries should be sufficient to support them and their families and opportunities for work should be available for all men. He is encouraged by the attention American Catholics have given to the social encyclicals of Leo and Pius XI.[25]

John XXIII: Social Doctrine Extended to the Rural Poor and to Impoverished Nations

The principal theme of John's first encyclical, *Ad Petri cathedram*, is the unity of the church and the challenges of ecumenism. Before he begins his analysis of the topic of unity, he first touches upon the problem of economic inequality. He shares Leo's view on the social order, declaring that

---

23. Fattorini, *Hitler, Mussolini, and the Vatican*, 168.

24. Christine Firer, "Commentary on *Quadragesimo anno (After Forty Years)*," in Himes, *Modern Catholic Social Teaching*, 151–74, 162.

25. Pius XII, *Sertum laetitiae*, 34–37, 41.

differences among social classes are part of the law of nature. He diverges from Leo, however, in that he does not view the current class stratification to be fixed and static.[26] According to Irish theologian Donal Dorr, "He accepted one aspect of the free enterprise ideology, namely, the assumption that it gives most people a reasonably equal chance of 'getting on,' that is, of moving upwards in society."[27] John laments, however, that "there is still too much disparity in the possession of material goods." He also introduces the topic of social justice, which will be the central theme of the encyclical *Mater et Magistra*. "With respect to social matters: it is Our paternal desire that relations among the various classes come under the guidance, control, and direction of the Christian value of justice. . . . [The church] preaches and inculcates a social doctrine and social norms which would eliminate every sort of injustice and produce a better and more equitable distribution of goods, if they were put into practice as they should be."[28]

Mater et Magistra marks a significant step in the development of Catholic doctrine. John begins by noting that "though the Church's first care must be for souls . . . she concerns herself too with the exigencies of man's daily life, with his livelihood and education, and his general, temporal welfare and prosperity." He then examines the pronouncements of his predecessors. *Rerum novarum* "is rightly regarded as a compendium of Catholic social and economic teaching." *Quadragesimo anno* dealt with "the Catholic's attitude to private property, the wage system, and moderate Socialism." Although Pius XII did not issue an encyclical devoted primarily to the social question, he had given a radio address in 1941 to commemorate the fiftieth anniversary of *Rerum novarum*. The reason that John offers for returning to the theme of the social question is that, in the twenty years since Pius's radio address, "the economic scene has undergone a radical transformation."[29]

The remainder of the encyclical consists of short, aphoristic paragraphs dealing with various aspects of the social question in no apparent order. On the issue of the just wage, he affirms Leo's teaching that the determination of such a wage cannot be left exclusively to market forces. He also criticizes the unjustified disparity in wages among various professions. He reiterates the continuing validity of the right of private property, which "is clearly sanctioned by the Gospel," although he does not cite any New Testament passage to support this assertion.

---

26. John XXIII, *Ad Petri cathedram*, 38–42.
27. Dorr, *Option for the Poor*, 95.
28. John XXIII, *Ad Petri cathedram*, 43, 127–28.
29. John XXIII, *Mater et Magistra*, 3, 15, 29, 41, 46.

His predecessors' social encyclicals focused on the plight of the urban working class, but John devotes a fair amount of space to the state of agriculture and the farmer. He laments the migration of farm workers to urban centers, caused by their inability to maintain an adequate standard of living through subsistence farming. He urges public authorities to address the needs of farmers through the creation of farm credit banks to supply loans, the establishment of social security systems, and the implementation of price protection for crops. He remains bound to the family farm as the ideal agricultural unit and urges family farmers to form cooperatives to obtain the advantages of economies of scale.[30]

For John, the social question extends beyond the internal economic life of a country to encompass the international community.[31] The demands of justice extend to nations as well. In particular, wealthier nations have a responsibility to assist undeveloped ones, and countries with agricultural surpluses are duty bound to aid countries with starving populations. But he warns that such aid must not be used as a subterfuge to gain political control over such nations. He acknowledges the concern about overpopulation and the adequacy of the world's food supply, but gives short shrift to those studies which suggest that the problem is a serious one. "Truth to tell, we do not seem to be faced with any immediate or imminent world problem arising from the disproportion between the increase of population and the supply of food. Arguments to this effect are based on such unreliable and controversial data that they can only be of very uncertain validity."[32] When *Mater et Magistra* was published in 1961, the world's population was in excess of three billion people, compared to more than seven billion today.

In terms of the relationship between nations, he observes a lack of mutual trust caused by ideological differences. Mutual trust can only be attained "by recognition of, and respect for, the moral order," which "has no existence except in God." This task is made more difficult by the existence of nations who "deny the existence of a moral order which is transcendent, absolute, universal, and equally binding upon all." He appears to be referring to the Soviet Union and China when he states that "the most fundamental modern error" is the effort to eradicate religion "as an anachronism and an obstacle to human progress."[33] An important innovation introduced by *Mater et Magistra* was its move away from a deductive approach and towards

---

30. Ibid., 70–71, 121–24, 134–37, 142–46.

31. Marvin L. Mich, "Commentary on *Mater et Magistra* (*Christianity and Social Progress*)," in Himes, *Modern Catholic Social Teaching*, 191–216, 199–202.

32. John XXIII, *Mater et Magistra*, 157–61, 171, 188.

33. Ibid., 208, 205, 214.

a more inductive approach to analyzing social questions, an approach that would be followed by Paul VI, then abandoned by John Paul II and Benedict XVI, and finally reintroduced by Francis.[34]

In *Pacem in terris*, John's discussion of inalienable human rights includes rights in the economic sphere. A corollary of the right to work is the right to a just wage. He reiterates the consistent teaching of his predecessors concerning "the right to the private ownership of property, including that of productive goods." With regard to the relationship among nations, they are governed by reciprocal rights and duties in the same way as individuals. An economically or militarily more powerful nation does not have the right "to exert unjust political domination over other nations." John is particularly sensitive to the condition of ethnic minorities who are forced by economic circumstances to leave their homeland in search of employment.[35]

The Second Vatican Council and the Universal Destination of Earthly Goods

The council in *Gaudium et spes* sought to apply the church's social doctrine to the social and economic situation of the mid-1960s. Since economic development is the concern of all people, the power to shape the economy cannot be left in the hands of self-appointed elites or the most powerful nations. Economic inequalities must be removed, and discrimination against migrants from foreign countries "must be carefully avoided." Human labor has a priority over capital; workers are not mere cogs in the economic engine. They are entitled to dignity as human beings, including time off from work to "enjoy sufficient rest and leisure to cultivate their familial, cultural, social and religious life." Workers have the right to unionize and the right to strike. The council emphasizes that the principle of the "universal destination of earthly goods" is superior to the right of private property, so that in extreme cases a person "has the right to procure for himself what he needs out of the riches of others." In underdeveloped regions, expropriation of uncultivated or under-cultivated estates may be appropriate, provided that just compensation is paid to the owners.[36]

---

34. Dorr, *Option for the Poor*, 119.
35. John XXIII, *Pacem in terrris*, 18–21, 80, 88, 94.
36. Second Vatican Council, *Gaudium et spes*, 65–71.

Paul VI: Social Doctrine Applied to Developing Nations and Their Inhabitants

Paul's lone social encyclical, *Populorum progressio*, issued in 1967, has a very different focus from those of his predecessors. *Rerum novarum* and *Quadragesimo anno* examined the plight of the urban working classes, while *Mater et Magistra* was concerned with problems facing small family farmers. Paul, on the other hand, discusses Catholic social doctrine from the perspective of developing nations and their citizens. "The progressive development of peoples is an object of deep interest and concern to the Church. This is particularly true in the case of those people who are trying to escape the ravages of hunger, poverty, endemic disease and ignorance; of those who are seeking a larger share in the benefits of civilization and a more active improvement of their human qualities; of those who are consciously striving for fuller growth."[37] The encyclical has been called "Catholic social teaching's Magna Carta on development."[38] This concern for developing nations and their inhabitants was prompted by what Paul perceived as a growing gap in prosperity between rich and poor nations and the worldwide increase in social unrest, a perception which may have grown as a result of his 1964 trip to India.[39] He had begun to address this concern in January 1967 with the establishment of the Pontifical Commission for Justice and Peace.[40]

Paul is quick to mention that "the Church . . . has no desire to be involved in the political activities of any nation." Instead, "she offers . . . a global perspective on man and human realities." He moves far beyond Leo XIII by emphasizing that "the right to private property is not absolute and unconditional." Instead, he points to the principle that "created goods should flow fairly to all. All other rights, whatever they may be, including the rights of property and free trade, are to be subordinated to this principle." It follows, therefore, that "no one may appropriate surplus goods solely for his own private use when others lack the bare necessities of life." He admits the possibility that the moral law, in certain circumstances, not only permits but may require the expropriation of private property for the common good. Paul unequivocally rejects those tenets of liberal economic theory which "present profit as the chief spur to economic progress, free competition as the guiding norm of economics, and private ownership of

---

37. Paul VI, *Populorum Progressio*, 1.

38. Allan Deck, "Commentary on *Populorum progressio* (*On the Development of Peoples*)," in Himes, *Modern Catholic Social Teaching*, 292–314, 296.

39. Paul VI, *Populorum progressio*, 4, 8–9; Hebblethwaite, *Paul VI*, 408–11, 483.

40. Paul VI, *Populorum progressio*, 5.

the means of production as an absolute right, having no limits nor concomitant social obligations."[41]

He recognizes that uncontrolled population growth threatens the prosperity of developing nations and that governments have a legitimate interest in controlling population growth. However, he is vague as to what actions a government may take to limit its population without infringing upon the primary rights of a married couple to determine the size of their family. He does not set down any hard and fast rules of family planning, suggesting that he had not yet resolved this issue in his own mind.[42]

The three major duties which wealthier nations have toward poorer ones are mutual solidarity, social justice, and universal charity. Wealthier nations should put surplus goods at the disposal of poorer ones. A portion of military expenditures should be set aside "for a world fund to relieve the needs of impoverished peoples." Creditor nations should provide interest rate relief and loan extensions to debtor nations. Relations between nations cannot be governed solely by contract principles where economic power is unequal, in the same way that market conditions alone cannot determine a just wage. Development and peace are intrinsically related, since lack of development jeopardizes peace.[43]

Paul's other major teaching on social issues is the 1971 apostolic letter *Octogesima adveniens*. Perhaps the most important aspect of the apostolic letter is Paul's acknowledgment that the diversity of economic conditions prevailing in the world does not permit Catholic social teaching to provide answers that are applicable to all economic systems. Not all answers to social questions need to originate in the Vatican.[44] Paul's emphasis on the role of local Christian communities in developing responses to social problems, rather than waiting for direction from the magisterium, represents a dramatic change from the top-down approach that had prevailed since Leo XIII.[45]

He is critical of the attraction of Marxism to certain Catholic thinkers, presaging the attacks on liberation theologians which would be a hallmark of the pontificate of John Paul II and his prefect of the Congregation for the Doctrine of the Faith, Cardinal Ratzinger. Paul rejects what he terms "technocratic capitalism" and "authoritarian democracy." As he had done

41. Ibid., 13, 22–26.
42. Ibid., 37.
43. Ibid., 44, 48–51, 54, 59, 76.
44. Paul VI, *Octogesima adveniens*, 4; Christine E. Gudorf, "Commentary on *Octogesima adveniens (A Call to Action on the Eightieth Anniversary of Rerum Novarum)*," in Himes, *Modern Catholic Social Teaching*, 315–32, 319.
45. Elsbernd, "What Ever Happened to *Octogesima Adveniens*?" 43.

in *Populorum progressio*, he emphasizes the importance of the development of nations. He concludes the apostolic letter by reiterating that flexibility is necessary in applying the social teaching of the church in practice.[46]

John Paul II: "Work Is for the Person, Not the Person for Work"

The central theme of John Paul II's first encyclical, *Redemptor hominis*, is redemption through Jesus Christ. Although it is not one of John Paul's social encyclicals, it anticipates some of the themes that will surface in greater depth in those later encyclicals. Human beings today suffer from feelings of alienation. They are threatened by the very goods they produce and view the environment simply as a source of consumption. Technological progress has not been accompanied by a corresponding development in the area of morals. He insists on "the priority of ethics over technology, in the primacy of the person over things, and in the superiority of spirit over matter." Misplaced priorities are evidenced by the excessive accumulation of goods by the privileged and the massive investment by nations in armaments rather than in food for the hungry.[47]

Laborem exercens is the first of John Paul's three encyclicals on Catholic social doctrine. It was published in 1981 to commemorate the ninetieth anniversary of *Rerum novarum* and was addressed to a worldwide audience. Before he takes up specific aspects of social doctrine, John Paul engages in a rather abstract, philosophical discussion of the nature of human work, which "revolves around two key notions: work is for the person, not the person for work; and labor has priority over capital."[48] He identifies human work as "*the essential key,* to the whole social question." In Genesis, God commands people to subdue and dominate the earth, which "dominion over the earth is achieved in and by means of work." He draws a distinction between work in its objective and subjective senses. Work in the objective sense involves the development of technology in fulfillment of the biblical injunction. Work in the subjective sense, on the other hand, is concerned with the worker rather than with the object of work. "As *a person, man is therefore the subject of work.*" It is the subjective sense of work which dominates the encyclical. In the ancient world, men were divided into classes based upon the type of work they performed. Physical labor was considered proper work only for slaves. Christianity ushered in a new era of respect for

---

46. Paul VI, *Octogesima adveniens*, 31–34, 37, 50.
47. John Paul II, *Redemptoris hominis*, 15–16.
48. Patricia A. Lamoureux, "Commentary on *Laborem exercens* (*On Human Work*)," in Himes, *Modern Catholic Social Teaching*, 389–414, 389.

the dignity of manual labor, because "one who, while *being God*, became like us in all things devoted most of the years of his life on earth to *manual work at the carpenter's bench*."[49] In the modern era, on the other hand, a materialistic approach to labor has predominated. Work has an impact on the personal, familial, and societal levels. On the personal level, "work is a good thing for man," because it promotes human dignity. On the familial level, "work is a condition for making it possible to found a family, since the family requires the means of subsistence which man normally gains through work." On the societal level, work connects an individual's labor with that of society at large for the development of the common good.[50]

The struggle between capital and labor was a hallmark of the rise of industrialization in the nineteenth and twentieth centuries. In this conflict, the church has shown a consistent preference for the priority of labor over capital.[51] On the question of the right to ownership of private property, the church's position differs from both capitalism and collectivism. Although Leo XIII and John XXIII confirmed the right to the ownership of private property, John Paul is much closer to the latter than the former in declaring that the right to ownership of private property is never absolute.[52] "Christian tradition has never upheld this right as absolute and untouchable. On the contrary, it has always understood this right within the broader context of the right common to all to use the goods of the whole of creation: *the right to private property is subordinated to the right to common use*, to the fact that goods are meant for everyone."[53] To say that the church has never upheld the right to private property as absolute is to read into *Rerum novarum* a qualifier which is found nowhere in that encyclical.

He prefers the term "family wage" to the traditional term "just wage." The former term connotes that a fair wage should take into account the number of dependents for whom a worker is financially responsible.

> ... Just remuneration for the work of an adult who is responsible for a family means remuneration which will suffice for establishing and properly maintaining a family and for providing security for its future. Such remuneration can be given either through what is called a *family wage*—that is, a single salary

---

49. John Paul II, *Laborem exercens*, 3–6. In fact, Jesus is referred to as a carpenter only in Mark 6:3. In Matt 13:55, he is referred to as "the carpenter's son." The other two Gospels contain no reference to Jesus performing manual labor.
50. John Paul II, *Laborem exercens*, 7–10.
51. Ibid., 11–12.
52. Lamoureux, "Commentary on *Laborem exercens*," 397–98.
53. John Paul II, *Laborem exercens*, 14.

given to the head of the family for his work sufficient for the needs of the family without the other spouse having to take up gainful employment outside the home—or through *other social measures* such as family allowances or grants to mothers devoting themselves exclusively to their families.[54]

It is difficult to conceive how such a family wage concept could be put into practice, and John Paul does not offer any suggestions. Gender equity laws, for example, would prohibit an employer from paying a father of four more for the same work than a single woman with no dependents. One consequence of such laws is that the wage paid to the father of four may be insufficient, requiring the mother to seek employment in the workplace as well. Does the principle of the family wage render gender equity laws unjust, because they fail to account for the familial situation of the worker? When the Vatican sets wages for its employees, the number of dependents an employee has is one of the factors which it considers.[55] Since the Vatican is governed only by its own laws, it can implement any salary program it wishes, an option not enjoyed by many public or private employers in other nations. The family wage appears not to be a concrete proposal intended to be implemented in the employment marketplace, but an ideal against which the justice of contractual wage arrangements may be judged. Nevertheless, the concept has been criticized because it "has perpetuated gender inequality and a patriarchal view of the family."[56]

John Paul appears to be of two minds on the issue of women in the workplace. On the one hand, he acknowledges that women hold jobs in all sectors of the work force and should not be subjected to employment discrimination. On the other hand, he expresses a clear preference that women devote themselves to the role of mother as opposed to that of wage earner.

> . . . It will redound to the credit of society to make it possible for a mother . . . to devote herself to taking care of her children and educating them in accordance with their needs, which vary with age. Having to abandon these tasks in order to take up paid work outside the home is wrong from the point of view of the good of society and of the family when it contradicts or hinders these primary goals of the mission of a mother.
>
> . . . The *true advancement of women* requires that labour should be structured in such a way that women do not have to pay for their advancement by abandoning what is specific

---

54. Ibid., 19.
55. Reese, *Inside the Vatican*, 211.
56. Lamoureux, "Commentary on *Laborem exercens*," 401.

> to them and at the expense of the family, in which women as mothers have an irreplaceable role.[57]

Donal Dorr has commented on John Paul's attitude toward women in the workplace. "There seems, then, to be a real ambivalence in the message of *Laborem exercens*. Its wording seems to have been carefully chosen to avoid the accusation that it is reaffirming the traditional teaching that a woman's place is in the home. On the other hand, it does not clearly dissociate itself from that older view of the nature and role of women."[58] John Paul expresses a similar ambivalence toward the role of women in the workplace in his apostolic exhortation *Familiaris consortio*, published two months after *Laborem exercens*.[59]

> There is no doubt that the equal dignity and responsibility of men and women fully justifies women's access to public functions. On the other hand the true advancement of women requires that clear recognition be given to the value of their maternal and family role, by comparison with all other public roles and all other professions....
>
> While it must be recognized that women have the same right as men to perform various public functions, society must be structured in such a way that wives and mothers are not in practice compelled to work outside the home, and that their families can live and prosper in a dignified way even when they themselves devote their full time to their own family.[60]

He insists on the continued importance of labor unions, the right of workers to strike without fear of penal sanctions, and the need for legal protection for the rights of agricultural workers and their families. Disabled workers should be offered work opportunities consistent with their abilities and dignity as persons. He supports the right of workers not only to emigrate from their native countries to find employment, but also their right not to be subject to employment discrimination in their adopted countries.[61]

The second of John Paul's encyclicals on social issues, *Sollicitudo rei socialis*, examines the changes in the social landscape in the twenty years since the publication of *Populorum progressio*. The aim of the encyclical is "to pay homage to this historic document of Paul VI" and "to reaffirm the

---

57. John Paul II, *Laborem exercens*, 19.

58. Dorr, *Option for the Poor*, 321.

59. Lisa Sowle Cahill, "Commentary on *Familiaris consortio (Apostolic Exhortation on the Family)*," in Himes, *Modern Catholic Social Teaching*, 363–88.

60. John Paul II, *Familiaris consortio*, 23.

61. John Paul II, *Laborem exercens*, 21–23.

continuity of the social doctrine as well as its constant renewal." He finds three points of originality in Paul's treatment of the social question. First, *Populorum progressio* had addressed "a matter which at first sight is solely economic and social: the development of peoples." Second, Paul affirmed "that the social question has acquired a worldwide dimension." Third, he explicitly equated development and peace. The expenditure of inordinate sums on nuclear weapons, on the other hand, has had a negative impact on development.[62]

In retrospect, John Paul views 1967 as having been a time of "widespread optimism" about the future of developing nations, an optimism which is no longer justified. He points to the widening inequalities between the developed countries of the North and the impoverished countries of the South. Among the major social problems in developing nations are the lack of housing, the lack of employment opportunities, and the increasing debt carried by these countries. In the political sphere, he expresses dismay over the growing tensions between the capitalist West and the Marxist East, both of which ideologies he characterizes as "imperfect and in need of radical correction." Developing nations in the Southern Hemisphere are grappling with unprecedented population growth, which can hinder development. He is dismayed, however, that the response of many governments has been to "launch systematic campaigns against birth," often to satisfy requirements placed by developing countries as a condition to financial assistance.[63]

He identifies certain positive aspects in the area of development, such as a growing awareness of human rights, a movement for peace, and an appreciation of the need to take ecology seriously. These ecological concerns have several consequences for how we live if we are to be responsible stewards of the planet. First, we cannot treat the environment as something to be exploited solely for our current needs. Second, there must be the realization "that natural resources are limited." Third, we must deal with the problem of pollution. This is the first encyclical to devote significant attention to ecology.[64]

He advances the concept of "solidarity" as a contrast to the political division of the world into Eastern and Western blocs.

> ... Interdependence must be transformed into solidarity, based upon the principle that the goods of creation are meant for all. ...

62. John Paul II, *Sollicitudo rei socialis*, 3, 8–10.
63. Ibid., 12–14, 17–21, 25.
64. Ibid., 26, 34; Curran, Himes, and Shannon, "Commentary on *Sollicitudo rei socialis* (*On Social Concern*)," in Himes, *Modern Catholic Social Teaching*, 415–35, 422.

> Surmounting every type of imperialism and determination to preserve their own hegemony, the stronger and richer nations must have a sense of moral responsibility for the other nations, so that a real international system may be established which will rest on the foundation of the equality of all peoples and on the necessary respect for their legitimate differences.

Since Leo XIII, one of the fundamental themes of papal encyclicals on the social question is "the option or love of preference for the poor." Equally important is the principle that "the goods of this world are originally meant for all." A corollary of this principle is that international systems of trade and finance must not function in such a way as to disadvantage poorer countries. An additional impediment to development is political corruption.[65]

Centesimus annus is John Paul's final social encyclical. The first section reexamines the teachings of *Rerum novarum*. He portrays that encyclical as a balanced critique of both socialism and liberal economic theory.[66] That characterization, however, is belied by Leo's scathing criticism of Socialism while upholding many of the tenets of capitalism.[67] John Paul sees Leo as having been prescient in his rebuke of Socialism. He expands on the critique of socialism which he had introduced in his two earlier social encyclicals. His fundamental problem with Socialism is not its economic theory, but its devaluation of the human being and its antireligious orientation. "We have to add that the fundamental error of socialism is anthropological in nature. Socialism considers the individual person simply as an element, a molecule within the social organism, so that the good of the individual is completely subordinated to the functioning of the socio-economic mechanism." As a result, the idea of a Christian Socialism is an oxymoron. He also uses the encyclical as the occasion to reflect on the fall of Communism. He views its collapse through the prism of the Solidarity movement in Poland, which allows him to link that movement to the struggle for the rights of workers generally.[68]

As he did in his first two encyclicals on the social question, John Paul both affirms the right to private property and stresses its limitations. However, the distribution of the goods of the earth is far from equal. Many people do not have the knowledge or training to participate in a meaningful way in the global economy, including a majority of people in the Third World. In these regions, many of the objectives announced in *Rerum novarum* still

---

65. John Paul II, *Sollicitudo rei socialis*, 36, 39, 42–44.
66. John Paul II, *Centesimus annus*, 10.
67. Dorr, *Option for the Poor*, 31.
68. John Paul II, *Centesimus annus*, 12–13, 23.

have not been achieved. The debts of developing nations may need to be renegotiated or canceled if the failure to do so would lead to "hunger and despair for entire peoples."[69]

John Paul introduces the concept of "human ecology" to indicate that, in addition to safeguarding the natural environment, human life must be safeguarded as well. This is to be done primarily through protection of the family, composed of a husband, a wife, and their offspring. "It is necessary to go back to seeing the family as the *sanctuary of life*. . . . In the face of the so-called culture of death, the family is the heart of the culture of life. Human ingenuity seems to be directed more towards limiting, suppressing or destroying the sources of life—including recourse to abortion, which unfortunately is so widespread in the world—than towards defending and opening up the possibilities of life."[70]

He admits that the church's role in the social question is limited to teaching general principles of social justice. Although the church does not have models of its own to propose, it is not neutral toward political systems. Totalitarianism denies human dignity and rejects the church. On the other hand, "the Church values the democratic system." He disputes the contention that religion and democracy are incompatible.

> . . . Nowadays there is a tendency to claim that agnosticism and sceptical relativism are the philosophy and the basic attitude which correspond to democratic forms of political life. Those who are convinced that they know the truth and firmly adhere to it are considered unreliable from a democratic point of view, since they do not accept that truth is determined by the majority, or that it is subject to variation according to different political trends. . . . As history demonstrates, a democracy without values easily turns into open or thinly disguised totalitarianism.

A key concept in Catholic social teaching is the "principle of subsidiarity." According to John Paul, the fundamental problem with the "welfare state" is that it violates the principle of subsidiarity. "Here again *the principle of subsidiarity* must be respected: a community of a higher order should not interfere in the internal life of a community of a lower order, depriving the latter of its functions, but rather should support it in the case of need and help to coordinate its activity with the activities of the rest of society, always with a view to the common good."[71]

69. Ibid., 30–35.
70. Ibid., 39.
71. Ibid., 43–46, 48.

The Congregation for the Doctrine of the Faith's Suppression of Liberation Theologies

During the pontificate of John Paul, the campaign to suppress liberation theology was spearheaded by the Congregation for the Doctrine of Faith. The seminal documents are the instructions *Libertatis nuntius* and *Libertatis conscientia*, issued in 1984 and 1986, respectively. The former is an attack on certain errors found in many theologies of liberation, whereas the latter is a more theoretical reflection upon the Christian understanding of liberation.

Varieties of liberation theology became popular in Latin American theological circles in the 1970s and 1980s. In his biography of Benedict XVI, John Allen has set forth a helpful summary of the main aspects shared by most of these liberation theologies.[72] Four ideas are central to this form of theology: (i) the preferential option for the poor; (ii) the charge that institutional violence is responsible for widespread hunger and poverty; (iii) a belief in structural sin; and (iv) orthopraxis, the notion that what is truly Christian is not correct belief but action to overthrow the structures of oppression. In addition to these shared fundamental concepts, liberation theologies also gave rise to tens of thousands of "base communities" of ten to thirty people each which operated outside of clerical control and episcopal oversight.

The purpose of *Libertas nuntius* is clearly stated in its introductory paragraphs. Although Christian liberation "is first and foremost liberation from the radical slavery of sin," some theologians mistakenly emphasize the priority of "liberation from servitude of an earthly and temporal kind." Therefore, the congregation deems it fitting to point out the errors of such theologies and their incompatibility with the Christian understanding of liberation and the church's social doctrine.[73] The instruction makes explicit that Marxist concepts cannot form the foundation of a Christian theology of liberation, because Marxism is a philosophy which is wholly immanent and denies the existence of a transcendent dimension. The kingdom of God proclaimed in the Gospels is one that is present here and now only incompletely; the fullness of the kingdom will not be realized in this world.[74] The congregation reaffirms the continuing validity in the church's social doctrine of the "preferential option for the poor" and acknowledges the reality of the growing inequality between the rich and the poor.[75] But the answer to the

---

72. Allen, *Benedict XVI*, 134–37.
73. Congregation for the Doctrine of the Faith, *Libertatis nuntius*, intro.
74. Ibid., conclusion.
75. Ibid., sec. 1, pars. 6–7.

problem of poverty is to be found in the Gospels and the Christian tradition rather than in a philosophy that at its core is atheistic and irreligious.

Liberation theology had its modern roots in the episcopal conferences held in Medellín, Colombia in 1968 and Puebla, Mexico in 1979, which were attended by Paul and John Paul, respectively.[76] But the theme of liberation goes back to the Bible. "The radical experience of 'Christian liberty' is our first point of reference. Christ, our Liberator, has freed us from sin and from slavery to the Law and to the flesh, which is the mark of the condition of sinful mankind." Liberation theologies tend to focus on the Book of Exodus, viewing the liberation of the Israelites from slavery in Egypt in purely political terms. The New Testament, although it is concerned with the poor and the suffering, is primarily on the liberation of all people form sin and its consequences.[77] Liberation theologies distort the New Testament teaching on the poor by confusing the "'poor' of the Scripture and the 'proletariat' of Marx."[78] The congregation rejects the notion of structural sin as a perversion of the Christian understanding of sin as a product of free and voluntary human choices.[79]

Marxism must be rejected because "atheism and the denial of the human person, his liberty and rights, are at the core of Marxist theory."[80] Human freedom is absent from Marxist analysis, as the class struggle is viewed as a necessary law of human history.[81] The class struggle, which is wholly immanent, by definition denies the reality of a transcendent dimension to life and limits the kingdom to the achievement of a classless society.[82]

The congregation also expresses distress as to the manner in which liberation theologians treat the magisterium as one of the structures of oppression. "There is a denunciation of members of the hierarchy and the magisterium as objective representatives of the ruling class which has to be opposed."[83] These theologians dismiss the church's social doctrine as a futile effort at compromise with the forces of oppression. Their insistence on the priority of orthopraxis over orthodoxy evidences the manner in which they relativize truth to "the imperatives of the class struggle."[84] The class struggle

---

76. Ibid., sec. 3, par. 2; sec. 5, par. 7.
77. Ibid., sec. 4, pars. 2–13.
78. Ibid., sec. 9, par. 10.
79. Ibid., sec. 4, par. 15.
80. Ibid., sec. 7, par. 9.
81. Ibid., sec. 8, pars. 5–7.
82. Ibid., sec. 9, par. 3.
83. Ibid., sec. 9, par. 13.
84. Ibid., sec. 10, pars. 3–4.

presupposes that the violence perpetrated by the structures of oppression can only be "overthrown by means of revolutionary violence." "One needs to be on guard against the politicization of existence which, misunderstanding the entire meaning of the Kingdom of God and the transcendence of the person, begins to sacralize politics and betray the religion of the people in favor of the projects of the revolution."[85]

Libertas conscientia, issued two years after *Libertas nuntius*, is a companion piece to the latter and the two "are to be read in the light of each other."[86] Some commentators have opined that the second instruction was issued to counteract the negativity of the first instruction.[87] The congregation attributes the driving forces behind freedom in the modern age to the Enlightenment and the French Revolution. Unfortunately, the age that began with freedom as its watchword and which strove for political and social equality later gave way to forms of totalitarianism that were unthinkable before the advent of modern technology. "Why do liberation movements which have roused great hopes result in regimes for which the citizens' freedom, beginning with the first of these freedoms which is religious freedom, becomes enemy number one?" One of the answers posed is that since the Enlightenment people have put a misplaced faith in science as a means for realizing freedom. The congregation reemphasizes one of the themes of its earlier instruction, that freedom from sin is the true meaning of Christian liberation. But in the modern age, a sense of sin has been lost.[88]

The church's social doctrine is geared toward the "putting into practice of the great commandment of love." This teaching by its nature is not static but continues to develop as new social, political, and economic conditions and structures arise. "Being essentially oriented toward action, this teaching develops in accordance with the changing circumstances of history. This is why, together with principles that are always valid, it also involves contingent judgments. Far from constituting a closed system, it remains constantly open to the new questions which continually arise; it requires the contribution of all charisma, experiences and skills." The church, in its social doctrine, strives to make existing political and social structures more just, but it does not endorse any one system as optimal. It condemns violent revolution, which only serves to substitute one form of oppression for another. Armed struggle against oppression is permissible only "as a

---

85. Ibid., sec. 11, pars. 10, 17.
86. Congregation for the Doctrine of the Faith, *Libertatis conscientia*, 2.
87. Curran, Himes, and Shannon, "Commentary on *Sollicitudo rei socialis*," 418.
88. Congregation for the Doctrine of the Faith, *Libertatis conscientia*, 6–14, 21, 37–41.

last resort to put an end to an obvious and prolonged tyranny which is gravely damaging the fundamental rights of individuals and the common good." The congregation reminds clergy who might be tempted to inject themselves into the forefront of the struggle for social and economic justice that the task of creating more just structures belongs properly to the laity rather than to the clergy.[89]

Benedict XVI: The Interdependence of Human Development and the Development of Nations

Benedict's contribution to Catholic social doctrine was set forth in his final encyclical, *Caritas in veritate*, and it was the only one which he addressed to a worldwide audience. It is a tribute to *Populorum progressio*, which Benedict refers to as "the *Rerum novarum* of the present age." He begins the encyclical by examining the dual virtues of charity and truth. "Charity is at the heart of the Church's social doctrine.... *Only in truth does charity shine forth*, only in truth can charity be authentically lived. Truth is the light that gives meaning and value to charity." Charity also is intimately related to justice, since they have the same end in mind, the common good. Charity, however, goes beyond the dictates of justice and extends to the neighbor more than his or her just due.[90]

The encyclical is divided into six chapters. Chapter 1 recapitulates the message of *Populorum progressio*. Paul had expanded the focus of the social question beyond the rights of workers to the struggles of developing nations; Benedict's goal is far more ambitious. He emphasizes the coherence present in those diverse encyclicals which constitute the seminal works in the development of Catholic social doctrine. He characterizes both *Populorum progressio* and *Humanae vitae* as social encyclicals, although he acknowledges that the latter does not have "any direct link to social doctrine." Benedict seeks to breathe new life into *Humanae vitae* by freeing it from the narrow constraints of a prohibition against artificial contraception, viewing it instead as an integral document of the church's magisterium on the social question.

> The Encyclical *Humanae Vitae* emphasizes both the unitive and the procreative meaning of sexuality, thereby locating at the foundation of society the married couple, man and woman, who accept one another mutually, in distinction and

---

89. Ibid., 71–80.
90. Benedict XVI, *Caritas in veritate*, 8, 2–3, 6–7.

> complementarity; a couple, therefore, that is open to life. This is not a question of purely individual morality: *Humanae Vitae* indicates the *strong links between life ethics and social ethics*, ushering in a new area of magisterial teaching that has gradually been articulated in a series of documents, most recently John Paul II's Encyclical *Evangelium Vitae*.[91]

Benedict has drawn a link between *Humanae vitae* and *Populorum progressio* that Paul never made.

Chapter 2 deals with the notion of human development. The development of nations and peoples has progressed in ways that Paul did not and could not have foreseen, primarily due to increasing economic globalization. The world as a whole possesses more wealth, but the inequalities between rich and poor, in terms of both individuals and nations, has increased greatly. Neither the production of goods nor the circulation of financial instruments are any longer circumscribed by national boundaries. Unfortunately, this globalization of commerce has been accompanied by an increase in unemployment and a reduction of social safety nets. As access to food and water become recognized "*as universal rights of all human beings, without distinction or discrimination*," the fight against hunger has gone global and "is an ethical imperative for the universal Church." Benedict combines the teachings of *Humanae vitae* and *Populorum progressio*, finding an essential link between the authentic development of the human person and the development of nations and peoples.

> One of the most striking aspects of development in the present day is the important question of *respect for life*, which cannot in any way be detached from questions concerning the development of peoples. . . .
>
> . . . In economically developed countries, legislation contrary to life is very widespread, and it has already shaped moral attitudes and praxis, contributing to the spread of an anti-birth mentality; frequent attempts are made to export this mentality to other States as if it were a form of cultural progress.
>
> Some non-governmental Organizations work actively to spread abortion, at times promoting the practice of sterilization in poor countries, in some cases not even informing the women concerned. Moreover, there is reason to suspect that development aid is sometimes linked to specific health-care policies which *de facto* involve the imposition of strong birth control measures. Further grounds for concern are laws permitting

---

91. Ibid., 12, 15.

euthanasia as well as pressure from lobby groups, nationally and internationally, in favor of juridical recognition.

He expresses grave concern about the rise in religious fundamentalism and the increase in terrorism which it has fostered, noting that development has stagnated in countries where religious fanaticism is prevalent.[92] Although he does not identify any particular religions or countries to which these remarks are addressed, his description best fits countries that combine Islamic fundamentalism with a lack of economic progress for the masses.

In chapter 3, which deals with economic development, Benedict rejects the notion that efficient markets, on their own, can satisfy the demands of economic justice. He is critical of contemporary corporate managers whose primary focus is the short term good of shareholders, while ignoring the long term best interests of the enterprise, as well as the interests of other constituencies, such as "the workers, the clients, the suppliers of various elements of production, the community of reference."[93]

Chapter 4 is devoted to human and environmental ecology. For Benedict, a critical issue in the development of peoples is how governments address the question of population growth. Although population growth is an important issue for many developing countries, the regulation of population is not a legitimate state activity. "It is irresponsible to view sexuality merely as a source of pleasure, and likewise to regulate it through strategies of mandatory birth control. In either case materialistic ideas and policies are at work, and individuals are ultimately subjected to various forms of violence. Against such policies, there is a need to defend the primary competence of the family in the area of sexuality, as opposed to the State and its restrictive policies, and to ensure that parents are suitably prepared to undertake their responsibilities." It is ironic that, whereas Benedict believes that government has no business regulating the activities of married couples in their own bedrooms, an all-male celibate hierarchy, under the leadership of the pope, considers itself entitled to intrude upon "the primary competence of the family in the area of sexuality."

Another critical issue in development is the relationship between humans and their environment, including the state of the environment that humans will leave to succeeding generations. He uses the language of "stewardship" and "covenant" to characterize the relationship between humans and their environment. He also suggests that environmental ecology can only be sustained if human ecology, as defined by the church, is defended

---

92. Ibid., 22–29.
93. Ibid., 35, 40.

and promoted.⁹⁴ The argument that human ecology and environmental ecology are inextricably linked is simply stated as a self-evident truth.

Chapter 5 focuses on the need for cooperation among members of the human family. He rejects the extremes of both religious indifferentism and religious fundamentalism, urging Christians to work with non-Christians and non-believers towards the goal of authentic human development. He closes this chapter with a plea that *"there is urgent need of a true world political authority."*⁹⁵ This final plea did not resonate with politically conservative Catholics in the United States.⁹⁶

The final chapter explores the challenges resulting from technological advances. In the field of bioethics, Benedict sees a "struggle between the supremacy of technology and human moral responsibility." His focus in this area is strictly on the problems posed by technology and not on the actual or potential benefits of that technology.

> . . . Yet we must not underestimate the disturbing scenarios that threaten our future, or the powerful new instruments that the "culture of death" has at its disposal. To the tragic and widespread scourge of abortion we may well have to add in the future—indeed it is already surreptitiously present—the systematic eugenic programming of births. At the other end of the spectrum, a pro-euthanasia mindset is making inroads as an equally damaging assertion of control over life that under certain circumstances is deemed no longer worth living.⁹⁷

This encyclical demonstrates Benedict's efforts to develop a doctrine that unifies the Church's social teaching with its sexual ethics in an all-encompassing human and environmental ecology.

Francis: Catholic Social Doctrine Demands Respect for the Environment

Francis's first publication on Catholic social doctrine is his apostolic exhortation *Evangelii gaudium*. Although evangelization is the primary theme of Francis's exhortation, one of the chapters is devoted to the challenges presented by the poor in society. What is new in Francis's approach to the social question is his understanding that wealth inequality is a structural

---

94. Ibid., 44, 48, 50–51.
95. Ibid., 53, 57, 67.
96. Dorr, *Option for the Poor*, 395.
97. Benedict XVI, *Caritas in veritate*, 74–75.

component of capitalism rather than an unintended byproduct. The structure of capitalism has resulted in the marginalization of the poor, who are deprived of the benefits that capitalism was supposed to bring to all.

> ... Today everything comes under the laws of competition and the survival of the fittest, where the powerful feed upon the powerless. As a consequence, masses of people find themselves excluded and marginalized: without work, without possibilities, without any means of escape....
>
> In this context, some people continue to defend trickle-down theories which assume that economic growth, encouraged by a free market, will inevitably succeed in bringing about greater justice and inclusiveness in the world. This opinion, which has never been confirmed by the facts, expresses a crude and naïve trust in the goodness of those wielding economic power and in the sacralized workings of the prevailing economic system. Meanwhile, the excluded are still waiting.

He laments the "idolatry of money" and the growing gap between the privileged few and the majority who do not share in the benefits of the market economy.[98]

The bulk of Francis's examination of the social question is contained in chapter 4, entitled "The Social Dimension of Evangelization." He dismisses the notion that the church properly should limit its influence to the spiritual realm; rather, the church has "a deep desire to change the world, to transmit values, to leave the earth somehow better than we found it." The "inclusion of the poor in society" becomes one of the most pressing social issues of our age. When private property is viewed through that prism, it becomes apparent that the right to private property is not absolute but is subordinate to the principle of the universal destination of goods. The marketplace has been unable on its own to achieve social justice, so that the inherent inequalities of the current economic system must be addressed and remedied.[99]

Francis's encyclical *Laudato si'* is devoted entirely to the environment and ecology. In its scope, the encyclical goes far beyond the statements on the subject found in the writings of John Paul and Benedict. The title refers to a canticle of St. Francis of Assisi, who "reminds us that our common home is like a sister with whom we share our life and a beautiful mother who opens her arms to embrace us." However, our sister is grieving due to our irresponsible use of her resources. "We have come to see ourselves as her lords and masters, entitled to plunder her at will." Francis pulls no

98. Francis, *Evangelii gaudium*, 53–56.
99. Ibid., 183, 185, 189, 202–4.

punches in his assessment of how humans have despoiled the planet. As a result of waste and pollution, "the earth, our home, is beginning to look more and more like an immense pile of filth." He accepts as an established scientific fact that global warming is real and that it is caused, in part, by our overreliance on fossil fuels. Even though access to potable drinking water is a universal human right, one of the effects of pollution has been to render much of the world's water supply unsafe for the poorest of people. This situation highlights the intrinsic relationship between ecology and justice. "Today, however, we have to realize that a true ecological approach always becomes a social approach; it must integrate questions of justice in debates on the environment, so as to hear both the cry of the earth and the cry of the poor."[100]

Francis finds in the creation accounts in Genesis the lesson that the fracturing of our relationship with the earth also has consequences for our relationship with God and our fellow human beings. "They suggest that human life is grounded in three fundamental and closely intertwined relationships: with God, with our neighbour and with the earth itself. According to the Bible, these three vital relationships have been broken, both outwardly and within us. This rupture is sin." In order to heal this rupture we need to recapture a sense of the world as the gift of God's creation.[101]

One of the primary motifs of the encyclical is the notion that social justice demands that environmental problems be examined from the perspective of how they impact the poorest and most marginalized people. He reiterates Benedict's injunction that our duty towards the environment extends to insuring that the planet we leave to future generations is not one filled with "debris, desolation and filth." Because the effect of pollution from fossil fuels is global, solutions must transcend national interests. Politicians should not allow their immediate electoral interests or near-term economic demands to trump long-term ecological planning. Francis is skeptical that environmental degradation can be slowed down or reversed solely through the operation of market forces. He also echoes John Paul's criticism of a culture that is driven by consumerism.[102]

In addition to enunciating general principles concerning the environment, Francis points to the daily choices that people can make to become better stewards of creation, "such as avoiding the use of plastic and paper, reducing water consumption, separating refuse, cooking only what can reasonably be consumed, showing care for other living beings, using public

---

100. Francis, *Laudato si'*, 1–2, 21, 23, 28–30, 49.
101. Ibid., 66, 76.
102. Ibid., 93, 161–75, 178, 190, 203–4.

transport or car-pooling, planting trees, turning off unnecessary lights, or any other number of other practices." In order to develop an attitude of stewardship toward the earth, he urges an "'ecological conversion,' whereby the effects of the encounter with Jesus Christ become evident in their relationship with the world around them."[103]

A unique feature of this encyclical is the extensive discussion of findings of environmental sciences concerning global warming and pollution. Prior popes have avoided scientific details in their encyclicals, but Francis's familiarity with science, as a result of his background in chemistry, make him comfortable with scientific terms and concepts. The encyclical is rife with references to the effects of greenhouse gases, the melting of the polar ice caps, carbon dioxide pollution, deforestation, diseases associated with unclean water, and the loss of biodiversity. One potential downside of this discussion is that if the science on which Francis relies turns out to be mistaken or superseded by future scientific developments, then doubt also may be cast on Francis's prescriptions.

From a theological perspective, a distinguishing feature of the encyclical is Francis's extensive reliance on statements of national and regional episcopal conferences. There are footnote references to reports of bishops' conferences from South Africa, Latin America and the Caribbean, the Philippines, Bolivia, Germany, Patagonia-Comahue, Canada, Japan, Brazil, the Dominican Republic, Paraguay, New Zealand, Argentina, Portugal, Mexico, and Australia. This reliance on the deliberations of episcopal conferences stands in sharp contrast to the practices of John Paul and Benedict, whose social encyclicals are devoid of references to declarations of such conferences.

In furtherance of the efforts of John Paul and Cardinal Ratzinger to centralize teaching on faith and morals in the Congregation for the Doctrine of the Faith, the teaching role of bishops' conferences was constrained through John Paul's apostolic letter *"motu proprio" Apostolos suos*, issued in 1998. The Second Vatican Council had supported regular conferences of national or regional bishops. Paul VI called for episcopal conferences to be established in areas where they did not exist, and the 1983 Code of Canon Law set forth regulations governing these conferences.[104] *Apostolos suos* places strict limits on the teaching authority of such conferences.

> . . . The Bishops assembled in the Episcopal Conference and jointly exercising their teaching office are well aware of the limits of their pronouncements. While being official and authentic and

---

103. Ibid., 211, 217.
104. John Pau II, *Apostolos suos*, 4–5.

in communion with the Apostolic See, these pronouncements do not have the characteristics of a universal magisterium. . . .

. . . When the doctrinal declarations of Episcopal Conferences are approved unanimously, they may certainly be issued in the name of the Conferences themselves, and the faithful are obliged to adhere with a sense of religious respect to that authentic magisterium of their own Bishops. However, if this unanimity is lacking, a majority alone of the Bishops of a Conference cannot issue a declaration as authentic teaching of the Conference to which all the faithful of the territory would have to adhere, unless it obtains the recogintio of the Apostolic See, which will not give it if the majority requesting it is not substantial.[105]

Although Francis has not abrogated *Apostolos suos*, his citations to on the declarations of bishops' conferences in *Laudato si'* may indicate an openness on his part to give to these conferences a recognized teaching authority which they have not previously enjoyed.

Conclusion

Not only has Catholic social doctrine come a long way since Leo XIII, but so have the popes themselves. Leo's critique of capitalism and support for the rights of organized labor were revolutionary when compared to his predecessor, who for much of his papacy ruled the Papal States as the absolute monarch that he was. But like Pius IX, Leo believed that the church had all the answers to society's ills. His analysis of the problems wrought by the Industrial Revolution was not based on any personal experience of the working and living conditions of the lower classes. As pope, he never set foot outside the walls of the Vatican; within those walls, he spoke not a single word to his coachman of twenty-five years.[106] His social doctrine was developed by deduction from general principles, an approach which would be emulated by some of his successors, including John Paul II.

Francis's social doctrine, on the other hand, was developed from the street up. When he wrote in *Laudato sì* of how "the earth, our home, is beginning to look more and more like an immense pile of filth," he was speaking from personal experience. As archbishop of Buenos Aires, he celebrated many Masses in the *villas miserias*, the slums "often built on illegal dumps

---

105. Ibid., 22.
106. Duffy, *Saints and Sinners*, 318.

or alongside contaminated water streams."[107] Unlike Leo, Francis does not have a coachman and is quite comfortable in personal dealings with his flock. In Buenos Aires, he did not wish to be addressed as "Your Eminence," preferring the less intimidating "Padre Jorge."[108]

Neoconservative Catholics sometimes dismiss papal teaching on social issues as nothing more than the personal political or economic viewpoint of the current pope from which Catholics are free to dissent. But that is not the manner in which the church views the authoritativeness of its social doctrine. The church maintains that it is competent to make moral judgments on the social order, as the council made clear in *Gaudium et spes*. "It is only right, however, that at all times and in all places, the Church should have true freedom to preach the faith, to teach her social doctrine, to exercise her role freely among men, and also to pass moral judgment in those matters which regard public order when the fundamental rights of a person or the salvation of souls require it."[109] The council's expression of the church's competence to teach authoritatively on social issues is echoed in the 1983 Code of Canon Law. "It belongs to the Church always and everywhere to announce moral principles, even about the social order, and to render judgment concerning any human affairs insofar as the fundamental rights of the human person or the salvation of souls requires it."[110]

However, in spite of its proclaimed competence to teach authoritatively on social issues, the church has never issued an infallible proclamation on a social issue. Due to the changing political, social, and economic landscapes with which the church has had to deal since the late nineteenth century, it is understandable that it would avoid issuing social judgments that are set in stone. Once an acknowledgement is made that certain teachings are noninfallible, however, Catholics who disagree with the teaching feel emboldened to dissent from them or to simply ignore them. This is another example of how "creeping infallibility" can undermine the respect which Catholics frequently display toward noninfallible papal teaching. It is this attitude which prompted Cardinal Ratzinger to characterize "the distinction between infallible and noninfallible teaching 'legalistic.'"[111] But that distinction was invented by the Vatican and not by its critics.

107. Tornielli and Galeazzi, *This Economy Kills*, 139–40.
108. Piqué, *Pope Francis*, 2.
109. Second Vatican Council, *Gaudium et spes*, 76.
110. *Code of Canon Law*, canon 747, sec. 2. For a comparison of canon 747 and *Gaudium et spes* 76, see John P. Boyle, "Church Teaching Authority in the 1983 Code," in Curran and McCormick, *Dissent in the Church*, 191–230, 198–201.
111. Charles Curran, "Public Dissent in the Church," in Curran and McCormick, *Dissent in the Church*, 387–407, 396.

9

Confusion: The Necessity of the Catholic Church for Salvation

> *There is one Universal Church of the faithful, outside of which there is absolutely no salvation.*
>
> —Fourth Lateran Council, 1215

> *However, this dogma must be understood in that sense in which the Church herself understands it.*
>
> —Letter of the Holy Office to the Archbishop of Boston, 1949

Extra Ecclesiam Nulla Salus

Perhaps no Catholic doctrine has proven more divisive or problematic than the four words *extra ecclesiam nulla salus* (outside the church no salvation). The literal meaning of the phrase has drastic implications. If there is no salvation outside the Catholic Church, then no member of any other Christian religion (Protestant or Orthodox), no adherent of any other monotheistic religion (Jew or Muslim) or any polytheistic religion (Hindu), no follower of any nontheistic religion (Buddhist), and certainly no agnostic or atheist has any possibility of reaching heaven. If the phrase means what it literally says, then it is a doctrine that the overwhelming majority of American Catholics do not accept. According to a 2007 Faith Matters Survey, 83 percent of American Catholics believe that non-Catholics, including non-Christians, can go to heaven.¹ Are these Catholics unaware of the official church teaching on this issue, or does *extra ecclesiam nulla salus* mean something less than or different from what its plain language commands?

Political scientists Robert Putnam and David Campbell attribute the results of the Faith Matters Survey to the experience of religious diversity in America, as members of one faith work and live in the same communities with members of other faiths, as well as people who profess no faith.

> ... We call it the "Aunt Susan Principle." We all have an Aunt Susan in our lives, the sort of person who epitomizes what it means to be a saint, but whose religious background is different from our own. Maybe you are Jewish and she is a Methodist. Or perhaps you are Catholic and Aunt Susan is not religious at all. But whatever her religious background (or lack thereof), you know that Aunt Susan is destined for heaven. And if she is going to heaven, what does that say about other people who share her religion or lack of religion? Maybe they can go to heaven too.²

One American who apparently did not have an Aunt Susan in his life was Leonard Feeney, a Jesuit who taught theology in Massachusetts during the 1940s. Feeney espoused the view that the doctrine outside the church no salvation, as promulgated by the Fourth Lateran Council, means what it says and allows of no exceptions. Archbishop Richard Cushing of Boston took a less restrictive view, and Feeney accused Cushing of heresy.³ This accusation prompted the Holy Office to send a lengthy letter to Cushing, declaring that the doctrine is not as restrictive as its plain language would seem to dictate.

> However, this dogma must be understood in that sense in which the Church herself understands it. ...
>
> ... Since, in order that one may obtain eternal salvation, it is not always required that he be incorporated into the Church actually as a member, but it is necessary that at least he be united to her by desire and longing.
>
> However, this desire need not always be explicit, as it is in catechumens; but when a person suffers from invincible ignorance, God accepts also an implicit desire, so called because it is included in that good disposition of soul whereby a person wishes his will to be conformed to the will of God.⁴

1. Putnam and Campbell, *American Grace*, 534–40.
2. Ibid., 526.
3. Sullivan, *Salvation Outside the Church?* 3.
4. Holy Office, *Letter to the Archbishop of Boston*, in Denzinger and Hünermann,

Feeney did not obediently accept the Holy Office's response; instead, he charged the Holy Office with heresy. He was ousted from the Jesuit order in 1949 and excommunicated four years later.[5]

Another Jesuit whose interpretation of *extra ecclesiam nulla salus* brought him to the attention of the Congregation for the Doctrine of the Faith is the Belgian Jesuit Jacques Dupuis. Dupuis had taught in India for more than thirty-five years, where he likely came into contact with many Aunt Susans among the Hindus, Muslims, and Buddhists he encountered there. In 1997 Dupuis published a book entitled *Toward a Christian Theology of Religious Pluralism*.[6] The book prompted a notification from the congregation, which was concerned that Dupuis may have strayed too far afield—in the opposite direction from Feeney—in his interpretation of the doctrine. The members of the congregation "found that his book contained notable ambiguities and difficulties on important doctrinal points, which could lead a reader to erroneous or harmful opinions. These points concerned the interpretation of the sole and universal salvific mediation of Christ, the unicity and completeness of Christ's revelation, the universal salvific action of the Holy Spirit, the orientation of all people to the Church, and the value and significance of the salvific function of other religions."[7] The congregation directed that the text of the notification be included in any future edition of the book.[8] The congregation stopped short of finding that Dupuis had deviated from Catholic teaching.[9]

If theologians like Feeney and Dupuis have trouble comprehending the precise boundaries of *extra ecclesiam nulla salus*, then how can those not trained in theology have any hope of understanding it? Does recent papal teaching provide any guidance? Sadly, papal teaching in this area has only compounded the confusion.

Enchiridion symbolorum, 3866–73.

5. Kerr, *Twentieth-Century Theologians*, 96–97; Sullivan, *Salvation Outside the Church?* 203.

6. Dupuis, *Religious Pluralism*.

7. Congregation for the Doctrine of the Faith, *On the Book by Jacques Dupuis*, 1–2.

8. Ibid., 2.

9. Heft, "Catholicism and Interreligious Dialogue," in Heft, *Catholicism and Interreligious Dialogue*, 1–22, 8.

Exclusivism, Inclusivism, and Pluralism Concerning Salvation

In recent years, the competing claims made by various religions to be the sole means for attaining salvation have preoccupied philosophers and theologians of religions, as Dominican theologian J. A. DiNoia has noted. "Can non-Christians attain salvation? Do other religions aim at salvation? . . . Together, these questions consume much of the attention of Christian theologians of religion."[10] The different approaches which religions have taken on these questions are identified under the broad labels of exclusivism, inclusivism, and pluralism. Philosopher of religion Robert McKim has provided a useful summary of these options. In its most extreme form, exclusivism about salvation holds both that that my religious tradition alone delivers salvation—exclusivism about the means of salvation—and that only members of my religious tradition can achieve salvation—exclusivism about the beneficiaries of salvation. Inclusivism, on the other hand, claims that salvation is available to members of other religious traditions. Although this position is inclusivist as to the beneficiaries of salvation, it may remain exclusivist as to the means of salvation—members of other religious traditions may attain salvation but only through my religious tradition, which is the sole means of salvation. Pluralism casts the widest net, holding not only that members of other religious traditions may attain salvation, but also that their religious traditions can serve as the vehicle for their salvation.[11]

Although papal teaching has not characterized the issue in terms of this threefold typology of the philosophy of religions, that framework can be useful in examining where the church's interpretation of *extra ecclesiam nulla salus* falls on this continuum. A shift from exclusivism to inclusivism concerning the beneficiaries of salvation began to take place during the pontificate of Pius IX, a move which was completed under Pius XII and the Second Vatican Council. By the time that Feeney had the temerity to teach that *extra ecclesiam nulla salus* means exactly what it says, that non-Catholics have no hope for salvation, the church already had moved away from this position. But how far the church has moved away from the exclusivism of the Fourth Lateran Council is far from clear. The church appears to be straddling the line between exclusivism and inclusivism as to the means of salvation. It continues to teach that the Catholic Church is necessary for salvation, while not denying that other religions may play some role in the salvation of their adherents. But the church has not clearly articulated the manner in which it remains necessary for the salvation of non-Catholics.

---

10. DiNoia, *Diversity of Religions*, 36.
11. McKim, *Religious Diversity*, 52–53, 72–73, 123–24.

The History of the Doctrine

The origin of the expression *extra ecclesiam nulla salus* has been traced to Cyprian, a third-century bishop of Carthage in North Africa. When Cyprian used the phrase, he was not directing his message to people who had never heard of Christ or the Gospel. Instead, he "addressed his warnings to people in danger of being separated from the Church or already separated from it, always supposing personal guilt on their part." Cyprian was admonishing heretics and schismatics who had voluntarily separated themselves from the church. However, after the church became the official religion of the Roman Empire in the early fourth century, others would extend the axiom to encompass pagans and Jews, who were presumed to have heard the message of Christ and voluntarily rejected him, as Jacques Dupuis has observed.

> It is after the Christian religion had become the official religion of the empire that we find the Church Fathers applying the axiom "Outside the Church no salvation" to the situation of Jews and pagans. As guilt had previously been supposed on the part of heretics and schismatics who had separated themselves from the Church, it is now equally presumed in the case of Jews and pagans who have failed to become Christians. The reason behind this judgment was the assumption that the Gospel had by then been promulgated everywhere and everyone had had the opportunity to accept it.[12]

The axiom became part of church doctrine in the thirteenth century, when the Fourth Lateran Council declared that "there is one Universal Church of the faithful, outside of which there is absolutely no salvation."[13] Less than one hundred years later, Boniface VIII upped the ante in his papal bull *Unam sanctam*, leaving no doubt that not only membership in the church, but also communion with and subservience to the bishop of Rome, was required in order to be saved. "Furthermore, we declare, we proclaim, we define that it is absolutely necessary for salvation that every human creature be subject to the Roman Pontiff."[14] Two centuries later, however, the church would be faced with the unexpected discovery of untold numbers of people in the Americas and the Far East to whom the message of Christ had never been preached and who had no opportunity to become members of the church.[15]

---

12. Dupuis, *Religious Pluralism*, 88–89.
13. Fourth Lateran Council, *Canons*, canon 1.
14. Boniface VIII, *Unam sanctam*, 1.
15. For a discussion of the manner in which theologians dealt with the issue

In spite of the questions which the discoveries of the fifteenth and sixteenth centuries raised as to the proper interpretation of the doctrine, the issue was not broached again by the Vatican until 1856, when Pius IX issued his encyclical *Singulari quidem* to the bishops of Austria. Pius repeats his earlier condemnations of indifferentism and rationalism. Indifferentism "makes no distinction between the different creeds." Rationalism errs by placing human reason above faith. "Full of confidence in themselves, they deny that we must believe in God for Himself and accept what He taught us about Himself." These errors must be rejected, because they fail to recognize the supremacy of the Catholic religion. "There is only one See founded in Peter by the word of the Lord, outside of which we cannot find either true faith or eternal salvation." Later in the encyclical, however, he adds an important qualifier to this exclusivist position. "Outside of the Church, nobody can hope for life or salvation unless he is excused through ignorance beyond his control."[16]

A similar qualifier appears a few years later in *Quanto conficiamur moerore*, an encyclical addressed to the bishops of Italy. Pius continues his attack on "the corruption of morals . . . the deadly virus of unbelief and indifferentism . . . contempt for ecclesiastical authority . . . and by the outrageous plundering of church possessions." He chastises those "Catholics who believe that it is possible to arrive at eternal salvation although living in error and alienated from the true faith and Catholic unity" and repeats the traditional admonition that "no one can be saved outside the Catholic Church."[17] But he expands on the qualifier he had introduced in *Singulari quidem*.

> . . . There are, of course, those who are struggling with invincible ignorance about our most holy religion. Sincerely observing the natural law and its precepts inscribed by God on all hearts and ready to obey God, they live honest lives and are able to attain eternal life by the efficacious virtue of divine light and grace. Because God knows, searches and clearly understands the minds, hearts, thoughts, and nature of all, his supreme kindness and clemency do not permit anyone at all who is not guilty of deliberate sin to suffer eternal punishments.[18]

Pius IX is the first pope to have declared that people who were ignorant of the Christian religion through no fault of their own could attain eternal

---

following the discoveries of the fifteenth and sixteenth centuries, see Sullivan, *Salvation Outside the Church?* 63–81.

16. Pius IX, *Singulari quidem*, 3–7.
17. Pius IX, *Quanto conficiamur moerere*, 3, 7–8.
18. Ibid., 7.

salvation.[19] Pius IX intended for the First Vatican Council to address the issue of *extra ecclesiam nulla salus* in a dogmatic constitution on the church. But the hastily adjourned council—due to the outbreak of the Franco-Prussian War—never took up the issue, one which would not be dealt with by any of Pius's successors for eighty years.[20]

The most controversial aspect of Pius XII's encyclical *Mystici corporis Christi* is his equation of the Mystical Body of Christ and the Catholic Church. He notes that the concept of the church as a body is found in scripture. The analogy is apt, he claims, because like a body the church has a multiplicity of members, each of whom serves a different function. The Mystical Body of Christ is not composed of all Christians; it is limited to baptized Catholics. Pius acknowledges, however, that non-Catholic Christians may be related in some imperfect manner to the Mystical Body. Christians who are separated from the church, "even though by an unconscious desire and longing they have a certain relationship with the Mystical Body of the Redeemer, they still remain deprived of the many heavenly gifts and helps which can only be enjoyed in the Catholic Church."[21] It was this concept of belonging to the church by an unconscious longing and desire which the Holy Office expounded on in its letter condemning the views of Feeney.

The Second Vatican Council: Inclusivism Endorsed in an Ill-Defined Manner

The Second Vatican Council addressed the doctrine of the necessity of the church for salvation in *Lumen gentium*. Salvation remains attainable only through the church for those who are aware of this rule and have the ability to join the church. But those who through no fault of their own do not know Christ or the church may attain salvation through alternative means.

> This Sacred Council wishes to turn its attention firstly to the Catholic faithful. Basing itself upon Sacred Scripture and Tradition, it teaches that the Church, now sojourning on earth as an exile, is necessary for salvation. Christ, present to us in His Body, which is the Church, is the one Mediator and the unique way of salvation. . . . Whosoever, therefore, knowing that the Catholic Church was made necessary by Christ, would refuse to enter or to remain in it, could not be saved. . . .

---

19. Sullivan, *Salvation Outside the Church?* 115.
20. Ibid., 119–20.
21. Pius XII, *Mystici corporis Christi*, 16–17, 22, 103.

> Finally, those who have not yet received the Gospel are related in various ways to the people of God. In the first place we must recall the people to whom the testament and the promises were given and from whom Christ was born according to the flesh. On account of their fathers this people remains most dear to God, for God does not repent of the gifts He makes nor of the calls He issues. But the plan of salvation also includes those who acknowledge the Creator. In the first place amongst these there are the Mohamedans, who, professing to hold the faith of Abraham, along with us adore the one and merciful God, who on the last day will judge mankind. Nor is God far distant from those who in shadows and images seek the unknown God, for it is He who gives to all men life and breath and all things, and as Saviour wills that all men be saved. Those also can attain to salvation who through no fault of their own do not know the Gospel of Christ or His Church, yet sincerely seek God and moved by grace strive by their deeds to do His will as it is known to them through the dictates of conscience.[22]

Although this interpretation of the axiom would apply to non-Christians who had never heard the message of Christ or the Catholic Church, it does not seem to cover non-Catholic Christians, who confess Christ but reject the Catholic Church. The council addressed the situation of Orthodox and Protestant Christians in its decree on ecumenism, *Unitatis redintegratio*, in which it held that other Christians are joined to the Catholic Church, albeit in an imperfect manner.

> Even in the beginnings of this one and only Church of God there arose certain rifts, which the Apostle strongly condemned. But in subsequent centuries much more serious dissensions made their appearance and quite large communities came to be separated from full communion with the Catholic Church—for which, often enough, men of both sides were to blame. The children who are born into these Communities and who grow up believing in Christ cannot be accused of the sin involved in the separation, and the Catholic Church embraces upon them as brothers, with respect and affection. For men who believe in Christ and have been truly baptized are in communion with the Catholic Church even though this communion is imperfect.[23]

Lumen gentium and *Unitatis redintegratio*, taken together, underscore how far the church has come from the exclusivist position of the Fourth Lateran

---

22. Second Vatican Council, *Lumen gentium*, 14, 16.
23. Second Vatican Council, *Unitatis redintegratio*, 3.

Council. With regard to other Christians, the church has adopted a position that is inclusivist not only as to the beneficiaries of salvation but also, in some ill-defined manner, as to the means of salvation.[24] The council also dealt with the issue of the salvation of non-Christians, at least indirectly, in *Gaudium et spes*, where it noted that God makes available his grace to non-Christians in a manner which the church does not yet comprehend.[25]

The status of the doctrine of the necessity of the Catholic Church for salvation in the period following Vatican II was summarized by the International Theological Commission in 1997.

> The primary question today is not whether men can attain salvation even if they do not belong to the visible Catholic Church; this possibility is considered theologically certain. The plurality of religions, something increasingly evident to Christians, better knowledge of these religions and the necessary dialogue with them, without leaving until the end the clearer awareness of the spatial and temporal frontiers of the Church—all these considerations make us ask whether one can nonetheless speak of the necessity of the Church for salvation and about the compatibility of this principle with the universal salvific will of God.[26]

Because the doctrine is one that the church asserts has been taught infallibly, it cannot simply be jettisoned, even if it engenders confusion among Catholics and non-Catholics alike.

The Current Status of the Doctrine

In *Redemptoris missio*, John Paul II links the urgency of the church's missionary activity with its long-standing teaching that membership in the Catholic Church is necessary for an individual to attain salvation. John Paul's travels had confronted him firsthand with the reality that a large percentage of the world's population does not know Christ or the church. Many of these people are adherents of non-Christian religions. Are all of these people ineligible for salvation as a result of the accident of where and when they were born? Can the religious traditions to which these people belong play any role in aiding them to attain salvation?

John Paul begins his analysis by exploring the centrality of Christ for salvation, which is the reason that missionary activity is always necessary.

---

24. Sullivan, *Salvation Outside the Church?* 145.
25. Second Vatican Council, *Gaudium et spes*, 22.
26. International Theological Commission, *Christianity and the World Religions*, 63.

"No one, therefore, can enter into communion with God except through Christ, by the working of the Holy Spirit. Christ's one, universal mediation, far from being an obstacle on the journey toward God, is the way established by God himself, a fact of which Christ is fully aware. Although participated forms of mediation of different kinds and degrees are not excluded, they acquire meaning and value *only* from Christ's own mediation, and they cannot be understood as parallel or complementary to his."[27] The vagueness of the last sentence appears to be deliberate. Statements later in the encyclical clarify it, indicating that the "participated forms of mediation" to which he refers are non-Christian religions. Although these religions cannot offer the fullness of salvation, they are not devoid of religious truth.

> ... It is necessary to keep these two truths together, namely, the real possibility of salvation in Christ for all mankind and the necessity of the Church for salvation....
>
> The universality of salvation means that it is granted not only to those who explicitly believe in Christ and have entered the Church. Since salvation is offered to all, it must be made concretely available to all. But it is clear that today, as in the past, many people do not have an opportunity to come to know or accept the gospel revelation or to enter the Church. The social and cultural conditions in which they live do not permit this, and frequently they have been brought up in other religious traditions. For such people salvation in Christ is accessible by virtue of a grace which, while having a mysterious relationship to the Church, does not make them formally part of the Church but enlightens them in a way which is accommodated to their spiritual and material situation.[28]

If billions may attain salvation, even though they have not heard the message of Christ and have had no opportunity to enter the church, then how can the church be necessary for salvation? The linchpin of John Paul's answer is the phrase "while having a mysterious relationship to the Church." In other words, while the Catholic Church is necessary for salvation, it is not necessary to be a member of it in order to attain salvation. Catholic doctrine is not exclusivist as to the beneficiaries of salvation, but it remains exclusivist as to the means of salvation. Then in what manner does the church participate in the salvation of those who are not members? John Paul provides no answer.

The lengths to which John Paul goes to hold together two seemingly contradictory propositions—"the real possibility of salvation in Christ for

---

27. John Paul II, *Redemptoris missio*, 27.
28. Ibid., 9–10.

all mankind and the necessity of the Church for salvation"—are necessitated by the typical papal unwillingness to openly question the continuing validity of a prior church teaching. The alternative would have been for him to hold that the almost eight hundred year old statement of the Fourth Lateran Council—that outside of the church there is no salvation—was incomplete, an oversimplification, or in need of revision. However, the Holy Office, only four decades before *Redemptoris missio*, had declared that *extra ecclesiam nulla salus* was an infallible teaching. Nevertheless, the interpretation of the axiom had already been revised to such an extent that it no longer meant what it plainly seemed to say. The result has been to leave Catholics and non-Catholics alike in a state of confusion as to the church's teaching on the necessity of the church for salvation. Yves Congar suggested that *extra ecclesiam nulla salus* be abandoned, "since in its formulation the axiom can no longer be taken *literally* and a correct understanding of it requires long explanations."[29]

Author James Carroll has noted that "there are mixed messages in recent Catholic history on the question of whether other religions offer 'ways' to salvation."[30] The Congregation for the Doctrine of the Faith, in the declaration *Dominus Jesus*, issued in 2000, attempted to clear up such mixed messages. The congregation reiterates the teaching of *Redmptoris missio* that Catholics must affirm both the real possibility of salvation in Christ for all mankind and the necessity of the Catholic Church for salvation.[31] The primary emphasis of the document, however, is on the manner in which other religions, Christian and non-Christian alike, are defective vis-à-vis the Catholic Church, the one and only way of salvation.

> . . . However, from what has been stated above about the mediation of Jesus Christ and the "unique and special relationship" which the Church has with the kingdom of God among men—which in substance is the universal kingdom of Christ the Saviour—it is clear that it would be contrary to the faith to consider the Church as *one way* of salvation alongside those constituted by other religions, seen as complementary to the Church or substantially equivalent to her, even if these are said to be converging with the Church toward the eschatological kingdom of God. . . .
>
> . . . If it is true that the followers of other religions can receive divine grace, it is also certain that *objectively speaking* they

---

29. Dupuis, *Religious Pluralism*, 101, emphasis in original.
30. Carroll, *Constantine's Sword*, 315.
31. Congregation for the Doctrine of the Faith, *Dominus Jesus*, 20.

are in a gravely deficient situation in comparison with those who, in the Church, have the fullness of the means of salvation.[32]

Dominus Jesus appears to adopt a tone of exclusivism that deviates from the documents of Vatican II. To define the situation of non-Catholic Christians as "gravely deficient" vis-à-vis Catholics strongly suggests that their ability to attain salvation is impeded because their traditions do not possess "the fullness of the means of salvation." *Dominus Jesus* was not well-received, not only by many outside of the church, but by some insiders as well. For example, German Cardinal Walter Kaspar, president emeritus of the Pontifical Council for Promoting Christian Unity, considered the declaration to be "ecumenically disastrous."[33] In a like manner, Australian Cardinal Edward Idris Cassidy, another former head of the same council, observed that "for a Christian community to be denied the title of 'church' is bitterly resented." Cassidy also noted that "Many members of the Jewish community worldwide . . . were worried by the assertion in *Dominus Jesus* that followers of religions other than Christianity were in a gravely deficient situation in regard to salvation."[34]

The Commission for Religious Relations with the Jews, which was established by Paul VI in 1974, has dealt squarely with the question of salvation for Jews in a 2015 reflection on Catholic-Jewish relations. It makes clear in the preface to the document that "the text is not a magisterial document or doctrinal teaching of the Catholic Church." Nevertheless, it is an accurate reflection of the state of current church teaching. The church's relationship with Jews is different than its relationship with members of other non-Christian religious groups, because Christianity grew out of Judaism and its central figure, Jesus of Nazareth, was Jewish. Moreover, the covenant between God and the Jews continues to occupy a place within salvation history and has not been superseded by Christ. "The covenant that God has offered Israel is irrevocable. . . . The New Covenant does not revoke the earlier covenants, but it brings them to fulfillment." Although "the Church is the definitive and unsurpassable locus of the salvific action of God. This however does not mean that Israel as the people of God has been repudiated or has lost its mission. (cf. *Nostra aetate*, No. 4). The New Covenant for Christians is therefore neither the annulment nor the replacement, but the fulfillment of the promises of the Old Covenant." Since Judaism has its own unique role to play in salvation history, the church has abandoned any missionary effort directed towards Jews. However, salvation for Jews, as for adherents of other

---

32. Ibid., 21–22.
33. Duffy, *Saints and Sinners*, 382.
34. Cassidy, *Ecumenism and Interreligious Dialogue*, 120, 248.

religions and those who profess no religion, is dependent in some unspecified manner on Christ and, by extension, on the church.[35]

Conclusion

Dominus Jesus is the church's most recent teaching on the meaning of *extra ecclesiam nulla salus*. Since the Holy Office had announced in 1949 that the doctrine was an infallible teaching, it is set in stone. It cannot be reversed or overruled; it can only be differently interpreted. Since the church is necessary for salvation, the only way in which non-Catholics, non-Christians, and non-believers can be saved is for them to be incorporated into the church in some manner. But how this takes place can only leave Aunt Susan scratching her head.

---

35. Commission for Religious Relations with the Jews, *Gifts and Calling*, 20, 27, 32, 40, 36.

10

Arrogance: Ecumenism and Interreligious Dialogue

> *There is something wrong with treating other religions as so far below par that we think we have nothing to learn from them.*
>
> —Robert McKim

> *Is real dialogue possible for a church and with a church which claims to have the absolute truth in an infallible way?*
>
> —Cardinal Walter Kasper

The Reformation at Five Hundred Years

On October 31, 1517, an Augustinian monk named Martin Luther nailed a piece of paper to the door of a church in Wittenberg, Germany. In that document, the "Ninety-Five Theses," Luther requested a debate over the sale of indulgences. The practice had been authorized by Leo X three years earlier in order to finance the completion of St. Peter's Basilica in Rome. (The practice would be abolished by Paul V in 1567.) Indulgences were popular because they reduced the time that a person—or a deceased relative—would have to spend in purgatory atoning for sins that had been forgiven in confession. The most prolific salesman of indulgences in Germany, the Dominican preacher Johann Tetzel, came up with the following advertising slogan to pitch the program to the masses. "'Place your penny on the drum, the pearly gates open and in strolls mum.'"[1] It was this cheap salvation offered by indulgences which explained both their appeal as well as Luther's revulsion to them.[2] Theologically, Luther could not accept the idea that the pope, in effect, was claiming to have authority over the amount of time a soul spent in purgatory. Politically, he objected to financing papal building projects on the backs of the impoverished German people.[3]

Luther could not be ignored by the Vatican, because his views were widely disseminated throughout Germany in pamphlets printed in the vernacular rather than in Latin. The importance of the printing press for the Reformation cannot be overestimated. "Without the advent of printing, there would have been no Reformation, and there might well have been no Protestantism either."[4] The pope did not remain silent in the face of this threat to his authority. In 1520, Leo X issued the papal bull *Exsurge Domine*. The bull lists forty-one specific errors (a technique that later will be used by Pius IX in his *Syllabus of Errors*), many of which were attacks on papal authority and the practice of indulgences. The pope gave Luther and his supporters sixty days to stop preaching and publishing their heretical opinions.[5] When Luther failed to comply, Leo issued a second papal bull, *Decet Romanum Pontificem*, excommunicating Luther and his followers.[6]

For most of the next five hundred years, popes did little to seek to bring about reunification of Catholic and Protestant Christians. Prior to the 1960s, the word "ecumenism" was seldom found in the papal lexicon. The attitude of popes toward the successors of Luther, Calvin, and the other reformers was to remind them that their only hope of salvation was to return to the Catholic fold and pledge fealty to the Roman Pontiff.[7] Since the Catholic Church possesses all religious truth, dialogue with Protestant (and Orthodox) Christians would be a futile exercise; the church has nothing to learn from them.

Like ecumenism, the term "interreligious dialogue" seldom made an appearance in papal documents. Non-Christian religions often were characterized as consisting of little more than superstitious and pagan practices; those religions played no role in whatever salvation their adherents

---

1. Duffy, *Saints and Sinners*, 200.
2. McGrath, *Christianity's Dangerous Idea*, 47.
3. González, *Reformation to the Present*, 21–35; McGrath, *Christianity's Dangerous Idea*, 45–49.
4. McGrath, *Christianity's Dangerous Idea*, 25.
5. Leo X, *Exsurge Domine*, 4.
6. Leo X, *Decet Romanum Pontificem*, 1.
7. Cassidy, *Ecumenism and Interreligious Dialogue*, 3.

might hope to attain while they remained in invincible ignorance of Christ and his church. The purpose of interaction with non-Christians was not dialogue but conversion.[8]

In the second half of the twentieth century, a dramatic shift took place in the church's attitude toward non-Catholic Christians and non-Christians, as well as toward their religions. John XXIII was the catalyst for this change. In *Ad Petri cathedram* he expresses the hope that non-Catholic Christians should be treated as "sons and brothers," rather than as heretics and schismatics. John also was the force behind the Second Vatican Council, which would issue groundbreaking documents on both ecumenism and non-Christian religions. Ecumenism, the dialogue with non-Catholic Christians aimed at the eventual reunification of all Christians, is the subject of the decree *Unitatis redintegratio*. Interreligious dialogue, which refers to dialogue between Catholics and non-Christians, is the subject of the declaration *Nostra aetate*. Ecumenism and interreligious dialogue have been important topics in the encyclicals of Paul VI and John Paul II, as well as the subject of several documents from the Congregation for the Doctrine of the Faith.

Nevertheless, it is fair to ask how far the church's attitude toward non-Catholic Christians and non-Christians really has changed. Dialogue presupposes that neither party to the dialogue believes that he or she possesses the whole truth and remains open to having his or her mind changed by the arguments of the other dialogue partner. If this understanding of dialogue is correct, then the Catholic Church is not prepared to engage in ecumenical or interreligious dialogue in any true sense of the terms. As Robert McKim has noted, "there is something wrong with treating other religions as so far below par that we think we have nothing to learn from them."[9] The Vatican remains adamant that only within the Catholic Church can one find the fullness of the means of salvation; all non-Catholic and non-Christian religions are objectively deficient by comparison. From the point of view of the other partner to the dialogue, what is the purpose of dialogue with a church who believes it has nothing to gain from the encounter, except for the opportunity to convince non-Catholics of the deficiencies of their religions?

The Ecumenical and Interreligious Landscape Prior to Vatican II

It is hardly surprising that Pius IX, the pope who presided over the council that promulgated the dogma of papal infallibility, was not a champion of ecumenism. Nevertheless, in *Quanto conficiamer moerore*, Pius takes a

8. Ibid., 125–26.
9. McKim, *Religious Diversity*, 45.

small step toward ecumenical outreach when he urges Catholics to assist separated Christians in returning to the fold. "First of all, let them rescue them from the darkness of the errors into which they have unhappily fallen and strive to guide them back to Catholic truth and to their most loving Mother who is ever holding out her maternal arms to receive them lovingly back into her fold. Thus, firmly founded in faith, hope, and charity and fruitful in every good work, they will gain eternal salvation."[10]

In the nineteenth century, the only ecumenical outreach the church was willing to make was to hold open the door for any separated Christians who were willing to confess their errors and return to the Catholic fold. Leo XIII, in his encyclical *Sapientiae Christianae*, sets forth a view of the church that would render futile any ecumenical dialogue. He describes the Catholic Church as "a perfect society far excelling every other."[11] The church, and specifically the pope, is the sole interpreter and teacher of divinely revealed truths. Leo's view of the respective roles of the pope, the bishops, and the faithful was summed up by an Irish Modernist, George Tyrell, as recounted by historian Jojn Ratté. "'*L'Eglise, c'est moi* is literally the pope's attitude. He is the steam engine; the episcopate is the carriages; the faithful are the passengers.' There was nothing for the layman to do but to 'pay his fare and take his seat as so much ballast in the bark of Peter, while the clergy pull him across the ferry.'"[12] Leo had an unshakeable belief in the superiority of the church in general, and the papacy in particular, over all other institutions, not only on matters of faith and morals, but in all areas of human thought and activity, as Eamon Duffy has noted.

> The fact is that however much Leo's tone of voice differed from that of his immediate predecessors, like them he believed that the Church—and therefore the Pope—had all the answers. If he thought less confrontationally, more historically, than Pio Nono [Pius IX], he had no doubt that the questionings and uncertainties of his age could all be resolved painlessly, by attention to what the Church, through St. Thomas, through the popes, had long since taught. There is a numbing smugness about the insistence in many of his encyclicals that the Church is responsible for all that is good in human society, human

---

10. Pius IX, *Quanto conficiamur moerere*, 9.
11. Leo XIII, *Sapientiae Christianae*, 17, 22–24.
12. Ratté, *Three Modernists*, 181–82. Tyrell was excommunicated in 1907 following a scathing review of Pius X's encyclical *Pascendi domenici gregis* which he had published in the London *Times*. Ibid., 206.

culture. It is the voice of a man who has worn a cassock and lived among clerics all his life.[13]

Satis cognitum is the encyclical most indicative of Leo's vision of ecumenism. Leo's hope is "to bring back to the *fold*, placed under the guardianship of Jesus Christ, the Chief Pastor of souls, sheep that have strayed." But it is no exaggeration to say that Leo's approach to ecumenism does not involve dialogue with separated churches, but instead their total submission to Rome. "The Church of Christ, therefore, is one and the same forever; those who leave it depart from the will and command of Christ, the Lord—leaving the path of salvation they enter on that of perdition." Submission to the teaching of the church means submission to each and every one of its doctrines.

> ... It was thus the duty of all who heard Jesus Christ, if they wished for eternal salvation, not merely to accept his doctrine as a whole, but to assent with their entire mind to all and every point of it, since it is unlawful to withhold faith from God even in regard to one single point....
>
> ... But he who dissents even in one point from divinely revealed truth absolutely rejects all faith, since he thereby refuses to honour God as the supreme truth and the *formal motive of faith*.[14]

His discussion of the relation between the pope and bishops seems clearly to be directed at the bishops of the Orthodox Churches who had broken away from communion with Rome. The pope does not have sole authority over the church, because the bishops also are an essential element and possess authority in their own right. "They are not to be looked as vicars of the Roman Pontiffs; because they exercise a power really their own." However, bishops lose their power and authority if they separate themselves from the pope.[15] He then raises an issue that had been a matter of debate for centuries: the authority of an ecumenical council independent of the pope. Disagreement on this issue had contributed to the schism between the churches of the East and the West in 1054.[16]

> But it is opposed to the truth, and in evident contradiction with the divine constitution of the Church, to hold that while each

---

13. Duffy, *Saints and Sinners*, 316.
14. Leo XIII, *Satis cognitum*, 1, 5, 8–9.
15. Ibid., 14–15.
16. MacCulloch, *Christianity*, 362; Pelikan, *Spirit of Eastern Christianity*, 273–74.

> Bishop is *individually* bound to obey the authority of the Roman Pontiffs, taken *collectively* the Bishops are not so bound....
>
> ... It has ever been unquestionably the office of the Roman Pontiffs to ratify or to reject the decrees of Councils.
>
> ... But the authority of the Roman Pontiff is supreme, universal, independent; that of the bishops limited, and dependent.[17]

Therefore, reconciliation between the Catholic Church and the Orthodox Churches of the East can only be accomplished on Rome's terms. This unbending precondition to reconciliation with the churches separated from Rome will reappear several times in the writings of John Paul II.

Leo's vision of ecumenism—a one-way street leading to Rome—is further evidenced by the manner in which he answered the question of the validity of Holy Orders conferred by the Anglican Communion, the subject of his apostolic letter *Apostolicae curae*. Leo affirms the traditional Catholic teaching that ordinations of priests and bishops by the Anglican rite are invalid. "For an opinion already prevalent, confirmed more than once by the action and constant practice of the Church, maintained that when in England, shortly after it was rent from the center of Christian Unity, a new rite for conferring Holy Orders was publicly introduced under Edward VI, the true Sacrament of Order as instituted by Christ lapsed, and with it the hierarchical succession." Not content simply to declare Anglican Orders a nullity, Leo concludes the letter by proclaiming that his teaching shall be valid for all time, thereby forcing his successors to either continue the teaching in force or explain how they could change what purports to be, by its express terms, a permanently valid papal teaching.

> We decree that these letters and all things contained therein shall not be liable at any time to be impugned or objected to ... but are and shall be always valid and in force and shall be inviolably observed both juridically and otherwise, by all of whatsoever degree and preeminence, declaring null and void anything which, in these matters, may happen to be contrariwise attempted, whether wittingly or unwittingly, by any person whatsoever, by whatsoever authority or pretext, all things to the contrary notwithstanding.[18]

Leo's teaching was confirmed and expanded by the Congregation for the Doctrine of the Faith in 1998. Although Leo's teaching had not been claimed by the magisterium to be divinely revealed, the Congregation stated that it

---

17. Leo XIII, *Satis cognitum*, 15.
18. Leo XIII, *Apsotolicae curae*, 3, 40.

was one of "those truths connected to revelation by historical necessity and which are to be held definitively" by all Catholics.[19]

The high points of the modern ecumenical movement in the first half of the twentieth century were the 1910 Missionary Conference in Edinburgh, the 1927 First World Conference on Faith and Order in Lausanne, and the founding of the World Council of Churches in 1948 in Amsterdam.[20] Conspicuous by their absence from these meetings were representatives of the Catholic Church. Neither Pius X nor Benedict XV addressed the birth of the ecumenical movement in any of their encyclicals. Benedict did, however, acknowledge the global growth of the non-Christian population in his apostolic letter *Maximum illud*, the subject of which was the status of the church's missionary activity. He begins with the acknowledgement that Jesus's command to the Apostles that the Gospel is to be preached to all the world is not a charge that ended with the apostolic age. The importance of this obligation is evidenced by the fact that the number of non-believers had grown to almost one billion people. One of the most pressing issues for Benedict was the development of native clergy in mission territories. If the church is not to be regarded as a foreign presence, then it is essential that mission churches be staffed as much as possible by local clergy.[21]

Many Italian priests in the early twentieth century displayed an anti-Protestant animus, and Pius XI was no exception.[22] The encyclical *Mortalium animos* sets forth his views on the ecumenical movement, which typify this prejudice. For Pius, the only effective ecumenism is for non-Catholic Christians to repudiate their heretical and schismatic ways, return to the church, and pledge loyalty to the Roman Pontiff, as Hubert Wolf has observed. "From a Roman perspective, ecumenism was possible, if at all, only as an ecumenism of return, in which Protestants rejected their false path and returned to Catholicism."[23] Nothing can be gained from ecumenical meetings between Catholics and other Christians. In fact, such conversations are strictly forbidden. "Conventions, meetings and addresses" of various Christian groups "can nowise be approved by Catholics, founded as they are on that false opinion which considers all religions to be more or less good and praiseworthy." A union of Christian Churches can only be found through the one, true church, which is the Catholic Church. "It is clear why this Apostolic

19. Congregation for the Doctrine of the Faith, *Doctrinal Commentary on "Professio fidei,"* 11.
20. González, *Reformation to the Present*, 512–19; Noll, *Turning Points*, 262–65.
21. Benedict XV, *Maximum illud*, 1, 6, 14.
22. Pollard, *Unknown Pope*, 204.
23. Wolf, *Pope and Devil*, 232.

See has never allowed its subjects to take part in assemblies of non-Catholics: for the union of Christians can only be promoted by promoting the return to the one true Church of Christ of those who are separated from it, for in the past they have unhappily left it."[24] In other words, Christian unity can only be realized by accepting and obeying the authority of the pope. In the words of Eamon Duffy, "The encyclical made it clear that the ecumenical message of the Vatican for the other churches was simple and uncompromising: 'Come in slowly with your hands above your head.'"[25]

Pius's ban on the participation of Catholics in meetings with Christians of other denominations is no longer in effect. Whereas the 1917 Code of Canon Law "forbade Catholic participation in ecumenical discussions without special permission," this proscription is absent from the 1983 Code.[26] In 1993, the Pontifical Council for Promoting Christian Unity declared that he participation of Catholics in ecumenical assemblies is encouraged, a sharp contrast to the conviction of Pius XI.

> Councils of Churches and Christian Councils are among the more permanent structures that are set up for promoting unity and ecumenical cooperation. . . .
>
> Since it is desirable for the Catholic Church to find the proper expression for various levels of its relation with other Churches and ecclesial Communities, and since Councils of Churches and Christian Councils are among the more important forms of ecumenical cooperation, the growing contacts which the Catholic Church is having with Councils in many parts of the world are to be welcomed.[27]

In *Mystici corporis Christi*, Pius XII echoes Leo XIII in his characterization of the church as "a perfect society of its kind" and "far superior to all other human societies."[28] A problem with this comparison, as one papal biographer has noted, is that it "erected a huge ecumenical obstacle simply by identifying the Mystical Body of Christ with the Roman Catholic Church."[29]

---

24. Pius XI, *Mortalium animos*, 2, 7–11.
25. Duffy, *Saints and Sinners*, 344.
26. Boyle, "Church Teaching Authority in the 1983 Code," 205.
27. Pontifical Council for Promoting Christian Unity, *Directory*, 166–67.
28. Pius XII, *Mystici corporis Christi*, 63.
29. Hebblethwaite, *Paul VI*, 183.

John XXIII and the Birth of Catholic Ecumenism

From the start of his papacy, John XXIII signaled that a new papal attitude toward non-Catholic Christian denominations was on the horizon. He begins the encyclical *Ad Petri cathedram* by noting that he recently had announced plans for the two most important projects of his papacy: the calling of an ecumenical council and a revision of canon law. The theme of the encyclical is unity, a subject which he introduces in the plainest language.

> We are called brothers. We actually are brothers. We share a common destiny in this life and the next. Why, then, do we act as though we are foes and enemies? Why do we envy one another? Why do we stir up hatred? Why do we ready lethal weapons for use against our brothers?
>
> There has already been enough warfare among men! Too many youths in the flower of life have shed their blood already! Legions of the dead, all fallen in battle, dwell within this earth of ours. Their stern voices urge us all to return at once to harmony, unity, and a just peace.
>
> All men, then, should turn their attention away from those things that divide and separate us, and should consider how they may be joined in mutual and just regard for one another's opinions and possessions.[30]

The principal theme of the encyclical, the unity of the church, had prompted John's call for an ecumenical council. He identifies the three unities of the Catholic Church as unity of doctrine, organization, and worship. The unity of doctrine is found in scripture and in the oral and written tradition of the church. The unity of doctrine does not mean that there is no room for debate on theological issues. "For discussion can lead to fuller and deeper understanding of religious truths; when one idea strikes against another, there may be a spark." He cites with approval the following maxim: "in essentials, unity; in doubtful matters, liberty; in all things, charity." Not a few Catholic theologians probably wish that some of John's successors would have followed this maxim when dealing with what the Vatican perceived as impermissible theological dissent. The unity of organization follows a hierarchical model: the faithful obey the priests, who obey the bishops, who are subject to the pope, a model similar to the one expressed by Leo in *Sapientiae Christianae*. Unity of worship is found in the seven sacraments, which were instituted by Christ and remain the same

---

30. John XXIII, *Ad Petri cathedram*, 3, 27–29.

up to the present day.[31] On this last point, John is on shaky ground historically. In the early church, only baptism and the Eucharist were universally agreed to be sacraments, and they remain the only two recognized by most Protestant denominations. The number of sacraments varied from two to twelve, with the first known list of seven dating from the twelfth century.[32] The *Catechism* acknowledges that agreement on the number of sacraments was a process of development. "Thus the Church has discerned over the centuries that among liturgical celebrations there are seven that are, in the strict sense of the term, sacraments instituted by the Lord."[33] John expresses his hope that the unity of the Catholic Church will strike a spark in those Christians who are separated from Rome. "May We, in fond anticipation, address you as sons and brothers? May We hope with a father's love for your return?" He invites these Christians of other denominations to join in prayers for the success of the council.[34]

His encyclical *Princeps pastorum* lays down certain guidelines to be followed by the church in the conduct of its mission activities. Social welfare projects in mission territories are encouraged, but they are secondary to the prime object of the missions, which is the propagation of the faith. He encourages lay involvement in the apostolic field, but does not delineate which tasks are best suited to be performed by the laity. It is important that converts provide whatever level of material support they can to their local church institutions. He rejects a one-size-fits-all missionary template for global use. "What has been done in one country cannot be carried over indiscriminately to another," because missionary activities must "be carefully adapted to local conditions and needs."[35]

The Second Vatican Council: A Positive Attitude towards Other Religions

The new attitude of the church toward non-Catholic Christians was boldly announced in one of the council's earliest documents, *Lumen gentium*. The council implicitly rejected the predominant understanding of the church that had pervaded papal teaching of the previous hundred years. Leo XIII and Pius XII, for example, had emphasized the great divide between the

---

31. Ibid., 59–62, 69–74.
32. Pelikan, *Growth of Medieval Theology*, 209; Pelikan, *Reformation of Church and Dogma*, 179.
33. *Catechism*, No. 1117.
34. John XXIII, *Ad Petri cathedram*, 80, 88.
35. John XXIII, *Princeps pastorum*, 22, 28, 39, 44.

Catholic Church as the perfect society and those Christians denominations which were separated from Rome. The council's approach is more nuanced and less triumphalist.

> This is the one Church of Christ which in the Creed is professed as one, holy, catholic and apostolic, which our Savior, after His Resurrection, commissioned Peter to shepherd, and him and the other apostles to extend and direct with authority, which He erected for all ages as "the pillar and mainstay of the truth." This Church constituted and organized in the world as a society, subsists in the Catholic Church, which is governed by the successor of Peter and by the Bishops in communion with him, although many elements of sanctification and of truth are found outside of its visible structure. These elements, as gifts belonging to the Church of Christ, are forces impelling toward catholic unity.[36]

The use of the term "subsists" (*subsistit in*) is the key to the paragraph. Previously, the Church saw an identity between the Church of Christ and the Catholic Church; the Catholic Church "is" (*est*) the Church of Christ and other Christian denominations are not. The change in terminology has profound theological implications, as Francis Sullivan has observed. "This is a positive statement about the Catholic Church, but it does not say or imply that the church of Christ exists nowhere else than in the Catholic Church. It leaves that question open, in a way that official Catholic doctrine had never done before."[37] This question will be answered in the succeeding years by the Congregation for the Doctrine of the Faith in a manner which would lead to complaints from non-Catholics that the church continues to deem other denominations to be second-class Christian organizations not worthy of the title "church." The council acknowledges that although the Catholic Church is not united with other Christian denominations in a formal, juridical sense, Catholics and other Christians are united by baptism and share many beliefs and practices.[38]

The church's new teaching on ecumenism is set forth in *Unitatis redintegratio*. The decree begins with the statement that "the restoration of unity among all Christians is one of the principle concerns of the Second Vatican Council." In chapter 1, entitled "Catholic Principles on Ecumenism," the council acknowledges the separation of Christian communities without laying blame for it solely at the feet of the Orthodox and Protestant communities, as was all too frequent in prior church teaching. However, although

---

36. Second Vatican Council, *Lumen gentium*, 8.
37. Sullivan, *Salvation Outside the Church?* 146.
38. Second Vatican Council, *Lumen gentium*, 25.

non-Catholic Christians "have a right to be called Christian," the council does not treat their respective denominations as on a par with the Catholic Church. Those denominations are "deficient in some respects . . . For it is only through Christ's Catholic Church, which is 'the all-embracing means of salvation,' that they can benefit fully from the means of salvation."[39]

In chapter 2, "The Practice of Ecumenism," the council turns to the ways in which Catholics properly may join together with other Christians in prayer and worship. Joint prayer is permissible, but "worship in common" is allowed only when permitted by the local bishop, a bishops' conference, or the Holy See. Catholics are urged "to acquire a more adequate understanding of the respective doctrines of our separated brethren, their history, their spiritual and liturgical life, their religious psychology and general background." In a statement directed at Catholic theologians, the council introduces the notion of a "hierarchy of truths."

> Moreover, in ecumenical dialogue, Catholic theologians standing fast by the teaching of the Church and investigating the divine mysteries with the separated brethren must proceed with love for the truth, with charity, and with humility. When comparing doctrines with one another, they should remember that in Catholic doctrine there exists a "hierarchy" of truths, since they vary in their relation to the fundamental Christian faith. Thus the way will be opened by which through fraternal rivalry all will be stirred to a deeper understanding and a clearer presentation of the unfathomable riches of Christ.[40]

Over the coming decades, the "hierarchy of truths" will be reduced to a purely formal concept involving only the logical relationship between theological doctrines and not an opening to ecumenical theological cooperation.

In chapter 3, "Churches and Ecclesial Communities Separated from the Roman Apostolic See," the council makes a crucial distinction between "Churches" and "ecclesial Communities," a distinction which will present an obstacle to ecumenical dialogue with denominations that arose out of the Reformation. According to the council, the Orthodox Churches, which separated completely from Rome in the eleventh century, properly may be called "Churches." "These Churches, although separated from us, yet possess true sacraments and above all, by apostolic succession, the priesthood and the Eucharist, whereby they are linked with us in closest intimacy. Therefore some worship in common (*communicatio in sacris*), given

---

39. Second Vatican Council, *Unitatis Redintegratio*, 1, 3.
40. Ibid., 8–9, 11.

suitable circumstances and the approval of Church authority, is not only possible but to be encouraged."[41]

The denominations that grew out of the Reformation, on the other hand, are not entitled to the designation "Church," but instead are referred to by the council as "ecclesial Communities." "Though the ecclesial Communities which are separated from us lack the fullness of unity with us flowing from Baptism, and though we believe they have not retained the proper reality of the Eucharistic mystery in its fullness, especially because of the absence of the sacrament of Orders, nevertheless when they commemorate His death and resurrection in the Lord's Supper, they profess that it signifies life in communion with Christ and look forward to His coming in glory."[42] It is ironic that a conciliar decree concerned with the reunification of Christian communities should begin the ecumenical conversation by announcing that certain Christian denominations are second class churches, characterized by a defective ministry and an imperfect Eucharist.

The council's declaration *Nostra aetate* is only four pages long, yet it is the cornerstone of Church teaching on interreligious dialogue. It stresses the common purpose of all religions, which is to attempt to answer the questions of the mystery of life and death. Probably the most important single sentence in the declaration is the statement that "The Catholic Church rejects nothing that is true and holy in these religions."[43] "Vatican II was the first church council to say something systematically and sympathetically about other world religions."[44]

The council gives examples of what it considers "true and holy" in four major religions. It commends Hinduism, a polytheistic religion, for its "searching philosophical inquiry" and its "ascetical practices." Buddhism, a nontheistic religion, "realizes the radical insufficiency of this changeable world" and aids its adherents in seeking to attain "supreme illumination." The council then turns to non-Christian monotheistic world religions. With respect to Islam, the council notes that its adherents worship the same creator God, link themselves to the faith of Abraham, revere Jesus as a prophet, honor Mary, and "value the moral life and worship God especially through prayer, almsgiving and fasting."[45]

Finally, the council confronts the thorny question of Jewish-Catholic relations, a relationship complicated by a history replete with examples of

41. Ibid., 15.
42. Ibid., 22.
43. Second Vatican Council, *Nostra aetate*, 2.
44. Heft, "Catholicism and Interreligious Dialogue," 4.
45. Second Vatican Council, *Nostra aetate*, 2–3.

Christian persecution of Jews and contempt for the Jewish religion. The council acknowledges the debt that the church owes to Judaism as the religion from which Christianity has sprung. As a result of this shared "spiritual patrimony," the Church must renounce any taint of anti-Semitism. "True, the Jewish authorities and those who followed their lead pressed for the death of Christ; still, what happened in His passion cannot be charged against all the Jews, without distinction, then alive, nor against the Jews of today. Although the Church is the new people of God, the Jews should not be presented as rejected or accursed by God, as if this followed from the Holy Scriptures."[46] The council ends the declaration on a note reminiscent of *Dignitatis humanae*. "The Church reproves, as foreign to the mind of Christ, any discrimination against men or harassment of them because of their race, color, condition of life, or religion."[47]

Nostra aetate marks a turning point in Catholic teaching concerning the Jews. It does not contain any call or hope for the conversion of Jews and recognizes that God's covenant with the Jews remains valid today.[48] In the decades following the council, the Commission for Religious Relations with the Jews has returned to *Nostra aetate* on several occasions. In its 1974 *Guidelines and Suggestions for Implementing the Conciliar Declaration "Nostra aetate" (n. 4)*, the commission emphasizes the need for Christian-Jewish dialogue.

> To tell the truth, such relations as there have been between Jews and Christian have scarcely ever risen above the level of monologue. From now on, real dialogue must be established.
>
> Dialogue presupposes that each side wishes to know the other, and wishes to increase and deepen its knowledge of the other. It constitutes a particularly suitable means of favouring a better mutual knowledge and, especially in the case of dialogue between Jews and Christians, of probing the riches of one's own tradition. Dialogue demands respect for the other as he is; above all, respect for his faith and his religious convictions.[49]

In a 1982 document the commission reiterates the statement from *Nostra aetate* that Israel remains a chosen people.[50] In a 2015 document the commission highlights the common heritage of Judaism and Christianity, which

---

46. Ibid., 4.
47. Ibid., 5.
48. Connelly, *From Enemy to Brother*, 239–72.
49. Commission for Religious Relations with the Jews, *Guidelines*, sec. 1.
50. Commission for Religious Relations with the Jews, *Notes*, sec. 6.

distinguishes Jewish-Christian relations from those between Christians and adherents of other non-Christian religions.

> Dialogue between Jews and Christians then can only be termed "interreligious dialogue" by analogy, that is, dialogue between two intrinsically separate and different religions. It is not the case that two fundamentally diverse religions confront one another after having developed independently of one another or without mutual influence....
>
> Nevertheless, from the theological perspective the dialogue with Judaism has a completely different character and is on a different level in comparison with the other world religions.... However, the dialogue with Judaism occupies a unique position for Christians; Christianity is by its roots connected with Judaism as with no other religion.

Finally, it states unequivocally that the Church does not have a mission to convert the Jews. "The Church is therefore obliged to view evangelisation to Jews, who believe in the one God, in a different manner from that to people of other religions and world views. In concrete terms this means that the Catholic Church neither conducts nor supports any specific institutional mission work directed towards Jews."[51]

Paul VI and the Call for a "New Evangelization"

Paul VI did not issue an encyclical devoted to ecumenism or interreligious dialogue, although he does touch upon these topics near the end of *Ecclesiam suam*. Dialogue is possible with non-Christian believers, including both monotheists (Jews and Muslims) and non-monotheists (e.g. Buddhists and Hindus). Although "the Christian religion is the one and only true religion," the church and these non-Christian faiths have shared values which make common cause possible. Paul realizes that many view the papacy as an obstacle to reconciliation of the Catholic Church and other Christian denominations. Although he holds firm to the notion that the papacy is necessary for the unity of the church, he welcomes representatives of separated churches to participate in the council.[52]

The cornerstone of modern papal teaching on evangelization is Paul's apostolic exhortation *Evangelii nuntiandi*. He began the practice, which has been followed by his successors, of issuing an apostolic exhortation

---

51. Commission for Religious Relations with the Jews, *Gifts and Calling*, 15, 20, 40.
52. Paul VI, *Ecclesiam suam*, 102–12.

following a synod of the world's bishops. The theme of the Third General Assembly of the Synod of Bishops, held in 1974, was evangelization. The primary significance of *Evangelii nuntiandi* is its introduction of the notion of the need for a "new evangelization" of people who are nominally Christian but are living in largely secularized societies.

Paul highlights the centrality of evangelizing to the mission of the church. "The presentation of the Gospel message is not an optional contribution for the Church. . . . It is a question of people's salvation." The church must follow the example of Christ, whose most important message was the proclamation of the kingdom of God. As set forth in Matthew 28: 19–20, Christ gave the disciples the "great commission" to evangelize the world. That command did not end with the apostolic age, but is a continuing duty of all Christians.[53]

He rejects a commonly-held belief that one can accept Christ while rejecting the Catholic Church. The challenge for the evangelizer is to meet these people where they are, speak their language, and offer answers to their deepest questions. The content of evangelization must include "a clear proclamation that, in Jesus Christ . . . salvation is offered to all men, as a gift of God's grace and mercy," together with a "prophetic proclamation of a hereafter." The good news which is proclaimed by the evangelizer is not a message of political liberation. The first proclamation of the kingdom was made by the apostles to people who did not know Christ. Today, there are people who were baptized Christians and yet remain in need of a first proclamation. "This first proclamation is addressed especially to those who have never heard the Good News of Jesus, or to children. But, as a result of the frequent situations of dechristianization in our day, it also proves equally necessary for innumerable people who have been baptized but who live quite outside Christian life."[54]

Paul makes a fundamental distinction between "secularization," a legitimate effort to seek to discover the laws which regulate the universe, from "secularism," "a concept of the world according to which the latter is self-explanatory, without any need for recourse to God." A first proclamation is necessary because many Christians live in countries where secularism is ascendant and religious practices are absent. In order to fulfill its task of evangelization, the church must confront these dual challenges.[55]

Paul's notion of a "new evangelization" is a concept which will be expanded upon and developed in depth by John Paul II in his encyclical

---

53. Paul VI, *Evangelii nuntiandi*, 13.
54. Ibid., 16, 20, 27–28, 32–37, 51–52.
55. Ibid., 55–56.

Redemptoris missio. It also will become the inspiration for Benedict XVI to create the Pontifical Council for Promoting the New Evangelization, which he established in 2010.[56]

John Paul II: Reunification of All Christians Embraced, But Only on Rome's Terms

The central theme of John Paul's first encyclical, *Redemptoris hominis*, is redemption through Jesus Christ. "The Church's fundamental function in every age and particularly in ours is to direct man's gaze, to point the awareness and experience of the whole of humanity towards the mystery of God, to help all men to be familiar with the profundity of the Redemption taking place in Christ Jesus."[57] This encyclical would become the first of a trilogy on the Trinity.[58] The audience for the encyclical includes not only bishops, clergy, and the Catholic laity, but "all men and women of good will." John Paul refers back to Paul's encyclical, *Ecclesiam suam*, and commends Paul's effort to open a dialogue with the modern world. Paul "knew how to display *ad extra*, externally, the true countenance of the Church, in spite of the various internal weaknesses that affected her in the postconciliar period." He admits that the church has been guilty of "triumphalism," but also complains that "criticism too should have its just limits." He praises the spirit of collegiality displayed at the Second Vatican Council. He is enthusiastic but cautious about the push toward ecumenism undertaken by John XXIII, Paul VI, and the council. "True ecumenical activity means openness, drawing closer, availability for dialogue, and a shared investigation of the truth in the full evangelical and Christian sense; but in no way does it or can it mean giving up or in any way diminishing the treasures of divine truth that the Church has constantly confessed and taught." Christ's redemptive action has ecumenical consequences. Because all Christians are redeemed by Christ, they should strive for unity, the first step of which is for the various Christian denominations to get to know each other.[59]

In *Redemptoris missio*, John Paul reaffirms the continuing validity of the church's missionary activity, which had become apparent to him during his extensive travels as pope. The growth in the number of people who

---

56. Benedict XVI, *Ubicumque et semper*, arts. 1–4.

57. John Paul II, *Redemptoris hominis*, 10.

58. John Paul informed his biographer George Weigel that the idea of a series of encyclicals on the Trinity did not arise until after the publication of *Redemptoris hominis*. Weigel, *Witness to Hope*, 386, 922 n. 7.

59. John Paul II, *Redemptoris hominis*, 4–6, 11–12.

have not been exposed to Christ is increasing, whereas "Missionary activity specifically directed 'to the nations' (*ad gentes*) appears to be waning." To counteract this trend, he "invites the Church *to renew her missionary commitment*."[60]

He identifies three different forms of missionary activity which are necessary today. The first involves preaching Christ and the gospel to those who have not heard of them. The second is the mission to established Christian communities, which takes the form of pastoral care. The third involves the recent phenomenon of the dechristianization of traditionally Christian countries. "There is an intermediate situation, particularly in countries with ancient Christian roots, and occasionally in the younger Churches as well, where entire groups of the baptized have lost a living sense of the faith, or even no longer consider themselves members of the Church, and live a life far removed from Christ and his Gospel. In this case what is needed is a 'new evangelization' or a 're-evangelization.'"[61]

With respect to the mission *ad gentes*, it is properly centered in urban areas in Asia, where Christians remain a small minority. In addition to the lack of Christians in traditional mission territories, there is also the phenomenon of large populations of non-Christians migrating to traditional Christian countries. Demographic shifts and the increase in the populations of non-Christian countries pose new challenges for the Church. A majority of the world's population has "not yet received an initial proclamation of Christ." There also is an ecumenical aspect to missionary activity, since the disunity among Christians negatively affects their missionary efforts.[62]

In the developing nations of the South, the church's missionary activity must go beyond preaching the Word to include activities to promote development, such as the establishment of "schools, hospitals, printing presses, universities and experimental farms." But even in these regions, such activity is not aimed primarily at economic development. This is even truer in the developed North, "which is prone to a moral and spiritual poverty caused by 'overdevelopment.'"[63]

In John Paul's major encyclical on ecumenism *Ut unum sint*, he takes up the challenge laid down by the Second Vatican Council in its decree *Unitatis redintegratio*. The council had decreed that "restoration of unity

---

60. Ibid., 1. The waning of Catholic missionary work in the post-conciliar period stands in sharp contrast to the growth of missionary activity in the global South by evangelical Protestants and Muslims. Weigel, *Witness to Hope*, 633.

61. John Paul II, *Redemptoris missio*, 33.

62. Ibid., 37, 40, 50.

63. Ibid., 58–59.

among all Christians is one of [its] principal concerns."[64] For John Paul, reunification is not an option for the church, but is part of its essence. "Believers in Christ, united in following in the footsteps of the martyrs, cannot remain divided. If they wish truly and effectively to oppose the world's tendency to reduce to powerlessness the Mystery of Redemption, they must *profess together the same truth about the Cross*." In undertaking its ecumenical activities, the church recognizes that there is value to be found in other Christian communities.[65]

John Paul emphasizes the primacy of prayer in ecumenism. "When brothers and sisters who are not in perfect communion with one another come together to pray, the Second Vatican Council defines their prayer as *the soul of the whole ecumenical movement*." He cites many examples of ecumenical prayer in which he has participated as pope. But he cautions that ecumenical prayer has its limits. "Certainly, due to disagreements in matters of faith, it is not yet possible to celebrate together the same Eucharistic Liturgy."[66]

He notes that ecumenical dialogue is trickier once one moves from the field of common prayer and enters into the domain of doctrine. "It must be stated that the dogmatic *formulas of* the Church's Magisterium were from the very beginning suitable for communicating revealed truth, and that as they are they remain forever suitable for communicating this truth to those who interpret them correctly."[67] This statement begs the question of whether any purpose can be served by ecumenical dialogue in the area of doctrine, if the Catholic Church remains firm in the belief that it already possesses the most suitable formulas for expressing revealed truths.

John Paul's approach to the denominations that arose out of the Reformation is ambivalent. He credits them with having begun the ecumenical movement, especially with the founding of the World Council of Churches, but he does not explain why the Catholic Church is not a member.[68] He then identifies five potential obstacles to Christian unity which need to be explored before true communion may be achieved.

> It is already possible to identify the areas in need of fuller study before a true consensus of faith can be achieved: 1) the relationship between Sacred Scripture, as the highest authority in matters of faith, and Sacred Tradition, as indispensable

64. Second Vatican Council, *Unitatis redintegratio*, 1.
65. John Paul II, *Ut unum sint*, 20, 1, 11.
66. Ibid., 21, 52–54, 45.
67. Ibid., 38.
68. Ibid., 65–69.

to the interpretation of the Word of God; 2) the Eucharist, as the Sacrament of the Body and Blood of Christ, an offering of praise to the Father, the sacrificial memorial and Real Presence of Christ and the sanctifying outpouring of the Holy Spirit; 3) Ordination, as a Sacrament, to the threefold ministry of the episcopate, presbyterate, and diaconate; 4) the Magisterium of the Church, entrusted to the Pope and the Bishops in communion with him, understood as a responsibility and an authority exercised in the name of Christ for teaching and safeguarding the faith; 5) the Virgin Mary, as Mother of God and Icon of the Church, the spiritual Mother who intercedes for Christ's disciples and for all humanity.[69]

One would expect to see the office of the Roman Pontiff on this list, if not at the top of it, but John Paul addresses that stumbling block separately in a later portion of the encyclical. "The Catholic Church's conviction that in the ministry of the Bishop of Rome she has preserved, in fidelity to the Apostolic Tradition and the faith of the Fathers, the visible sign and guarantor of unity, constitutes a difficulty for most other Christians, whose memory is marked by certain painful recollections. To the extent that we are responsible for these, I join my Predecessor Paul VI in asking forgiveness." John Paul does not propose a solution to this seemingly insurmountable problem, but he is encouraged that the problem is the subject of serious study He leaves no doubt, however, as to where he and the Catholic Church stand on this question. "The Catholic Church, both in her *praxis* and in her solemn documents, holds that the communion of the particular Churches with the Church of Rome, and of their Bishops with the Bishop of Rome, is—in God's plan—an essential requisite of full and visible communion."[70] In other words, reconciliation between the Catholic Church and the churches and ecclesial communities which are separated from it is possible only if those denominations are willing to submit to the primacy of the Roman Pontiff. Both the World Council of Churches and the World Alliance of Reformed Churches reacted negatively to the encyclical and rejected the notion that the papal office should be seen as "the visible sign and guarantor of unity" among Christians.[71] Although John Paul proclaimed his commitment to ecumenism, especially with the Orthodox Churches, his view that reunification can only be accomplished on Rome's terms reflects a pre-conciliar attitude.

69. Ibid., 79.
70. Ibid., 88–89, 97.
71. Cassidy, *Ecumenism and Interreligious Dialogue*, 40.

Ecclesia de Eucharistia is the only encyclical authored by John Paul between 1998 and his death in 2005. It is a rather dense work of ecclesiology in which he explores the role played by the Eucharist in the life of the church. He links together the Eucharist and apostolic succession in a manner that places significant limitations on ecumenical worship. The Eucharist was instituted by Christ in the presence of the apostles and entrusted to them, and they in turn handed it down to their successors. Therefore, the celebration of the Eucharist by a Christian denomination which lacks apostolic succession, as defined by the Catholic Church, is defective. As a result, there can be no joint Eucharistic celebration between Catholics and those ecclesial communities.[72]

One area of fundamental disagreement between Catholics and Protestants is the role of Mary in the history of salvation and in the life of the church.[73] *Redemptoris Mater* is John Paul's meditation on the role of Mary. He engages in an in-depth examination of the New Testament record of Mary's activities from the Annunciation through Pentecost. The Annunciation is the manifestation of Mary's complete faith in God, a faith he compares to that of Abraham. He refers to her time in Nazareth after the return from Egypt as "the long period of the hidden life."[74] He understands the story of the wedding feast at Cana (John 2:1–11) as prefiguring Mary's role as mediator with Christ. When the host of the wedding runs out of wine, Mary seeks Jesus's help and instructs the attendants to do whatever he directs. The result is Jesus's miracle of turning water into wine.[75]

The concept of the "pilgrim church" was employed by the Second Vatican Council, establishing an analogy with Israel's journey through the desert during the Exodus. John Paul uses this analogy to describe the relationship between Mary and the church. "The moment of Pentecost in Jerusalem had been prepared for by the moment of the Annunciation in Nazareth, as well as by the Cross. In the Upper Room Mary's journey meets the Church's journey of faith. In what way?" His answer is that, although "Mary did not directly receive this apostolic mission," her presence in the Upper Room with the Apostles in some unexplained way united her with their mission to be witnesses to Christ.[76]

He discusses several unrelated Marian themes in no particular order. He refers to places of Marian apparitions—Guadalupe, Lourdes, Fatima,

---

72. John Paul II, *Ecclesia de Eucharistia*, 27, 29, 44.
73. Noll and Nystrom, *Is the Reformation Over?* 133–37.
74. John Paul II, *Redemptoris Mater*, 13–14, 17.
75. Ibid., 21.
76. Ibid., 26.

Jasna Gora—as constituting "a specific 'geography' of faith and Marian devotion." He acknowledges that a significant obstacle to the unification of the Catholic Church, on the one hand, with other churches and ecclesial communities, on the other hand, is "the role of Mary in the work of salvation." He finds common ground in the fact that "they recognize her as the Mother of the Lord." In particular, he emphasizes the role that Mary plays in the worship and iconography of the Orthodox Churches.[77]

These statements underestimate the seriousness of the divide between the Catholic Church and most Protestant denominations concerning the role of Mary. Those denominations do not have statues of her in their churches, nor do they sanction prayer to her. In particular, her role as mediator with Christ is in no way a part of their theology. He pays lip service to the notion that Jesus is the sole mediator between God the Father and humans. But it is hard to reconcile that position with the following statement. "Through her mediation, subordinate to that of the Redeemer, Mary contributes in a special way to the union of the pilgrim Church on earth with the eschatological and heavenly reality of the Communion of Saints, since she has already been 'assumed into heaven.'"[78] Either Jesus is the sole mediator, or he is the primary mediator and Mary is a subordinate mediator. John Paul maintains that he subscribes to the former interpretation, although his words suggest that he leans toward the latter.

Francis: Interreligious Dialogue and the Quest for Peace

In chapter 4 of *Evangelli gaudium*, entitled "The Social Dimension of Evangelization," Francis examines the issue of "dialogue," which had been the leitmotiv of Paul's encyclical *Ecclesiam suam*. "Evangelization also involves the path of dialogue. For the Church today, three areas of dialogue stand out where she needs to be present in order to promote full human development and to pursue the common good: dialogue with states, dialogue with society—including dialogue with cultures and the sciences—and dialogue with other believers who are not part of the Catholic Church." Francis follows the approach of the Second Vatican Council's decree on ecumenism when he explains the manner in which the concept of a "hierarchy of truths" can be employed to foster ecumenical dialogue. "If we concentrate on the convictions we share, and if we keep in mind the principle of the hierarchy of

---

77. Ibid., 28–33.
78. Ibid., 38, 41.

truths, we will be able to progress decidedly towards common expressions of proclamation, service and witness."[79]

He situates his discussion of the relationship between Christians and Judaism in between his discussion of ecumenical dialogue and his discussion of interreligious dialogue. This placement is consistent with the Vatican's practice of treating Judaism separately from other non-Christian religions. In the curia, the Commission for Religious Relations with the Jews is linked organizationally to the Pontifical Council for Promoting Christian Unity rather than with the Pontifical Council for Interreligious Dialogue. "As Christians, we cannot consider Judaism a foreign religion. . . . With them, we believe in the one God who acts in history, and with them we accept his revealed word." He expresses regret for the persecutions that Jews have been forced to endure, "especially those that have involved Christians." Christians and Jews share not only the Hebrew Scriptures but also a "common concern for justice and the development of peoples."[80]

Francis links interreligious dialogue and the quest for world peace, a tacit acknowledgment that religious wars have been a major source of armed conflict not only in the past but even today, especially between Christian and Muslim groups in Africa. The relationship between Christians and Muslims is strained by their different visions of church-state relations. Whereas Muslims in traditionally Christian countries enjoy freedom to practice their religion and worship publicly, the same in not true for Christians residing in many Muslim countries. He makes a plea that "countries of Islamic tradition . . . grant Christians freedom to worship and to practice their faith, in light of the freedom which followers of Islam enjoy in Western countries!" He also reaches out to secularists who do not practice any religion, people whom religious pollsters in the United States have labeled "the nones." "As believers, we also feel close to those who do not consider themselves part of any religious tradition, yet sincerely seek the truth, goodness and beauty which we believe have their highest expression and source in God. We consider them as precious allies in the commitment to defending human dignity, in building peaceful coexistence between peoples and in protecting creation."[81]

---

79. Francis, *Evangelii gaudium*, 238, 246.
80. Ibid., 247–49.
81. Ibid., 250, 253, 257.

The Congregation for the Doctrine of the Faith: Catholic Triumphalism Returns

In the last two decades, the Congregation for the Doctrine of the Faith has issued documents on ecumenism and interreligious dialogue which are at variance from the optimistic and welcoming tone of *Unitatis redintegratio* and *Nostra aetate*. The congregation has endeavored to chill what it perceived to be overbroad and overenthusiastic readings of those conciliar documents by certain theologians. It stresses not opportunities for ecumenism and interreligious dialogue but the limits of such activities, repeatedly emphasizing the necessity of the Roman Pontiff for Christian unity and the uniqueness of the life, death, and resurrection of Jesus Christ in God's plan of salvation. The conclusion drawn by Protestant and non-Christian religious leaders from these documents is that the Catholic Church no longer places a priority on ecumenism and interreligious dialogue; instead, it has returned to its pre-conciliar attitude towards other Christian denominations and non-Christian religions.

In *Ut unum sint*, John Paul stated that he had been asked by members of other Christian communities to "find a way of exercising the primacy which, while in no way renouncing what is essential to its mission, is nonetheless open to a new situation."[82] In 1997, the congregation took up this task in *The Primacy of the Successor of Peter in the Mystery of the Church*. The document, which is characterized as "reflections," has as its purpose "only to recall the *essential* points of Catholic doctrine on the primacy."[83]

The origins of papal primacy are found in the New Testament, where Peter was expressly appointed by Christ as the first among the Apostles; his presence and death in Rome establish the preeminence of that see over other ancient centers of the early church. Any attempt to reduce the primacy of Rome to a primacy of honor (the position adopted by the Orthodox Churches) is rebuffed. The office of the Roman Pontiff is a teaching office of a particular character; "it is an office that involves a charism: the Holy Spirit's special assistance to the Successor of Peter, which also involves, in certain cases, the prerogative of infallibility." As such, the pope's power is supreme and "there is no other authority to which the Roman Pontiff must juridically answer for his exercise of the gift he has received," such as an ecumenical council. The congregation is careful, however, to distinguish the "supreme" power which the pope possesses from the power of an absolute monarch. There are inherent limitations on the pope, since he "is subject to

---

82. John Paul II, *Ut unum sint*, 95.

83. Congregation for the Doctrine of the Faith, *Primacy of the Successor of Peter*, 2.

the Word of God, to the Catholic faith. . . . He does not make arbitrary decisions, but is the spokesman for the will of the Lord." As God's spokesman, he alone has the final say on what constitutes Catholic doctrine. Although the congregation admits that "human errors and even serious failings can be found in the history of the papacy," it invites all Christians to embrace the pope as the true sign of the unity of the Church of Christ.[84]

Any hopes that non-Catholic Christians might accept this invitation to embrace the pope as the living symbol of Christian unity were dashed in the wake of the congregation's publication of the declaration *Dominus Jesus*. The congregation makes clear, in stark and sometimes insensitive language, that those Christian denominations arising out of the Reformation are not entitled to be called "churches" in the proper sense of the term.

The stated purpose of the declaration is to set forth Catholic doctrine on the issue of ecumenism and interreligious dialogue in refutation of certain errors that have arisen.[85] The congregation seeks to put an end to such uncertainty by the frequent repetition throughout the document of what "must be *firmly held*" or what "must be *firmly believed*" by Catholics concerning salvation through Jesus Christ and the Catholic Church.

In section 1, "The Fullness and Definitiveness of the Revelation of Jesus Christ," the congregation reemphasizes Catholic doctrine concerning the uniqueness and universal applicability of salvation in Jesus Christ. "In fact, it must be *firmly believed* that, in the mystery of Jesus Christ . . . the full revelation of divine truth is given." Any suggestion that there are complements to the revelation of Jesus Christ in other religions would undermine the belief that the complete and final revelation of God has been given in Jesus Christ. The congregation draws a sharp distinction Christian *faith* (a divine gift) and the *belief* possessed by non-Christians (a matter of human wisdom).[86] "*Dominus Jesus* (section 7) appears to say that non-Christian traditions are purely human creations."[87] Only the books of the Old Testament and New Testament may be considered inspired texts. Whatever value the sacred writings of other religions have for their adherents they "receive from the mystery of Christ" in some unexplained manner.[88]

Section 2, "The Incarnate Logos and the Holy Spirit in the Work of Salvation," rejects any theological understanding of Jesus Christ as complementary to salvific figures in other religions. Section 3, "Unicity and Universality

---

84. Ibid., 3, 7, 9–10, 13, 15.
85. Congregation for the Doctrine of the Faith, *Dominus Jesus*, 4.
86. Ibid., 5–7.
87. McKim, *Religious Diversity*, 11 n. 7.
88. Congregation for the Doctrine of the Faith, *Dominus Jesus*, 8.

of the Salvific Mystery of Jesus Christ," affirms that Jesus Christ is the sole and unique mediator of the Father's salvific action.[89] The role of the church is explained in section 4, "Unicity and Unity of the Church," the section which caused the most volatile reaction from Protestants. The congregation explores the meaning of the term *subsistit in* in conciliar documents and its implications for ecumenism.

> Therefore, in connection with the unicity and universality of the salvific mediation of Jesus Christ, the unicity of the Church founded by him must be *firmly believed* as a truth of the Catholic faith....
>
> The Catholic faithful *are required to profess* that there is a historical continuity—rooted in apostolic succession—between the Church founded by Christ and the Catholic Church.... With the expression *subsistit in*, the Second Vatican Council sought to harmonize two doctrinal statements: on the one hand, that the Church of Christ, despite the divisions which exist among Christians, continues to exist fully only in the Catholic Church, and on the other hand, that "outside of her structure, many elements can be found of sanctification and truth," that is, in those Churches and ecclesial communities which are not yet in full communion with the Catholic Church.
>
> Therefore, there exists a single Church of Christ, which subsists in the Catholic Church, governed by the Successor of Peter and by the Bishops in communion with him....
>
> On the other hand, the ecclesial communities which have not preserved the valid Episcopate and the genuine and integral substance of the Eucharistic mystery, are not Churches in the proper sense; however, those who are baptized in these communities are, by Baptism, incorporated in Christ and thus are in a certain communion, albeit imperfect, with the Church.[90]

The negative reaction of Protestant and non-Christian religious leaders to the document did not go unnoticed among members of the church's hierarchy. According to Cardinal Kasper, Protestants were particularly outraged by the assertion that their denominations are not worthy of the title "church."

> ... This statement angered many Protestant Christians, who perceived it as bold and offensive. The question arose: Is real dialogue possible for a church and with a church which claims to have the absolute truth in an infallible way? For dialogue presupposes openness toward other positions and an encounter of

---

89. Ibid., 10, 13–14.
90. Ibid., 16.

equals. So the question was, and for many still is: Is this document not a sign that the Catholic Church understands ecumenism only as a simple return of the separated brethren into the fold of the Catholic Church and thus she withdraws from the spirit and the precepts of the Second Vatican Council and relinquishes the concept of dialogue? An ecumenical cooling, a doubt and—as many see it—an ecumenical crisis ensued.[91]

Lutheran-Catholic Relations and the Future of the Ecumenical Enterprise

The Congregation for the Doctrine of the Faith has been criticized, from both inside and outside the Church, for its emphasis on the manner in which non-Catholic churches and ecclesial Communities are deficient vis-a-vis the Catholic Church. The focus of the Pontifical Council for Promoting Christian Unity, on the other hand, has been on those matters of faith which Catholics and other Christians share in common. This has been especially apparent in connection with Lutheran-Catholic relations. In 1999 the Catholic Church and the Lutheran World Federation issued their *Joint Declaration on the Doctrine of Justification*. The doctrine of justification by faith was a central tenet of Luther's Reformation. The conflict over the doctrine of justification was not some abstract theological disputation; it had serious implications for the Church's doctrine of purgatory, its sacramental system, and the authority of the pope to grant indulgences, as Alister McGrath has remarked. "The most radical element of Luther's doctrine of justification is its conception of salvation as a matter affecting God and the individual. The individual's relationship with God is direct, determined by faith in God's promises and the salvation procured by Christ's death and resurrection. There is no longer any need for intermediaries—for the intercession of Mary or the saints. There is no necessary role for the church, its sacraments, or its priests in the dynamic of salvation."[92] If there is no purgatory, then there is no theological basis for the papal system of indulgences.

The upshot of the dispute was reciprocal condemnations between the Catholic Church and the Lutheran Confessions. "From the Reformation perspective, justification was the crux of all the disputes. Doctrinal condemnations were put forward both in the Lutheran Confessions and by the Roman Catholic Church's Council of Trent. These condemnations are still

91. Kaspar, *That They May All Be One*, 34–35.
92. McGrath, *Christianity's Dangerous Idea*, 43–44.

valid today and thus have a church-dividing effect." By means of the Joint Declaration, the Catholic Church and the Lutheran World Federation demonstrate that the reciprocal condemnations should not continue; the Joint Declaration shows that the Catholic Church and the Lutheran Confessions share "a consensus on basic truths of the doctrine of justification and shows that the remaining differences in its explication are no longer the occasion for doctrinal condemnations."[93]

In contemplation of the five hundredth anniversary of the beginning of the Reformation, in 2013 the council issued *From Conflict to Communion: Lutheran-Catholic Common Commemoration of the Reformation in 2017*. The document acknowledges that the Catholic Church may have something to learn from that movement. "The upcoming year of 2017 challenges Catholics and Lutherans to discuss in dialogue the issues and consequences of the Wittenberg Reformation, which centered on the person and thought of Martin Luther, and to develop perspectives for the remembrance and appropriation of the Reformation today. Luther' reforming agenda poses a spiritual and theological challenge for both contemporary Catholics and Lutherans."[94] Luther's posting of the Ninety-Five Theses was not intended as an attack on the church but as a call for an academic discussion "regarding the theory and practice of indulgences." Luther offered arguments in support of his position that, as there was no scriptural basis for the doctrine of purgatory, there is no theological basis for the system of indulgences. Rome, on the other hand, eschewed dialogue, offering Luther the choice "to recant or be proclaimed a heretic." The Church feared that Luther's arguments, if accepted, would undermine papal authority.[95]

Some critics of religion argue that religions are by their very nature intolerant of opposing beliefs, because they all make exclusive claims to the truth. For example, Sam Harris states that "while all faiths have been touched, here and there, by the spirit of ecumenicalism, the central tenet of every religious tradition is that all others are mere repositories of error or, at best, dangerously incomplete. Intolerance is thus intrinsic to every creed."[96] Perhaps the situation is not as dire as Harris suggests. The answer to the question raised by Cardinal Kasper at the start of this chapter is that dialogue is possible if the church confronts honestly the history of its relations with other religions and admits that its arrogance has proven to be a

---

93. Pontifical Council for Promoting Christian Unity, *Joint Declaration on Justification*, 1, 5.

94. Pontifical Council for Promoting Christian Unity, *From Conflict to Communion*, 3.

95. Ibid., 40, 45–46, 52–53.

96. Harris, *The End of Faith*, 13.

stumbling block to both ecumenism and interreligious dialogue. As *From Conflict to Communion* notes, the church is not doomed to repeat the mistakes of the past. "What happened in the past cannot be changed, but what is remembered of the past and how it is remembered can, with the passage of time, indeed change. Remembrance makes the past present. While the past itself is unalterable, the presence of the past in the present is alterable. In view of 2017, the point is not to tell a different history, but to tell that history differently."[97] Ecumenism and interreligious dialogue require the humility to accept the damage caused by past (and present) arrogance. But infallibility seldom is accompanied by humility.

---

97. Pontifical Council for Promoting Christian Unity, *From Conflict to Communion*, 16.

11

Constancy: Human Sexuality—Marriage and Divorce, Birth Control, and Homosexuality

> *It is only in the marital relationship that the use of sexual faculty can be morally good.*
>
> —Congregation for the Doctrine of the Faith

> *Augustine speculated wistfully about the time before the Fall in Eden, when Adam and Eve's private parts had behaved in an orderly fashion. The Church has been trying to tell private parts what to do ever since.*
>
> —Diarmaid MacCulloch

The Supreme Court and the Catholic Church Confront Contraception and the Gay Rights Movement

IN THE SECOND HALF of the twentieth century, two developments touching upon human sexuality—contraception and the emergence of the gay rights movement—presented particular challenges not only to the Catholic Church but also to the legal systems of many countries. In the United States, laws against contraception and homosexual activities were on the books, even if seldom enforced. Church teachings against contraception and homosexual practices date back to the earliest days of Christianity. The manner in which the highest legal and religious authorities have dealt with their respective precedents in the face of these challenges is instructive. The United States Supreme Court would display a willingness to overrule its precedents on sexual conduct, going so far as to say not only that such precedents had outlived their usefulness, but that they were bad law from the inception. Popes, on the other hand, would hold fast to the centuries old teachings of the church on human sexuality, fearing that any deviation from prior teaching might undermine the credibility of papal teaching authority.

The development of the progesterone pill in the 1950s, and its approval by the United States Food and Drug Administration in 1960, helped to usher in the sexual revolution of the 1960s.[1] The widespread availability of the pill and its undisputed effectiveness at preventing pregnancy made it the preferred means of contraception for married and unmarried women alike. Legal attacks on laws outlawing artificial contraception quickly followed. In 1961, two executives of the Planned Parenthood League of Connecticut were found guilty and fined one hundred dollars for violating a statute that prohibited the supplying of medical advice to married couples concerning the means for preventing pregnancy. The case, *Griswold v. Connecticut*, reached the United States Supreme Court in 1965.[2] The Court held that Connecticut's ban on the use of artificial contraception by married couples violated their constitutional right to privacy. Although a right to privacy is not expressly set forth in the Constitution, the Court found that such a right resided in the "penumbra" of the Bill of Rights. Marriage is a fundamental right, and sexual relations within marriage are no business of the state. "Would we allow the police to search the sacred precincts of marital bedrooms for telltale signs of the use of contraceptives? The very idea is repulsive to the notions of privacy surrounding the marriage relationship. We deal with a right of privacy older than the Bill of Rights——older than our political parties, older than our school system. Marriage is a coming together for better or for worse, hopefully enduring, and intimate to the degree of being sacred."[3]

The ruling in *Griswold* was reaffirmed and expanded a few years later when the Court invalidated a Massachusetts law banning the dispensing of contraceptive devices to unmarried persons.[4] *Griswold*'s greatest impact, however, would be on the question of the constitutionality of laws criminalizing abortion. The right of privacy which *Griswold* had introduced into the legal lexicon would form one of the pillars of the Supreme Court's decision

---

1. Noonan, *Contraception*, 460.
2. 381 U.S. 479 (1965).
3. *Id.* at 485–86.
4. Eisenstadt v. Baird, 405 U.S. 438 (1972).

in *Roe v. Wade*,[5] where it held that a woman had a constitutional right to terminate a pregnancy through abortion.[6]

The emergence of the gay rights movement presented the Supreme Court with even more difficult challenges. The first case to reach the Court was in 1986. In *Bowers v. Hardwick*, the defendant had been charged with violating a Georgia sodomy statute by engaging in sexual relations with another man in his home.[7] The Court gave short shrift to the defendant's argument that he had a fundamental right to engage in consensual homosexual acts with another adult male in private, noting that until 1961, homosexual activity was a crime in all fifty states.[8]

Only seventeen years later, the Court again faced the question of a state law which criminalized private, consensual, adult homosexual conduct. In *Lawrence v. Texas*, two adults were convicted of "'deviate sexual intercourse, namely anal sex, with a member of the same sex (man).'"[9] The defendants challenged their convictions as violations of the Equal Protection Clause of the Fourteenth Amendment, a challenge which would require the Court to reconsider its recent precedent in *Bowers*.

> It must be acknowledged, of course, that the Court in *Bowers* was making the broader point that for centuries there have been powerful voices to condemn homosexual conduct as immoral. The condemnation has been shaped by religious beliefs, conceptions of right and acceptable behavior, and respect for the traditional family. . . . These considerations do not answer the question before us, however. The issue is whether the majority may use the power of the State to enforce those views on the society through the operation of the criminal law.[10]

The Court would proceed to answer that question in the negative and, in the process, expressly overrule a precedent that was less than two decades old. "*Bowers* was not correct when it was decided, and it is not correct today. It ought not to remain binding precedent. *Bowers v. Hardwick* shall be and now

---

5. 410 U.S. 113 (1973).

6. For a discussion of the impact of *Griswold* on the Court's decision in *Roe v. Wade*, see Sunstein, *Radicals in Robes*, 81–109.

7. 478 U.S. 186 (1986).

8. *Id.* at 193–96.

9. 539 U.S. 558, 563 (2003).

10. *Id.* at 571.

is overruled."[11] Justice Scalia, in a prescient dissent, predicted that the decision would place in jeopardy state laws against same-sex marriage.[12]

It is one thing for the Court to hold that a state may not criminalize private, consensual, adult homosexual activity; it is quite another thing for it to decide that two members of the same sex could compel a state to issue a marriage license to them in contravention of a state law defining marriage as a union of one man and one woman. That was the issue that was presented to the Court in *Obergefell v. Hodges*.[13] Once again, the Court was confronted with a prior ruling that seemingly should have disposed of the case summarily. In the 1972 case of *Baker v. Nelson*, the Court had held that "the exclusion of same-sex couples from marriage did not present a substantial federal question."[14] Nevertheless, the Court in *Obergefell* held that state laws excluding same-sex couples from contracting a civil marriage violated the Due Process and Equal Protection Clauses of the Fourteenth Amendment. In so doing, the Court expressly overruled *Baker v. Nelson*.

By overruling its precedents, the Court implicitly acknowledges that any opinion it issues is subject to revision or even reversal; they always remain provisional judgments. The Court is not blessed with the charism of infallibility possessed by the Roman Pontiff or by the worldwide college of bishops in union with the pope. In the famous dictum of Justice Robert Jackson, "We are not final because we are infallible, but we are infallible only because we are final."[15] The doctrine of infallibility, on the other hand, has tempted popes to treat most teachings of their predecessors as irreformable, even those teachings that have never been claimed to be infallible. If the possibility of papal error were to be forthrightly acknowledged, the faithful might be emboldened to believe that they can dissent from any papal teaching not expressly declared to be infallible.

At the same time that the Supreme Court in Washington was facing the question of contraception, the Second Vatican Council was meeting in Rome. "The timing of the Council and the Supreme Court's decision legalizing the sale of oral contraceptives in 1965 were preternaturally close."[16] Paul VI would remove the issue of contraception from the council, as he awaited the findings of a papal commission that was studying the matter. Any change in church teaching on contraception, however, would neces-

11. *Id.* at 578.
12. *Id.* at 590 (Scalia, J., dissenting).
13. 135 S. Ct. 2584 (2015).
14. 409 U.S. 810 (1972).
15. Brown v. Allen, 344 U.S. 443, 540 (1953) (Jackson, J., concurring).
16. McDonough, *Catholic Labyrinth*, 15.

sitate a reconsideration of centuries of prior consistent and unambiguous teaching. As John Noonan has noted, "The teachers of the Church have taught without hesitation or variation that certain acts preventing procreation are gravely sinful. . . . The teaching on contraception is clear and apparently fixed forever."[17] The manner in which Paul would handle the issue is emblematic of modern papal teaching on human sexuality, marriage and divorce, and birth control. Church teaching on those subjects is the same today as it was in 1870 when the doctrine of papal infallibility was announced; constancy, rather than development or contradiction, is the papal watchword on matters of human sexuality.

Constancy in teaching should be expected in a religious community whose history stretches back to the first century. Popes always have considered themselves custodians of an unchanging faith. According to John O'Malley, "The church is by definition a conservative institution. Its sole reason for existence is to pass on unadulterated a message received long ago."[18] Constancy in teaching is present above all in those doctrines of faith which are at the heart of Christian belief. For example, the key Christological dogmas of the human and divine nature of Christ were defined authoritatively by ecumenical councils in the fourth and fifth centuries.[19] These dogmas are seldom the subject of modern papal teaching, because they are settled doctrine which rarely generate controversy.

Constancy has been a hallmark of Catholic doctrine in certain matters of morals as well as in matters of faith. Although papal teaching on human sexuality has been constant, such constancy has not resulted in universal acceptance by Catholics of papal teaching in this area. A large percentage of the laity do not respond to such teaching with the docility that Rome expects from Catholics.[20] Instead, the teaching has produced widespread dissent, especially among Catholics in North America and Europe. Much of the dissent takes the form of simply ignoring church teaching on matters of sexual relations. Many Catholics refuse to follow rules which have been decreed by celibate males who do not have to live with the consequences of their dictates. The divide between the hierarchy and rank and file Catholics

---

17. Noonan, *Contraception*, 6.

18. O'Malley, *Catholic History*, 1. "Orthodoxy was the ancient Petrine tradition, and what threatened it was novelty. New ideas and practices were essentially wrong by virtue of their very newness, however trivial they might seem" (Collins, *Keepers of the Keys*, 60).

19. Jenkins, *Jesus Wars* and Kelly, *Ecumenical Councils*, contain informative accounts of the early ecumenical councils.

20. "The faithful receive with docility the teachings and directives that their pastors give them in different forms" (*Catechism*, No. 87).

is the widest over divorce and contraception. Bishops have acknowledged the pastoral challenge presented by the denial of the sacraments to Catholics who have divorced and remarried. With respect to the church's ban on certain forms of birth control, the use of artificial contraception by Catholic women of childbearing years actually increased following the publication of Paul's encyclical *Humanae vitae*.[21]

Homosexuality has not been the subject of any major papal teaching, but it has been addressed on several occasions in the last thirty years by the Congregation for the Doctrine of the Faith. The congregation's position on homosexual activity is unyielding: while a homosexual orientation is not sinful in itself, all homosexual acts are inherently disordered and gravely sinful. As a result, the church has steadfastly opposed any legal recognition of civil unions or same-sex marriages. Although the congregation has stated—albeit not loudly or often—that homosexuals should not be the subject to legal discrimination due to their sexual orientation, it has supported the exclusion of homosexuals from certain professions and the denial of their right to adopt children.

The Indissolubility of Marriage Affirmed

The church's teaching on marriage and divorce has been constant throughout the age of infallibility. The best summary of this teaching is found in the *Catechism*.[22] The twofold purpose of marriage is unitive and procreative. "The spouses' union achieves the twofold end of marriage: the good of the spouses themselves and the transmission of life." Each act of marital sexual activity must "remain ordered *per se* to the procreation of human life." Divorce is an offense against the dignity of marriage and "introduces disorder into the family and into society." Any sexual activity outside of marriage is a grave sin.[23]

The first modern papal teaching to deal with marriage was Leo XIII's encyclical *Arcanum*.[24] He explores the history of marriage from its biblical beginnings up to the time of Christ, highlighting the deficiencies of marriage among both the Jews and the Gentiles. Marriage was instituted by God in the Garden of Eden. But marriage among the Jews departed from the ideal of one

---

21. Tentler, *Catholics and Contraception*, 220.

22. The "*Catechism* . . . provides the most accessible, complete statement of official Roman Catholic teaching that exists today" (Noll and Nystrom, *Is the Reformation Over?* 14).

23. *Catechism*, Nos. 2363, 2366, 2385, 2390.

24. Pollard, *Papacy in the Age of Toralitarianism*, 183.

man and one woman that God had established, as the patriarchs practiced polygamy and Moses permitted husbands to divorce their wives. Marriage was further corrupted by the Gentiles, as husbands could have sexual relations with prostitutes and female slaves as they pleased. Jesus brought back the dignity of marriage through his miracle at Cana and by his rejection of the Mosaic permission of divorce, raising marriage to the level of a sacrament. Leo laments the modern tendency of states to treat marriage as merely a contractual relation subject solely to civil authorities rather than the church. He cautions Catholics against entering into marriages with non-Catholics, since such unions may "endanger the faith of the Catholic partner" and can lead "to the belief that all religions are equally good."[25]

Marriage and divorce legislation in certain predominantly Catholic countries was the subject of three of Leo's encyclicals. *Quod multum* was addressed to the bishops of Hungary. He urges the bishops to remind the faithful that marriage between a Catholic and a non-Catholic Christian is not permitted except as authorized by the church. He also commends Catholic legislators who had rejected a proposal to validate marriages between Christians and Jews.[26] In spite of the prevalence today of marriages between Catholics and non-Catholics, the church continues to insist on prior ecclesiastical approval of such unions. The *Catechism* distinguishes between a "*mixed marriage* (between a Catholic and a baptized non-Catholic)" and "marriage with *disparity of cult* (between a Catholic and a non-baptized person)." The former requires "*express permission* of ecclesiastical authority," whereas for the latter "an *express dispensation* from this impediment is required for the validity of the marriage." In each case, the Catholic party must confirm the obligation that any children will be baptized and educated in the church.[27]

In *Quam religiosa*, Leo examines legislation from Peru which introduced civil marriage. He rejects the notion that civil authorities, independent of the church, have the right to regulate marriages.[28] In *Dum multa*, issued only a few months before his death in 1903, Leo condemns certain civil marriage and divorce legislation that had been enacted in Ecuador.[29]

Pius XI twice addressed the nature of marriage and the regulation of sexual activity within marriage. The first occasion was in 1930 with the encyclical *Casti connubii*, the seminal modern encyclical on human

---

25. Leo XIII, *Arcanum*, 5–9, 17–23, 43.
26. Leo XIII, *Quod multum*, 7.
27. *Catechism*, No. 1635.
28. Leo XIII, *Quam religiosa*, 4.
29. Leo XIII, *Dum multa*, 3.

sexuality. Marriage is of divine origin because it was instituted by God, but it also contains a human element, since the free consent of the spouses is necessary to the sacrament. The first blessing of marriage is offspring, the second is the conjugal love of the spouses, and the third is sacramental. The relation of the spouses, however, is not one of equality. A proper marriage "includes both the primacy of the husband with regard to the wife and children, the ready subjection of the wife and her willing obedience." Since Jesus declared in the Gospels that marriage is indissoluble, divorce is not permissible.[30] In *Dilectissima nobis*, he criticizes certain laws of the new Spanish Republic. Church and state were officially separated, which led to legislation Pius considers harmful to the interests of Catholics, due in part to the legalization of divorce.[31]

The church's view of the marital state stands in contrast with the manner in which it has extolled consecrated virginity, holding it up as a nobler calling than marriage. Diarmaid MacCulloch has stated that "The greatest fault-line in Christian attitudes to sex lies in the status of virginity and celibacy relative to heterosexual marriage."[32] In *Sacra virginitas* Pius XII states the case for the superiority of consecrated virginity over the marital state. Those who "exalt marriage as to rank it ahead of virginity" are guilty of error. The purpose of virginity is "to aim only at the divine," which is easier to accomplish if one is free from the duties and obligations of marriage.[33] Pius repeatedly reminds his readers of the superiority of consecrated virginity over marriage.

> ... According to the teaching of the Church, holy virginity surpasses marriage in excellence. ...
>
> This doctrine of the excellence of virginity and of celibacy and of their superiority over the married state was ... revealed by our Divine Redeemer and by the Apostle of the Gentiles; so too, it was solemnly defined as a dogma of divine faith by the holy council of Trent, and explained in the same way by all the holy Fathers and Doctors of the Church. ...
>
> ... Yet whoever ... argues that it is preferable to live in matrimony than to consecrate oneself completely to God, without doubt perverts the right order.[34]

---

30. Pius XI, *Casti connubii*, 6, 11, 19, 79, 26, 32.
31. Pius XI, *Dilectissima nobis*, 24.
32. MacCulloch, *Reformation*, 608.
33. Pius XII, *Sacra virginitatis*, 8, 15, 20.
34. Ibid., 24, 32, 42.

He denounces as a dangerous error the position that marriage is superior to virginity because marriage is a sacrament and virginity is not.[35] But he does not explain the reason for consecrated virginity's lack of sacramental status.

The Second Vatican Council took up the theme of marriage and the family in *Gaudium et spes*. The council reaffirms the traditional teaching that "marriage and conjugal love are by their nature ordained toward the begetting and educating of children." However, procreation is not the sole end of marriage, and a childless marriage still can be a valuable one. Paul had directed that the council not take up the issue of birth control, which he would make the subject of a papal encyclical. Therefore, the council limited itself to an acknowledgement that although some couples may need to temporarily limit the size of their families, they must do so in a manner which does not run afoul of church law.[36]

In his apostolic exhortation *Familiaris consortio*, John Paul echoes Pius XII's teaching on the supremacy of consecrated virginity and celibacy over marriage.

> Virginity or celibacy, by liberating the human heart in a unique way, "so as to make it burn with greater love for God and all humanity," bears witness that the Kingdom of God and His justice is that pearl of great price which is preferred to every other value no matter how great, and hence must be sought as the only definitive value. It is for this reason that the Church, throughout her history, has always defended the superiority of this charism to that of marriage, by reason of the wholly singular link which it has with the Kingdom of God.

He reminds Catholics in mixed marriages of their obligation to have their children baptized and raised in the Catholic faith. He rejects as unacceptable certain alternatives to sacramental marriage, such as trial marriages, unions without religious or civil recognition, and civil marriages between Catholics. He urges pastors that, in their dealings with divorced and remarried Catholics, they should "make sure that they do not consider themselves as separated from the Church," while reaffirming the practice of denying the Eucharist to them.[37]

Benedict XVI focused on the issue of divorced and remarried Catholics in his apostolic exhortation *Sacramentum caritatis*. The Eleventh Ordinary Synod of Bishops in 2005 had "confirmed the Church's practice . . . of not

---

35. Ibid., 37.
36. Second Vatican Council, *Gaudium et spes*, 50–51.
37. John Paul II, *Familiaris consortio*, 16, 78, 80–84.

admitting the divorced and remarried to the sacraments." However, Benedict is quick to point out that they remain members of the Church.[38]

Francis dealt at length with issues of marriage and divorce in his apostolic exhortation *Amoris laetitia*. This document was the culmination of two synods devoted to marriage and family life—the Third Extraordinary General Assembly of the Synod of Bishops in 2014 and the Fourteenth Ordinary General Assembly of the Synod of Bishops in 2015. In a departure from the practice of his two immediate predecessors, Francis quotes liberally and at length from the documents produced by the synod, which documents reflect the concerns of bishops from all parts of the globe. This approach is in keeping with Francis's belief that everything the church has to teach, especially in the area of morals, need not originate in the Vatican. He is critical of the manner in which the church often has presented its teaching on marriage. "We need a healthy dose of self-criticism. Then too, we often present marriage in such a way that its unitive meaning, its call to grow in love and its ideal of mutual assistance are overshadowed by an almost exclusive insistence on the duty of procreation. . . . At times we have also proposed a far too abstract and almost artificial theological ideal of marriage, far removed from the concrete situations and practical possibilities of real families."[39] Francis's reference to "duty of procreation" is curious, since Catholic teaching has never imposed such a duty upon married couples, often extolling abstinence in marriage.[40] He likely intends this phrase as a criticism of the tendency of the church to overemphasize the procreative end of marriage at the expense of the unitive end.

Francis acknowledges that not all unions live up to the ideal of a Catholic marriage, such as unmarried couples who are cohabiting and those who are divorced and remarried in a civil ceremony, not having obtained annulments of their prior unions. But he urges pastors not to be too quick to judge such couples without an understanding of their particular situations. He reiterates Benedict's reminder that divorced and remarried Catholics remain a part of the church and should be welcomed as such.[41]

Whereas both Pius XII and John Paul II taught the superiority of consecrated virginity and celibacy over marriage, Francis takes a different approach. Although he carefully avoids expressly contradicting his predecessors, he opines that a focus on the superiority of consecrated virginity and celibacy tends to devalue the married state. "Rather than speak absolutely of

---

38. Benedict XVI, *Sacramentum caritatis*, 29.
39. Francis, *Amoris laetitia*, 3, 36.
40. Noonan, *Contraception*, 438.
41. Francis, *Amoris laetitia*, 78–79, 243, 299.

the superiority of virginity, it should be enough to point out that the different states of life complement one another, and consequently that some can be more perfect in one way and others in another."[42]

The Papal Ban on Artificial Contraception: Well-Known, Widely Ignored

Although various forms of contraception were employed in the ancient world, neither the Old Testament nor the New Testament contains an express prohibition against the practice. Early Christian writers treated abortion as a grave sin, but not contraception. No ecumenical council has ever addressed the sinfulness of contraception; prior to the twentieth century, no pope had written an encyclical on the question.[43] By the late nineteenth and early twentieth centuries, however, the use of contraception in Europe and North America became a subject of increasing debate, due to the growing availability of condoms and diaphragms.

Papal silence on the issue ended with the publication of *Casti connubii*. In the midst of a worldwide economic depression, several religious organizations decided that it was an appropriate time to ease the traditional restrictions against the use of artificial contraception by married couples. In the early 1930s, the use of artificial forms of birth control was approved by the Universalist and Unitarian churches, the Federal Council of Churches, and the Central Council of American Rabbis. Most important for Pius XI, although not mentioned in the encyclical, was the action of the Lambeth Conference of the Anglican Communion in 1930 in authorizing the use of artificial contraception by married couples, under certain limited conditions.[44] For Pius, this action by the Anglican Communion required a firm reiteration by the Catholic Church of its long-held prohibition on such forms of birth control, because they frustrate the primary purpose of martial sexual relations.

> But no reason, however grave, may be put forward by which anything intrinsically against nature may become comfortable to nature and morally good. Since, therefore, the conjugal act is destined primarily by nature for the begetting of children, those who in exercising it deliberately frustrate its natural power and

---

42. Ibid., 159.

43. Noonan, *Contraception*, 30–55, 104–6, 231.

44. Küng, *Infallible?* 45; McGreevy, *Catholicism and American Freedom*, 161–62; O'Malley, *Vatican II*, 82.

purpose sin against nature and commit a deed which is shameful and intrinsically vicious. . . .

. . . Our mouth proclaims anew; any use whatsoever of matrimony exercised in such a way that the act is deliberately frustrated in its natural power to generate life is an offense against the law of God and of nature, and those who indulge in such are branded with the guilt of a grave sin.[45]

It is difficult to imagine a married Catholic, as opposed to a celibate cleric, characterizing any act of consensual sexual intercourse between a husband and wife as "a deed which is shameful and intrinsically vicious."[46] Nevertheless, this characterization was common among early twentieth century Catholic theologians. "In declaring evil an act of contraception performed by lawfully wedded persons, the theologians had condemned an act which was literally beyond their experience."[47] A negative view of sexual activity, coupled with a desire to control such activity, has a long history in the church. In the words of Diarmaid MacCulloch, "Augustine speculated wistfully about the time before the Fall in Eden, when Adam and Eve's private parts had behaved in an orderly fashion. The Church has been trying to tell private parts what to do ever since."[48]

Pius is not unmindful that the Great Depression had reduced many to a condition of chronic unemployment and poverty. Families had difficulty providing for their children and lacked the financial resources to support additional children. His prescription, however, is not to permit the use of artificial contraception. Instead, he refers back to Leo XIII's call for workers to receive a living wage sufficient to permit a husband and father to provide for the needs of his wife and children. Of course, a living wage provides no relief to those who are unable to find employment. In that situation, Pius believes that it is necessary for the state to step in and provide support.[49]

This encyclical will have a profound impact on the decision of Paul VI to reaffirm the church's ban on artificial contraception. It also will serve as a precedent for John Paul's development of the contrast between the "culture of life" (represented by the Gospels) and the "culture of death" (represented by artificial contraception and abortion).

From the time of the publication of *Casti connubii* until the 1960s, there was a divide among theologians as to whether the teaching of *Casti*

45. Pius XI, *Casti connubii*, 54, 56.
46. Kerr, *Twentieth-Century Catholic Theologians*, 215.
47. Noonan, *Contraception*, 488.
48. MacCulloch, *Reformation*, 611.
49. Pius XI, *Casti connubii*, 60, 117, 120–21.

connubii on artificial contraception was infallible.[50] This question would become a major issue in the deliberations of the commission that would advise Paul VI on whether the church's position as to the sinfulness of artificial contraception could and should be changed.

Pius XII did not issue an encyclical on birth control, but he dealt with the subject in depth in an address to a professional association of midwives. He does not announce any new doctrine, but unequivocally reaffirms the teaching of Pius XI on the issue. He understands the proscription against the use of artificial contraception as a logical corollary of the primary end of marriage, which is not the fulfillment of the married couple "but the procreation and upbringing of a new life." He distinguishes, however, between artificial contraception, which is a violation of natural law, and the rhythm method, which is licit because it is in accord with natural law. "Husband and wife may use their matrimonial right even during the days of natural sterility . . . . In this case they do not hinder or jeopardize in any way the consummation of the natural act and its ulterior natural consequences."[51] Although the church previously had permitted Catholic couples to use the rhythm method, it forbade Catholic publications from providing information about it.[52]

Paul's most memorable encyclical is *Humanae vitae*, which he issued in 1968. It is surprisingly short, comprising less than thirteen pages (without notes) in the official English translation. The subject is artificial birth control, an issue that had become urgent due to the rapid increase in the world's population and the financial difficulties of providing for a large family. Paul asks whether it is time to reexamine the church's traditional teaching on the subject, even though the issue already had been addressed by his two immediate predecessors. "Could it not be admitted, in other words, that procreative finality applies to the totality of married life rather than to each single act? A further question is whether, because people are more conscious today of their responsibilities, the time has not come when the transmission of life should be regulated by their intelligence and will rather than through the specific rhythms of their own bodies."[53]

An examination of the backstory behind the encyclical is instructive. John XXIII had set up a commission to study scientific advances in contraception. The official name of the commission was the Pontifical Commission

---

50. McClory, *Turning Point*, 21–22, 70; Noonan, *Contraception*, 428; Tentler, *Catholics and Contraception*, 74.

51. Pius XII, *Address to Midwives*, 5, 3.

52. Pollard, *Papacy in the Age of Totalitarianism*, 184.

53. Paul VI, *Humanae vitae*, 2–3.

for the Study of Population, Family and Births, which was commonly referred to as the Birth Control Commission. The initial makeup of the commission in 1963 was six members: a sociologist, a neurologist, a demographer, a diplomat, an economist, and an internist, two of whom were priests. An additional seven members were appointed by Paul prior to the commission's second meeting in 1964: five of the new members were theologians (all of them priests) and two were lay sociologists. Two additional priests were appointed prior to the third meeting in 1964. The fourth meeting in 1965 saw the appointment of an additional forty-three members, including three married couples. The fifth and final meeting in 1965 saw the addition of fourteen more members, all but one of whom was an archbishop or a cardinal.[54] In separate votes, both the entire commission and the theologians on it voted that artificial contraception was not intrinsically evil. The final vote of a group of bishops was nine to three in favor of changing the church's teaching, with three abstentions. But Paul already had made up his mind that he could not change the clear church teaching which had held that all forms of artificial contraception were sinful. A change would constitute an admission that earlier papal teachings had been in error.[55]

Paul begins the encyclical by reminding his readers "that the Church is competent in her magisterium to interpret the natural moral law," including issuing pronouncements "on the nature of marriage, the correct use of conjugal rights, and the duties of spouses." He acknowledges that the question had been the subject of a study by a commission initially established by his predecessor. However, Paul refuses to follow the commission's recommendations, ostensibly on the ground that there was not unanimity among its members.

> However, the conclusions arrived at by the commission could not be considered by Us as definitive and absolutely certain, dispensing Us from the duty of examining personally this serious question. This was all the more necessary because, within the commission itself, there was not complete agreement concerning the moral norms to be proposed, and especially because certain approaches and criteria for a solution to this question had emerged which were at variance with the moral doctrine on marriage constantly taught by the magisterium of the Church.[56]

---

54. McClory, *Turning Point*, 38–56, 67–76, 96–128, 188–90.
55. Küng, *Infallible?* 27–52; McClory, *Turning Point*, 96–128; Wills, *Papal Sin*, 89–98.
56. Paul VI, *Humanae vitae*, 5–6.

Although it is true that the commission was not unanimous in its recommendations, Paul fails to disclose that the vast majority of the commission, including a majority of the theologians on the commission, voted in favor of abolishing the ban on artificial contraception. He does not explain why he should disregard the commission's recommendations simply because they were not unanimous. At the First Vatican Council, there were dissenting votes on the question of papal infallibility, but that did not prevent the council from issuing a dogmatic constitution proclaiming the dogma. None of the documents issued by the Second Vatican Council had received unanimous approval. Accepting the commission's recommendation, however, would have required Paul to hold either that *Casti connubii* had been wrong in outlawing the use of artificial contraception, or that its teachings were no longer normative less than forty years later. That is a road that Paul refused to take, since it could put in doubt the deference that must be shown to all papal pronouncements on matters of faith and morals, whether or not they are accompanied by an exercise of infallibility. In fact, Paul intentionally omitted from *Humanae vitae* any proclamation of the infallibility of its teaching.[57]

Paul also reaffirms Pius XI's reliance on natural law principles as the foundation for both the ban on artificial contraception and the permission to use natural means of birth control. "The Church . . . teaches that each and every marital act must of necessity retain its intrinsic relationship to the procreation of human life." Married couples "if they further reflect, they must also recognize that an act of mutual love which impairs the capacity to transmit life which God the Creator, through specific laws, has built into it, frustrates His design which constitutes the norm of marriage, and contradicts the will of the Author of life." Consistent with the precedent of *Casti connubii*, Paul declares as unlawful "any action which either before, at the moment of, or after sexual intercourse, is specifically intended to prevent procreation—whether as an end or as a means."[58] Under Paul's interpretation of natural law, the only permissible forms of birth control are abstinence and the rhythm method. "Married people may then take advantage of the natural cycles immanent in the reproductive system and engage in marital intercourse only during those times that are infertile." In addition, he recommends periodic abstinence as "a shining witness to the chastity of husband and wife."[59]

---

57. Hebblethwaite, *Paul VI*, 517.
58. Paul VI, *Humanae vitae*, 11, 13–14.
59. Ibid., 16, 21.

Humanae vitae generated dissent among both clergy and laity, much to Paul's amazement and dismay. Episcopal conferences in some northern European countries and Canada gave Catholics in their countries permission to dissent in conscience from the encyclical's dictates.[60] Paul was not prepared for the hostility with which the encyclical was received, as Garry Wills has observed. "The Pope was stunned. He would spend the remaining ten years of his pontificate as if sleepwalking, unable to understand what had happened to him, why such open dissent was entertained at the very top of the episcopate."[61] Married Catholics simply ignored its teaching. In fact, the percentage of American Catholics who viewed contraception as always wrong decreased dramatically in the years following publication of the encyclical.[62] Although Paul would continue as pope for ten more years after the encyclical's publication, it was the last one that he would issue.

Homosexuality: An "Objectively Disordered" Orientation

Modern popes have not issued any encyclicals on the morality of homosexual practices, but the Congregation for the Doctrine of the Faith has opined on the subject on several occasions during the pontificate of John Paul. The issue was first briefly raised by the congregation under Paul in a document dealing with the issue of human sexuality. The 1975 declaration *Persona humana* unequivocally rejects the notion that there are no absolute norms governing human sexual conduct. "In this domain there exist principles and norms which the Church has always unhesitatingly transmitted as part of her teaching, however much the opinions and morals of the world may have been opposed to them.... They therefore cannot be considered as having become out of date or doubtful under the pretext that a new cultural situation had arisen." One short section of the declaration deals with homosexual relations. The Congregation attempts to disabuse those who advocate that, since there are "homosexuals who are definitively such because of some kind of innate instinct or a pathological constitution judged to be incurable," homosexual relations between such persons are justifiable. "For according to the objective moral order, homosexual relations are acts which lack an essential and indispensable finality. In Sacred Scripture they are condemned as a serious depravity and even presented as the sad consequence

---

60. McBrien, *Catholicism*, 990.
61. Wills, *Papal Sin*, 96.
62. The percentage of American Catholics who believed that contraception always was wrong fell from 56 percent in 1963 to 17 percent in 1974. Putnam and Campbell, *American Grace*, 583 n. 5.

of rejecting God. This judgment of Scripture does not of course permit us to conclude that all who suffer from this anomaly are personally responsible for it, but it does attest to the fact that homosexual acts are intrinsically disordered and can in no case be approved of."[63]

The congregation's first document devoted to the subject under Cardinal Ratzinger's prefecture was a 1986 letter to bishops. The reason for the issuance of the letter was twofold. First, because "the issue of homosexuality and the moral evaluation of homosexual acts have increasingly become a matter of public debate," the congregation considered it appropriate to address the bishops of the world on the pastoral care of homosexual persons. Second, the congregation notes that since the publication of its 1975 declaration, some people erroneously have viewed homosexuality as "neutral, or even good."[64] The congregation sets forth certain principles that will appear repeatedly in future documents of the Congregation and later in the *Catechism*.[65]

First, a persons' homosexual orientation is not a sin. Second, this orientation is "objectively disordered," since it does not reflect the complementarity of the sexes which is God's plan for the transmission of life. Third, the homosexual orientation tends "toward an intrinsic moral evil." Fourth, all homosexual acts are sinful, since "it is only in the marital relationship that the use of the sexual faculty can be morally good." Fifth, homosexuals are called to exercise Christian self-control and refrain from engaging in such acts. Sixth, homosexuals are entitled to human dignity and their civil rights must be respected. Seventh, pastoral care of homosexuals must assert the church's position concerning the immorality of homosexual activity.[66]

In 1992 the congregation addressed the manner in which Catholics should respond to legislative proposals concerning adoption by homosexuals, employment of homosexuals, and housing for homosexuals. Such responses should be guided by the principle that discrimination based on sexual orientation is inherently different from other forms of discrimination and, therefore, is not per se a violation of civil rights. "'Sexual orientation' does not constitute a quality comparable to race, ethnic background etc. in respect to non-discrimination. Unlike these, homosexual orientation is an objective disorder and evokes moral concern." Laws seeking to outlaw discrimination against homosexuals may improperly be used as an endorsement of homosexuality. The congregation expresses the hope that those

---

63. Congregation for the Doctrine of the Faith, *Persona humana*, secs. 5, 8.
64. Congregation for the Doctrine of the Faith, *Letter to Bishops*, 1, 3.
65. *Catechism*, Nos. 2357–59.
66. Congregation for the Doctrine of the Faith, *Letter to Bishops*, 3, 6–7, 12, 10, 15.

homosexuals who follow the church's teaching and live a chaste life will not be subject to discrimination, because they "do not publicize their sexual orientation. Hence the problem of discrimination in terms of employment, housing, etc., does not usually arise." Moreover, certain forms of discrimination against homosexuals are acceptable, such as in areas like adoption and foster care, employment of teachers and coaches, and the military.[67]

Civil unions and same-sex marriage were addressed by the congregation in 2003. Its starting point is the creation story in Genesis, where God created humans as male and female. Therefore, it is God's plan that "marriage exists solely between a man and a woman." There can be no correlation between Christian marriage and homosexual unions; the former is a sacrament, the latter is not. Catholics are duty-bound to oppose legislation seeking to grant legal status to homosexual unions. Permitting homosexual couples to adopt children "would actually mean doing violence to these children," since they "would be deprived of the experience of either fatherhood or motherhood." Catholic politicians have a responsibility to vote against any law seeking to give legal recognition to homosexual unions.[68]

The Congregation for the Doctrine of the Faith has been the main, but not the sole dicastery to address questions about homosexuality. In 2005 the Congregation for Catholic Education issued an instruction that sets forth in unequivocal language the church's position on the admission of gay men to the seminary and the priesthood. "The Church, while profoundly respecting the persons in question, cannot admit to the seminary or to holy orders those who practice homosexuality, present deep seated homosexual tendencies or support the so-called 'gay culture.'"[69] The instruction did not address the thornier question of how the church should deal with gay men who already have been ordained as priests.

Francis has dealt briefly with homosexuality in his apostolic exhortation *Amoris laetitia*. He reiterates the Church's rejection of same-sex marriage and acceptance of legal bans on the ability of same-sex couples to adopt children. But he reminds the clergy and the faithful of the clear teaching of the *Catechism* that a person's sexual orientation is not a basis for "unjust discrimination" against them, while avoiding a discussion of what forms of discrimination against homosexuals the Church considers to be just.[70]

---

67. Congregation for the Doctrine of the Faith, *Considerations concerning Legislative Proposals*, 10–14.

68. Congregation for the Doctrine of the Faith, *Considerations regarding Legal Recognition*, 2–5, 7, 10.

69. Congregation for the Doctrine of the Faith, *Instructions concerning Homosexual Tendencies*, 2.

70. Francis, *Amoris laetitia*, 52, 251, 172, 250.

Catholic Employers and the Affordable Care Act's Contraceptive Mandate

The Connecticut statute at issue in *Griswold* had been passed by a predominantly Protestant legislature, but it had remained on the books for decades (even though seldom enforced) due to the opposition to its repeal or replacement by Catholic legislators.[71] The Planned Parenthood League of Connecticut had sought since the 1930s to introduce legislation that would permit doctors to give their married patients information about contraceptives, but those efforts proved unsuccessful. Doctors at Catholic hospitals who publicly supported these efforts found their services terminated.[72] Planned Parenthood then sought a judicial rather than a legislative challenge to the ban and ultimately won a victory in the Supreme Court in 1965.

Fifty years later, contraception again came before the Supreme Court, although the issue was quite different. The twenty-first-century battle is not over whether doctors may provide birth control information to their patients. This time, the contested issue is whether the federal government may mandate that employer-provided health insurance plans provide coverage for FDA-approved contraceptives at no cost to employees. The first challenge to reach the Court was brought by employers. The owners of three closely-held corporations argued that the regulations which had been adopted by the Department of Health and Human Services, pursuant to the Affordable Care Act, violated their religious beliefs in contravention of the Religious Freedom Restoration Act of 1993. In the *Hobby Lobby* case, the employers contended that certain of the covered methods of contraception were abortifacients.[73] Providing coverage for such birth control methods would make the owners complicit in abortions in violation of their sincerely held religious beliefs. The Court sided with the employers, accepting their argument that the goals of the ACA could be reached without forcing them to go against the religious beliefs of their owners. The Court noted that an opt-out provision that was available to certain non-profit religious institutions could be tailored to such private employers as well. Although churches themselves were exempt from the contraception mandate, other religious affiliated employers, such as colleges and health care systems, were not. But the regulations provided them with a means to avoid having to pay for such coverage through the simple expedient of providing notice of their objection to the federal government or to their insurance carrier.

---

71. Noonan, *Contraception*, 413 n. 92.
72. Hull and Hoffer, *Roe v. Wade*, 76–77.
73. Burwell v. Hobby Lobby Stores, Inc., 134 S. Ct. 2751 (2014).

Religious groups, however, launched an attack on the opt-out provision itself, arguing that the mere fact of having to provide the notice violated their religious beliefs, because it would make them complicit in a scheme that provided contraceptive coverage to their employees. The objectors included Catholic dioceses, Catholic bishops, Priests for Life, and the Little Sisters of the Poor. The issue was expected to be decided by the Court in June 2016, but the untimely death of Justice Antonin Scalia left the Court with only eight members. In order to avoid the possibility of a four-to-four split and a decision with no general precedential value, the Court returned the cases to the Courts of Appeals to determine whether an accommodation between HHS and the objectors could be reached.[74] But the staunch opposition of Catholic groups to the ACA's contraception mandate is evidence that the church's teaching on artificial means of birth control remains the same today as it has been for centuries, even if widely ignored by a large percentage of the laity.

One question remains, however. If the bishops throughout the centuries, in communion with the pope, universally have taught that artificial contraception is always sinful, why is this teaching not an exercise of the infallibility of the college of bishops? Paul did not so claim in *Humanae vitae*, and most theologians have held that the teaching of the encyclical is not infallible.[75] As we shall see in the next chapter, John Paul exercised the infallibility of the college of bishops in declaring abortion and euthanasia always to be gravely sinful, but stopped short of making the same claim for artificial contraception, even while he constantly decried the "contraceptive mentality" and its devaluation of human life. This hesitancy may reflect an uneasiness with setting in stone the teaching of *Humanae vitae*. Such unease is appropriate, because, as Francis Sullivan reminds us, "Doctrine that has been infallibly proposed cannot be reversed."[76]

---

74. Zubik v. Burwell, 578 U.S. (2016).

75. Charles Curran, "Public Dissent in the Church," in Curran and McCormick, *Dissent in the Church*, 387–407, 395; Komonchak, "*Humanae Vitae* and its Reception," 222. But see Ford and Grisez, "Contraception," 258–312, claiming that the church's teaching on contraception has been declared infallibly.

76. Sullivan, "Secondary Object," 546.

12

Certainty: Murder, Abortion, Euthanasia, and the Death Penalty

> *I declare that direct abortion, that is, abortion willed as an end or as a means, always constitutes a grave moral disorder, since it is the deliberate killing of an innocent human being.*
>
> —John Paul II

> *Sometimes morally flawed laws already exist. In this situation, the process of framing legislation to protect life is subject to prudential judgment and "the art of the possible."*
>
> —United States Conference of Catholic Bishops

The German Bishops' Responses to the Nazi Programs of Forced Sterilization and Euthanasia

Sometimes, the church's teaching on moral issues compels its leaders to take positions that puts the church at odds with political powers in a country. For example, in the 1930s the bishops of Germany were confronted with newly enacted laws on compulsory sterilization and euthanasia that contradicted unambiguous church teaching.[1] On January 1, 1934, less than a year after Adolf Hitler had come to power, the Law

---

1. The following account is taken from Lewy, *Catholic Church and Nazi Germany*, 258–67.

for the Prevention of Hereditary Diseased Offspring took effect. It sought to accomplish the goal set forth in its title through the forced sterilization of persons with certain disabilities. Three years earlier, Pius XI had condemned compulsory sterilization for eugenic purposes in *Casti connubii*.[2] The German government refused to exempt state-employed Catholic healthcare workers and judges from participating in the program. The bishops were concerned that Catholics would have to choose between participation in forced sterilizations, in violation of church teaching and their consciences, or risk dismissal from their positions.

Contrary to the bishops' expectations, most Catholic physicians and judges complied with the law without complaint. In the first three years of the law's operation, more than 160,000 sterilizations were carried out. Through a deft bit of casuistry, bishops arrived at a compromise that would permit Catholic physicians to participate in the program without violating church law. They could report to the authorities the names of patients under their care who, under the law, were subject to forced sterilization. Guenter Lewy has described the manner by which the bishops analyzed the morality of Catholic participation in the program. "*Reporting* was 'material cooperation' which was lawful, since the act of reporting in itself was morally indifferent, and since the official in question would otherwise suffer harm, that is, lose his job. To submit an *application* for the sterilization of a person, on the other hand, was 'formal cooperation' which, being an essential part of an evil action, was sinful; but this position . . . the Church did not attempt to enforce."[3] The issue of whether nurses could assist in the sterilization procedures was passed along to the Holy Office in Rome. It ruled that such assistance was morally permissible, if the refusal to assist would result in termination of employment and their places might be taken by non-Catholic nurses who were hostile to the church.

On September 1, 1939, the same day that German troops invaded Poland, Hitler ordered the euthanizing of all persons with incurable diseases. The order was not publicly disclosed, but the scale of the killings insured that word of the program could not remain secret indefinitely. The program lasted for two years, resulting in 70,000 executions by gunshot or gassing. Formal protests to the government by Cardinal Bertram of Breslau and Cardinal Faulhaber of Munich were ignored. In August 1941 Bishop Galen of Münster preached a sermon denouncing the killings and calling for the prosecution for murder of those who had performed the executions. Copies of the sermon were disseminated throughout the country. The Nazi

---

2. Pius XI, *Casti Connubii*, 67–71.
3. Lewy, *Catholic Church and Nazi Germany*, 262–63, emphasis in original.

leadership was furious, some arguing that Galen should be hanged for treason. Goebbels and Hitler, not wanting to make a martyr out of Galen, decided instead to officially end the program.

As the above two examples disclose, there is no single template for how the leaders of the church respond to public policies that violate express Catholic moral teaching. The bishops' reaction to forced sterilizations was to try and minimize the participation of Catholics in the program while not putting them at risk of losing their livelihoods. In the end, the church acquiesced in the program, so long as Catholic physicians did not apply for the sterilization of a person or perform the operation. The policy of forced sterilizations itself was not assailed. In the case of euthanasia, after the failure of formal protests from Germany's highest Catholic prelates, Bishop Galen denounced the executions directly, at grave risk to his own life. Neither response was dictated by the church's unambiguous teachings against forced sterilization and euthanasia. They were driven by prudential judgments made in the light of the political realities of the time and place. Regardless of the clarity of Catholic moral teaching, that teaching often provides little guidance to clergy and laity alike as to how they should respond as Catholics and citizens to laws which permit or compel actions in violation of such teaching.

The Infallibility of the College of Bishops in Matters of Morals

Church teaching against forced sterilization and euthanasia was unambiguous, but that did not provide the bishops of Germany with clear guidance on how they should respond to Nazi policies requiring actions in violation of moral law. More than fifty years later, John Paul II would confirm that the infallibility of the college of bishops extends to matters of morals. He would declare that the worldwide college of bishops has taught that the killing of innocents, abortion, and euthanasia are always gravely sinful, without exception. He also would state in no uncertain terms that the death penalty is seldom if ever warranted as a punishment of the criminal justice system. John Paul's clear teaching, however, does not answer the difficult questions raised by public policies permitting abortion and euthanasia and imposing death sentences on convicted criminals. Are Catholics morally obliged to oppose such policies and vote for candidates who vow to repeal them?

In his 1995 encyclical *Evangelium vitae*, John Paul unveils his concept of the struggle between the "culture of death," which has been fostered by modern secularism, and the "culture of life," which is exemplified by the teachings of the church. The battleground on which this struggle plays out is the beginning and end of life. The culture of life promotes natural birth and death, whereas contraception, abortion, and euthanasia are products of the culture of death. John Paul sees no middle ground between these two cultures.

"The Gospel of life is at the heart of Jesus' message." This message, however, is under attack, due to the pervasiveness of a culture of death in modern society.

> ... This reality is characterized by the emergence of a culture which denies solidarity and in many cases takes the form of a veritable "culture of death." This culture is actively fostered by powerful cultural, economic and political currents which encourage an idea of society excessively concerned with efficiency. Looking at the situation from this point of view, it is possible to speak in a certain sense of a war of the powerful against the weak: a life which would require greater acceptance, love and care is considered useless, or held to be an intolerable burden, and is therefore rejected in one way or another.[4]

Looking first at the beginning of life, he rejects as "unfounded" the accusation that the church, by its ban on the use of artificial contraception, in effect promotes abortions. He argues that contraception and abortion, although they "are specifically different evils," stem from the same source—"the negative values inherent in the 'contraceptive mentality.'"[5] The phrase "contraceptive mentality" had been embraced by some Catholic apologists in the period following the Second World War as the debate over the sinfulness of artificial contraception was intensifying.[6] According to John Paul, contraception and abortion both "are rooted in a hedonistic mentality," and the distance from the former to the latter is a slippery slope. "The life which could result from a sexual encounter thus becomes an enemy to be avoided at all costs, and abortion becomes the only possible decisive response to failed contraception."[7] John Paul sees a linkage between the use of contraception to avoid a pregnancy and the decision to end an unwanted pregnancy through abortion. He assumes that a woman who uses artificial contraception will be less hesitant to terminate an unwanted pregnancy by means of an abortion. John Noonan has pointed out that this argument had been advanced by opponents of contraception since the mid-twentieth century. Statistics from England, Sweden, Switzerland, Hungary, Poland,

---

4. John Paul II, *Evangelium vitae*, 1, 12.
5. Ibid., 13.
6. Tentler, *Catholics and Contraception*, 138.
7. John Paul II, *Evangelium vitae*, 13.

and Japan were used to support the argument that those who use contraception were more likely to abort an unwanted pregnancy.[8] In the United States, twenty million abortions were performed between 1973 and 1989, a period when both contraceptives and abortions were legally available. "One-third of all pregnancies in America ended in abortions, and abortion was the most common elective surgery in the country."[9] As is common in papal encyclicals, however, John Paul makes no reference to any empirical data; he simply states the relation between contraception and abortion as a self-evident truth.

But John Paul does not stop there. He also finds the culture of death present in the practice of in vitro fertilization, in the treatment of terminally ill patients, and in policies enacted by governments to curtail population growth. It may seem strange that in vitro fertilization should be included in this list, since the procedure is not an attempt to avoid life but to create a new life. But John Paul maintains that the only creation of a new life fully consistent with the culture of life is one brought about through a natural sexual encounter between husband and wife. For him, the rise of the culture of death is a result of the growing secularism of modern society, with a concomitant loss of the sense of the divine. This struggle between the two cultures is nothing less than a manifestation of the primordial "clash between good and evil."[10]

The Bible contains no specific prohibition against abortion or euthanasia, even though abortion was widespread in the world in which Christianity came of age. Nevertheless, John Paul finds this omission to be neither strange nor inexplicable. "Although there are no direct and explicit calls to protect human life at its very beginning, specifically life not yet born, and life nearing its end, this can easily be explained by the fact that the mere possibility of harming, attacking, or actually denying life in these circumstances is completely foreign to the religious and cultural way of thinking of the People of God."[11] This argument is unlikely to convince anyone not already predisposed to believe that abortion and euthanasia are murder.

How is the commandment "you shall not kill" to be applied to the situations of taking the life of another in self-defense (or in defense of another) and the taking of life by the state through capital punishment? To answer these questions, John Paul looks to the recently published *Catechism*. The right to self-defense is grounded in "the intrinsic value of life and the duty

---

8. Noonan, *Contraception*, 518–19.
9. Hull and Hoffer, *Roe v. Wade*, 228.
10. John Paul II, *Evangelium vitae*, 21–23, 28.
11. Ibid., 61, 44.

to love oneself no less than others."[12] Capital punishment presents a more difficult situation. The answer found in the *Catechism* and in the encyclical is that whereas capital punishment may be justified in certain situations, those circumstances rarely are present today.[13]

> This is the context in which to place the problem of the death penalty. On this matter there is a growing tendency, both in the Church and in civil society, to demand that it be applied in a very limited way or even that it be abolished completely. ... Public authority must redress the violation of personal and social rights by imposing on the offender an adequate punishment for the crime, as a condition for the offender to regain the exercise of his or her freedom. In this way authority also fulfils the purpose of defending public order and ensuring people's safety, while at the same time offering the offender an incentive and help to change his or her behaviour and be rehabilitated.
>
> It is clear that, for these purposes to be achieved, the nature and extent of the punishment must be carefully evaluated and decided upon, and ought not to go to the extreme of executing the offender except in cases of absolute necessity: in other words, when it would not be possible otherwise to defend society. Today however, as a result of steady improvements in the organization of the penal system, such cases are very rare, if not practically non-existent.[14]

The late Justice Antonin Scalia, a conservative Catholic, was an outspoken critic of John Paul's teaching on the death penalty. Scalia was a longstanding supporter of the death penalty, believing that a judge who had moral qualms against imposing capital punishment had a duty to resign his office. At a 2002 forum held at the University of Chicago Divinity School, he addressed how he could square his view on the death penalty with Catholic teaching as enunciated in *Evangelium vitae*. While he acknowledged the clarity and certainty of John Paul's teaching on the subject, he felt free to dissent from it because it was not an *ex cathedra* infallible pronouncement.[15] This is another example of how infallibility has operated to diminish the authoritativeness of noninfallible papal teaching in the minds of some of the faithful.

12. Ibid., 55.

13. According to John Paul's biographer George Weigel, the *Catechism* was revised to bring its teaching on capital punishment in line with the encyclical. Weigel, *Witness to Hope*, 758; *Catechism*, No. 2267.

14. John Paul II, *Evangelium vitae*, 56.

15. Murphy, *Scalia*, 281–97.

A unique aspect of this encyclical is John Paul's issuance of three seemingly infallible pronouncements. These are not *ex cathedra* infallible papal statements as defined by the First Vatican Council. Instead, they reflect an exercise of infallibility by the college of bishops as set forth by the Second Vatican Council in article 25 of *Lumen gentium*. John Paul confirms the exercise of infallibility by the ordinary and universal magisterium of the Church—when the bishops of the world outside of an ecumenical council, but united with each other and the pope, teach on a matter of faith or morals which is to be definitively held by all Catholics.[16] The first of these pronouncements relates to voluntary killing of an innocent human life.

> Therefore, by the authority which Christ conferred upon Peter and his Successors, and in communion with the Bishops of the Catholic Church, I confirm that the direct and voluntary killing of an innocent human being is always gravely immoral. This doctrine, based upon that unwritten law which man, in the light of reason, finds in his own heart (cf. Rom. 2:14–15), is reaffirmed by Sacred Scripture, transmitted by the Tradition of the Church and taught by the ordinary and universal Magisterium.[17]

The second of these pronouncements concerns "procured abortion," which John Paul defines as "the deliberate and direct killing, by whatever means it is carried out, of a human being in the initial phase of his or her existence, extending from conception to birth."[18] There has never been any question as to the church's teaching on the sinfulness of abortion; the prohibition against abortion has been a constant throughout the church's history. In the early twentieth century, it was reaffirmed by Pius XI in *Casti connubii*. John Paul is emphatic in holding that abortion is in every instance intrinsically evil, even when performed to save the life of the mother. In order to enforce this prohibition, public officials have a duty to pass appropriate legislation to protect the lives of the innocent.[19] The Second Vatican Council did not issue a document devoted to abortion, but in *Gaudium et spes* it declares that "from the moment of conception life must be safeguarded with greatest care while abortion and infanticide are unspeakable crimes."[20]

---

16. For a discussion of the manner in which the ordinary and universal magisterium of the church is exercised, see Gaillardetz, "Ordinary Universal Magisterium," 447–71.

17. John Paul II, *Evangelium vitae*, 57.

18. Ibid., 58–60, 62.

19. Pius XI, *Casti connubii*, 63–64, 67.

20. Second Vatican Council, *Gaudium et spes*, 51.

The question of abortion was the subject of a 1974 declaration of the Congregation for the Doctrine of the Faith. In light of the debate in the 1970s in many nations over the decriminalization of abortion, the congregation sought to reaffirm the church's teaching as to the sinfulness of abortion. "The tradition of the Church has always held that human life must be protected and favored from the beginning, just as at various stages of its development."[21] The congregation outlines the history of the Church's opposition to abortion from the first centuries up to the Middle Ages. During this time, there was debate over when a fetus became infused with a soul, which debate was influenced by the Aristotelian notion that a fetus did not become a human being until forty days after conception for a boy and ninety days after conception for a girl.[22] But the church consistently taught that abortion was illicit at every stage of fetal development, however early.[23]

According to John Paul, the parties who are morally responsible for a procured abortion include not only the mother, but others who aid or abet the offense, such as the father, family and friends, doctors and nurses, elected officials who pass laws permitting abortion, and associations which campaign for its legalization.[24] Since life begins at conception, the lack of fetal viability does not permit abortion in the early stages of a pregnancy. Even "the mere probability that a human person is involved" would justify the prohibition. In any event, he asserts that the prohibition on abortion has been constantly taught throughout the church's history. Recent popes and the Second Vatican Council have been unanimous in their condemnation of abortion. The Code of Canon Law also provides for excommunication not only of the participants but also of "those accomplices without whose help the crime would not have been committed." He then provides the second instance in the encyclical of the exercise of infallible teaching authority.

> . . . Therefore, by the authority which Christ conferred upon Peter and his Successors, in communion with the Bishops . . . I declare that direct abortion, that is, abortion willed as an end or as a means, always constitutes a grave moral disorder, since it is the deliberate killing of an innocent human being. This doctrine is based upon the natural law and upon the written Word of God, is transmitted by the Church's Tradition and taught by the ordinary and universal Magisterium.[25]

21. Congregation for the Doctrine of the Faith, *Questio de aborto procurato*, 6.
22. Noonan, *Contraception*, 90.
23. Congregation for the Doctrine of the Faith, *Questio de aborto procurato*, 7.
24. John Paul II, *Evangelium vitae*, 58.
25. Ibid., 60–62.

The ban on direct abortions extends as well to experimentation with human embryos.[26]

He draws a bright line between euthanasia and the decision not to use extraordinary means to keep alive a terminally ill patient. The former is proscribed, whereas the latter is permissible.

> ... Euthanasia in the strict sense is understood to be an action or omission which of itself and by intention causes death, with the purpose of eliminating all suffering. ...
>
> Euthanasia must be distinguished from the decision to forego so-called "aggressive medical treatment," in other words, medical procedures which no longer correspond to the real situation of the patient, either because they are by now disproportionate to any expected results or because they impose an excessive burden on the patient and his family. In such situations, when death is clearly imminent and inevitable, one can in conscience "refuse forms of treatment that would only secure a precarious and burdensome prolongation of life, so long as the normal care due to the sick person in similar cases is not interrupted."[27]

John Paul then makes his third infallible pronouncement.

> ... Taking into account these distinctions, in harmony with the Magisterium of my Predecessors and in communion with the Bishops of the Catholic Church, I confirm that euthanasia is a grave violation of the law of God, since it is the deliberate and morally unacceptable killing of a human person. This doctrine is based upon the natural law and upon the written word of God, is transmitted by the Church's Tradition and taught by the ordinary and universal Magisterium.[28]

Although he has closely linked abortion and contraception in this encyclical and elsewhere, he makes no infallible declaration as to the sinfulness of artificial contraception. In fact, Catholic theologians generally agree that the sinfulness of contraception has not been infallibly taught.[29] The three infallible pronouncements in this encyclical are especially noteworthy, because "previously the church had never spoken infallibly on a question of the moral law."[30]

26. Ibid. 63.
27. Ibid., 65.
28. Ibid.
29. Sullivan, *Magisterium*, 120; Sullivan, "Note: *Evangelium Vitae*," 565.
30. Sullivan, *Creative Fidelity*, 159. Sullivan sets forth several arguments which

Moral Guidance to Catholic Voters on the Election of Public Officials

John Paul's statement that abortion is gravely sinful and never morally permissible could not be any clearer. However, the clarity of this doctrinal statement does not, by itself, provide guidance to Catholics as to how they should vote for candidates for public office. Are Catholics required to be single-issue voters for whom a candidate's stance on abortion trumps all other issues? Is it ever legitimate for a Catholic to vote for a candidate who is avowedly pro-choice? How is a Catholic to evaluate candidates, one of whom is anti-abortion but pro-death penalty, when the opposing candidate is pro-choice but anti-death penalty? These and related questions cannot be answered simply by reference to the infallible teaching that abortion is always gravely sinful.

In 2015, the United States Conference of Catholic Bishops issued revised guidelines to aid Catholics in their voting choices. The bishops do not presume to lecture Catholics on which candidates they should support. "We recognize that the responsibility to make choices in political life rests with each individual in light of a properly formed conscience." They acknowledge the difficult choices which Catholics face in trying to exercise their obligations as citizens in a manner consistent with the church's moral teaching. Candidates for public office take positions on a variety of issues that have moral consequences. Some of these positions are consistent with Catholic teaching and others are not. A voter must weigh the overall consistency of a candidate's position with Catholic teaching rather than the candidate's position on a single issue. Although a candidate's position on a single issue should not be a sufficient reason to vote in favor of that candidate, it may suffice to disqualify him or her from receiving a Catholic's vote.[31]

The bishops make the astounding claim that "It is important to be clear that the political choices faced by citizens not only have an impact on general peace and prosperity but also may affect the individual's salvation."[32] The statement itself is anything but clear. Does it mean what it seems to imply, that a vote for a particular candidate could be a mortal sin? The bishops

---

cast doubt on whether the three declarations in *Evangelium vitae* satisfy the condition for infallible teaching of the college of bishops established by *Lumen gentium* 25. Ibid., 154–61. However, as will be explored in the postscript, the Congregation for the Doctrine of the Faith in 1998 left no doubt that the teaching of *Evangelium vitae* constitutes papal confirmation of doctrines that have been taught infallibly by the college of bishops.

31. United States Conference of Catholic Bishops, *Forming Consciences*, 7, 35–36, 42.

32. Ibid., 38.

provide no explanation; but during the 2004 presidential election campaign, some bishops had opined that it might be sinful for a Catholic to vote for fellow Catholic John Kerry, due to his pro-choice stance on abortion.[33]

The bishops acknowledge that they are not writing on a clean slate. Abortion has been legal in all states since the Supreme Court's 1973 decision in *Roe v. Wade*. Americans disagree as to whether *Roe* should remain the law of the land, whether the Constitution should be amended to protect life from conception, or whether restricting abortion to the greatest extent possible is the most that can be accomplished. "Sometimes morally flawed laws already exist. In this situation, the process of framing legislation to protect life is subject to prudential judgment and 'the art of the possible.'"[34]

When the pope speaks infallibly on an issue of faith, such as a Marian dogma, the matter is settled. When he announces that a matter of morals has been taught infallibly by the ordinary and universal magisterium, it is not the end of the discussion but only the beginning. Doctrine may be clear, but life is messy.

---

33. Kaveny, *Prophecy without Contempt*, 267.
34. United States Conference of Catholic Bishops, *Forming Consciences*, 31.

13

Not an Option: The Priestly Ordination of Women

> *The Church, in fidelity to the example of the Lord, does not consider herself authorized to admit women to priestly ordination.*
>
> —Congregation for the Doctrine of the Faith

> *The Church's teaching about women . . . is a body of teaching about women and for women that has been worked out and proclaimed almost entirely by men.*
>
> —Donal Dorr

The Fear of the Return of a "Pope Joan"

THE 1492 CONCLAVE THAT resulted in the election of the Spanish cardinal Rodrigo Borgia as Alexander VI was one of the most corrupt in history, as Borgia's election was secured by purchasing the votes of many of the cardinal-electors.[1] One of the first orders of business following his election likely was to ensure that he was a male. He would have been seated on a chair with a circular hole cut out of the bottom while one of the clerics reached underneath to feel his genitalia. The practice of using a *chaise percées* (pierced chair) following a papal election is attested to by a source from 1490, only two years before Borgia's election. "Up to the present day

---

1. McBrien, *Lives of the Popes*, 267; McGrath, *Christianity's Dangerous Idea*, 22.

the seat is still in the same place and is used at the election of the pope. And in order to demonstrate his worthiness, his testicles are felt by the junior cleric present as testimony of his male sex. When this is found to be so, the person who feels them shouts out in a loud voice, 'He has testicles!' And all the clerics present reply 'God be praised!' Then they proceed joyfully to the consecration of the pope-elect."[2] This strange practice was a hangover from the specter of "Pope Joan," a medieval legend that circulated for centuries. Richard McBrien describes two versions of the story, neither of which has any historical validity.

> Joan, "Pope," subject of a medieval fable that was widely accepted in the thirteenth century and until the seventeenth, when a French Protestant, David Blondel (d. 1655), disproved the belief in a treatise published in Amsterdam in 1647 and 1657. It was thought that Pope Victor III (d. 1087) was succeeded by a woman who, having disguised her gender, had worked in the Curia and been named a cardinal. She is said to have been elected pope, but that her disguise was disclosed when she gave birth to a child while mounting her horse. In another version of the story, Pope Leo IV (d. 855) was succeeded by John Anglicus, who was in fact a woman but whose brilliant lectures in Rome and whose edifying life resulted in her unanimous election as pope. She is said to have served as pope for more than two years. Like the other putative female pope, this one also was exposed when, riding in procession from St. Peter's to the Lateran, she gave birth to a child.[3]

It is ironic that the cardinal-electors felt a need to ensure themselves of Borgia's gender, since he was notorious for having fathered several children prior to his election.[4]

Although the story of Pope Joan is apocryphal, the church's unwillingness to contemplate the ordination of women to the priesthood is quite real, prompting John Paul II to issue an infallible pronouncement intended to end debate on the subject. Despite his best efforts, the controversy persists.

Mandatory Celibacy and the Shortage of Priests

In the 1960s the Catholic Church faced a perceived shortage of priests. During the preceding decade, the church in Europe had experienced a decline

---

2. Norwich, *Absolute Monarchs*, 67.
3. McBrien, *Lives of the Popes*, 480.
4. Ibid., 267.

in vocations to the priesthood, a shortage that was acute in France and Italy.[5] Two possible solutions to the problem were proposed: one was to make priestly celibacy voluntary rather than mandatory; the other was to permit the priestly ordination of women. Paul VI had refused to allow the topic of clerical celibacy to be discussed at the Second Vatican Council, preferring instead to address it in his 1967 encyclical *Sacerdotalis caelibatus*.[6]

He begins the encyclical by asking "Has the time not come to break the bond linking celibacy with the priesthood in the Church? Could the difficult observance of it not be made optional?" Although he readily admits that celibacy has not always been demanded of priests, he is not swayed by arguments that the abolition of mandatory celibacy is the appropriate response to reverse the decline in priestly vocations. "Hence We consider that the present law of celibacy should today continue to be linked to the ecclesiastical ministry."[7] But the rationale he puts forth is better suited toward recommending celibacy than it is toward mandating it.

Celibacy was not required of priests in the early church, and the Fathers of the church spoke only of the growth of voluntary celibacy. Popes from the fourth century forward promoted the practice of celibacy. Eventually, the requirement of mandatory celibacy was decreed by the Council of Trent and subsequently enacted into the Code of Canon Law. Even today, celibacy remains voluntary in Eastern Rite Catholic Churches, "due to the different historical background of that most noble part of the Church." Unfortunately, Paul does not detail these historical differences, so that it is not possible to evaluate whether they are sufficient to justify a difference in the discipline of celibacy between the Eastern and Western rites. He is quick to point out, however, that there are limitations on the ability of Eastern Rite priests to marry. "In the East only celibate priests are ordained bishops, and priests themselves cannot contract marriage after their ordination to the priesthood." Although he is unwilling to change the existing church discipline, he is prepared to authorize a study of whether to permit married ministers of other denominations who convert to Catholicism to become priests.[8] Two years later, he would authorize the ordination of four married former Anglican priests who had converted to Catholicism.[9]

Paul is unconvinced that a relaxation of the celibacy requirement would relieve the shortage of priests, because "the contemporary experience

---

5. O'Malley, *Vatican II*, 231.
6. Collins, *Keepers of the Keys*, 486; Reese, *Inside the Vatican*, 38.
7. Paul VI, *Sacerdotalis caelibatus*, 3, 5, 8, 14.
8. Ibid., 17, 35–36, 38, 40, 42.
9. Hebblethwaite, *Paul VI*, 496.

of those Churches and ecclesial communities which allow their ministers to marry seems to prove the contrary." Since Paul cites no support for this proposition, it is unclear whether it is based on statistically valid research, anecdotal evidence, or a preconceived opinion. He rejects the notions that celibacy is contrary to human nature and that full human development can only be found through marriage and family.[10] Paul poses the issue in absolute terms—either all priests must be celibate in order to properly fulfill their clerical duties, or all priests must be married in order to be fully human. Regardless of the persuasiveness of Paul's arguments, his rejection of voluntary celibacy for priests left one other option to redress the shortage of priests: the ordination of women.

The Priestly Ordination of Women is not an Option

Paul delegated the task of addressing this proposed solution to the Congregation for the Doctrine of the Faith, which took up the question in its declaration *Inter insigniores* in 1976. The congregation began by announcing its conclusion: "The Church, in fidelity to the example of the Lord, does not consider herself authorized to admit women to priestly ordination."[11] Therefore, unlike the issue of clerical celibacy, the ordination of women is not a disciplinary matter but a doctrinal one. It is not a question of the church not wanting to ordain women; it has no power to do so. The congregation did not simply announce its conclusion; it went on to advance several reasons supporting the ban on the priestly ordination of women.

The first argument is based on the church's "constant tradition" of ordaining only men, a practice which "has enjoyed peaceful and universal acceptance." Second, Jesus did not choose any women as apostles, not even his mother. Third, the apostles did not select Mary to fill a vacancy in the "College of the Twelve," electing Mathias instead. Fourth, the practices of Jesus and his apostles set forth in the previous two arguments are of permanent value. "The practice of the Church therefore has a normative character: in the fact of conferring priestly ordination only on men, it is a question of unbroken tradition throughout the history of the Church, universal in the East and in the West, and alert to repress abuses immediately. This norm, based on Christ's example, has been and is still observed because it is considered to conform to God's plan for his Church." The fifth argument is framed theologically, but it appears to be more psychological. Since Christ was a man, it would be difficult to see a female priest as exercising Christ's role in the

10. Paul VI, *Sacerdotalis caelibatus*, 49, 53–56.
11. Congregation for the Doctrine of the Faith, *Inter insigniores*, intro.

sacrament of the Eucharist. The sixth and final argument rejects any notion that the refusal to ordain women is a result of institutional gender discrimination or that it violates women's right to equality. "The priesthood does not form part of the rights of the individual, but stems from the economy of the mystery of Christ and the Church."[12] In other words, this is not a matter of employment discrimination, because the priesthood is not a career which one chooses but a vocation to which one is called by God.

Although *Inter insigniores* left no doubt as to the church's official position on the issue of women's ordination, it did not put to rest the doubts of many within the Catholic theological community. Karl Rahner, generally regarded as the leading Catholic theologian of the twentieth century, did not consider the document to be definitive, but possibly erroneous.[13] Many were unpersuaded by its reasoning. At the same time, an increasing number of women were entering Protestant ministry, and women were being ordained as priests by some churches in the Anglican Communion. But the fact that *Inter insigniores* was not issued by the pope himself did not mean that it could be ignored or its teaching disputed.

In 1990 the Congregation for the Doctrine of the Faith issued its instruction *Donum veritatis*. The instruction is concerned primarily with explicating the proper relationship between the Catholic theologian and the magisterium. But it also discusses the appropriate response required of all the faithful, not just theologians, to the pronouncements of the magisterium, noninfallible as well as infallible. Although its focus is not on the priestly ordination of women, the instruction confirms that the teaching of the congregation in *Inter insigniores* may not be disregarded or disagreed with simply because it is not a papal teaching. The official teaching of the magisterium is not limited to papal and conciliar documents, but extends to those issued by the Roman Curia, especially the Congregation for the Doctrine of the Faith. The congregation makes clear that, although the response of Catholics to noninfallible teaching is not on the same level as that called for by infallible pronouncements, that response must be one of acceptance rather than dissent.[14] Although the congregation acknowledges that statements of the magisterium may, over time, prove to be mistaken—or, in the words of the Congregation "might not be free from all deficiencies," such mistakes presumably are rare. "But it would be contrary to the truth, if, proceeding from some particular cases, one were to conclude the Church's Magisterium can be habitually mistaken in its prudential judgments, or that

12. Ibid., 1–6.
13. Kerr, *Twentieth-Century Catholic Theologians*, 102.
14. Congregation for the Doctrine of the Faith, *Donum veritatis*, 18, 23.

it does not enjoy divine assistance in the integral exercise of its mission." As a result, "the willingness to submit loyally to the teaching of the Magisterium on matters *per se* not irreformable must be the rule."[15]

This discussion of infallible versus noninfallible teaching in *Donum veritatis* highlights the problem of what has been called "creeping infallibility" or "creeping infallibilism." Richard McCormick has noted that "Yves Congar . . . stated that the ordinary magisterium 'has been almost assimilated, in current opinion, to the prerogatives of the extraordinary magisterium.' Thus, we have what is known as 'creeping infallibilism.'"[16] Richard McBrien has described the problem in the following terms. "Moreover, if there were no practical difference between infallible and noninfallible teaching, all noninfallible teaching would have to be taken *as if* it were infallible (the problem of 'creeping infallibility'). In that case, all church teaching would be unchangeable. But, in fact, church teachings *do* change, and therein lies the problem."[17] Francis Sullivan has opined that creeping infallibility may have the unintended consequence of diminishing, rather than enhancing, the authority of papal teaching.

> The tendency to obscure the difference between the infallible and the non-infallible exercise of magisterium, by treating papal encyclicals as though they were practically infallible, has, I believe, been largely responsible for the fact that many people, when they learn that encyclicals are not infallible after all, jump to the conclusion that one need pay no attention to them. If people have been led to think of the infallibility of the pope as the basic motive for giving their assent to his teaching, it is not surprising that when this motive is no longer available, their assent will fail as well.[18]

To the extent that the Vatican frets about the willingness of Catholics to freely dissent from noninfallible teachings, the distinction between the levels of papal teaching is one of Rome's own invention.

John Paul II: The Final Word on the Ordination of Women?

In order to settle once and for all the issue of the priestly ordination of women, John Paul II issued his apostolic letter *Ordinatio sacerdotalis* in

---

15. Ibid., 24.

16. McCormick, "The Search for Truth in the Catholic Context," in Curran and McCormick, *Dissent in the Church*, 421–34, 426.

17. McBrien, "Theologians under Fire," in ibid., 484–90, 487, emphasis in original.

18. Sullivan, *Magisterium*, 172.

1994. He briefly repeats some of the arguments that had been advanced in *Inter insigniores*, and then attempts to shut down debate in no uncertain terms. "Wherefore, in order that all doubt may be removed regarding a matter of great importance, a matter which pertains to the Church's divine constitution itself, in virtue of my ministry of confirming the brethren (cf. Lk 22:32) I declare that the Church has no authority whatsoever to confer priestly ordination on women and that this judgment is to be definitively held by all the Church's faithful."[19]

In the famous dictum attributed to Augustine, "Rome has spoken, the debate is over"; or so John Paul believed. However, there was a divide among theologians as to whether this teaching was an infallible pronouncement.[20] The following year, the Congregation for the Doctrine of the Faith weighed in on the dispute in a one page document concerning the teaching of *Ordinatio sacerdotalis*.

> This teaching requires definitive assent, since, founded on the written Word of God, and from the beginning constantly preserved and applied in the Tradition of the Church, it has been set forth infallibly by the ordinary and universal Magisterium (cf. Second Vatican Council, Dogmatic Constitution on the Church *Lumen Gentium* 25, 2). Thus, in the present circumstances, the Roman Pontiff, exercising his proper office of confirming the brethren (cf. Lk 22:32), has handed on this same teaching by a formal declaration, explicitly stating what is to be held always, everywhere, and by all, as belonging to the deposit of the faith.[21]

This document, in spite of its brevity, is a groundbreaking one, as Francis Sullivan has pointed out. "While Catholic theologians have commonly taught that there are some articles of faith which have never been solemnly defined, but have nonetheless been taught by the 'ordinary and universal magisterium,' the recent declaration of the CDF marks the first time, to my knowledge, that an authoritative document of the Holy See has specifically declared that a particular doctrine has been taught in this way."[22]

John Paul did all that he could to make sure that women may never become priests. Although one does not have to be a priest to be elected pope, canon law limits papal eligibility to males over the age of reason. Therefore, absent a change in canon law and an acknowledgment that *Ordinatio*

19. John Paul II, *Ordinatio sacerdotalis*, 4.

20. Cornwell, *Pontiff in Winter*, 133–34; McClory, *Power and the Papacy*, 206; Weigel, *Witness to Hope*, 728–33.

21. Congregation for the Doctrine of the Faith, *Responsum ad propositum dubium*.

22. Sullivan, *Creative Fidleity*, 182.

sacerdotalis was not an infallible teaching, there can never be any repeat of Pope Joan. No woman has, nor ever will, occupy the throne of Peter as pope. But it appears that at least one woman has exercised papal authority on occasion. When Alexander VI was away from Rome on papal (or family) business, he often left his "daughter Lucrezia ... in charge of the papacy, as virtual regent."[23] So long as *Ordinatio sacerdotalis* continues to be regarded as infallible teaching, no women will have the possibility of exercising priestly, much less, papal authority.

May Women Be Ordained as Deacons?

One aspect of the papal ban on the ordination of women that sometimes is overlooked is that it extends only to the ordination of women to the priesthood and does not foreclose the possibility of their ordination to the diaconate. The sacrament of Holy Orders "includes three degrees: episcopate, presbyterate, and diaconate."[24] The role of deacons is to assist the bishops and the priests in their ministry of service. "Among other tasks, it is the task of deacons to assist the bishops and priests in the celebration of the divine mysteries, above all the Eucharist, in the distribution of Holy Communion, in assisting at and blessing marriages, in the proclamation of the Gospel and preaching, in presiding over funerals, and in dedicating themselves to the various ministries of charity."[25]

In *Lumen gentium*, the Second Vatican Council determined that the possibility of reestablishing a permanent diaconate should be considered.[26] Following the conclusion of the council, Paul set forth norms for the establishment of the permanent diaconate.[27] Today, there are more than 42,000 men in the permanent diaconate.[28] The question remains, however, whether the order of permanent deacons could be opened to women.

In 2016, this question was posed to Francis by an assembly of women religious. Francis responded positively, appointing a twelve member commission, six of whom are female theologians, to study the issue. It is impossible to predict what conclusion such a commission might reach or whether that conclusion will prompt the pope to make a change in current Church practice. A commission would not be starting from scratch. In 2002 the

23. McBrien, *Lives of the Popes*, 268.
24. *Catechism*, No. 1536.
25. Ibid., No. 1570.
26. Second Vatican Council, *Lumen gentium*, 29.
27. Paul VI, *General Norms*.
28. Phyllis Zagano, "Introduction," in Zagano, *Women Deacons?* xii.

International Theological Commission issued a study document on the question.[29] Included in this study was an examination of the role played by deaconesses in the early Church. Although the commission's findings were inconclusive, the document could serve as a starting point for any papal commission. Moreover, there have been a number of scholarly studies of the female diaconate in the early church.[30] Given the speed with which the Vatican moves, the work of the commission may not even be completed during Francis's pontificate. A successor may not be as positively disposed toward the possibility of a female diaconate as Francis. Will a woman ever be ordained to the diaconate? One may, but only time will tell.

---

29. International Theological Commission, *From the Diakonia of Christ*.
30. See the studies contained in Zagano, *Women Deacons?*

14

Avoidance: The Problem of Evil and Suffering

> *How can Jews believe in an omnipotent, beneficial God after Auschwitz?*
>
> —Richard Rubenstein

> *In the Cross of Christ not only is the Redemption accomplished through suffering, but also human suffering itself has been redeemed.*
>
> —John Paul II

The Theodicy Problem: How Can God Permit Evil and Suffering?

No issue has been more troubling for philosophers and theologians than the problem of how an all-loving and all-powerful God can permit evil and suffering to exist in the world, a problem referred to by the term "theodicy." But until the 1980s, papal teaching had been virtually silent on the problem.

The term was coined by the German philosopher Gottfried Wilhelm Leibniz in his early eighteenth-century treatise *Theodicy: Essays on the Goodness of God, the Freedom of Man, and the Origin of Evil*. The theodicy problem has been expressed through various formulas, but a recent summary of the issue offered by American biblical scholar Bart Ehrman has the advantage of capturing the essence of the issue without resort to philosophical or theological jargon.

As philosophers and theologians have discussed theodicy over the years, they have devised a kind of logical problem that needs to be solved to explain the suffering in the world. This problem involves three assertions that all appear to be true, but if true appear to contradict one another. The assertions are these:

God is all powerful.

God is all loving.

There is suffering.

How can all three be true at once? If God is all powerful, then he is able to do whatever he wants (and can therefore remove suffering). If he is all loving, then he obviously wants the best for people (and therefore does not want them to suffer). And yet people suffer. How can that be explained?[1]

A variation on this formula, suggested by theologian David Ray Griffin, concludes that the presence of evil and suffering in the world negates the existence of an all-powerful and all-loving God.

The problem of evil is generally formalized as a syllogism using only ... three premises, as follows:

A. If God is omnipotent, God would prevent all evil.

B. If God is perfectly good, God would want to prevent all evil.

C. There is evil.

D. Therefore, [an omnipotent, perfectly good] God does not exist.[2]

Some of the most famous theological and philosophical minds have sought to answer this problem, but a consensus has never been reached.[3] All of the proposed "solutions", however, share a common element—they are unsatisfying, both intellectually and existentially.

---

1. Ehrman, *God's Problem*, 8.
2. Griffin, *God, Power, and Evil*, 18–19.
3. For an historical overview of the most significant philosophical and theological contributions to the theodicy problem, see ibid.

Novelists Rebel Against a God Who Permits Children to Suffer

Novelists have addressed the theodicy problem as well. Unlike philosophers and theologians, however, they have not felt compelled to offer answers. For example, characters in the novels of Fyodor Dostoevsky and Albert Camus rebel against a God who permits children to suffer from abuse and disease. For them, the problem of theodicy results in an indictment of God. A God who permits suffering cannot in any sense be considered all-loving, regardless of what recompense may be provided in the afterlife.

In Dostoevsky's novel *The Brothers Karamazov*, in the chapter entitled "Rebellion," Ivan Karamazov rails against a God who would permit children to suffer at the hands of an invading army or cruel parents. His brother Aloysha, a novice at a local monastery, acts as his sounding board. Ivan first cites an example of wartime atrocities committed by Turkish troops in Bulgaria. "'Here is another scene that I thought very interesting. Imagine a trembling mother with her baby in her arms, a circle of invading Turks around her. They've planned a game; they pet the baby, laugh to make it laugh. They succeed, the baby laughs. At that moment a Turk points a pistol four inches from the baby's face. The baby laughs, holds out its little hands to the pistol, and the Turk pulls the trigger in the baby's face and blows out its brains. Artistic, wasn't it?'"[4] Ivan then cites the example of a mother who abuses her young daughter.

> "This poor child of five was subjected to every possible torture by those cultivated parents. They beat her, kicked her for no reason till her body was one bruise. Then, they went to greater refinements of cruelty—shut her up all night in the cold and frost in a privy . . . they smeared her face and filled her mouth with excrement. . . . Can you understand why a little creature, who can't even understand what's done to her, should beat her little aching heart with her tiny fist in the dark and the cold, and weep her meek unresentful tears to dear, kind God to protect her?"[5]

Ivan refuses to take solace in the idea that all earthly suffering will be requited by an eternity spent in heaven. "'It's not worth the tears of that one tortured child who beat itself on the breast with its little fist and prayed in its stinking outhouse, with its tears to 'dear, kind God'! It's not worth it, because those tears are unatoned for. . . . And if the sufferings of children go to swell

---

4. Dostoevsky, *The Brothers Karamazov*, 220.
5. Ibid., 223.

the sum of sufferings which was necessary to pay for truth, then I protest that the truth is not worth such a price."⁶

In his encyclical *Spe salvi*, Benedict XVI acknowledges the seriousness of the moral problem of evil and suffering raised by Ivan Karamazov. He finds a partial answer to the theodicy problem in the fact that the perpetrators of evil, the Turkish soldiers and the abusive mother, will not share eternal life with their victims. "Grace does not cancel out justice. It does not make wrong into right. . . . Dostoevsky, for example, was right to protest against this kind of Heaven and this kind of grace in his novel *The Brothers Karamazov*. Evildoers, in the end, do not sit at table at the eternal banquet beside their victims without distinction, as though nothing had happened."⁷

The Plague is Camus' post-World War II novel about an epidemic of bubonic plague that strikes the North African city of Oran. At its heart, the novel is a story of those who refuse to succumb to the terror and who strive to protect what there is of value in human life. The religious response to the plague is represented by the local priest, Father Paneloux, who preaches that the plague is a punishment from God for the sins of the Oranians. In a sermon, he admonishes the citizens of Oran to accept God's providential care in spite of the plague. In contrast, the humanist response to the plague is represented by Doctor Rieux, whose job it is to combat the epidemic and treat its victims. He revolts against a world in which people die of plague and refuses to accept suffering as a trial imposed by God. He speaks to Father Paneloux in terms reminiscent of Ivan Karamazov's speech to his brother Aloysha. "'No, Father. I've a different idea of love. And until my dying day I shall refuse to love a scheme of things in which children are put to torture.'"⁸

The Theodicy Problem and the Holocaust

The issue of theodicy has acquired an existential urgency in the wake of the Holocaust. Franciscan theologian Thomas Weinandy, a member of the International Theological Commission since 2014, has referred to Auschwitz as "the contemporary icon of human suffering."⁹ The centrality of the Holocaust for theology today is evidenced by the following passage from Jewish theologian Richard Rubenstein.

---

6. Ibid., 225–26.
7. Benedict XVI, *Spe salvi*, 44.
8. Camus, *The Plague*, 196–97.
9. Weinandy, *Does God Suffer?* 262.

> I believe the greatest single challenge to modern Judaism arises out of the question of God and the death camps. I am amazed at the silence of contemporary Jewish theologians on this most crucial and agonizing of all Jewish issues. How can Jews believe in an omnipotent, beneficent God after Auschwitz? Traditional Jewish theology maintains that God is the ultimate, omnipotent actor in the historical drama. It has interpreted every major catastrophe in Jewish history as God's punishment of a sinful Israel. I fail to see how this position can be maintained without regarding Hitler and the SS as instruments of God's will. The agony of European Jewry cannot be likened to the testing of Job. To see any purpose in the death camps, the traditional believer is forced to regard the most demonic, antihuman explosion in all history as a meaningful expression of God's purposes. The idea is simply too obscene for me to accept.[10]

Traditional Jewish theology is not alone in viewing God as "the ultimate actor in history." Catholic and Protestant theologians over the centuries have advocated the same belief. For Augustine, "*nothing* happens other than what God wills to happen." Aquinas held "that God actually *does* everything that is done, that God causes everything that occurs." Luther held that "God does *all things* according to God's infallible will. And part of Luther's reasoning is that the necessity of all things follows from the fact that God surely wills and does what God foreknows––and this includes all things." For Calvin, "God is called omnipotent because 'he so regulates all things that nothing takes place without his deliberation.'"[11] The inescapable, but unacceptable, conclusion of this approach to the theodicy problem is that the death camps must be viewed as having been willed by God.

The Papal Response: Suffering Has Been Redeemed Through the Suffering and Death of Christ

Jewish theologians are not the only ones who have remained silent in the face of the challenge posed by the Holocaust to the belief in an omnipotent and all-loving God; so have most popes from Pius XII to Francis. The Catholic Church made no official response to the Holocaust until 1998, when the Holy See's Commission for Religious Relations with the Jews issued *We Remember: A Reflection on the Shoah*. The document states that "the Church approaches with deep respect and great compassion the experience

---

10. Rubenstein, *After Auschwitz*, 153.
11. Griffin, *God, Power, and Evil*, 63, 76, 104, 116, emphasis in original.

of extermination, the *Shoah*, suffered by the Jewish people during World War II," but it offers no insight into the theodicy problem.[12]

Although John Paul II did not raise the problem of theodicy in any of his encyclicals, he addressed the question in his apostolic letter *Salvifici doloris* in 1984, "the first official Roman Catholic document that specifically treats the subject of suffering."[13] John Paul mentions the suffering caused by the last two world wars, but he makes no reference to the Holocaust. Instead, he discusses the question of evil and suffering simply as part of the general human condition. "Within each form of suffering endured by man, and at the same time at the basis of the whole world of suffering, there inevitably arises *the question: why?*... Why does evil exist? Why is there evil in the world? When we put the question in this way, we are always, at least to a certain extent, asking a question about suffering too."[14]

John Paul first examines how the Bible explains suffering, starting with the author of the Book of Job in the Old Testament. Job was a wealthy man from the land of Uz who was blessed with sons and daughters, vast holdings of sheep, camels, oxen, and donkeys, and attended by vast number of servants. The book begins with a discussion between God and Satan. God describes Job as "'a blameless and upright man who fears God and turns away from evil'" (Job 1:8). But Satan responds that if God were to take away Job's blessings, Job would "'curse you to your face'" (Job 1:11). God accepts Satan's dare. Job's oxen, donkeys, and camels are stolen, his servants are put to the sword, and his children are killed when a desert windstorm caused a house to collapse upon them (Job 1:13–20).

Job's friends seek to explain the sufferings that had befallen him by reference to the traditional Old Testament belief that suffering is punishment for sin. But God acknowledges that Job is not guilty of any sin which would justify his suffering. According to John Paul, the answer to the theodicy question offered by the writer of Job is that suffering "must be accepted as a mystery, which the individual is unable to penetrate completely by his own intelligence."[15]

John Paul's analysis of the manner in which the Book of Job answers the theodicy question fails to mention how God responds to Job. God rewards Job by blessing him with twice the number of animals that he had before and by giving him seven new sons and three new daughters to "replace" those that had been taken away from Job (Job 42:10–17). Thus,

12. Commission for Religious Relations with the Jews, *We Remember*, 8.
13. Weinandy, *Does God Suffer?* 243 n. 2.
14. John Paul II, *Salvifici doloris*, 8–9.
15. Ibid., 10–11.

there is no theodicy problem, because Job is rewarded in this life for his faithfulness to God.

In the New Testament, John Paul says that the answer to the question of suffering is found in the redemptive death of Christ, who overcomes sin and death by his voluntary and innocent suffering. "In the Cross of Christ not only is the Redemption accomplished through suffering, but *also human suffering itself has been redeemed*." The suffering of a Christian is not in vain, because it is through suffering that a Christian shares in the suffering of Christ for the sake of the kingdom.[16] Although John Paul's explanation may satisfy an adult Christian that his or her suffering, however inexplicable, is not in vain, it would appear to offer little solace to a non-Christian victim of the Holocaust, a five-year-old abused at the hands of her mother, or a child-victim of the plague.

John Paul's solution to the theodicy problem is similar to one offered by John Hick, a preeminent philosopher of religion, who rejects the Augustinian/Calvinist explanation that suffering is just punishment for sins, whether original or personal. But like John Paul, Hick has no answer except an appeal to mystery. "Moreover, I do not now have an alternative theory to offer that would explain in any rational or ethical way why men suffer as they do. The only appeal left is to mystery. . . . Our 'solution,' then, to this baffling problem of excessive and undeserved suffering is a frank appeal to the positive value of mystery. Such suffering remains unjust and inexplicable, haphazard and cruelly excessive."[17]

Francis devotes one paragraph of his first encyclical, *Lumen fidei*, to the theodicy problem. The encyclical had been drafted by Benedict XVI but it was not published before his resignation. Francis issued it under his own name, having added "a few contributions" of his own. He points to Francis of Assisi and Mother Teresa as Christians who found those who suffer to be mediators of faith.[18]

Physical Evil and Moral Evil: Two Distinct Problems

The *Catechism* takes on the question of theodicy in some detail. Due to the lack of papal guidance, this section of the *Catechism* contains no citations to papal documents, relying instead on the teachings of Augustine and Aquinas. The *Catechism* recognizes that the theodicy problem is, in fact, two separate problems: the problem of physical evil (such as natural

---

16. Ibid., 15–21.
17. Hick, *Evil and the God of Love*, 333–35.
18. Francis, *Lumen fidei*, 7, 57.

disasters), and the problem of moral evil (such as the Holocaust). The answer which is given to the problem of moral evil is the classical free will defense. God gave people free will knowing that some people would abuse it and choose evil over good. God does not cause evil, but he permits it because he respects human freedom. The *Catechism* states that God is able to derive good from evil, but it offers no historical examples.[19] It is fair to ask what good has been derived from the Holocaust which could justify the extermination of six million Jews.

Theology always has had even more difficulty justifying physical evil. Free will and sin cannot explain floods, tsunamis, and earthquakes, despite the occasional rants of certain bloviating televangelists. The *Catechism* fails to explain why God, who could have created a perfect natural world, chose not to do so.

Although both religious and irreligious minds have wrestled with the question of evil and suffering for more than two thousand years, solutions have proven to be illusive. To say, as the *Catechism* does, that "Only Christian faith as a whole constitutes the answer to this question" is tantamount to an admission that no satisfactory answer can be found.[20] Like Job, we can do no more than accept the mystery, acknowledge God's power, and hope that we attain our reward, if not in this life then in the next. While the answers offered by John Paul and the *Catechism* present sound Catholic doctrine, they are manifestly unsatisfying. The deficiency lies not so much in the answers they proffer but in the manner in which they frame and analyze the question. Neither treats theodicy with the existential urgency of Rubenstein (a Jew) or exhibits the moral outrage of Dostoevsky (an Orthodox Christian) or Camus (an atheist). Instead, they discuss the issue in a clinical, academic manner that is the antithesis of the feelings that have compelled people over the centuries to raise the question of how an omnipotent and all-loving God can permit evil and suffering.[21]

Conclusion

When the pope speaks, he expects the faithful to listen. According to the *Catechism*, "the faithful receive with docility the teachings and directives

---

19. *Catechism*, Nos. 309–11.
20. Ibid., No. 309.
21. This approach is similar to the one taken by medieval theologians, for whom the existence of evil "was not regarded as an obstacle to belief, but simply as an academic theological problem" (McGrath, *Historical Theology*, 187).

that their pastors give them in different forms."[22] However, one can only receive with docility a teaching which is expressed without equivocation. Popes are not accustomed to addressing questions for which the Church does not have ready answers. They are most comfortable offering teachings and directives about those matters on which Catholic doctrine is settled, even if those doctrines are sometimes ones which the faithful find difficult to accept. The theodicy problem is not susceptible to an easy answer or solution. It is difficult to pontificate on a question to which Catholic teaching has pronounced no satisfactory answer.

---

22. *Catechism*, No. 87.

Postscript

Uncertainty: The Boundaries of the Infallibility of the College of Bishops

> *The history of Catholic doctrine suggests the need of great caution in claiming that something has been taught infallibly by the ordinary universal magisterium, if there is reason to judge that a position on which there was a consensus in the past no longer enjoys such a consensus.*
>
> —Francis Sullivan

> *It is possible for a teaching to have been taught by the ordinary universal magisterium without that fact being readily evident at a given point in time.*
>
> —Richard Gaillardetz

IN 1998 THE CONGREGATION for the Doctrine of the Faith under Cardinal Ratzinger issued its *Doctrinal Commentary on the Concluding Formula of the Professio fidei*. The *Doctrinal Commentary* contains a detailed discussion concerning the various doctrines which have been declared infallibly by the church, while at the same time downplaying the distinction between infallible and noninfallible teaching. Unfortunately, the result of the *Doctrinal Commentary* has been to further obscure the boundaries of the infallibility of the college of bishops and to exacerbate the problem of "creeping infallibility."

The *Professio fidei* begins with a recitation of the Nicene-Constantinopolitan Creed, and then adds the following three paragraphs.

> With firm faith, I also believe everything contained in the word of God, whether written or handed down in Tradition, which the Church, either by a solemn judgement or by the ordinary and universal Magisterium, sets forth to be believed as divinely revealed.
>
> I also firmly accept and hold each and everything definitively proposed by the Church regarding teaching on faith and morals.
>
> Moreover, I adhere with religious submission of will and intellect to the teachings which either the Roman Pontiff or the College of Bishops enunciate when they exercise their authentic Magisterium, even if they do not intend to proclaim these teachings by a definitive act.[1]

The *Doctrinal Commentary*, issued under the signature of the congregation's prefect, Cardinal Ratzinger, contains the most thorough curial statement on both infallibility and on the degree of deference owed by Catholics to the teachings of the magisterium, including those which are noninfallible. Although it would be difficult to overstate the importance of this document for an understanding of the nature and scope of infallibility, as well as for the manner in which it may be exercised, two caveats are in order. First, a statement of the congregation for the Doctrine of the Faith, even though approved by the pope, is not a papal declaration.[2] Second, the *Doctrinal Commentary* is by definition noninfallible, since the charism of infallibility granted to popes may not be delegated.[3] The congregation sets forth the purpose of the *Doctrinal Commentary* in the following manner. "This new formula of the *Professio fidei* restates the Nicene-Constaninopolitan Creed and concludes with the addition of three propositions or paragraphs intended to better distinguish the order of the truths to which the believer adheres. The correct explanation of these paragraphs deserves a clear presentation, so that their authentic meaning, as given by the Church's Magisterium, will be well understood, received and integrally preserved."[4] The "explanation" which follows may be clear to professional theologians and curial insiders, but probably not to the vast majority of the laity, or even many members of

---

1. Congregation for the Doctrine of the Faith, *Professio fidei*, 1.
2. Sullivan, "Magisterial Documents and Public Dissent," 511.
3. Orsy, "Magisterium," 479.
4. Congregation for the Doctrine of the Faith, *Doctrinal Commentary on Professio fidei*, 4.

the clergy. Any lack of clarity is not due to poor drafting. To the contrary, the *Doctrinal Commentary* is very carefully worded and precise in its terminology. The difficulty in understanding the document is due to its attempt to give a systematic explanation of the doctrine of infallibility, a doctrine which had developed in a haphazard manner over the preceding century.

The first paragraph or proposition of the *Professio fidei* deals with those doctrines of Catholic faith

> ... which the Church proposes as divinely and formally revealed and, as such, as irreformable.
>
> These doctrines *are contained in the word of God, written or handed down, and defined with a solemn judgment as divinely revealed truths either by the Roman Pontiff when he speaks "ex cathedra," or by the College of Bishops gathered in council, or infallibly proposed for belief by the ordinary and universal Magisterium.*
>
> These doctrines require *the assent of theological faith* by all members of the faithful. Thus, whoever obstinately places them in doubt or denies them falls under the censure of heresy, as indicated by the respective canons of the Code of Canon Law.[5]

The object of the first paragraph, therefore, is truths which the church has declared to be divinely revealed and which are to be believed by all Catholics. Later in the document, the congregation gives examples of divinely revealed doctrines which are covered by the first paragraph of the profession of faith.

> *To the truths of the first paragraph* belong the articles of faith of the Creed, the various Christological dogmas and Marian dogmas; the doctrine of the institution of the sacraments by Christ and their efficacy with regard to grace; the doctrine of the real and substantial presence of Christ in the Eucharist and the sacrificial nature of the eucharistic celebration; the foundation of the Church by the will of Christ; the doctrine on the primacy and infallibility of the Roman Pontiff; the doctrine on the existence of original sin; the doctrine on the immortality of the spiritual soul and on the immediate recompense after death; the absence of error in the inspired sacred texts; the doctrine on the grave immorality of direct and voluntary killing of an innocent human being.[6]

Although these truths are declared by the congregation to be divinely revealed, they are not doctrines which have been universally accepted as divinely revealed from the birth of Christianity. The key Christological

5. Ibid., 5.
6. Ibid., 11.

dogmas defining the divine and human natures of Christ were not dealt with authoritatively until the councils of the fourth and fifth centuries. The nature and number of the sacraments, especially the dogma of the real presence of Christ in the Eucharist, were definitively ruled upon by the Council of Trent in the sixteenth century, in reaction to the beliefs expressed by leaders of the Reformation. The doctrine of papal infallibility was not defined until the First Vatican Council in 1870. The Marian dogmas of the Immaculate Conception and the Assumption were not defined until 1854 and 1950, respectively. To address this point, the congregation will distinguish between the divinely revealed nature of a doctrine and the process by which it came to be recognized as divinely revealed.

The object of the second paragraph of the profession of faith concerns non-revealed truths which the magisterium has infallibly defined. These truths are those which the congregation referred to in *Mysterium ecclesiae* as "those matters without which that deposit [of faith] cannot be rightly preserved and expounded."[7]

> The object taught by this formula includes *all those teachings belonging to the dogmatic or moral area, which are necessary for faithfully keeping and expounding the deposit of faith, even if they have not been proposed by the Magisterium of the Church as formally revealed.*
>
> Such doctrines *can be defined solemnly by the Roman Pontiff when he speaks "ex cathedra" or by the College of Bishops gathered in council, or they can be taught infallibly by the ordinary and universal Magisterium of the Church as a "sententia definitve tenenda".* Every believer, therefore, is required to give firm and definitive assent to these truths, based on faith in the Holy Spirit's assistance to the Church's Magisterium, and on the Catholic doctrine of the infallibility of the Magisterium in these matters. Whoever denies these truths would be in a position of *rejecting a truth of Catholic doctrine and would therefore no longer be in full communion with the Catholic Church.*[8]

Therefore, regardless of whether a truth is a divinely revealed truth (first paragraph) or a non-revealed truth which has been definitively proposed by the magisterium (second paragraph), each is an infallible doctrine to which all Catholics must consent.[9]

---

7. Congregation for the Doctrine of the Faith, *Mysterium ecclesiae*, 3.

8. Congregation for the Doctrine of the Faith, *Doctrinal Commentary on Professio fidei*, 6.

9. Ibid., 8.

The congregation gives several unrelated examples of truths of the second paragraph: the development of the doctrine of papal infallibility; the doctrine that priestly ordination is limited to men; the illicitness of euthanasia; the illicitness of prostitution and fornication; and doctrines relating to papal elections, canonization of saints, and the invalidity of Anglican ordinations.[10]

The congregation boldly asserts that belief in primacy of the bishop of Rome "was always believed as a revealed fact" from the beginning by the church.[11] This assertion rests on shaky historical ground. Historians have found little evidence of Peter's presence in Rome, in spite of Paul VI's claim in 1968 that the bones of St. Peter had been discovered under the basilica in Rome that bears his name. The first real bishop of Rome may not have been in place until the middle of the second century or perhaps even later.[12] The substance of the congregation's argument concerning papal infallibility rests on a distinction between two facts, one of which is of a historical nature and the other a matter of faith alone. The fact that the infallibility of the pope is a divinely revealed truth is a faith claim, not an historical event subject to verification. The fact that the divinely revealed nature of this truth was not recognized until the doctrine was defined by the First Vatican Council in 1870 is a historical event. During the period prior to Vatican I, the doctrine of infallibility was a truth of the second paragraph; since the council, it has been a truth of the first paragraph. Following this logic, it would appear that the Marian dogmas are of a similar character. According to the apostolic constitutions which defined the dogmas of the Immaculate Conception and the Assumption, those doctrines were long held to be true—but not confirmed as divinely revealed—until 1854 and 1950, respectively.

The second example given by the congregation of a doctrine belonging to the second paragraph is the doctrine of the limitation of priestly ordination to men.

> A similar process can be observed in the more recent teaching regarding the doctrine that priestly ordination is reserved only to men. The Supreme Pontiff, while not wishing to proceed to a dogmatic definition, intended to reaffirm that this doctrine is to be held definitively, since, founded on the written word of God, constantly preserved and applied in the Tradition of the Church, it had been set forth infallibly by the ordinary and universal Magisterium. As the prior example illustrates, this

---

10. Ibid., 9.
11. Ibid.
12. Collins, *Keepers of the Keys*, 5–14; Sullivan, *From Apostles to Bishops*, 14–15.

> does not foreclose the possibility that, in the future, the consciousness of the Church might progress to the point where this teaching could be defined as a doctrine to be believed as divinely revealed.[13]

The intention of the pope to "reaffirm" the doctrine is a reference to John Paul's apostolic letter *Ordiantio sacerdotalis*.

The third example given by the congregation of a proposition of the second paragraph is the illicitness of euthanasia, which John Paul had addressed in his encyclical *Evangelium vitae*.

> The doctrine on the illicitness of euthanasia, taught in the Encyclical Letter *Evangelium Vitae*, can also be recalled. Confirming that euthanasia is "a grave violation of the law of God", the Pope declares that "this doctrine is based upon the natural law and upon the written word of God, is transmitted by the Church's Tradition and taught by the ordinary and universal Magisterium." It could seem that there is only a logical element in the doctrine on euthanasia, since Scripture does not seem to be aware of the concept. In this case, however, the interrelationship between the orders of faith and reason becomes apparent: Scripture, in fact, clearly excludes every form of the kind of self-determination of human existence that is presupposed in the theory and practice of euthanasia.[14]

Recall that the prohibition on euthanasia was one of the three declarations of infallibility which John Paul made in *Evangelium vitae*. In that same encyclical, he infallibly declared that direct abortion is a grave sin. Like euthanasia, abortion is not mentioned in scripture. Abortion would seem to be the same "kind of self-determination of human existence" as euthanasia and proscribed for the same reason. But the congregation did not choose to include the illicitness of abortion as an example of a proposition of the second paragraph.

The next example of sins that have been definitively held to be gravely immoral is "the teaching of the illicitness of prostitution and of fornication."[15] The congregation does not explicitly state in what manner these actions have been infallibly declared to be sinful. The footnotes refer to the *Catechism*, but it contains no reference to an infallible declaration of the sinfulness of these activities. Fornication is condemned in the *Catechism*

---

13. Congregation for the Doctrine of the Faith, *Doctrinal Commentary on Professio fidei*, 11.
14. Ibid.
15. Ibid.

as "gravelly contrary to the dignity of persons and of human sexuality."[16] Likewise, prostitution is decried because it "reduces the person to an instrument of sexual pleasure."[17]

It would appear that the illicitness of euthanasia has been held definitively by a non-defining act of John Paul in *Evangelium vitae*, wherein he confirmed the teaching of the ordinary and universal magisterium but did not give a solemn definition. According to theologian Richard Gaillardetz "The pope may exercise his own ordinary papal magisterium to confirm the teaching of the bishops. We have seen this papal confirmation at work implicitly in *Ordinatio sacerdotalis* and explicitly in *Evangelium vitae*."[18] The illicitness of prostitution and fornication, on the other hand, can only have been held definitively by a non-defining act which has not been confirmed by the pope, since there is no statement anywhere that their sinfulness is to be definitively held. The exercise of infallibility by a non-defining act, where such infallibility has not been confirmed or reaffirmed by the pope, is difficult to discern. As Gaillardetz also has noted, "Today it is commonly recognized that one of the vexing features of the exercise of the ordinary universal magisterium arises because no clearly defining act is involved. This creates serious difficulties for verifying that a given teaching has, in fact, been taught infallibly by the ordinary universal magisterium."[19] The same section of the *Catechism* referred to above also declares lust, masturbation, pornography, and rape to be violations of the Sixth Commandment.[20] Should one understand that these activities are also held to be sinful by a non-defining act of the ordinary and universal magisterium? The range of doctrines which might be held to be infallible due to the exercise of a non-defining act of the ordinary and universal magisterium appears to be theoretically limitless.

The final examples given by the congregation of doctrines within the second paragraph are the following ecclesiological ones. "With regard to those truths connected to revelation by historical necessity and which are to be held definitively, but are not able to be declared as divinely revealed, the following examples can be given: the legitimacy of the election of the Supreme Pontiff or of the celebration of an ecumenical council, the canonizations of saints (*dogmatic facts*), the declarations of Pope Leo XIII in the Apostolic

---

16. *Catechism*, No. 2353.
17. Ibid., No. 2355.
18. Gaillardetz, "Ordinary Universal Magisterium," 468.
19. Ibid., 462.
20. *Catechism*, Nos. 2351–56.

Letter *Apostolicae Curae* on the invalidity of Anglican ordinations."[21] Since these doctrines have not been declared to be held definitively by a defining act, they are further instances of non-defining declarations of infallibility. The surprising inclusion in this list is the one involving the invalidity of Anglican ordinations. It is not an example different in kind from the other two included in the same paragraph, so that its inclusion was superfluous. Its only effect, whether intended or otherwise, was to ignite an ecumenical firestorm with the Anglican hierarchy.[22]

Finally, the third paragraph of the profession of faith concerns the assent required to be given to noninfallible teachings of the magisterium. The reach of this paragraph encompasses all noninfallible doctrines taught by the magisterium.

> To this paragraph belong *all those teachings—on faith and morals—presented as true or at least as sure, even if they have not been defined with a solemn judgement or proposed as definitive by the ordinary and universal Magisterium.* Such teachings are, however, an authentic expression of the ordinary Magisterium of the Roman Pontiff or of the College of Bishops and therefore require *religious submission of will and intellect.* They are set forth in order to arrive at a deeper understanding of revelation, or to recall the conformity of a teaching with the truths of faith, or lastly to warn against ideas incompatible with those truths or against dangerous opinions that could lead to error.[23]

The congregation provides no concrete examples of any doctrines belonging to the third paragraph. Would the *Syllabus of Errors* of Pius IX be one of those doctrines? The *Syllabus* appears to meet the criteria established by the congregation for a doctrine of the third paragraph. The vast majority of propositions condemned by the *Syllabus* are matters of faith and morals. They certainly were denounced in order "to warn against . . . dangerous opinions that could lead to error." If the *Syllabus* belongs to a doctrine of the third paragraph, then what degree of deference must be given to its pronouncements? The "nature of the document" testifies to its seriousness. Pius IX frequently repeated his condemnation of the errors of the modern age, especially liberalism, indifferentism, and socialism. These condemnations were echoed by Pius X in *Lametabili sane,* which also added a condemnation

---

21. Congregation for the Doctrine of the Faith, *Doctrinal Commentary on Professio fidei,* 11.

22. Allen, *Benedict XVI,* 230.

23. Congregation for the Doctrine of the Faith, *Doctrinal Commentary on Professio fidei,* 10.

of Modernist opinions. The "tenor of the verbal expression" of the *Syllabus* could hardly be stronger.

All of these points would suggest that a high degree of assent is required to the *Syllabus*. However, there is a mitigating factor, which is the deafening silence from the magisterium over the *Syllabus* since Vatican II. Does a doctrine still require assent if that doctrine has for all practical purposes been abandoned? There is a legal concept known as "desuetude," whereby a statute will lapse for its failure to be enforced for a lengthy period of time, even though it has not formally been repealed. This raises the question whether assent to a doctrine is required if that doctrine has in practice been abandoned through silence. Assent certainly cannot be required regarding those "erroneous" propositions on religious freedom and church-state relations which were condemned by the *Syllabus*, since they have become the normative church doctrine as established by the Second Vatican Council. This issue has not been addressed in any encyclical or in any document issued by the Congregation for the Doctrine of the Faith.

It is not logically possible to assent to both a nineteenth century expression of church teaching on religious freedom and church-state relations and also to assent to Vatican II's contrary teaching. The church cannot expect believers to docilely accept as true two logically inconsistent doctrines. If the church's position is that the faithful should accept the current teaching and ignore the prior teaching, then it should say so. A straightforward acknowledgement that the church's teaching on religious freedom and church-state relations is noninfallible and subject to change would be refreshing, but not likely forthcoming.

Bibliography

Ahlstrom, Sydney E. *A Religious History of the American People*. 2nd ed. New Haven: Yale University Press, 2004.
Allen, John L., Jr. *The Future Church: How Ten Trends are Revolutionizing the Catholic Church*. New York: Doubleday, 2009.
———. *Pope Benedict XVI: A Biography of Joseph Ratzinger*. New York: Continuum, 2000.
Alvarez, David. *Spies in the Vatican: Espionage and Intrigue from Napoleon to the Holocaust*. Lawrence: University Press of Kansas, 2002.
Bell, Daniel M., Jr. *Just War as Christian Discipleship: Recentering the Tradition in the Church rather than the State*. Grand Rapids: Brazos, 2009.
Benedict XV. Apostolic letter *Maximun illud: On the Propagation of the Faith throughout the World*. 1919. http://www.svdcuria.org/public/mission/docs/encycl/mi-en.htm.
———. Encyclical *Ad beatissimi Apostolorum: Appealing for Peace*. 1914. http://w2.vatican.va/content/benedict-xv/en/encyclicals/documents/hf_ben-xv_enc_01111914_ad-beatissimi-apostolorum.html.
———. Encyclical *Annus iam plenus: On Children of Central Europe*. 1920. http://w2.vatican.va/content/benedict-xv/en/encyclicals/documents/hf_ben-xv_enc_01121920_annus-iam-plenus.html.
———. Encyclical *Pacem, Dei munus pulcherrimum: On Peace and Christian Reconciliation*. 1920. http://w2.vatican.va/content/benedict-xv/en/encyclicals/documents/hf_ben-xv_enc_23051920_pacem-dei-munus-pulcherrimum.html.
———. Encyclical *Paterno iam diu: On the Children of Central Europe*. 1919. http://w2.vatican.va/content/benedict-xv/en/encyclicals/documents/hf_ben-xv_enc_24111919_paterno-iam-diu.html.
———. Encyclical *Quod iam diu: On the Future Peace Conference*. 1918. http://w2.vatican.va/content/benedict-xv/en/encyclicals/documents/hf_ben-xv_enc_01121918_quod-iam-diu.html.
Benedict XVI. *Address of His Holiness Benedict XVI to the Members of the Roman Curia at the Traditional Exchange of Christmas Greetings*. 2006. http://w2.vatican.va/content/benedict-xvi/en/speeches/2006/december/documents/hf_ben_xvi-spe_20061222_curia-romana.html.

———. Apostolic exhortation *Africae Munus: On the Church in Africa in Service to Reconciliation, Justice, and Peace*. 2011. http://w2.vatican.va/content/benedict-xvi/en/apost_exhortations/documents/hf_ben-xvi_exh_20111119_africae-munus.html.

———. Apostolic exhortation *Sacramentum Caritatis: On the Eucharist as the Source and Summit of the Church's Life and Mission*. 2007. http://w2.vatican.va/content/beneddict-xvi/en/apost_exhortations/documents/hf_ben-xvi_exh_20070222_sacramentum-caritatis.html.

———. Apostolic exhortation *Verbum Domini: On the Word of God in the Life and Mission of the Church*. 2010. http://w2.vatican.va/content/benedict-xvi/en/apost_exhortations/documents/hf_ben-xvi_exh_20100930_verbum-domini.html.

———. Apostolic letter *"motu proprio" Ubicumque et semper: Establishing the Pontifical Council for Promoting the New Evangelization*. 2010. http://w2.vatican.va/content/benedict-xvi/en/apost_letters/documents/hf_ben-xvi_apl_20100921_ubicumque-et-semper.html.

———. Encyclical *Caritas in veritate: On Integral Human Development in Charity and Truth*. 2009. http://w2.vatican.va/content/benedict-xvi/en/encyclicals/documents/hf_ben-xvi_enc_20090629_caritas-in-veritate.html.

———. Encyclical *Deus caritas est: On Christian Love*. 2005. http://w2.vatican.va/content/benedict-xvi/en/encyclicals/documents/hf_ben-xvi_enc_20051225_deus-carits-est.html.

———. Encyclical *Spe salvi: On Christian Hope*. 2007. http://w2.vatican.va/content/benedict-xvi/en/encyclicals/documents/hf_ben-xvi_enc_20071130_spe-salvi.html

———. *Reflections of His Holiness Benedict XVI Published for the First Time on the Fiftieth Anniversary of the Opening of the Second Vatican Council*. 2012. http://www.vatican.va/special/annus_fidei/documents/annus-fidei_bxvi_inedito-50-concilio_en.html.

Blet, Pierre. *Pius XII and the Second World War: According to the Archives of the Vatican*. Translated by Lawrence J. Johnson. Mahwah, NJ: Paulist, 1999.

Boniface VIII. Papal bull *Unam sanctam*. 1302. http://www.papalencyclicals.net/Bono8/B8unam.htm.

Brettler, Marc Zvi. *How to Read the Jewish Bible*. New York: Oxford University Press, 2007.

Camus, Albert. *The Plague*. Translated by Stuart Gilbert. New York: Vintage, 1972.

Carroll, James. *Constantine's Sword: The Church and the Jews; A History*. New York: Mariner, 2002.

Cassidy, Edward Idris. *Ecumenism and Interreligious Dialogue: Unitatis Redintegratio, Nostra Aetate*. Mahwah, NJ: Paulist, 2005.

Catechism of the Catholic Church: With Modifications from the Editio Typica. 2nd ed. Translated by United States Catholic Conference. New York: Doubleday, 1997.

Chadwick, Owen. *A History of the Popes, 1830–1914*. New York: Oxford University Press, 1998.

Chiron, Yves. *Pope Pius IX: The Man and the Myth*. Translated by Graham Harrison. Kansas City, MO: Angelus, 2005.

Clark, Meghan J. *The Vision of Catholic Social Thought: The Virtue of Solidarity and the Praxis of Human Rights*. Minneapolis: Fortress, 2014.

Clement XII. Papal bull *In eminenti: On Freemasonry*. 1738. http://www.papal encyclicals.net/Clem12/cl5inemengl.htm.

Collins, Roger. *Keepers of the Keys of Heaven: A History of the Papacy*. New York: Basic, 2009.

Commission for Religious Relations with the Jews. *"The Gifts and the Calling of God are Irreviocable" (Rom 11:29): A Reflection on Theological Questions Pertaining to Catholic Jewish Relations on the Occasion of the Fiftieth Anniversary of "Nostra Aetate" (n. 4)*. 2015. http://www/vatican.va/roman_curia/pontifical_councils/chrstuni/relations-jews-docs/rc_pc_chrstuni_doc_20151210_ebraismo-nostra-aetate_en.html.

———. *Guidelines and Suggestions for Implementing the Conciliar Declaration "Nostra Aetate" (n. 4)*. 1974. http://www/vatican.va/roman_curia/pontifical_councils/chrstuni/relations-jews-docs/rc_pc_chrstuni_doc_19741201_nostra-aetate_en.html.

———. *Notes on the Correct Way to Present the Jews and Judaism in Preaching and Catechesis in the Roman Catholic Church*. 1982. http://www/vatican.va/roman_curia/pontifical_councils/chrstuni/relations-jews-docs/rc_pc_chrstuni_doc_19820306_jews-judaism_en.html.

———. *We Remember: A Reflection on the Shoah*. 1998. http://www/vatican.va/roman_curia/pontifical_councils/chrstuni/documents/rc_pc_chrstu ni_doc_16031998_shoah_en.html.

Concordat between the Holy See and France. 1801. http://www.concordatwatch.eu/kb-1496.834.

Concordat between the Holy See and Germany. 1933. http://www.concordatwatch.eu/kb-1211.834.

Concordat between the Holy See and Spain. 1851. http://www.concordatwatch.eu/showtopic.php?org_id=845&kb_header_id=34511.

Congregation for Catholic Education. Decree *On the Reform of Ecclesiastical Studies of Philosophy*. 2011. http://www.vatican.va/roman_curia/congregations/ccatheduc/documents/rc_con_ccatheduc_doc_20110128_dec-rif-filosofia_en.html.

———. Instruction *Concerning the Criteria for the Discernment of Vocations with regard to Persons with Homosexual Tendencies in View of Their Admission to the Seminary and to Holy Orders*. 2005. http://www.vatican.va/roman_curia/congregations/ccatheduc/documents/rc_con_ccatheduc_doc_20051104_instruzione_en.html.

Congregation for the Doctrine of the Faith. *Considerations regarding Proposals to Give Legal Recognition to Unions between Homosexual Persons*. 2003. http://www.vatican.va/roman_curia/congregations/cfaith/documents/rc_con_cfaith_doc_20030731_homosexual-unions_en.html.

———. Declaration *"Dominus Jesus": On the Unicity and Salvific Universality of Jesus Christ and the Church*. 2000. http://www.vatican.va/roman_curia/congregations/cfaith/documents/rc_con_cfaith_doc_20000806_dominus-jesus_en.html.

———. Declaration *Inter insigniores: On the Question of Admission of Women to the Ministerial Priesthood*. 1976. http://www.vatican.va/roman_curia/congregations/cfaith/documents/rc_con_cfaith_doc_19761015_inter-insigniores_en.html.

———. Declaration *On Masonic Associations*. 1983. http://www.vatican.va/roman_curia/congregations/cfaith/documents/rc_con_cfaith_doc_19831126_declaration-masoinc_en.html.

———. Declaration *Mysterium ecclesiae: In Defense of the Catholic Doctrine on the Church against Certain Errors of the Present Day*. 1973. http://www.vatican.va/roman_curia/congregations/cfaith/documents/rc_con_cfaith_doc_19730705_mysterium-ecclesiae_en.html.

———. Declaration *Persona Humana: On Certain Questions concerning Sexual Ethics*. 1975. http://www.vatican.va/roman_curia/congregations/cfaith/documents/rc_con_cfaith_doc_19751229_persona-humana_en.html.

———. Declaration *Questio de abortu procurator: On Procured Abortion*. 1974. http://www.vatican.va/roman_curia/congregations/cfaith/documents/rc_con_cfaith_doc_19741118_declaration-abortion_en.html.

———. *Doctrinal Commentary on the Concluding Formula of the "Professio fidei."* 1998. http://www.vatican.va/roman_curia/congregations/cfaith/documents/rc_con_cfaith_doc_1998_professio-fidei_en.html.

———. Instruction *Donum veritatis: On the Ecclesial Vocation of the Theologian*. 1990. http://www.vatican.va/roman_curia/congregations/cfaith/documents/rc_con_cfaith_doc_19900524_theologian-vocation_en.html.

———. Instruction *Libertatis conscientia: On Christian Freedom and Liberation*. 1986. http://www.vatican.va/roman_curia/congregations/cfaith/documents/rc_con_cfaith_doc_19840322_freedom-liberation_en.html.

———. Instruction *Libertatis nuntius: On certain Aspects of the "Theology of Liberation."* 1984. http://www.vatican.va/roman_curia/congregations/cfaith/documents/rc_con_cfaith_doc_19840806_theology-liberation_en.html.

———. *Letter to the Bishops of the Catholic Church on the Pastoral Care of Homosexual Persons*. 1986. http://www.vatican.va/roman_curia/congregations/cfaith/documents/rc_con_cfaith_doc_19861001_homosexual-persons_en.html.

———. Notification *On the book Toward a Christian Theology of Religious Pluralism by Father Jacques Dupuis, SJ*. 2001. http://www.vatican.va/roman_curia/congregations/cfaith/documents/rc_con_cfaith_doc_20010124_dupuis_en.html.

———. *The Primacy of the Successor of Peter in the Mystery of the Church*. 1998. http://www.vatican.va/roman_curia/congregations/cfaith/documents/rc_con_cfaith_doc_19981031_primato-successore-pietro_en.html.

———. *Responsum ad propositum dubium concerning the Teaching contained in "Ordinatio sacerdotalis."* 1995. http://www.vatican.va/roman_curia/congregations/cfaith/documents/rc_con_cfaith_doc_19951028_dubium-ordinatio-sac_en.html.

———. *Some Considerations concerning the Response to Legislative Proposals on the non-Discrimination of Homosexual Persons*. 1992. http://www.vatican.va/roman_curia/congregations/cfaith/documents/rc_con_cfaith_doc_19920724_homosexual-persons_en.html.

Connelly, John. *From Enemy to Brother: The Revolution in Catholic Teaching on the Jews, 1933–1965*. Cambridge, MA: Harvard University Press, 2012.

Copleston, Frederick. *A History of Philosophy*. Vol. 2, *Medieval Philosophy, Part 2: Albert the Great to Duns Scotus*. Garden City, NY: Image, 1962.

———. *A History of Philosophy*. Vol. 5, *Modern Philosophy: The British Philosophers, Part 1; Hobbes to Paley*. Garden City, NY: Image, 1964.

Coppa, Frank, Jr., ed. *Controversial Concordats: The Vatican's Relations with Napoleon, Mussolini, and Hitler*. Washington, DC: Catholic University of America Press, 1999.

———. *The Life and Pontificate of Pope Pius XII: Between History and Controversy.* Washington, DC: Catholic University of America Press, 2013.

———. *Politics and the Papacy in the Modern World.* Westport, CT: Praeger, 2008.

Cornwell, John A. *Hitler's Pope: The Secret History of Pius XII.* New York: Viking, 1999.

———. *The Pontiff in Winter: Triumph and Conflict in the Reign of John Paul II.* New York: Image, 2005.

Council of Trent, Fourth Session. *Decree concerning the Edition, and the Use, of the Sacred Books.* 1546. http://history.hanover.edu/texts/trent/ct04.html.

Council of Trent, Thirteenth Session. *Decree concerning the Most Holy Sacrament of the Eucharist.* 1551. http://history.hanover.edu/texts/trent/ct13.html.

Crossan, John Dominic. *Who Killed Jesus? Exposing the Roots of Anti-Semitism in the Gospel Story of the Death of Jesus.* New York: HarperSanFrancisco, 1995.

Crossan, John Dominic, and Jonathan L. Reed. *Excavating Jesus: Beneath the Stones, Behind the Texts.* New York: HarperSanFrancisco, 2001.

Curran, Charles E. *Catholic Social Teaching, 1891–Present: A Historical, Theological, and Ethical Analysis.* Washington, DC: Georgetown University Press, 2002.

———, ed. *Change in Official Catholic Moral Teachings.* Readings in Moral Theology 13 Mahwah, NJ: Paulist, 2003.

Curran, Charles E., and Richard A. McCormick, eds. *Dissent in the Church.* Readings in Moral Theology 6: Mahwah, NJ: Paulist, 1988.

D'Agostino, Peter R. *Rome in America: Transnational Catholic Ideology from the Risorgimento to Fascism.* Chapel Hill: University of North Carolina Press, 2004.

Dawkins, Richard. *The God Delusion.* New York: Mariner, 2008.

De Mattei, Roberto. *Pius IX.* Translated by John Laughland. Herefordshire, UK: Gracewing, 2004.

Denzinger, Heinrich, and Peter Hünermann. *Enchiridion symbolorum definitionum et declarationum de rebus fidei et morum: Compendium of Creeds, Definitions, and Declarations on Matters of Faith and Morals.* 43rd ed. San Francisco: Ignatius, 2012.

DiNoia, J. A. *The Diversity of Religions: A Christian Perspective.* Washington, DC: Catholic University of America Press, 1992.

Dorr, Donal. *Option for the Poor and for the Earth: Catholic Social Teaching.* Rev. ed. Maryknoll, NY: Orbis, 2012.

Dostoevsky, Fyodor. *The Brothers Karamazov.* Translated by Constance Garnett. New York: Signet Classics, 1957.

Dreisbach, Daniel L., and Mark David Hall, eds. *Faith and the Founders of the American Republic.* New York: Oxford University Press, 2014.

Duffy, Eamon. *Saints and Sinners: A History of the Popes.* 3rd ed. New Haven: Yale University Press, 2006.

———. *Ten Popes Who Shook the World.* New Haven: Yale University Press, 2011.

Dulles, Avery. *The Craft of Theology: From Symbol to System.* Rev. ed. New York: Crossroad, 1995.

Dupuis, Jacques. *Toward a Christian Theology of Religious Pluralism.* Maryknoll, NY: Orbis, 2001.

Ehrman, Bart D. *God's Problem: How the Bible Fails to Answer Our Most Important Question—Why We Suffer.* New York: HarperOne, 2008.

Elsbernd, Mary. "What Ever Happened to *Octogesima Adveniens*?" *Theological Studies* 56 (1995) 39–60.

Fattorini, Emma. *Hitler, Mussolini, and the Vatican: Pope Pius XI and the Speech that Was Never Made.* Translated by Carl Ipsen. Cambridge: Polity, 2011.

Feldman, Noah. *Divided by God: America's Church-State Problem—and What We Should Do about It.* New York: Farrar, Strauss & Giroux, 2005.

First Vatican Council. Dogmatic constitution *Dei Filius: On the Catholic Faith.* 1870. http://vaxxine.com/pjm/vatican1.htm.

———. Dogmatic constitution *Pastor Aeternus: On the Church of Christ.* 1870. http://fisheaters.com/pastoraeternus.html.

Ford, John C., and Germain Grisez. "Contraception and the Infallibility of the Ordinary Magisterium." *Theological Studies* 39 (1978) 258–312.

Fourth Lateran Council. *Canons of the Fourth Lateran Council.* 1215. http://www.fordham.edu/halsall/basis/lateran4.html.

Francis. Apostolic exhortation *Amoris Laetitia: On Love in the Family.* 2016. http://w2.vatican.va/content/francesco/en/apost_exhortations/documents/papa-francesco_esortazione-ap_20160319_amoris-laetitia.html.

———. Apostolic exhortation *Evangelii gaudium: On the Proclamation of the Gospel in Today's World.* 2013. http://w2.vatican.va/content/francesco/en/apost_exhortations/documents/papa-francesco_esortazione-ap_20131124_evangelli-gaudium.html.

———. Encyclical *Laudato si': On Care for our Common Home.* 2015. http://w2.vatican.va/content/francesco/en/encyclicals/documents/papa-francesco_20150524_enciclica-laudato-si.html.

———. Encyclical *Lumen fidei: On Faith.* 2013. http://w2.vatican.va/content/francesco/en/encyclicals/documents/papa-francesco_20130629_enciclica-lumen-fidei.html.

Gaillardetz, Richard R. "The Ordinary Universal Magisterium: Unresolved Questions." *Theological Studies* 63 (2002) 447–71.

Gardella, Peter. *American Civil Religion: What Americans Hold Sacred.* New York: Oxford University Press, 2014.

Gill, Anthony. *The Political Origins of Religious Liberty.* New York: Cambridge University Press, 2008.

González, Justo L. *The Story of Christianity.* Vol. 1, *The Early Church to the Dawn of the Reformation.* Rev. ed. New York: HarperOne, 2010.

———. *The Story of Christianity.* Vol. 2, *The Reformation to the Present Day.* Rev. ed. New York: HarperOne, 2010.

Gottschalk, Peter. *American Heretics: Catholics, Jews, Muslims, and the History of Religious Intolerance.* New York: Palgrave MacMillan, 2013.

Green, Steven. *The Bible, the School, and the Constitution: The Clash that Shaped Modern Church-State Doctrine.* New York: Oxford University Press, 2012.

———. *Inventing a Christian America: The Myth of the Religious Founding.* New York: Oxford University Press, 2015.

———. *The Second Disestablishment: Church and State in Nineteenth-Century America.* New York: Oxford University Press, 2010.

Gregory XVI. Encyclical *Inter Praecipuas: On Biblical Societies.* 1844. http://www.papalencyclicals.net/Greg16/g16inter.htm.

———. Encyclical *Mirari vos: On Liberalism and Religious Indifferentism.* 1832. http://www.papalencyclicals.net/Greg16/g16mirar.htm.

———. Encyclical *Singulari nos: On the Errors of Lammenais*. 1834. http://www.papalencyclicals.net/Greg16/g16singu.htm.
Griffin, David Ray. *God, Power, and Evil: A Process Theodicy*. Louisville: Westminster John Knox, 2004.
Guarino, Thomas G. "*Fides et Ratio*: Theology and Contemporary Pluralism." *Theological Studies* 62 (2001) 675–700.
Gunn, T. Jeremy, and John Witt, Jr., eds. *No Establishment of Religion: America's Original Contribution to Religious Liberty*. New York: Oxford University Press, 2012.
Hasler, August B. *How the Pope Became Infallible: Pius IX and the Politics of Persuasion*. Translated by Peter Heinegg. Garden City, NY: Doubleday, 1981.
Hamburger, Philip. *Separation of Church and State*. Cambridge, MA: Harvard University Press, 2002.
Harris, Sam. *The End of Faith: Religion, Terror, and the Future of Reason*. New York: Norton, 2004.
Hart, David Bentley. *Atheist Delusions: The Christian Revolution and Its Fashionable Enemies*. New Haven: Yale University Press, 2009.
Hastings, Max. *Inferno: The World at War, 1939–1945*. New York: Vintage, 2012.
Hatch, Nathan O., and Mark A. Noll, eds. *The Bible in America: Essays in Cultural History*. New York: Oxford University Press, 1982.
Hebblethwaite, Peter. *Paul VI: The First Modern Pope*. London: Fount, 1994.
Heft, James L., ed. *Catholicism and Interreligious Dialogue*. New York: Oxford University Press, 2012.
Hick, John. *Evil and the God of Love*. Rev. ed. New York: Palgrave Macmillan, 2010.
Himes, Kenneth R., ed. *Modern Catholic Social Teaching: Commentaries and Interpretations*. Washington, DC: Georgetown University Press, 2005.
Hitchens, Christopher. *god is not Great: How Religion Poisons Everything*. New York: Twelve, 2009.
Holy Office. Decree *Lamentabili sane: Syllabus Condemning the Errors of the Modernists*. 1907. http://www.papalencyclicals.net/Pius10/p10lamen.htm.
Huddock, Barry. *Struggle, Condemnation, Vindication: John Courtney Murray's Journey toward Vatican II*. Collegeville, MN: Michael Glazier, 2015.
Hughes, John Jay. "Hans Küng and the Magisterium." *Theological Studies* 41 (1980) 368–89.
Hull, N. E. H., and Peter Charles Hoffer. *Roe v. Wade: The Abortion Rights Controversy in American History*. 2nd ed. Lawrence: University Press of Kansas, 2010.
Hutchinson, William R. *Religious Pluralism in America: The Contentious History of a Founding Ideal*. New Haven: Yale University Press, 2003.
International Theological Commission. *Christianity and the World Religions*. 1997. http://www.vatican.va/roman_curia/congregations/cfaith/cti_documents/rc_cti_1997_cristainesimo-religioni_en.html.
———. *From the Diakonia of Christ to the Diakonia of the Apostles*. 2002. http//www.vatican.va/roman_curia/congregations/cfaith/cti_documents/rc_con_cfaith_pro_05072004_diaconate_en.html.
Jacoby, Susan. *Freethinkers: A History of American Secularism*. New York: Owl, 2005.
Jenkins, Philip. *The Great and Holy War: How World War I Became a Religious Crusade*. New York: HarperOne, 2014.

———. *Jesus Wars: How Four Patriarchs, Three Queens, and Two Emperors Decided What Christians Would Believe for the Next 1,500 Years.* New York: HarperOne, 2011.

John XXII. Papal bull *Quia quorundum.* 1323. http://www.papalencyclicals.net/John22/qquor-e.htm.

John XXIII. Encyclical *Ad Petri Cathedram: On Truth, Unity and Peace, in a Spirit of Charity.* 1959. http://w2.vatican.va/content/john-xxiii/en/encyclicals/documents/hf_j-xxiii_enc_29061959_ad-petri.html.

———. Encyclical *Mater et Magistra: On Christianity and Social Progress.* 1961. http://w2.vatican.va/content/john-xxiii/en/encyclicals/documents/hf_j-xxiii_enc_15051961_mater.html.

———. Encyclical *Pacem in terris: On Establishing Universal Peace in Truth, Justice, Charity, and Liberty.* 1963. http://w2.vatican.va/content/john-xxiii/en/encyclicals/documents/hf_j-xxiii_enc_11041963_pacem.html.

———. Encyclical *Princeps pastorum: On the Missions, Native Clergy, and Lay Participation.* 1959. http://w2.vatican.va/content/john-xxii/en/encyclicals/documents/hf_j-xxiii_enc_28111959_princeps.html.

John Paul II. *Address of His Holiness Pope John Paul II to the Diplomatic Corps.* 2003. http://w2.vatican.va/content/john-paul-ii/en/speeches/2003/january/documents/hf_jp-ii_spe_20030113_diplomatic-corps.html.

———. *Address to the Plenary Session of the Pontifical Academy of Sciences on "The Emergence of Complexity in Mathematics, Physics, Chemistry, and Biology."* 1992. http://www.pas.va/content/academia/en/magisterium/johnpaulii/31october1992.html.

———. Apostolic exhortation *Ecclesia in Africa: On the Church in Africa and Its Evangelizing Mission towards the Year 2000.* 1995. http://w2.vatican.va/content/john-paul-ii/apost_exhortations/documents/hf_jp-ii_exh_14091995_ecclesia-in-africa.html.

———. Apostolic exhortation *Ecclesia in America: On the Encounter with the Living Jesus Christ; the Way to Conversion, Communion and Solidarity in America.* 1999. http://w2.vatican.va/content/john-paul-ii/apost_exhortations/documents/hf_jp-ii_exh_22011999_ecclesia-in-america.html.

———. Apostolic exhortation *Ecclesia in Asia: On Jesus Christ the Saviour and His Mission of Love and Service in Asia.* 1999. http://w2.vatican.va/content/john-paul-ii/apost_exhortations/documents/hf_jp-ii_exh_06111999_ecclesia-in-asia.html.

———. Apostolic exhortation *Ecclesia in Europa: On Jesus Christ Alive in His Church the Source of Hope for Europe.* 2003. http://w2.vatican.va/content/john-paul-ii/apost_exhortations/documents/hf_jp-ii_exh_20030628_ecclesia-in-europe.html.

———. Apostolic exhortation *Familiaris consortio: On the Role of the Christian Family in the Modern World.* 1981. http://w2.vatican.va/content/john-paul-ii/apost_exhortations/documents/hf_jp-ii_exh_19811122_familiaris-consortio.html.

———. Apostolic letter *Inter Munera Academiarum.* 1999. http://w2.vatican.va/content/john-paul-ii/en/apost_letters/1999/documents/hf_jp-ii_apl_19990128_inter-munera-academiarum.html.

———. Apostolic letter *Ordinatio Sacerdotalis: On Reserving Priestly Ordination to Men Alone.* 1994. http://w2.vatican.va/content/john-paul-ii/en/apsot_letters/1994/documents/hf_jp-ii_apl_22051994_ordinatio-sacerdotalis.html.

———. Apostolic letter *Salvifici doloris: On the Christiaan Meaning of Human Suffering*. 1984. http://w2.vatican.va/content/john-paul-ii/en/apsot_letters/1984/documents/hf_jp-ii_apl_11021984_salvifici-doloris.html.

———. Apostolic letter *"motu proprio" Apostolos suos: On the Theological and Juridical Nature of Episcopal Conferences*. 1998. http://w2.vatican.va/content/john-paul-ii/en/motu_proprio/documents/hf_jp-ii_motu_proprio_22071998_apostolos-suos.html.

———. Encyclical *Centesimus annus: On the Hundredth Anniversary of Rerum novarum*. 1991. http://w2.vatican.va/content/john-paul-ii/en/encyclicals/documents/hf_jp-ii_enc_01051991_centesimuss-annus.html.

———. Encyclical *Ecclesia de Euchariastia: On the Eucharist in Its Relationship to the Church*. 2003. http://w2.vatican.va/content/john-paul-ii/en/encyclicals/documents/hf_jp-ii_enc_20030417_eccl-de-euch.html.

———. Encyclical *Evanglium vitae: On the Value and Inviolability of Human Life*. 1995. http://w2.vatican.va/content/john-paul-ii/en/encyclicals/documents/hf_jp-ii_enc_25031995_evangelium-vitae.html.

———. Encyclical *Fides et ratio: On the Relationship between Faith and Reason*. 1998. http://w2.vatican.va/content/john-paul-ii/en/encyclicals/documents/hf_jp-ii_enc_14091998_fides-et-ratio.html.

———. Encyclical *Laborem exercens: On Human Work on the Nineteeth Anniversary of Rerum Novarum*. 1981. http://w2.vatican.va/content/john-paul-ii/en/encyclicals/documents/hf_jp-ii_enc_14091981_laborem-exercens.html.

———. Encyclical *Redemptoris Mater*. 1987. http://w2.vatican.va/content/john-paul-ii/en/encyclicals/documents/hf_jp-ii_enc_25031987_redemptoris-mater.html.

———. Encyclical *Redemptoris missio*. 1990. http://w2.vatican.va/content/john-paul-ii/en/encyclicals/documents/hf_jp-ii_enc_07121990_redemptoris-missio.html.

———. Encyclical *Redemptoris hominis*. 1979. http://w2.vatican.va/content/john-paul-ii/en/encyclicals/documents/hf_jp-ii_enc_04031979_redemptoris-hominis.html.

———. Encyclical *Solicitudo rei socialis: For the Twentieth Anniversary of Populorum Progressio*. 1987. http://w2.vatican.va/content/john-paul-ii/en/encyclicals/documents/hf_jp-ii_enc_30121987_solicitudo-rei-socialis.html.

———. Encyclical *Ut unum sint: On Commitment to Ecumenism*. 1995. http://w2.vatican.va/content/john-paul-ii/en/encyclicals/documents/hf_jp-ii_enc_25051995_ut-unum-sint.html.

———. Encyclical *Veritatis splendor*. 1993. http://w2.vatican.va/content/john-paul-ii/en/encyclicals/documents/hf_jp-ii_enc_06081993_veritatis-splendor.html.

———. *Message du Saint-Père Jean-Paul II aux Membres de L'Assemblée Plénière de L'Académie des Sciences*. 1996. http://w2.vatican.va/content/john-paul-ii/fr/messages/pont_messages/1996/document/hf_jp-ii_mes_19961022_evoluzione.html.

Kaspar, Walter. *That They May All Be One: The Call to Unity*. New York: Burns & Oates, 2004.

Kaveny, Cathleen. *A Culture of Engagement: Law, Religion, and Morality*. Washington, DC: Georgetown University Press, 2016.

———. *Prophecy without Contempt: Religious Discourse in the Public Square*. Cambridge, MA: Harvard University University Press, 2016.

Keegan, John. *The First World War*. New York: Knopf, 1999.

———. *The Second World War*. New York: Viking, 1990.
Kelly, Joseph F. *The Ecumenical Councils of the Catholic Church: A History*. Collegeville, MN: Michael Glazier, 2009.
Kerr, Fergus. *Thomas Aquinas: A Very Short Introduction*. New York: Oxford University Press, 2009.
———. *Twentieth-Century Theologians: From Neoscholasticism to Nuptial Mysticism*. Malden, MA: Blackwell, 2007.
Kershaw, Ian. *To Hell and Back: Europe, 1914–1949*. New York: Penguin, 2016.
Kertzer, David I. *The Pope and Mussolini: The Secret History of Pius XI and the Rise of Fascism in Europe*. New York: Random House, 2014.
———. *Prisoner of the Vatican: The Popes' Secret Plot to Capture Rome from the New Italian State*. New York: Houghton Mifflin, 2004.
Koester, Helmut. *Paul and His World: Interpreting the New Testament in Its Context*. Minneapolis: Fortress, 2007.
Komonchak, Joseph A. "*Humanae Vitae* and its Reception: Ecclesiological Reflections." *Theological Studies* 39 (1978) 221–57.
Kruse, Kevin M. *One Nation under God: How Corporate America Invented Christian America*. New York: Basic, 2015.
Küng, Hans. *Infallible? An Unresolved Enquiry*. Rev. ed. Translated by Eric Mosbacher. New York: Continuum, 1994.
Lambert, Frank. *The Founding Fathers and the Place of Religion in America*. Princeton: Princeton University Press, 2003.
———. *Religion in American Politics: A Short History*. Princeton: Princeton University Press, 2008.
Larson, Edward J. *Summer for the Gods: The Scopes Trial and America's Continuing Debate over Science and Religion*. New York: Basic, 1997.
Lateran Accords. *Conciliation Treaty*. 1929. http://www.aloha.net/~mikesch/treaty.htm.
———. *Concordat*. 1929. http://www.aloha.net/~mikesch/treaty.htm.
———. *Finanacial Convention*. 1929. http://www.aloha.net/~mikesch/treaty.htm.
Leo X. Papal bull *Decet Romanum Pontificem: On the Condemnation and Excommunication of Martin Luther, the Heretic, and his Followers*. 1521. http://www.papalencyclicals.net/Leo10/l10decet.htm.
———. Papal bull *Exsurge Domine: Condemning the Errors of Martin Luther*. 1520. http://www.papalencyclicals.net/Leo10/l10exdom.htm.
Leo XIII. Apostolic letter *Apsotolicae curae: On the Nullity of Anglican Orders*. 1896. http://www.papalencyclicals.net/Leo13/l13curae.htm.
———. Encyclical *Aeterni Patris: On the Restoration of Christian Philosophy*. 1879. http://w2.vatican/va/content/leo-xiii/en/encyclicals/documents/hf_l-xiii_enc_04081879_aeterni-patris.html.
———. Encyclical *Arcanum: On Christian Marriage*. 1880. http://w2.vatican/va/content/leo-xiii/en/encyclicals/documents/hf_l-xiii_enc_10021880_arcanum.html.
———. Encyclical *Au milieu des sollicitudes: On the Church and State in France*. 1892. http://w2.vatican/va/content/leo-xiii/en/encyclicals/documents/hf_l-xiii_enc_16021892_au-milieu-sollicitudes.html.

———. Encyclical *Caritatis studium: On the Church in Scotland*. 1898. http://w2.vatican/va/content/leo-xiii/en/encyclicals/documents/hf_l-xiii_enc_25071898_caritatis-studium.html.

———. Encyclical *Custodi di quella fede: On Freemasonry*. 1892. http://w2.vatican/va/content/leo-xiii/en/encyclicals/documents/hf_l-xiii_enc_08121892_custodi-di-quella-fede.html.

———. Encyclical *Dall'alto dell'Apostolico Seggio: On Freemasonry*. 1890. http://w2.vatican/va/content/leo-xiii/en/encyclicals/documents/hf_l-xiii_enc_18901015_apostolico-seggio.html.

———. Encyclical *Diuturnum: On the Origin of Civil Power*. 1881. http://w2.vatican/va/content/leo-xiii/en/encyclicals/documents/hf_l-xiii_enc_29061881_diuturnum.html.

———. Encyclical *Dum multa: On Marriage Legislation*. 1902. http://w2.vatican/va/content/leo-xiii/en/encyclicals/documents/hf_l-xiii_enc_24121902_dum-multa.html.

———. Encyclical *Etsi nos: On Conditions in Italy*. 1882. http://w2.vatican/va/content/leo-xiii/en/encyclicals/documents/hf_l-xiii_enc_15021882_etsi-nos.html.

———. Encyclical *Graves de communi re: On Christian Democracy*. 1901. http://w2.vatican/va/content/leo-xiii/en/encyclicals/documents/hf_l-xiii_enc_18011901_graves-de-communi-re.html.

———. Encyclical *Humanum Genus: On Freemasonry*. 1884. http://w2.vatican/va/content/leo-xiii/en/encyclicals/documents/hf_l-xiii_enc_18840420_humanum-genus.html.

———. Encyclical *Immortali Dei: On the Christian Constitution of States*. 1885. http://w2.vatican/va/content/leo-xiii/en/encyclicals/documents/hf_l-xiii_enc_01111885_immortale-dei.html

———. Encyclical *Inimica vis: On Freemasonry*. 1892. http://w2.vatican/va/content/leo-xiii/en/encyclicals/documents/hf_l-xiii_enc_08121892_inimica-vis.html.

———. Encyclical *Inscrutabili Dei consilio: On the Evils of Society*. 1878. http://w2.vatican/va/content/leo-xiii/en/encyclicals/documents/hf_l-xiii_enc_21041878_inscrutabili-dei-consilio.html.

———. Encyclical *Libertas: On the Nature of Human Liberty*. 1888. http://w2.vatican/va/content/leo-xiii/en/encyclicals/documents/hf_l-xiii_enc_20061888_libertas.html.

———. Encyclical *Longinqua: On Catholicism in the United States*. 1895. http://w2.vatican/va/content/leo-xiii/en/encyclicals/documents/hf_l-xiii_enc_06011895_longinqua.html.

———. Encyclical *Providentissimus Deus: On the Study of Holy Scripture*. 1893. http://w2.vatican/va/content/leo-xiii/en/encyclicals/documents/hf_l-xiii_enc_18111893_providentissimus-deus.html.

———. Encyclical *Quam religiosa: On Civil Marriage Law*. 1898. http://w2.vatican/va/content/leo-xiii/en/encyclicals/documents/hf_l-xiii_enc_16081898_quam-religiosa.html.

———. Encyclical *Quod apostolici muneris: On Socialism*. 1878. http://w2.vatican/va/content/leo-xiii/en/encyclicals/documents/hf_l-xiii_enc_28121878_quod-apostolici-muneris.html.

———. Encyclical *Quod multum: On the Liberty of the Church*. 1886. http://w2.vatican/va/content/leo-xiii/en/encyclicals/documents/hf_l-xiii_enc_22081886_quod-multum.html.

———. Encyclical *Rerum novarum: On Capital and Labor*. 1891. http://w2.vatican/va/content/leo-xiii/en/encyclicals/documents/hf_l-xiii_enc_15051891_rerum-novarum.html.

———. Encyclical *Sapientiae Christianae: On Christians as Citizens*. 1890. http://w2.vatican/va/content/leo-xiii/en/encyclicals/documents/hf_l-xiii_enc_10011890_sapientiae-christianae.html.

———. Encyclical *Satis cognitum: On the Unity of the Church*. 1896. http://w2.vatican/va/content/leo-xiii/en/encyclicals/documents/hf_l-xiii_enc_29061896_satis-cognitum.html.

———. Encyclical *Spesse volte: Suppression of Catholic Institutions*. 1898. http://w2.vatican/va/content/leo-xiii/en/encyclicals/documents/hf_l-xiii_enc_05081898_spesse-volte.html.

———. Letter to James Cardinal Gibbons, *Testem benevolentiae nostrae: Concerning New Opinions, Virtue, Nature and Grace, with regard to Americanism*. 1899. http://papalencyclicals.net/Leo13/l13teste.htm.

Levada, William, *Dei Verbum—Forty Years Later*. 2005. http://www.vatican.va/roman_curia/congregations/cfaith/documents/rc_con_cfaith_doc_20051010_dei-verbum-levada_en.html.

Lewy, Guenter. *The Catholic Church and Nazi Germany*. New York: Da Capo, 2000.

Lincoln, Abraham. *Second Inaugural Address*. 1865. htpp://www.nationalcenter.org/LincolnSecondinaugural.html.

MacCulloch, Diarmaid. *Christianity: The First Three Thousand Years*. New York: Viking, 2010.

———. *The Reformation: A History*. New York: Penguin, 2005.

Marchione, Margherita. *Man of Peace: Pope Pius XII*. Mahwah, NJ: Paulist, 2003.

Marsden, George M. *Fundamentalism and American Culture*. 2nd ed. New York: Oxford University Press, 2006.

McBrien, Richard P. *Catholicism*. Rev. ed. New York: HarperOne, 1994.

———. *Lives of the Popes: The Pontiffs from St. Peter to Benedict XVI*. Rev. ed. New York: HarperOne, 2000.

McClory, Robert. *Power and the Papacy: The People and Politics behind the Doctrine of Infallibility*. Liguori, MO: Triumph, 1997.

———. *Turning Point: The Inside Story of the Papal Birth Control Commission and How "Humanae Vitae" Changed the Life of Patty Crowley and the Future of the Church*. New York: Crossroad, 1995.

McDonough, Peter. *The Catholic Labyrinth: Power, Apathy, and a Passion for Reform in the American Church*. New York: Oxford University Press, 2013.

McGrath, Alister E. *Christianity's Dangerous Idea: The Protestant Revolution—A History from the Sixteenth Century to the Twenty-First*. New York: HarperOne, 2008.

———. *Historical Theology: An Introduction to the History of Christian Thought*. 2nd ed. Malden, MA: Wiley-Blackwell, 2013.

McGreevy, John T. *Catholicism and American Freedom: A History*. New York: Norton, 2003.

McKim, Robert. *On Religious Diversity*. New York: Oxford University Press, 2012.

McMullin, Ernan, ed. *The Church and Galileo*. Notre Dame: University of Notre Dame Press, 2005.

Monsma, Steven V., and J. Christopher Soper. *The Challenge of Pluralism: Church and State in Five Democracies*. 2nd ed. Lanham, MD: Rowman & Littlefield, 2009.

Morris, Charles R. *American Catholic: The Saints and Sinners Who Built America's Most Powerful Church*. New York: Vintage, 1997.

Murphy, Bruce Allen. *Scalia: A Court of One*. New York: Simon & Schuster, 2015.

Murphy, Cullen. *God's Jury: The Inquisition and the Making of the Modern World*. New York: Houghton Mifflin Harcourt, 2012.

Murray, John Courtney. "The Church and Totalitarian Democracy." *Theological Studies* 13 (1952) 525–63.

———. "The Problem of Religious Freedom." *Theological Studies* 25 (1964) 503–75.

Newman, John Henry. *An Essay on the Development of Christian Doctrine*. 6th ed. Notre Dame: University of Notre Dame Press, 1989.

Nicholas III. Constitution *Exiit qui seminat*. 1279. http://www.papalencyclicals.net/Nichol03/exit-e.htm.

Noll, Mark A. *America's God: From Jonathan Edwards to Abraham Lincoln*. New York: Oxford University Press, 2002.

———. *The Civil War as a Theological Crisis*. Chapel Hill: University of North Carolina Press, 2006.

———. *A History of Christianity in the United States and Canada*. Grand Rapids: Eerdmans, 1992.

———. *Turning Points: Decisive Moments in the History of Christianity*. 3rd ed. Grand Rapids: Baker Academic, 2012.

Noll, Mark A., and Luke E. Harlow, eds. *Religion and American Politics: From the Colonial Period to the Present*. 2nd ed. New York: Oxford University Press, 2007.

Noll, Mark A., and Carolyn Nystrom, eds. *Is the Reformation Over? An Evangelical Assessment of Contemporary Roman Catholicism*. Grand Rapids: Baker Academic, 2005.

Noonan, John T., Jr. *A Church that Can and Cannot Change: The Development of Catholic Moral Teaching*. Notre Dame: University of Notre Dame Press, 2005.

———. *Contraception: A History of Its Treatment by the Catholic Theologians and Canonists*. Cambridge, MA: Belknap, 1986.

———. *The Lustre of Our Country: The American Experience of Religious Freedom*. Berkeley: University of California Press, 1998.

Norwich, John Julius. *Absolute Monarchs: A History of the Papacy*. New York: Random House, 2011.

O'Connell, Marvin R. *Critics on Trial: An Introduction to the Catholic Modernist Crisis* Washington, DC: Catholic University of America Press, 1994.

O'Malley, John W. *Catholic History for Today's Church: How Our Past Illuminates Our Present*. Lanham, MD: Rowman & Littlefield, 2015.

———. *Trent: What Happened at the Council*. Cambridge, MA: Belknap, 2013.

———. *What Happened at Vatican II*. Cambridge, MA: Belknap, 2010.

Orsy, Ladislas. "Magisterium: Assent and Dissent." *Theological Studies* 48 (1987) 473–97.

Our Sunday Visitor. *2016 Catholic Almanac*. Huntington, IN: Our Sunday Visitor, 2016.

Passelecq, George, and Bernard Suchecky. *The Hidden Encyclical of Pius XI*. Translated by Steven Rendall. New York: Harcourt Brace, 1997.

Paul VI. Apostolic exhortation *Evangelii nuntiandi*. 1975. http://w2.vatican.va/content/paul-vi/en/apost_exhortations/documents/hf_p-vi_exh_19751208_evangelii-nuntiandi.html.

———. Apostolic letter *Octogesima adveniens: On the Occasion of the Eightieth Anniversary of the Encyclical "Rerum Novarum."* 1971. http://w2.vatican.va/content/paul-vi/en/apost_letters/documents/hf_p-vi_apl_19710514_octogesima-adveniens.html.

———. Apostolic letter *"motu proprio" Sacrum diaconatus ordinem: General Norms for Restoring the Permanent Diaconate in the Latin Church*. 1967. http://w2.vatican.va/content/paul-vi/en/motu_proprio/documents/hf_p-vi_motu-proprio_19670618_sacrum-diaconatus.html.

———. Encyclical *Ecclesiam suam: On the Church*. 1964. http://w2.vatican.va/content/paul-vi/en/encyclicals/documents/hf_p-vi_enc_06081964_ecclsiam.html.

———. Encyclical *Humanae vitae: On the Regulation of Birth*. 1968. http://w2.vatican.va/content/paul-vi/en/encyclicals/documents/hf_p-vi_enc_25071968_humanae-vitae.html.

———. Encyclical *Mysterium fidei: On the Holy Eucharist*. 1965. http://w2.vatican.va/content/paul-vi/en/encyclicals/documents/hf_p-vi_enc_03091965_mysterium.html.

———. Encyclical *Populorum progressio: On the Development of Peoples*. 1967. http://w2.vatican.va/content/paul-vi/en/encyclicals/documents/hf_p-vi_enc_26031967_populorum.html.

———. Encyclical *Sacerdotalis caelibatus: On the Celibacy of the Priest*. 1967. http://w2.vatican.va/content/paul-vi/en/encyclicals/documents/hf_p-vi_enc_24061967_sacerdotalis.html.

Pelikan, Jaroslav. *Christian Doctrine and Modern Culture (since 1700)*. The Christian Tradition: A History of the Development of Doctrine 5. Chicago: University of Chicago Press, 1989.

———. *The Growth of Medieval Theology (600–1300)*. The Christian Tradition: A History of the Development of Doctrine 3. Chicago: University of Chicago Press, 1978.

———. *Reformation of Church and Dogma (1300–1700)*. The Christian Tradition: A History of the Development of Doctrine 4. Chicago: University of Chicago Press, 1983.

———. *The Spirit of Eastern Christendom (600–1700)*. The Christian Tradition: A History of the Development of Doctrine 2. Chicago: University of Chicago Press, 1974.

Phayer, Michael. *The Catholic Church and the Holocaust, 1930–1965*. Bloomington: Indiana University Press, 2000.

———. *Pius XII, the Holocaust, and the Cold War*. Bloomington: Indiana University Press, 2008.

Piqué, Elisabetta. *Pope Francis: Life and Revolution; A Biography of Jorge Bergoglio*. Translated by Anna Mazzotti and Lydia Colin. Chicago: Loyola, 2014.

Pius II. Papal bull *Execrabilis*. 1460. http://geocities.ws/caleb1x/documents/execrabilis.html.

Pius V. Papal bull *Regnans in excelsis: Excommunicating Elizabeth I of England*. 1570. http://www.papalencyclicals.net/Pius05/p5regnans.htm.

Pius IX. Apostolic constitution *Ineffabilis Deus: The Immaculate Conception*. 1854. http://www.papalencyclicals.net/Pius09/p9ineff.htm.

———. Encyclical *Incredibili: On Persecution in New Granada*. 1863. http://www.papalencyclicals.net/Pius09/p9incred.htm.

———. Encyclical *Inter multiplices: Pleading for Unity of Spirit*. 1853. http://www.papalencyclicals.net/Pius09/p9interm.htm.

———. Encyclical *Nostis et nobiscum: On the Church in the Pontifical States*. 1849. http://www.papalencyclicals.net/Pius09/p9nostis.htm.

———. Encyclical *Probe noscitis venerabilis: On the Discipline for Clergy*. 1852. http://www.papalencyclicals.net/Pius09/p9proben.htm.

———. Encyclical *Quanta cura: Condemning Current Errors*. 1864. http://www.papalencyclicals.net/Pius09/p9quanta.htm.

———. Encyclical *Quanto conficiamur moerore: On Promotion of False Doctrines*. 1863. http://www.papalencyclicals.net/Pius09/p9quanto.htm.

———. Encyclical *Qui nuper: On Pontifical States*. 1859. http://www.papalencyclicals.net/Pius09/p9quinup.htm.

———. Encyclical *Qui pluribus: On Faith and Religion*. 1846. http://www.papalencyclicals.net/Pius09/p9quiplu.htm.

———. Encyclical *Quod nunquam: On the Church in Prussia*. 1875. http://www.papalencyclicals.net/Pius09/p9quodnu.htm.

———. Encyclical *Respicientes: Protesting the Taking of the Pontifical States*. 1870. http://www.papalencyclicals.net/Pius09/p9respic.htm.

———. Encyclical *Singulari quidem: On the Church in Austria*. 1856. http://www.papalencyclicals.net/Pius09/p9singul.htm.

———.Encyclical *Ubi nos: On Pontifical States*. 1871. http://www.papalencyclicals.net/Pius09/p9ubinos.htm.

———. Encyclical *Ubi Primum: On the Immaculate Conception*. 1849. http://www.papalencyclicals.net/Pius09/p9ubipr2.htm.

———. Encyclical *Vix dum a nobis: On the Church in Austria*. 1874. http://www.papalencyclicals.net/Pius09/p9vixdum.htm.

———. *Syllabus of Errors*. 1864. http://www.papalencyclicals.net/Pius09/p9syll.htm.

Pius X. Encyclical *Il fermo propsito: On Catholic Action in Italy*. 1905. http://w2.vatican.va/content/pius-x/en/encyclicals/documents/hf_p-x_enc_11061905_il-fermo-proposito.html.

———. Encyclical *Gravisimo officii munere: On French Associations of Worship*. 1906. http://w2.vatican.va/content/pius-x/en/encyclicals/documents/hf_p-x_enc_10081906_gravissimo-officii-munere.html.

———. Encyclical *Iamdudum: On the Law of Separation in Portugal*. 1911. http://w2.vatican.va/content/pius-x/en/encyclicals/documents/hf_p-x_enc_24051911_iamdudum.html.

———. Encyclical *Pascendi dominici gregis: On the Doctrine of the Modernists*. 1907. http://w2.vatican.va/content/pius-x/en/encyclicals/documents/hf_p-x_enc_19070908_pascendi-dominici-gregis.html.

———. Encyclical *Une fois encore: On the Separation of Church and State*. 1907. http://w2.vatican.va/content/pius-x/en/encyclicals/documents/hf_p-x_enc_06011907_une-fois-encore.html.

---. Encyclical *Vehementer nos: On the French Law of Separation*. 1906. http://w2.vatican.va/content/pius-x/en/encyclicals/documents/hf_p-x_enc_11021906_vehementer-nos.html.

---. *The Oath against Modernism*. 1910. http://www.papalencyclicals.net/Pius10/p10moath.htm.

Pius XI. Encyclical *Acerba animi: On Persecution of the Church in Mexico*. 1932. http://w2.vatican.va/content/pius-xi/en/encyclicals/documents/hf_p-xi_enc_29091932_acerba-animi.html.

---. Encyclical *Casti connubii: On Christian Marriage*. 1930. http://w2.vatican.va/content/pius-xi/en/encyclicals/documents/hf_p-xi_enc_19301231_casti-connubii.html.

---. Encyclical *Dilectissima nobis: On Oppression of the Church in Spain*. 1933. http://w2.vatican.va/content/pius-xi/en/encyclicals/documents/hf_p-xi_enc_03061933_dilectissima-nobis.html.

---. Encyclical *Divini illius magistri: On Christian Education*. 1929. http://w2.vatican.va/content/pius-xi/en/encyclicals/documents/hf_p-xi_enc_31121929_divini-illius-magistri.html.

---. Encyclical *Divini Redemptoris: On Atheistic Communism*. 1937. http://w2.vatican.va/content/pius-xi/en/encyclicals/documents/hf_p-xi_enc_19370319_divini-redemptoris.html.

---. Encyclical *Firmissimam constantiam: On the Religious Situation in Mexico*. 1937. http://w2.vatican.va/content/pius-xi/en/encyclicals/documents/hf_p-xi_enc_19370328_firmissimam-constantiam.html.

---. Encyclical *Iniquis afflictisque: On the Persecution of the Church in Mexico*. 1926. http://w2.vatican.va/content/pius-xi/en/encyclicals/documents/hf_p-xi_enc_18111926_iniquis-afflictisque.html.

---. Encyclical *Maximam gravisimamque: On French Diocesan Associations*. 1924. http://w2.vatican.va/content/pius-xi/en/encyclicals/documents/hf_p-xi_enc_18011924_maximam-gravissimamque.html.

---. Encyclical *Mit brennender Sorge: On the Church and the German Reich*. 1937. http://w2.vatican.va/content/pius-xi/en/encyclicals/documents/hf_p-xi_enc_14031937_mit-brennender-sorge.html.

---. Encyclical *Mortalium animos: On Religious Unity*. 1928. http://w2.vatican.va/content/pius-xi/en/encyclicals/documents/hf_p-xi_enc_19280106_mortalium-animos.html.

---. Encyclical *Non abbiamo bisogno: On Catholic Action in Italy*. 1931. http://w2.vatican.va/content/pius-xi/en/encyclicals/documents/hf_p-xi_enc_29061931_non-abbiamo-bisogno.html.

---. Encyclical *Quadragesimo anno: On Reconstruction of the Social Order*. 1931. http://w2.vatican.va/content/pius-xi/en/encyclicals/documents/hf_p-xi_enc_19310515_quadragesimo-anno-.html.

Pius XII. *Address to Midwives on the Nature of their Profession*. 1951. http://www.papalencyclicals.net/Pius12/P12midwives.htm.

---. Apostolic constitution *Munificentissimus Deus: Defining the Doctrine of the Assumption*. 1950. http://w2.vatican.va/content/pius-xii/en/apost_constitutions/documents/hf_p-xii_apc_19501101_munifcentissimus-deus.html

---. Christmas Message *Democracy and a Lasting Peace*. 1944. http://www.papalencyclicals.net/Pius12/P12XMAS.HTM.

———. Christmas Message *The Internal Order of States and Peoples*. 1942. http://www.papalencyclicals.net/Pius12/P12CH42.HTM.
———. Encyclical *Ad Apostolorum principis: On Communism and the Church in China*. 1958. http://w2.vatican.va/content/pius-xii/en/encyclicals/documents/hf_p-xii_enc_29061958_ad-apostolorum-principis.html.
———. Encyclical *Ad Sinarum gentem: On the Supranationality of the Church*. 1954. http://w2.vatican.va/content/pius-xii/en/encyclicals/documents/hf_p-xii_enc_07101954_ad-sinarum-gentem.html.
———. Encyclical *Communium interpretes dolorum: Appealing for Prayers for Peace during May*. 1945. http://w2.vatican.va/content/pius-xii/en/encyclicals/documents/hf_p-xii_enc_15041945_communium-interpretes-dolorum.html.
———. Encyclical *Datis nuperrime: Lamenting the Sorrowful Events in Hungary and Condemning the Ruthless Use of Force*. 1956. http://w2.vatican.va/content/pius-xii/en/encyclicals/documents/hf_p-xii_enc_05111956_datis-nuperrime.html.
———. Encyclical *Deiparae Virginis Mariae: On the Possibility of Defining the Assumption of Mary as a Dogma of Faith*. 1946. http://w2.vatican.va/content/pius-xii/en/encyclicals/documents/hf_p-xii_enc_01051946_deiparae-virginis-mariae.html.
———. Encyclical *Divino afflante Spiritu: On Promoting Biblical Studies*. 1943. http://w2.vatican.va/content/pius-xii/en/encyclicals/documents/hf_p-xii_enc_30091943_divino-afflante-spiritu.html
———. Encyclical *Humani generis: Concerning some False Opinions Threatening to the Undermine the Foundations of Catholic Doctrine*. 1950. http://w2.vatican.va/content/pius-xii/en/encyclicals/documents/hf_p-xii_enc_12081950_humani-generis.html.
———. Encyclical *Laetamur admodum: Renewing Exhortation for Prayers for Peace for Poland, Hungary, and the Middle East*. 1956. http://w2.vatican.va/content/pius-xii/en/encyclicals/documents/hf_p-xii_enc_01111956_laetamur-admodum.html.
———. Encyclical *Luctuosissimi eventus: Urging Public Prayers for Peace and Freedom for the People of Hungary*. 1956. http://w2.vatican.va/content/pius-xii/en/encyclicals/documents/hf_p-xii_enc_28101956_lucuosissimi-eventus.html.
———. Encyclical *Mystici corporis Christi: On the Mystical Body of Christ*. 1943. http://w2.vatican.va/content/pius-xii/en/encyclicals/documents/hf_p-xii_enc_29061943_mystici-corporis-christi.html.
———. Encyclical *Sacra virginitatis: On Consecrated Virginity*. 1954. http://w2.vatican.va/content/pius-xii/en/encyclicals/documents/hf_p-xii_enc_25031954_mystici-sacra-virginitatis.html.
———. Encyclical *Sertum laetitiae: On the Hundred and Fiftieth Anniversary of the Hierarchy in the United States*. 1939. http://w2.vatican.va/content/pius-xii/en/encyclicals/documents/hf_p-xii_enc_01111939_sertum-laetitiae.html.
———. Encyclical *Summi Pontificatus: On the Unity of Human Society*. 1939. http://w2.vatican.va/content/pius-xii/en/encyclicals/documents/hf_p-xii_enc_20101939_summi-pontificatus.html.
Phillips, Peter. *The Tragedy of Nazi Germany*. New York: Pegasus, 1969.
Pollard, John F. *Money and the Rise of the Modern Papacy: Financing the Vatican, 1850–1950*. London: Geoffrey Chapman, 1999.
———. *The Papacy in the Age of Totalitarianism, 1914–1958*. New York: Oxford University Press, 2014.

———. *The Unknown Pope: Benedict XV (1914–1922) and the Pursuit of Peace.* New York: Geoffrey Chapman, 2000.
Pontifical Council for Justice and Peace. *Compendium of the Social Doctrine of the Church.* 2004. http://www.vatican.va/roman_curia/pontifical_councils/justpeace/documents/rc_pc_justpeace_doc_20060526_compendio-dott-soc_en.html.
Pontifical Council for Promoting Christian Unity. *Directory for the Application of Principles and Norms on Ecumenism.* 1993. http://www.vatican.va/roman_curia/pontifical_councils/chrstuni/general-docs/rc_pc_chrstuni_doc_19930325_directory_en.html.
———. *From Conflict to Communion: Lutheran-Catholic Common Commemoration of the Reformation in 2017.* 2013. http://www.vatican.va/roman_curia/pontifical_councils/chrstuni/lutheran-fed-docs/rc_pc_chrstuni_doc_2013_dal-conflitto-alla-comunione_en.html.
———. *Joint Declaration on the Doctrine of Justification by the Lutheran World Federation and the Catholic Church.* 1999. http://www.vatican.va/roman_curia/pontifical_councils/chrstuni/documents/rc_pc_chrstuni_doc_31101999_cath-luth-joint-declaration_en.html.
Powell, Mark E. *Papal Infallibility: A Protestant Evaluation of an Ecumenical Issue.* Grand Rapids: Eerdmans, 2009.
Putnam, Robert D., and David E. Campbell. *American Grace: How Religion Divides and Unites Us.* New York: Simon & Schuster, 2010.
Rable, George C. *God's Almost Chosen Peoples: A Religious History of the American Civil War.* Chapel Hill: University of North Carolina Press, 2010.
Rapport, Mike. *1848: Year of Revolution* New York: Basic, 2009.
Ratté, John. *Three Modernists: Alfred Loisy, George Tyrell, William L. Sullivan.* New York: Sheed & Ward, 1967.
Ratzinger, Joseph. *Jesus of Nazareth: From the Baptism in the Jordan to the Transfiguration.* Translated by Adrian J. Walker. San Francisco: Ignatius, 2007.
———. *Light of the World: The Pope, the Church, and the Signs of the Times; A Conversation with Peter Seewald.* Translated by Michael J. Miller and Adrian J. Walker. San Francisco: Ignatius, 2010.
———. *On the One Hundredth Anniversary of the Pontifical Biblical Commission: Relationship between Magisterium and Exegetes.* 2003. http://www.doctrinafidei.va/pcb_documents_con_cfaith_doc_20030510_ratzinger-com_en.html.
Reese, Thomas J. *Inside the Vatican: The Politics and Organization of the Catholic Church.* Cambridge, MA: Harvard University Press, 1996.
Rowland, Wade. *Galileo's Mistake: A New Look at the Epic Confrontation between Galileo and the Church.* New York: Arcade, 2012.
Rubenstein, Richard L. *After Auschwitz: Radical Theology and Contemporary Judaism.* Indianapolis: Bobbs-Merrill, 1966.
Sánchez, José M. *Pius XII and the Holocaust: Understanding the Controversy.* Washington, DC: Catholic University of America Press, 2002.
Second Vatican Council. Declaration *Dignitatis humanae: On the Right of the Person and of Communities to Social and Civil Freedom in matters of Religion,* 1965. http://www.vatican.va/archive/hist_councils/ii_vatican_council/documents/vat-ii_decl_19651207_dignitatistis-humanae_en.html.

———. Declaration *Nostra aetate: On the Relation of the Church to Non-Christian Religions*. 1965. http://www.vatican.va/archive/hist_councils/ii_vatican_council/documents/vat-ii_decl_19651028_nostra-aetate_en.html.

———. Decree *Unitatis redintegratio: On Ecumenism*. 1964. http://www.vatican.va/archive/hist_councils/ii_vatican_council/documents/vat-ii_decree_19641121_unitatis-redintegratio_en.html.

———. Dogmatic constitution *Dei Verbum: On Divine Revelation*. 1965. http://www.vatican.va/archive/hist_councils/ii_vatican_council/documents/vat-ii_const_19651118_dei-verbum_en.html.

———. Dogmatic constitution *Lumen gentium: On the Church*. 1964. http://www.vatican.va/archive/hist_councils/ii_vatican_council/documents/vat-ii_const_19641121_lumen-gentium_en.html.

———. Pastoral constitution *Gaudium et spes: On the Church in the Modern World*. 1965. http://www.vatican.va/archive/hist_councils/ii_vatican_council/documents/vat-ii_const_19651207_gaudium-spes_en.html.

Sehat, David. *The Myth of American Religious Freedom*. New York: Oxford University Press, 2011.

Stark, Rodney, and Roger Finke. *Acts of Faith: Explaining the Human Side of Religion*. Berkeley: University of California Press, 2000.

Steinfals, Peter. *A People Adrift: The Crisis of the Roman Catholic Church in America*. New York: Simon & Schuster, 2004.

Stout, Harry S. *Upon the Altar of the Nation: A Moral History of the Civil War*. New York: Penguin, 2006.

Sullivan, Francis A. *Creative Fidelity: Weighing and Interpreting Documents of the Magisterium*. Eugene, OR: Wipf & Stock, 2003.

———. *From Apostles to Bishops: The Development of the Episcopacy in the Early Church*. Mahwah, NJ: Newman, 2001.

———. *Magisterium: Teaching Authority in the Catholic Church*. Eugene, OR: Wipf & Stock, 2002.

———. "Note: The Doctrinal Weight of *Evangelium Vitae*." *Theological Studies* 56 (1995) 560–65.

———. "Note: The 'Secondary Object" of Infallibility." *Theological Studies* 54 (1993) 536–50.

———. "Recent Theological Observations on Magisterial Documents and Public Dissent." *Theological Studies* 58 (1997) 509–15.

———. *Salvation Outside the Church? Tracing the History of the Catholic Response*. Eugene, OR: Wipf & Stock, 2002.

Sunstein, Cass R. *Radicals in Robes: Why Extreme Right-Wing Courts Are Wrong for America*. New York: Basic, 2005.

Taler, C. J. T. "Swearing Against Modernism: *Sacrorum Antistitum* (September 1, 1910)." *Theological Studies* 71 (2010) 454–66.

———. "'The Synthesis of all Heresies'—100 Years On." *Theological Studies* 68 (2007) 491–514.

Tentler, Leslie Woodcock. *Catholics and Contraception: An American History*. Ithaca, NY: Cornell University Press, 2004.

Tornielli, Andrea, and Giacomo Galeazzi. *This Economy Kills: Pope Francis on Capitalism and Social Justice*. Translated by Demetrio S. Yocum. Collegeville, MN: Liturgical, 2015.

United States Conference of Catholic Bishops. *Forming Consciences for Faithful Citizenship: A Call to Political Responsibility*. 2015. http://www.usccb.org/issues-and-action/faithful-citizenship/upload/forming-consciences-for-faithful-citizenship-title.cfm.

Urofsky, Melvin. *Dissent and the Supreme Court: Its Role in the Court's History and the Nation's Constitutional Dialogue*. New York: Vintage, 2015.

Vermes, Geza. *The Changing Faces of Jesus*. New York: Viking Compass, 2001.

Walzer, Michael. *Just and Unjust Wars: A Moral Argument with Historical Illustrations*. 4th ed. New York: Basic, 2006.

Weigel, George. *Witness to Hope: The Biography of John Paul II*. New York: HarperPerennial, 2005.

Weinandy, Thomas G. *Does God Suffer?* Notre Dame: Notre Dame University Press, 2000.

Whalen, William J. *Christianity and American Freemasonry*. 3rd ed. San Francisco: Ignatius, 1989.

White, L. Michael. *From Jesus to Christianity*. New York: HarperOne, 2005.

Wills, Garry. *Papal Sin: Structures of Deceit*. New York: Image, 2001.

Wolf, Hubert. *Pope and Devil: The Vatican's Archives and the Third Reich*. Translated by Kenneth Kronenberg. Cambridge, MA: Belknap, 2010.

Wood, Gordon S. *The Radicalism of the American Revolution*. New York: Vintage, 1993.

Yallop, David. *The Power and the Glory: Inside the Dark Heart of John Paul II's Vatican*. New York: Carroll & Graf, 2007.

Zagano, Phyllis, ed. *Women Deacons? Essays with Answers*. Collegeville, MN: Michael Glazier, 2016.

Zuccotti, Susan. *Under His Very Windows: The Vatican and the Holocaust in Italy*. New Haven: Yale University Press, 2002.

www.ingramcontent.com/pod-product-compliance
Lightning Source LLC
Chambersburg PA
CBHW061432300426
44114CB00014B/1657